£2.50
W10

CW00672468

Exploring the Thought of
Rabbi Joseph B. Soloveitchik

Exploring the Thought of Rabbi Joseph B. Soloveitchik

edited by

Marc D. Angel

KTAV Publishing House, Inc.

Copyright ©1976, 1980, 1984, 1988, 1994, 1996
New matter: Copyright ©1997

Rabbinical Council of America

Library of Congress Cataloging-in-Publication Data

Exploring the thought of Rabbi Joseph B. Soloveitchik / edited by Marc
D. Angel.
    p.   cm.
    Includes bibliographical references.
    ISBN 0-88125-578-5 (hc) : ISBN 0-88125-583-1 (pbk)
    1. Soloveitchik, Joseph Dov. 2. Judaism. 3. Philosophy, Jewish.
    4. Repentance—Judaism. I. Angel, Marc.
    BM755.S6114E95   1997
    296.8'32'092—dc21   97–21918
[B]   CIP

Manufactured in the United States of America
KTAV Publishing House, Inc.
900 Jefferson St., Hoboken, NJ 07030

Contents

Acknowledgments

I thank Rabbi Rafael Grossman, President of the Rabbinical Council of America, for having invited me to serve as editor of this volume. I also express gratitude to Rabbi Steven Dworken, Executive Vice President of the Rabbinical Council of America, for his cooperation. Appreciation is expressed to the Editorial Boards of *Tradition*, past and present, for their wisdom in publishing writings of Rabbi Joseph B. Soloveitchik, as well as many serious studies on the thought of the Rav.

It has been a pleasure working with Mr. Bernard Scharfstein of Ktav Publishing House. I thank the staff of Ktav for their work in the preparation and production of this volume.

The essays in this volume have previously appeared in *Tradition*, the quarterly journal published by the Rabbinical Council of America. Since 1958, *Tradition* has been a world-renowned journal of Orthodox Jewish thought. Its pages have included articles of great significance by leading thinkers and scholars, and the Rav himself chose *Tradition* for a number of his seminal works.

I thank the authors of the articles included in this volume for their cooperation. We express deep respect for the memories of Professors Marvin Fox and Pinchas Peli. They are both very much missed, but their writings and teachings continue to influence a wide circle of admirers.

With gratitude to the Almighty, we are pleased to make this book available to the public. We pray that the memory of the Rav will continue to be a source of blessing and inspiration to our generation and generations to come.

Marc D. Angel

Hanukkah 5757

About the Contributors

Marc D. Angel is Rabbi of Congregation Shearith Israel, the historic Spanish and Portuguese Synagogue in the City of New York. A past President of the Rabbinical Council of America, Rabbi Angel serves on the Editorial Board of *Tradition*. He has authored and edited fourteen books, including *The Orphaned Adult: Confronting the Death of a Parent*, which won the 1988 National Jewish Book Award in the category of Jewish Thought; *Voices In Exile: A Study in Sephardic Intellectual History*; and *Seeking Good, Speaking Peace*, a collection of essays.

Yitzchak Blau teaches at the Yeshivah of Flatbush and Drisha Institute.

Gerald Blidstein is M. Hubert Professor of Halakhic Thought at Ben Gurion University and a member of *Tradition*'s editorial board.. His most recent book is *Prayer in Maimonidean Halakha*. His *Political Principles in Maimonidean Halakha* won the Jerusalem Prize in 1985.

Shalom Carmy is Consulting Editor of *Tradition*. He has published widely on Bible and Jewish thought and has recently edited *Modern Scholarship in the Study of Torah: Contributions and Limitations*, and *Traditional Jewish Approaches to Suffering*, both in the Orthodox Forum series. He is currently engaged in preparing for publication Rabbi Soloveitchik's manuscripts on prayer.

Marvin Fox was Director Emeritus of the Lown School of Near Eastern and Judaic Studies and Philip W. Lown Professor Emeritus of Jewish Philosophy at Brandeis University. His work in general philosophy includes studies on Plato, Hume, Dewey, as well as work in ethical theory and in the philosophy of religion. Among his books are *Modern Jewish Ethics: Theory and Practice* and *Interpreting Maimonides: Studies in Methodology, Metaphysics and Moral Philosophy*. He was a founding member of *Tradition*'s editorial board.

William Kolbrener lectures at Bar Ilan University. He is the author of *Milton's Warring Angels: A Study of Critical Engagements*.

Pinchas Hacohen Peli was Professor of Jewish Thought and Literature at Ben Gurion University, and was a prolific author and lecturer. He edited a Hebrew book of the Rav's writings, *Besod ha-Yahid ve-ha-Yahad* as well as *Al ha-Teshuvah*.

Jonathan Sacks is Chief Rabbi of the United Hebrew Congregations of the British Commonwealth. He is the former Principal of Jews' College and was Visiting Professor of Philosophy at the University of Essex. He has written and edited a number of books dealing with the Orthodox Jewish confrontation with modernity, and is a member of *Tradition*'s editorial board.

Moshe Sokol is Associate Professor and Chairman of the Department of Philosophy at Touro College, and Rabbi of the Yavneh Minyan of Flatbush. He has published essays on Jewish ethics and philosophy, and has edited two volumes in the Orthodox Forum series.

Moshe Sosevsky serves as Dean of Yeshivat Ohr Yerushalayim in Israel, and is editor of *Jewish Thought: A Journal of Torah Scholarship*, a semi-annual publication of the Orthodox Union. Prior to making *aliyah*, he served as Rabbi of Congregation Shomrei Emunah of Englewood, New Jersey (1976–1980).

Shubert Spero is Irving Stone Professor of Jewish Thought at Bar Ilan University. He is author of *Morality, Halakhah and the Jewish Tradition, God in All Seasons*, and articles on Jewish philosophy which have appeared in a variety of journals.

Walter S. Wurzburger is Rabbi Emeritus of Congregation Shaaray Tefila in Lawrence, New York, and is Adjunct Professor of Philosophy at Yeshiva University. A past President of the Rabbinical Council of America and Editor Emeritus of *Tradition*, he is the author of *Ethics of Responsibility: Pluralistic Approaches to Jewish Covenantal Ethics*.

Introduction

෴

Marc D. Angel

෴

The modern era in the Western world has witnessed numerous assaults on the patterns of traditional religious life. Science has changed the way people think; technology has changed the way they live. Autonomous, human-centered theology has come to replace heteronomous, God-centered theology. Rationalism and positivism have constricted metaphysics. Respect for authority and hierarchies has been replaced by an emphasis on individuality and egalitarianism. The challenges of modernity are symbolized by such names as Darwin, Schleiermacher, Freud, Einstein, Ayn Rand.

The modern era has also seen dramatic changes in the physical patterns of life: vast migrations from the farms to the cities; mass emigration (often as refugees) from one country or continent to another; shrinking family size; increased mobility; expansion of educational opportunities; phenomenal technological change.

Peter Berger has described modern individuals as suffering "spiritual homelessness." People have lost their sense of being part of a comprehensive, cohesive and understandable world.

For the Jewish people, the modern period has been particularly challenging. Jews were given the possibility of entering the mainstream

of Western civilization. As the first winds of change swept into Jewish
neighborhoods and ghettos, many Jews were enticed to leave traditional
Jewish life behind. They hoped to gain acceptance into the general
society by abandoning or modifying their religious beliefs and observances. Some went so far as to convert to other religions. The
Haskalah—Jewish "enlightenment"—attracted numerous intellectuals
who sought to modernize Jewish culture. The result was a secularization
and objectification of Judaism.

The traditional religious framework was threatened by the Reform
movement. Reform was an attempt of 19th century Western European
Jews to "sanitize" Judaism by discarding Jewish laws and traditions.
Reform wanted to make Judaism appear more "cultured" and socially
respectable.

Whereas in previous eras, the masses of Jews accepted the authority
of Torah and Halakhah, the modern period experienced a transition
to the opposite situation—the masses of Western Jews no longer
accepted the authority of Torah and Halakhah. In their desire to
succeed in the modern world, many were ready to cast aside the
claims of Jewish tradition. When large numbers of European Jews
came to the United States during the late 19th and early 20th centuries,
this phenomenon continued and expanded. A sizeable majority of
American Jews came to be affiliated with non-Orthodox movements
or chose to remain unaffiliated with any movement at all.

In the face of tremendous defections from classic halakhic Judaism,
the Orthodox community fought valiantly to maintain the time-
honored beliefs and observances which they had inherited from their
ancestors. But the Orthodox responses to the challenges of the modern
situation were not monolithic. Some advocated a rejectionist stand,
arguing that modern Western culture was to be eschewed to the
extent possible. The "outside world," including non-Orthodox society,
presented a danger to the purity of Jewish religious tradition; isolation
was the best approach for Jews who wished to remain loyal to Torah
and Halakhah. On the other hand, another Orthodox approach called
for the active participation of Jews in general society while at the

same time maintaining a strict allegiance to Halakhah. The task was to keep a balance of Torah with *derekh eretz*, Torah with *madda*. These attitudes within Orthodoxy, as well as variations within the themes, have characterized Orthodox Jewish life since the mid-19th century.

The strength of Orthodoxy has been its heroic devotion to Torah and Halakhah, even in the face of criticism and hostility. Orthodoxy alone maintains a total commitment to the Divine nature of the Torah and the binding authority of Halakhah. Orthodoxy is inextricably bound to all past generations of Torah observant Jews, and is faithfully confident that with the coming of the Messiah all Jews will return to traditional Torah life. Yet, it is the peculiar genius of modern Orthodoxy to be thoroughly loyal to Torah and Halakhah while being open to modern thought and participating creatively in society.

Non-Orthodox detractors accuse Orthodoxy of being too bound by tradition, inflexible, unreceptive to modernity. Non-Orthodox Jews have often found it expedient to stereotype Orthodox Jews as being "pre-modern," narrow-minded, irrational, insular, those who use religion as an escape from the realities of the world. They criticize Jewish law as being dry and tedious. They describe followers of Halakhah as unthinking slaves of ritual and detail, lacking in deeper spiritual feelings.

These criticisms and stereotypes are refuted in one name: Rabbi Joseph Baer Soloveitchik.

The Rav and Modernity
Rabbi Joseph B. Soloveitchik, known to his students and followers as the Rav (the rabbi par excellence), is Orthodoxy's most eloquent response to the challenges of modernity and to the critics of modern Orthodoxy. A Torah giant of the highest calibre, the Rav was also a world-class philosopher. In his studies in Lithuania, he attained the stature of a rabbinic luminary. At the University of Berlin, he achieved the erudition of a philosophical prodigy.

A Midrash teaches that the path of Torah is flanked on the right by fire and on the left by ice. If one moves too far to the right, he is consumed by fire. If he moves too close to the left, he freezes to death. Rabbi Soloveitchik was that model personality who walked the path of the Torah, veering neither to the right nor to the left.

The Rav's unique greatness made him the ideal symbol and spokesman of modern Orthodoxy. In his own person, he demonstrated that the ideal Torah sage is creative, open-minded, compassionate, righteous, visionary, realistic and idealistic. He showed that one could be profoundly committed to the world of Torah and Halakhah and at the same time be a sophisticated modern thinker. Rabbi Soloveitchik was the paradigmatic 20th century figure for those seeking a mediation between classic halakhic Judaism and Western modernity. He was the spiritual and intellectual leader of Yeshiva University, the Rabbinical Council of America and Mizrachi; his influence, directly and through his students, has been ubiquitous within modern Orthodox Jewish life. He was the singular rabbinic sage of his generation who was deeply steeped in modern intellectual life, who understood modernity on its own terms; he was, therefore, uniquely qualified to guide Orthodoxy in its relationship with modernity.

The Rav was appreciative of many of the achievements of Western civilization. But he could not ignore the shortcomings of modernity. He was pained by the discrepancy between dominant modern values and the values of traditional religion. It is lonely being a person of faith in "modern society which is technically-minded, self-centered, and self-loving, almost in a sickly narcissistic fashion, scoring honor upon honor, piling up victory upon victory, reaching for the distant galaxies, and seeing in the here-and-now sensible world the only manifestation of being" ("The Lonely Man of Faith," p. 8). Utilitarianism and materialism, as manifestations of the modern worldview, are inimical to the values of religion.

In pondering the dilemma of a person of faith, the Rav explores a universal dilemma of human beings: inner conflict. He draws on the Torah's descriptions of the creation of Adam to shed light on human nature. Adam I is majestic; he wants to build, to control, to succeed. He is dedicated to attaining dignity. Adam II is covenantal; he is introspective, lonely, in search of community and meaning. He seeks a redeemed existence. Each human being, like Adam, is an amalgam of these conflicting tendencies. In creating humans in this way, God thereby underscored the dual aspect of the human personality. Human fulfillment involves the awareness of both Adams within, and the ability to balance their claims.

The Rav suggests that Western society errs in giving too much weight to Adam I. The stress is on success and control, pragmatic benefits. Even when it comes to religion, people seem to be more concerned with operating quantifiably successful institutions rather than coming into a relationship with God. In the words of the Rav: "Western man diabolically insists on being successful. Alas, he wants to be successful even in his adventure with God. If he gives of himself to God, he expects reciprocity. He also reaches a covenant with God, but this covenant is a mercantile one. . . . The gesture of faith for him is a give-and-take affair" ("The Lonely Man of Faith," p. 64). This attitude is antithetical to authentic religion. True religious experience necessitates surrender to God, feelings of being defeated—qualities identified with Adam II.

By extension, the Rav is critical of modernizers and liberalizers of Judaism who have tried to "market" Judaism by changing its content. Any philosophy of Judaism not firmly rooted in Halakhah is simply not true to Judaism. The non-halakhic movements did not grow out of classic Judaism; rather, they emerged as compromising responses to modernity. Had it not been for the external influences on Western Jews, non-halakhic movements would not have arisen as they did. The litmus test of an authentic philosophy of Judaism is: is it true to Torah and Halakhah, does it spring naturally and directly from them, is it faithful to their teachings? If Torah and Halakhah are made subservient to external pressures of modernity, this results in a corruption of Judaism.

Modernity, then, poses serious problems for traditional religion.

However, counter-currents within modernity offer opportunities. Already in the early 1940's, Rabbi Soloveitchik felt that the time had come for a new approach to the philosophy of religion. The "uncertainty principle" of quantum physics was an anodyne to the certainty of Newtonian physics. Thinkers in psychology, art and religion were proclaiming that human beings are not computers, but are complex organisms with religious, emotional and aesthetic sensibilities. Rationalism could not sustain and nourish the human soul. The Holocaust exploded the idealized myths of Western humanism and culture. Western civilization was moving into a post-modern phase which should be far more sympathetic to the spiritual character of human beings, more receptive to the eternal teachings of religion.

The Rav felt that a philosophy of Judaism rooted in Torah and Halakhah needed to be expressed in modern terms. Orthodox Jews needed to penetrate the eternal wisdom of the halakhic tradition, deepening their ability to cope with the challenges and opportunities of modernity and post-modernity. And non-Orthodox Jews needed to study classic Judaism on its own terms, freed from the negative propaganda of anti-Orthodox critics. After all, Torah and Halakhah are the patrimony of all Jews.

In his various lectures and writings, the Rav has provided a meaningful and powerful exposition of halakhic Judaism. He is a modern thinker, rooted in tradition, who has laid the foundation for post-modern Jewish thought.

Conflict and Creativity

The Rav has stated that "man is a great and creative being because he is torn by conflict and is always in a state of ontological tenseness and perplexity." The creative gesture is associated with agony ("Majesty and Humility," p. 25). As the Rav pointed out in "The Lonely Man of Faith," God created human beings with a built-in set of conflicts and tensions; this inner turmoil is a basic feature of the human predicament.

Religion is not an escape from conflict: it is a way of confronting and balancing the tensions that go with being a thinking human being. One must learn to be a creative free agent and, at the same time, an obedient servant of God.

Detractors of religion often portray religionists as seeking peace of mind by losing themselves in the spiritual realm. Critics say: "it is easy to be religious; you do not have to think; you only have to accept the tenets of faith and you can avoid the responsibility of making decisions and facing conflict." To such critics, the Rav would say simply: you do not understand the true nature of religion. Religion is not a place for cowards to hide; it is a place for courageous people to face a totally honest revelation of their own inner being. Halakhic Judaism does not shield the Jew from ontological conflict: it compels him to face it directly, heroically.

It is precisely this inner tension and struggle which generates a lofty and creative understanding of life. Rabbi Soloveitchik's writings and lectures are vivid examples of religious struggle and creativity at their best. His use of typologies, his first-person reminiscences, his powerfully emotive use of language—all contribute to express his singular message: a religious person must live a creative, heroic life.

In his *Ish ha-Halakhah* (Halakhic Man), the Rav notes that the halakhic Jew approaches reality with the Torah, given at Sinai, in hand. "Halakhic man, well furnished with rules, judgments, and fundamental principles, draws near the world with an a priori relation. His approach begins with an ideal creation and concludes with a real one" (*Halakhic Man*, p. 19). Intellectual effort is the hallmark of the ideal religious personality, and is a sine qua non of understanding the halakhic enterprise.

The Rav compares the domain of theoretical Halakhah with mathematics. The mathematical theoretician develops a system in the abstract; this theoretical construct is then applied to the practical world. The theoretical system helps define and shape practical reality. So it is with Halakhah. The classic halakhists immerse themselves in the world of theoretical Halakhah and apply halakhic constructs to the mundane world. The Rav observes that "both the halakhist and the mathematician live in an ideal realm and enjoy the radiance of their own creations" (*Halakhic Man*, p. 25).

The ideal halakhic personality lives in constant intimacy with Halakhah. Halakhah is as natural and central to him as breathing. His concern for theoretical Halakhah is an expression of profound love and commitment to the entire halakhic worldview. This love and commitment are manifested in a scrupulous concern for the observance of the rules of practical Halakhah.

The sage who attains the highest level of relationship with Halakhah is one "to whom the Torah is married." This level is achieved not merely by intellectual acumen, but by imagination and creativity. "The purely logical mode of halakhic reasoning draws its sustenance from the pre-rational perception and vision which erupt stormily from the depths of this personality, a personality which is enveloped with the aura of holiness. This mysterious intuition is the source of halakhic creativity and innovative insight. . . . Creative halakhic activity begins not with intellectual calculation, but with vision; not with clear formulations, but with unease; not in the clear light of rational discourse, but in the pre-rational darkness" (*Besod ha-Yahid ve-ha-Yahad*, p. 219). The halakhic personality, then, is characterized by conflict, creativity, imagination, vision. The world of Halakhah is vast and all-encompassing. One who reaches the level of being "married" to the Torah and Halakhah has come as close to eternal truth as is possible for a human being.

Halakhic Activism

Rabbi Soloveitchik emphasized the Torah's focus on this-worldy concerns. "The ideal of halakhic man is the redemption of the world not via a higher world but via the world itself, via the adaptation of empirical reality to the ideal patterns of Halakhah. . . . A lowly world is elevated through the Halakhah to the level of a divine world" (*Halakhic Man*, pp. 37–8).

Whereas the universal *homo religiosus* believes that the lower spiritual domain of this world must yearn for the higher spiritual realms, halakhic man declares that "the higher longs and pines for the lower." God created human beings to live in this world; in so doing, He endowed human life in this world with dignity and meaning.

Halakhah can be actualized only in the real world. "Halakhic man's most fervent desire is the perfection of the world under the dominion of righteousness and loving-kindness—the realization of the a priori, ideal creation, whose name is Torah (or Halakhah), in the realm of concrete life" (*Halakhic Man*, p. 94). The halakhic life, thus, is necessarily committed to this-worldly activism; the halakhic personality is devoted to the creation of a righteous society.

The Halakhah is not confined to sanctuaries, but "penetrates into every nook and cranny of life." Halakhah is in the home, the marketplace, the banquet hall, the street, the office—everywhere. As important as the synagogue is, it does not occupy the central place in halakhic Judaism. Halakhah is too vast and comprehensive to be confined to a synagogue.

Rabbi Soloveitchik argues that non-halakhic Judaism erred grievously in putting the temple at the heart of religion. "The Halakhah, the Judaism that is faithful to itself . . . which brings the Divine Presence into the midst of empirical reality, does not center about the synagogue or study house. These are minor sanctuaries. The true sanctuary is the sphere of our daily, mundane activities, for it is there that the realization of the Halakhah takes place" (*Halakhic Man*, pp. 94–5).

Consequently, halakhic Judaism is realistic, idealistic and demanding. Halakhah is concerned with every moment, with every place. Its sanctity fills the universe.

Halakhah is unequivocally committed to righteous, ethical life. The Rav points out that the great sages of Halakhah have always been known for their lofty ethical standards. The Halakhah demands high respect for the dignity of others. "To recognize a person is not just to identify him physically. It is more than that: it is an act of identifying him existentially, as a person who has a job to do, that only he can do properly. To recognize a person means to affirm that he is irreplaceable. To hurt a person means to tell him that he is expendable, that there is no need for him. The Halakhah equated the act of publicly embarrassing a person with murder" ("The Community," p. 16).

The ethical demands of Halakhah are exacting. One's personal life must be guided by halakhic teachings in every situation, in every relationship. The halakhic worldview opposes mystical quietism which is tolerant of pain and suffering. On the contrary, halakhic Judaism "wants man to cry out aloud against any kind of pain, to react indignantly to all kinds of injustice or unfairness" ("Redemption, Prayer, Talmud Torah," p. 65; see also, *U-Vikkashtem mi-Sham*, p. 16). The Rav's stress on ethical activism manifested itself in his views on religious Zionism. He accepted upon himself the mantle of leadership for religious Zionism; this placed him at odds with many Orthodox leaders who did not ascribe religious legitimacy to the State of Israel. Rabbi Soloveitchik eloquently insists that the Halakhah prohibits the missing of opportunities. After the Holocaust, the Jewish people were given the miraculous opportunity to re-establish a Jewish state in the land of Israel. For centuries, Jews had prayed for the return of Jewish sovereignty in Israel. Now, in this generation, the opportunity was being offered. For the Rav, it would be tragic and unforgivable to miss the gift of the moment. Not to respond to "the knocking of the beloved," not to respond to God's message to the suffering people of Israel—this would be a tragic error of terrible magnitude. This was not a time for hesitation: this was a time to embrace the opportunity of a Jewish State, an opportunity granted to us by the Almighty. The Rav conveyed a certain impatience with those who did not respond religiously to the new Jewish State. Like the Shulamith maiden in the Song of Songs, they were drowsy and hesitant at the very moment the beloved had returned. They were not fully awake to the significance of the moment, and the halakhic and ethical imperatives which flowed from it.

Interiority

All true religious action must be accompanied by appropriate inner feelings and thoughts. The exterior features of religious behavior must be expressions of one's interior spiritual sensibilities.

Yet in non-Orthodox circles, it has long been fashionable to deride halakhic Jews as automatons who slavishly adhere to a myriad of ancient rules and regulations. They depict Orthodox Jews as unspiritual beings who only care about the letter of the law, who nitpick over trifling details, whose souls are lost in a labyrinth of medieval codes of law. To such critics, Rabbi Soloveitchik would answer quite simply: you do not understand the Halakhah; you do not understand the nature of halakhic Judaism. Interiority is a basic feature of the halakhic way of life.

Halakhah relates not merely to an external pattern of behavior. Rather, it infuses and shapes one's inner life. "The Halakhah wishes to objectify religiosity not only through introducing the external act and the psychophysical deed into the world of religion, but also through the structuring and ordering of the inner correlative in the realm of man's spirit" (*Halakhic Man*, p. 59).

For the halakhic Jew, Halakhah is not a compilation of random laws; it is the expression of God's will. Through Halakhah, God provides a means of drawing nearer to Him, even of developing a sense of intimacy with Him. To the outsider, a person fulfilling a halakhic prescription may seem like an unthinking robot; but this skewed view totally ignores the inner life of the halakhic Jew. It does not see or sense the inner world of thought, emotion, spiritual elevation.

The halakhic Jew must expect to be misunderstood. How can others who do not live in the world of Halakhah possibly understand the profundity of halakhic life? How can those who judge others by surface behavior be expected to penetrate into the mysterious depths of a halakhic Jew's inner life? Those who stereotype Orthodoxy are thereby revealing their own ignorance of the true halakhic personality.

"Halakhic man does not quiver before any man; he does not seek out compliments, nor does he require public approval. . . . He knows that the truth is a lamp unto his feet and the Halakhah a light unto his path" (*Halakhic Man*, p. 89). The halakhic personality strives to maintain and develop inner strength. One must have the courage and self-confidence to be able to stand alone. Self-validation comes from within one's self, not from others. "Heroism is the central category in practical Judaism." The halakhic Jew needs the inner confidence "which makes it possible for him to be different" ("The Community," p. 13).

Knesset Israel

Halakhic Jews feel inextricably bound to all Jews, even those who are unsympathetic to them and their beliefs. "Judaism has stressed the wholeness and the unity of Knesset Israel, the Jewish community. The latter is not a conglomerate. It is an autonomous entity, endowed with a life of its own. . . . However strange such a concept may appear to the empirical sociologist, it is not at all a strange experience for the halakhist and the mystic, to whom Knesset Israel is a living, loving and suffering mother" ("The Community," p. 9). In one of his *teshuvah* lectures, Rabbi Soloveitchik stated that "the Jew who believes in Knesset Israel is the Jew who lives as part of it wherever it is and is willing to give his life for it, feels its pain, rejoices with it, fights in its wars, groans at its defeats and celebrates its victories" (*Al ha-Teshuvah*, p. 98). By binding oneself to the Torah, which embodies the spirit and destiny of Israel, the believer in Knesset Israel thereby is bound to all the generations of the community of Israel, past, present and future.

The Rav speaks of two types of covenant which bind Jews to Knesset Israel. The *berit goral*, the covenant of fate, is that which makes a Jew identify with Jewishness due to external pressure. Such a Jew is made conscious of Jewish identity when under attack by anti-Semites; when Israel is threatened by its enemies; when Jews around the world are endangered because of their Jewishness. The *berit goral* is connected to Jewish ethnicity and nationalism; it reminds the Jew that, like it or not, he is a Jew by fate.

The *berit yeud*, the covenant of mission and destiny, links the Jew to the positive content of Jewishness. He is Jewish because he chooses the Jewish way of life, the Torah and Halakhah; he seeks a living relationship with the God of Israel. The *berit yeud* is connected with Jewish ideals, values, beliefs, observances; it inspires the Jew to choose to live as a Jew.

The *berit goral* is clearly on a much lower spiritual level than the *berit yeud*; the ideal Jew should see Jewish identity primarily in the positive terms of the *berit yeud*. However, the Rav does not negate the significance of the *berit goral*. Even if a Jew relates to Jewishness only on the ethnic level, this at least manifests some connection to the Jewish people. Such individuals should not be discounted from Knesset Israel, nor should they be disdained as hopelessly lost as Jews. Halakhic Jews, although they cling to the *berit yeud*, must recognize their necessary relationship with those Jews whose connection to Jewishness is on the level of *berit goral*.

Ultimately, though, Jewish tradition is passed from generation to generation by those Jews who are committed to Torah and Halakhah. Thus, it is critical that all Jews be brought into the category of those for whom Jewishness is a positive, living commitment. Jewishness based on ethnicity will not insure Jewish continuity.

The Rav credited the *masorah* community with transmitting Judaism from generation to generation. The *masorah* community is composed of those Jews for whom transmission of Torah and Halakhah is the central purpose of life. It was founded by Moses and will continue into the times of the Messiah. Members of the *masorah* community draw on the traditions of former generations, teach the present generation, plan for future generations. "The *masorah* community cuts across the centuries, indeed millenia, of calendaric time and unites those who already played their part, delivered their message, acquired fame, and withdrew from the covenantal stage quietly and humbly, with those who have not yet been given the opportunity to appear on the covenantal stage and who wait for their turn in the anonymity of the 'about to be'" ("The Lonely Man of Faith," p. 47).

The *masorah* community actually embodies two dimensions—the *masorah* community of the fathers and that of the mothers. The Rav clarifies this point by a personal reminiscence. "The laws of Shabbat, for instance, were passed on to me by my father; they are part of *mussar avikha*. The Shabbat as a living entity, as a queen, was revealed to me by my mother; it is a part of *torat imekha*. The fathers *knew* much about the Shabbat; the mothers *lived* the Shabbat, experienced her presence, and perceived her beauty and splendor. The fathers taught generations how to observe the Shabbat; mothers taught generations how to greet the Shabbat and how to enjoy her twenty-four hour presence." ("A Tribute to the Rebbitzen of Talne," p. 77).

The Rav teaches that Knesset Israel is a prayerful community and a charitable community. "It is not enough to feel the pain of many, nor is it sufficient to pray for the many, if this does not lead to charitable action" ("The Community," p. 22). A responsible member of Knesset Israel must be spiritually awake, must be concerned for others, must work to help those in need. "The prayerful-charity community rises to a higher sense of communion in the teaching community, where teacher and disciple are fully united" ("The Community," p. 23). The community must engage in teaching, in transmitting, in passing the teachings of Torah to new generations.

The Rav, Our Teacher

The Rav, through his lectures and writings, was the most powerful and effective teacher of Orthodoxy of our times. In his lectures, he was able to spellbind huge audiences for hours on end. His talmudic and halakhic lessons pushed his students to the limits of their intellects, challenging them to think analytically. His insights in Torah thought were breathtaking in their depth and scope. Those who were privileged to study with him cherish their memories of the Rav. And those who have read his writings have been grateful for the privilege of learning Torah from one of the Torah giants of our time.

The Rav described his own experience when he studied Talmud. "When I sit to 'learn' I find myself immediately in the fellowship of the sages of tradition. The relationship is personal. Maimonides is at my right. Rabbenu Tam at the left. Rashi sits at the head and explicates the text. Rabbenu Tam objects, the Rambam decides, the Ra'abad attacks. They are all in my small room, sitting around my table."

Learning Torah is a trans-generational experience. It links the student with the sages of all previous generations. It creates a fellowship, a special tie of friendship and common cause. It binds together the community in a profound bond of love, and provides the foundation for future generations. Halakhic Judaism represents a millenial Jewish tradition dedicated to Torah and Halakhah, truth and righteousness, love and fear of God. It demands—and yearns to bring out—the best in us. One who strives to be a member of the trans-generational community does not suffer from spiritual homelessness.

When we and future generations sit down to study Torah, we will be privileged to share our room with Rashi and Maimonides, with Rabbenu Tam and the Rashba. And sitting right next to us will be Rabbi Joseph B. Soloveitchik, his penetrating insights leading us to greater heights in our quest to become "married" to the Torah.

References

Al ha-Teshuvah, written and edited by Pinchas Peli, Jerusalem, 5735.
Besod ha-Yahid ve-ha-Yahad, edited by Pinchas Peli, Jerusalem, 5736.
"The Community," *Tradition* 17:2 (1978), pp. 7–24.
"Confrontation," *Tradition* 6:2 (1964), pp. 5–29.
Halakhic Man, translated by Lawrence Kaplan, Philadelphia, 1983.
"The Lonely Man of Faith," *Tradition* 7:2 (1965), pp. 5–67.
"Majesty and Humility," *Tradition* 17:2 (1978), pp. 25–37.
"Redemption, Prayer and Talmud Torah," *Tradition* 17:2 (1978), pp. 55–72.
"A Tribute to the Rebbitzen of Talne," *Tradition* 17:2 (1978), pp. 73–83.
"U-Vikkashtem mi-Sham," *Hadarom*, Tishri 5739, pp. 1–83.

Rabbi Soloveitchik's spiritual leadership was manifest in his role as posek. His halakhic decisions were sought by his many students and followers; for many years, he was the chairman of the Halakhah Commission of the Rabbinical Council of America.

In this essay (Tradition *29:1*), *Walter Wurzburger examines the Rav's role as posek. The Rav combined his phenomenal mastery of Halakhah was his keen insight into the dilemmas of modern life. The Rav was deeply committed to the unity of the Jewish people, to the significance of the State of Israel, and to the ethical responsibility of Jews towards the world at large. He was a pioneer in fostering the intensive study of Talmud by women.*

The Rav respected the right of individuals to form their own opinions on matters not subject to halakhic legislation. In respecting the autonomy and freedom of individuals, and in demanding that they take responsibility and think through their own decisions, the Rav stood apart from the trend in some circles to seek authoritative guidance from halakhic luminaries on all policy matters.

Rabbi Joseph B. Soloveitchik as *Posek* of Post-Modern Orthodoxy

Walter Wurzburger

In the circles of what is labelled "Modern Orthodoxy" or "Centrist Orthodoxy," Rabbi Joseph B. Soloveitchik *z.tz.l.* is referred to as "the Rav." This appellation is not merely a sign of respect and reverence accorded a charismatic luminary, the mentor of generations of Rabbis, academicians and communal leaders, but it also attests to his role as *the* authority figure of those segments of the Orthodox community which see no conflict between commitment to Torah and full participation in scientific and cultural activities of modern society.

To the popular mind, unfortunately, "Modern Orthodoxy" represents a movement which is characterized by willingness to make all sorts of concessions to modernity at the expense of genuine religious commitment. It is perceived as a "moderate" brand of halakhic Judaism which lacks the fervor and passion associated with the *Haredi* community.

In this misinterpretation of the ideology of "Modern Orthodoxy," the adjective "modern" is treated as a modifier rather than as an attribute. To illustrate this distinction, there are all kinds of presidents: popular or unpopular, dynamic or passive, honest or corrupt. In these cases, the adjective functions as an attribute, characterizing a president. But when we speak of a past president, an honorary president, or a dead president, we are no longer dealing with presidents; the adjective does not merely add a qualification to the noun, but completely modifies the meaning of the noun. Similarly, it is widely taken for granted that "Modern Orthodoxy" is not really an authentic form of Orthodoxy, but a hybrid of an illicit union between modernity and Orthodoxy, a kind of oxymoron. Its opponents ridicule it as a compromise designed to facilitate entry into a modern lifestyle by offering less stringent interpretations of Halakhah and even condoning laxity in religious observance.

Because the term "Modern Orthodoxy" has acquired such a pejorative meaning, Rabbi Norman Lamm has proposed that we replace it with "Centrist Orthodoxy."[1] In my opinion, "Post-Modern Orthodoxy" would be the most appropriate designation for a movement which stands not for evasion or accommodation but for uncompromising confrontation of modernity.

It is this type of halakhic Judaism which can invoke the spiritual authority of the Rav, who never wavered in his demand for scrupulous adherence to Halakhah. His aim was not to make halakhic observance more convenient. On the contrary, in many areas, such as *hilkhot avelut*, the construction of *eruvin* in cities, refusal to grant a *shetar mekhirah* authorizing non-Jewish workers to operate Jewish factories or commercial establishments on Shabbat, the Rav has consistently issued rulings that surpass in stringency those of right-wing authorities. He was especially particular in observing all the Brisker stringencies pertaining to the writing of *shetarot*. I recall spending close to two hours with the Rav on writing a simple *shetar prozbol*. As opposed to other poskim, he did not condone the signing of a *ketubah* before *shekiah* when the actual *huppah* would take place *bein ha-shemashot*. Similarly, he did not permit the scheduling of weddings *bein ha-shemashot*, even when this would have been more convenient for the concerned parties. For that matter, he was opposed to the modernization of synagogue services. He even objected to announcements of pages during *hazarat ha-shatz*, the composition of prayers for special occasions, and the recital of invocations, because they smacked of the attempt to dilute traditional Jewish approaches with prevailing American practices.

The Rav's traditionalism can also be discerned in his emphasis upon what he called *mesorah ma'asit* (established practice). Once a halakhic practice was agreed upon, it could no longer be modified by reliance on opinions which had previously been rejected.[2] This respect for established norms manifested itself in his aversion to utilizing even newly discovered manuscripts of Rishonim for halakhic purposes.[3]

Notwithstanding the Rav's traditionalism, I disagree with Moshe Sokol's and David Singer's[4] contention that the Rav, for all his philosophical brilliance and his extensive scientific knowledge, really cannot be invoked as an authority figure for Modern Orthodoxy, since in his halakhic decision-making he operates exclusively with traditional methods and does not permit philosophical ideas or the findings of modern textual scholarship to impinge upon the formation of his halakhic rulings. They claim that his halakhic positions and methodologies do not differ basically from those of other *poskim*, who have insulated themselves against modernity. The traditional nature of his halakhic reasoning is also evidenced by the fact that his vast Talmudic erudition and the profundity and originality of his scholarship is widely admired even by many of the leading figures of the *Haredi* community ("right-wing" Orthodoxy), which demands total isolation from modern, secular culture.

What differentiates the approach of Rav Soloveitchik from that of *Haredi poskim* and makes him the authority figure of so-called "Modern Orthodoxy" is his endorsement of secular studies, including philosophy, his espousal of religious Zionism, and his pioneering of intensive Jewish education for women. Although these policies are not logically connected, they are closely related to each other, because they arise from the conviction that a *Torat Hayyim* addresses the realities of the world rather than seeks an escape from them. It is this religious philosophy, which engenders a unique approach to Halakhah, which has made him into the *posek par excellence* of Modern Orthodoxy.

The Rav's objection to the employment of modern historic and textual scholarship to ascertain the meaning of Halakhah reflects not naive traditionalism but highly sophisticated post-modern critical thought. He insists that Halakhah operate with its own unique canons of interpretation. According to R. Soloveitchik, scientific methods are appropriate only for the explanation of natural phenomena but have no place in the quest for the understanding of the normative and cognitive concepts of Halakhah, which imposes its own *a priori* categories, which differ from those appropriate in the realm of science. It is for this reason that the Rav completely ignores Bible criticism and eschews the "positive historical" approach of the "Science of Judaism."

Whole-hearted endorsement of traditional halakahic methodology and concomitant rejection of historicism is, however, fully compatible with a positive attitude towards some values of modernity. The Rav always insisted that historic contingencies have no bearing upon the halakhic process. In his view, Halakhah represented an *a priori* system of ideas and concepts to be applied to empirical realities. When Rav Soloveitchik looks upon the study of sciences and the development of technology as religiously desirable, it cannot be said that he reads the value system of the Enlightenment[5] into the halakhic tradition. After all, he unequivocally opposes many of the most fundamental tenets of the Enlightenment. Thus he rejects its belief that religion lacks cognitive significance and that its function is to manifest itself in the realms of feeling and actions rather than to concern itself with dogmas or articles of faith pertaining to theoretical beliefs.[6] Similarly, he categorically rejects the Enlightenment conception of the superiority of natural religion over the various revealed religions.[7] For the Rav, Halakhah represents not a human construct designed to relate to Transcendence, but a divinely revealed cognitive approach to God and the world. He

denies the fundamental premises of liberal religion, because on epistemological grounds he maintains that human efforts to search for God
are doomed to failure[8] and that man can find Him only when overwhelmed by His Presence. He stresses the primacy not of the religious
experience but of Halakhah. The Rav's rejection of natural theology,
while similar to Karl Barth's position, arises from his conviction that
Halakhah is not merely a normative discipline, but must provide the
foundation for Jewish philosophy.[9] Such an orientation is diametrically
opposed to the ethos of the Enlightenment, which, as Kant formulated
it, constitutes "man's exodus from self-incurred tutelage."[10]

Since the Rav stresses heteronomous divine Revelation rather than
the autonomy of human reason and conscience, his notion of Adam I,
the "man of majesty," is not a concession to modernity but an authentic
interpretation of the Jewish value system. Those who follow in the
footsteps of Rambam, need not expound the Jewish tradition in
conformity with the quietistic and pietistic mindset of European
Orthodoxy.

It must, however, be emphasized that for the Rav the endorsement
of scientific methods is strictly limited to the realm of Adam I, whose
function it is to harness the world of nature for the benefit of humanity. But causal explanations are irrelevant in the domain of Adam II,
who can overcome his existential loneliness only through the establishment of a "covenantal community," enabling him to relate to
transcendence.

The Rav's approach is reminiscent of the Kantian dichotomy between
science and ethics. According to Kant, determinism, while indispensable to the perception of phenomena, renders impossible the moral
"ought." He therefore regarded freedom as an indispensable postulate
of ethics. Similarly, Rav Soloveitichik insists that it is totally illicit to
"explain" (in reality, explain away) religious phenomena by application
of methods which are legitimate only with respect to the concerns of
Adam I.

The dichotomy between Adam I and Adam II, which in the Rav's
view arises from the very ontological nature of man, mirrors the

conflict which the Rav personally experienced with his move to Berlin. Reminiscing about his student days, the Rav once remarked to me: "You have no idea how enormously difficult it was for me to move from the world of R. Hayyim to that of Berlin University. Even my children cannot appreciate it, because they already found a paved road. But my generation was challenged to become pioneers."

It was out of this tension that Rav Soloveitchik developed a formula which enabled him to encounter the value system of modernity while remaining fully committed to traditional halakhic methodology. To apply scientific methods or the tools of modern historic scholarship to Halakhah would do violence to the integrity of the system. Those who insist upon applying historic scholarship to the analysis of Halakhah commit the "genetic fallacy." In the Rav's view, Halakhah must encounter reality by imposing upon it its own autonomous set of *a priori* categories, which are completely independent of scientific or historic factors.

It is, however, one thing to affirm that halakhic concepts are *a priori*, and another to maintain that subjective factors play no role in halakhic decision-making. As a matter of fact, Rav Soloveitchik always emphasized that halakhic decision-making is not purely mechanical but highly creative. A *posek* is not a computer. It is therefore inevitable that like everyone else's, the Rav's halakhic rulings, especially the perception and assessment of the realities to which halakhic *a priori* notions are to be applied, reflect to some extent his personal philosophical convictions. From his perspective, human creativity and initiative in science and technology are not merely legitimate but eminently desirable, because they reflect the dignity conferred upon creatures bearing the divine image.[11]

This stance is usually rejected by the so called "yeshivah world," which assigns religious significance to creativity only insofar as it is directly and immediately related to the field of Torah. R. Hayyim of Volozhin makes the point that while human beings are mandated to imitate the creativity of the Creator, this emulation is possible only in the exercise of spiritual creativity. This is in keeping with Kabbalistic doctrines which affirm that only Torah study and observance of the Commandments create new spiritual worlds in the higher regions of being and are instrumental in helping bring about the re-unification of God with the *Shekhinah*.[12] In the view of the classical yeshivah world, science and technology do not qualify as genuine creativity, since they rely exclusively on purely natural processes. The Rav objects to this denigration of "secular" activities and contends that scientific and technological creativity also constitutes an intrinsically valuable mode of imitating the divine Creator.

It is against this background that we can appreciate the Rav's enthusiasm for scientific and philosophical studies. Whereas in the Yeshiva world, secular studies are condoned only to the extent necessary to making a living, the Rav endowed them with intrinsic value, because they enable human beings to realize the ideals of Adam I. This explains why he encouraged many of his disciples to pursue graduate studies in secular fields.

The Rav's *z.tz.l.* endorsement of Religious Zionism is also closely related to his belief that taking the initiative in ameliorating natural, economic, social or political conditions, far from being a usurpation of divine prerogatives, represents a religiously mandated activity of becoming partners with God in the process of Creation.[13] This position is radically different from that prevailing in the *Haredi* community. Although they may not be quite as extreme as the *Neturei Karta*, who refuse to acknowledge the legitimacy of the State of Israel, the rest of the *Haredi* community, nevertheless, is not prepared to ascribe any religious value to the existence of a sovereign Jewish state in the pre-Messianic era. While reconciling themselves to the recognition of Israel as a *de facto* reality, they cannot view as a religious desideratum a Jewish state that came into being as a result of political activity and not through supernatural intervention. In their opinion, reliance on human initiatives to establish a "secular" Jewish state cannot be reconciled with belief in God the Redeemer, who would restore the Jewish people to its national homeland when the process of catharsis was completed and Israel would become worthy of the Redemption.

Significantly, so dominant was the quietistic streak in traditional circles that the devotees of the Hatam Sofer opposed any involvement in the political arena, even for the limited purpose of improving the socio-political conditions of Diaspora Jewry. It was argued that if God really wanted the Jewish people to enjoy more rights and more tolerable conditions, He did not need the assistance of the Jewish community to accomplish this and there was no point in petitioning the rulers of the various nations for better conditions. With religious faith being equated with such a sense of total dependence upon God that all human efforts were dismissed as essentially inconsequential, one could hardly expect sympathy for the Zionist revolution, which, instead of merely passively awaiting the arrival of the Messiah, insisted upon human initiatives leading eventually to the birth of a Jewish state.[14]

Although the Rav's advocacy of Religious Zionism is closely connected with his conception of Adam I, it would, of course, have been possible for him to follow in the footsteps of R. Samson Raphael Hirsch and endorse human initiatives in general, while insisting that the return to a national Jewish homeland had to await the Messianic Redemption. He could have chosen the course charted by the German Agudat Yisrael, which enthusiastically subscribed to the ideal of *Torah im Derekh Eretz* while maintaining all-out opposition to Zionism. As a matter of fact, it was only after his arrival in the United States that he left Agudah and identified with Mizrachi, of which he subsequently became the leading ideologist.

The Rav shared with Yitzchak Breuer the conviction that the time had arrived when Torah ideals (especially those relating to Adam I) could best be realized by building a Jewish society in *Eretz Yisrael.* As opposed to Breuer, who developed and transformed the Hirschian doctrine of *Torah im Derekh Eretz* into that of *Torah im Derekh Eretz Yisrael,* the Rav's approach to the building of a Jewish state was completely devoid of Messianic overtones but focused upon the material and spiritual needs of the Jewish people and the obligation to do whatever is in one's power to ameliorate their conditions.[15] Similarly, the absence of Messianic motifs prevented the Rav from subscribing to the Gush Emunim philosophy, which of late has made such inroads into Mizrachi circles.

This realistic approach to the State of Israel was responsible for his reluctance to authorize the recital of *Hallel* on *Yom Ha'atzmaut* and *Yom Yerushalayim*. If the chapters of *Tehillim* which comprised *Hallel* were to be recited, he recommended saying them some time after *Kaddish Titkabel* and not immediately following the *Shemoneh Esreh* as is customary on *Yom Tov* or *Rosh Hodesh*.

The Rav's commitment to Religious Zionism was possible only because he opposed the secessionist tendencies which Yitzchak Breuer had inherited from his grandfather, Samson Raphael Hirsch. Breuer disapproved of membership in the Zionist movement and, for that matter, frowned upon any association with groups which were not totally committed to the ideals of halakhic Judaism. The Rav maintained that Halakhah demands a sense of identification with all Jews, regardless of their religious convictions or practices.

Although the rise of Hitler may have strengthened the Rav's conviction that Jews formed a community of fate[16] and not merely one of faith, opposition to total separation from non-observant segments of the Jewish community was a long standing family tradition, which can be traced back to Netziv.[17] The Rav frequently referred to the example of his illustrious grandfather, R. Hayyim of Brisk, who, on a Yom Kippur evening before *Kol Nidrei*, asked the community to desecrate the holiness of Yom Kippur in order to gather the funds needed to save the life of a follower of the Bund from execution. The fact that this "Bundist" was an atheist and an opponent of halakhic Judaism had no bearing upon the requirement to concern oneself with the fate of every Jew.

In his insistence that failure to observe Halakhah does not affect one's status as a full fledged member of the Jewish people, the Rav went so far as to urge kohanim who were not Sabbath observers to participate in *Birkat Kohanim*. According to his ruling, only transgressions of prohibitions specifically governing kohanim, but not violation of other halakhic norms (with the exception of homicide), disqualify a kohen from *dukhening*.

The emphasis upon the nationalistic dimension of Jewishness comes also to the fore in the Rav's frequent references to the halakhic opinion that anyone who loses his life because of his Jewishness is regarded as having died *al kiddush haShem*. He regarded this as precedent for his belief that any one who gives up his life in the defense of the State of Israel should be viewed as having died *al kiddush ha-Shem*.[18]

It was because of his solicitude for the material and spiritual well-being of every Jew that despite his insistence that a *mehitzah* was an absolute halakhic requirement, the Rav occasionally permitted rabbis to accept pulpits in synagogues which flouted this norm. His leniency was due to his belief that the presence of a dedicated rabbi was likely to result in the raising of religious standards (e.g., establishment of day schools, *kashrut, taharat ha-Mishpahah*, etc.). I vividly recall the Rav's address to a Rabbinical Council convention where he discussed the dilemma facing the *posek* who is torn between the prohibition against worshiping in a synagogue which violates halakhic standards and the responsibility to prevent the total assimilation of a Jewish community. The Rav cited this as an illustration of the difficulties inherent in the *Derekh ha-Benoni*, a philosophy of moderation, which, unlike extremist positions, must mediate between a plurality of conflicting values and obligations.

The emphasis placed upon the ethnic and nationalistic components of Jewish identity inspired the Rav's interpretation of the meaning and implications of the *B'rit Avraham* and the *B'rit Mitzrayim* which established the Jewish community of fate.[19] These covenants mandate a sense of solidarity and kinship among all the members of the Jewish Covenantal community of fate and affirm the need to recognize the centrality of *Eretz Yisrael* for the destiny of the Jewish people. Since these covenants preceded the community of faith established by the Sinaitic Covenant and constitute integral and indispensable components of the Jewish faith, we must not limit our concern to the protection of the interests of the religious sector. We should aim not merely at the preservation of isolated religious enclaves, but at the creation of a society which will foster loyalty to Torah on the part of the entire Jewish people.[20] The Torah is addressed not to a religious elite but to the entire Jewish people.

The importance the Rav attached to the *B'rit Avraham* also explains his refusal to concur with the famous *issur* (prohibition) banning participation in the Syngagogue Council of America and the New York Board of Rabbis, which was issued by a group of prominent *roshei yeshivah*.

To be sure, the Rav could not have harbored the slightest sympathy for Jewish religious movements which deviated from halakhic norms. His conception of Judaism was so Halakhah-centered that he denied any Jewish religious significance to purely subjective attempts to reach out for Transcendence. Moreover, his followers in Boston did not belong to the interdenominational Rabbinical Association or to The Associated Synagogues, a lay body consisting of some Orthodox and a large number of Conservative and Reform congregations. He went so far as to rule that one should not worship in a Conservative synagogue, even when there was no other opportunity to listen to the sounding of the *shofar*. What prevented the Rav from joining other *roshei yeshivah* in demanding withdrawal from interdenominational umbrella groups was his fear that leaving organizations in which Orthodoxy had participated for many years would be a divisive move at a time when Jewish unity was so essential. Although ideally he would have preferred that these umbrella groups would not have come into existence, his ideological considerations were subordinated to his overriding concern for the welfare of the Jewish people and the security of the State of Israel. He therefore did not object to the participation of Orthodox organizations in the Synagogue Council of America, as long its functions were limited to representing the total Jewish community to governmental agencies or non-Jewish denominations (*kelappei hutz*).

There are some revisionist accounts of the Rav's attitude to the Synagogue Council. It has been reported that while the Rav opposed the continued membership of Orthodox groups, the Rabbinical Council refused to abide by his instructions. To point out the absurdity of this claim, one need only take into consideration the indisputable fact that as the chairman of its Halakhah commission, the Rav was the unchallenged halakhic authority of the Rabbinical Council of America. I cannot help but be amused by fanciful accounts of the Rav's views on the issue. I vividly recall a session with the Rav and the late Rabbi Klavan, when we mapped strategy to prevent the Union from seceding from the Synagogue Council.

The Rav's opposition to moves which threatened the unity of the Jewish community also manifested itself in his attitudes towards non-Orthodox groups. He counselled against denying Conservative or Reform Rabbis the right to use communal *mikva'ot* for conversions. Moreover, he once instructed me that Reform conversions that were accompanied by circumcision and immersion in a *mikvah* had to be treated as a *safek giyur*. (Accordingly, a *get* would be required to dissolve a marriage in which one of the partners previously underwent a Conservative or Reform conversion which conformed to the requirement of *milah* and *tevilah*.)

Rav Soloveitchik's emphasis upon Jewish particularism, which prompted him to attach so much weight to the welfare and security of the State of Israel and of all Jews regardless of their religious orientation, stood in marked contrast to the universalism and outright hostility to Zionism of Hermann Cohen, whose philosophical doctrines he not only analyzed in his Ph.D. dissertation but which also impacted upon the development of his own thought. Cohen's influence is especially noticeable in the *Ish ha-Halakhah* and in the conception of Adam I of "The Lonely Man of Faith," which extol intellectual, cultural, scientific, technological and political activities as *religious* desiderata. But, despite his admiration for some aspects of neo-Kantianism, the Rav categorically rejected Cohen's uncompromising rationalism and radical universalism, which were utterly incompatible with belief in supernatural Revelation or the affirmation of Jewish particularism.

Notwithstanding these fundamental disagreements concerning the very essence of Judaism, R. Soloveitchik adopted Cohen's thesis that the Rambam's ethical views reflected a Platonic rather than an Aristotelian approach. According to Aristotle, human beings became most God-like through intellectual perfection. Plato, however, maintained that ethical conduct and attainment of virtue constituted *imitatio Dei*. This accounts for the centrality of ethics in the Rav's religious philosophy. Throughout his writings he repeatedly makes the point that the Torah is not a metaphysical treatise but the source of normative guidance.

Professor Ravitzki[21] has advanced some cogent arguments against Cohen's interpretation of Maimonides' ethical views. But for our purposes, this controversy is irrelevant, since it is of interest only to the student of the history of ideas. What matters for us is that, basing himself on the Rambam, the Rav unequivocally declared that striving for ever higher rungs of moral perfection is the pre-eminent approach to *imitatio Dei*.

This emphasis upon ethics must be seen not as a concession to modern Jewish thinkers such as Mendelssohn, Luzzatto, Ahad Ha'am and Cohen, but it reflects his affinity for Maimonidean approaches. Unlike Yehudah Halevi, who relegated ethical norms to the domain of social necessities and assigned to the performance of ritual laws the function of cultivating the religious faculty (*Inyan ha-Eloki*), Maimonides stresses the religious significance of ethics. The Rav frequently pointed out that all our ethical norms are grounded in *imitatio Dei*. I show elsewhere[22] that Rambam himself (in his more mature formulation in the *Mishneh Torah*, as opposed to his earlier conception in the *Sefer haMitzvot*) did not go so far; he invoked *imitatio Dei* only as prooftext for the cultivation of ethical traits of character but not for performance of ethical actions.

It should also be noted that the Rav had serious doubts whether a purely secular ethics is possible. In this he anticipated the critique of Alistair McIntyre of all post-Enlightenment attempts to found ethics without any reference to a divine source.[23] Moreover, R. Soloveitchik maintained that, at the very most, a purely secular ethics can do justice only to those aspects of human nature which reflect Adam I. But since the ontological nature of human beings also involves Adam II, a purely secular ethics is bound to be inadequate.

Since the Rav maintains that the entire ethical domain is founded upon *imitatio Dei*, he was extremely sensitive to ethical demands. Out of ethical principles, he refused to grant a *shetar mekhirah* to one of the most important benefactors of his Day School in Boston, who wanted to be able to operate his plants on Shabbat. When questioned why another renowned halakhic authority had no difficulty in arranging a *shetar mekhirah* for the same plants, the Rav explained that his refusal was motivated by his concern that enabling industrialists to operate their business on Shabbat by transferring ownership to a non-Jew would make it much more difficult for *shomrei Shabbat* to obtain employment in firms owned by Orthodox Jews.

Even more revealing of the Rav's emphasis upon ethical values is his conviction that in a democratic society which grants equal rights and opportunities to Jews, some of the halakhic provisions regarding *mesirah* do not apply. He therefore unequivocally stated that governmental employees must apply the law to Jew and non-Jew alike. His sense of gratitude to America for according Jews full equality also comes to the fore in his positive attitude towards the observance of Thanksgiving as a national holiday.

Ethical considerations also played a major role in his revolutionary ruling that yeshivot had the right to institute a lottery for the chaplaincy,[24] compelling rabbis, who were exempted from the draft, to "volunteer" to serve in the armed forces as chaplains. The Rav endorsed this procedure in spite of the fact that it was probable that the chaplain might be forced to desecrate the Sabbath. In support of his opinion, R. Soloveitchik cited halakhic precedents demonstrating that one may embark on religiously worthwhile projects even at the risk that they might lead to serious transgressions of halakhic norms. It is, however, significant that the Rav's *z.tz.l.* solicitude for the welfare of personnel serving in the armed forces prompted him even to endorse sanctions against rabbis refusing to serve in the chaplaincy. His conviction that there was a moral obligation not to abandon Jews in need of rabbinic guidance overrode his reluctance to put observant Jews in a position where they had no choice but to desecrate the Sabbath. He made this ruling in spite of the generally accepted halakhic norm that "one does not encourage an individual to commit a sin in order to benefit another individual."[25]

Because of his deep-rooted conviction that Jews have an ethico-religious responsibility to the world at large, the Rav found it necessary to devise a formula to enable Jewish participation in inter-religious consultations and activities without jeopardizing the integrity and uniqueness of the Jewish faith experience. Contrary to widespread misconceptions, his essay "Confrontation" and the guidelines for interfaith discussions were not intended to forestall meaningful exchanges between representatives of Judaism and of other religions. Rabbi Isadore Twersky, the Rav's son-in-law, told me that at one time the Rav considered an invitation to deliver a lecture at the Christian-Jewish colloquium held at the Harvard Divinity School. Moreover, the Rav's classic article "The Lonely Man of Faith" was first presented as an oral lecture at a Catholic seminary in Brighton, Massachusets. While he looked upon interreligious discussions of purely theological issues as exercises in futility, he approved of discussions devoted to socio-political issues, in spite of the fact that as he noted in a footnote to "Confrontation,"[26] for people of faith such issues are not secular concerns but are grounded in theological convictions.

The Rav's sensitivity to ethical concerns also led him to sponsor research to find more humane methods than hoisting and shackling to prepare animals for *shechitah*. As a general rule, the Orthodox establishment was concerned only with blocking legislation affecting *shechitah*. But the Rav felt that it was irresponsible to ignore the clamor for reducing the pain animals endured prior to *shechitah*.

The Rav's sharp reaction to the tragic massacres in Lebanon,[27] when large segments of the Jewish community wanted to sweep the problem under the rug, also attests to his extraordinary concern for ethical propriety. It was because of the threat that unless Mafdal pressed for the appointment of an independent investigation commission, he would publicly resign from membership in Mizrachi, that the leadership of Religious Zionism had no choice but to comply with his request.

His extraordinary ethical sensitivity engendered what at first blush strikes us as non-traditional attitudes towards women. Although he never advocated egalitarianism or questioned the halakhic stipulations governing the respective roles of the genders, he emphasized that these distinctions by no means implied an inferior status. Significantly, he interpreted the verse that Eve was to function as Adam's *eizer kenegdo* in the sense that Eve was not simply to function as Adam's helpmeet, but that she was supposed to help him by being *kenegdo*, i.e., complementing Adam by offering opposing perspectives. In a similar vein, the Rav invoked the special dignity of women as an explanation for the halakhic rule disqualifying women from serving as witnesses. He compared their status to that of a king, who, according to Jewish law, is disqualified from serving as a witness because it is incompatible with royal dignity to be subjected to cross-examination. By the same token, he took pains to point out that the reason why *kevod ha-Tzibbur* was invoked as the ground for barring women from receiving an *aliyah* reflected not inferior status but the fear that males when hearing the Torah read by an attractive woman might have improper thoughts.

Ethical considerations also prompted the Rav's refusal to participate in granting a *heter me'ah rabbanim* to husbands whose wives were unwilling to accept a get. The Rav explained that his policy was based upon the realization that, if the shoe were on the other foot, corresponding procedures would not be available to the wife.

Especially revolutionary was his pioneering of the intensive study of *Gemara* by women. He was convinced that under contemporary conditions, it was necessary to confront the challenge of modernity, and therefore Jewish women must be provided with the intellectual resources needed to appreciate the meaning of halakhic Judaism. Mere familiarity with the do's and don'ts of religious observance would no longer be adequate, especially at a time when mothers rather than fathers exercise the strongest influence upon children. If Jewish mothers were to provide proper guidance to their children in an era when relatively few Jews abided by Halakhah, they had to possess a real understanding of the halakhic process, since without knowledge of Halakhah one could not possibly acquire a genuinely Jewish perspective. It was for this reason that the Rav insisted that girls receive thorough instruction in *Gemara* at his Maimonides Day School in Boston. Many years later, Stern College and some other institutions followed suit, and, despite the traditional aversion to instructing girls in *Gemara*, initiated programs for intensive study not merely of the practical aspects needed for proper observance, but also of the theoretical underpinnings of the Halakhah.

We have so far discussed a number of specific issues which pointed to the uniqueness of the Rav as an authority figure for Modern Orthodoxy. But even more important is the Rav's general approach to the nature of rabbinic authority, which in his view was limited to the domain of *pesak halakhah*. He respected the right of individuals to form their own opinions and attitudes with respect to matters which were not subject to halakhic legislation. Because of his respect for human autonomy and individuality, he never wanted to impose his particular attitudes upon others or even offer his personal opinions as *Da'at Torah*.[28] On the contrary, when I turned to him for guidance on policy matters, which at times also involved halakhic considerations, he frequently replied that I should rely upon my own judgment. Similarly, whenever the Rav expounded on his philosophy of Halakhah, he stressed that these were merely his personal opinions which he was prepared to share with others but which did not possess any kind of authoritative status.

This non-authoritarian approach runs counter to current trends in the Orthodox community which seeks authoritative guidance from halakhic luminaries on all policy matters. Nowadays, fundamentalism flourishes because, as Eric Fromm has pointed out, there are many who desperately seek an escape from personal responsibility. Although

the Rav's approach does not satisfy the demand for dogmatic pro-
nouncements, in the long run it holds the greatest promise for those
seeking to combine commitment to Halakhah with a selective acceptance of the ethos of modernity, which emphasizes the preciousness
of individual autonomy and freedom. According to the Rav, these
"modern" values are implicit in the biblical and rabbinic doctrine of
kevod ha-beriot, the dignity due to human beings by virtue of their
bearing the *tzelem Elokim.*[29]

One might argue that such a stance, far from constituting a concession
to modernity, represents a reaffirmation of classical teachings of Biblical
and Rabbinic Judaism, which frequently have been neglected. One
therefore might conclude that Orthodoxy would be spiritually far
healthier if the Rav would be accepted as a role model not merely by
"Modern Orthodoxy" but rather by all halakhically committed Jews
of the modern era.

Notes

1. See my article "Centrist Orthodoxy," *Journal of Jewish Thought*, Rabbinical Council of America, 1985, pp. 67–75.

2. R. Joseph B. Soloveitchik, *Shiurim le-Zekher Abba Mari z.l.*, (Jerusalem, 1984), pp. 220–239.

3. Rav Soloveitchik's attitude resembles that of the Hazon Ish, whose views on this issue were discussed by Zvi A. Yehudah, "Hazon Ish on Textual Criticism and Halakhah," *Tradition*, 18:2, Summer 1980, pp. 172–80.

4. David Singer and Moshe Sokol, "Joseph Soloveitchik: Lonely Man of Faith," *Modern Judaism*, vol. 2, 1982, pp. 227–272.

5. See my article "The Enlightenment, the Emancipation and the Jewish Religion," *Judaism*, Fall 1989, pp. 309–407.

6. Ernst Cassirer, *The Philosophy of the Enlightenment*, Fritz B. Koellin and James A. Pettegrove, trans. (Princeton, NJ: Princeton University Press, 1951), p. 169.

7. *Ibid.*, pp. 170–171.

8. See R. Joseph B. Soloveitchik, *Ish ha-Halakhah—Galui ve-Nistar*, World Zionist Organization, Jerusalem, 1979, pp. 122–134.

9. Joseph B. Soloveitchik, *The Halakhic Mind* (New York: MacMillan), 1986, pp. 85–89.

10. See Ernst Cassirer, *Ibid.*, p. 163.

11. Joseph B. Soloveitchik, "The Lonely Man of Faith," *Tradition*, 7:2, Summer 1965, pp. 5–67, especially pp. 13–16. See also my article, "The Maimonidean Matrix of Rabbi Soloveitchik's Two-Tiered Ethics," in J.V. Plaut, ed., *Through the Sound of Many Voices* (Toronto: Lester and Orpen Dennys, 1982), pp. 172–183.

12. See Rabbi Chaim of Volozhin, *Nefesh Hayyim*. See also my article "Confronting the Challenge of the Values of Modernity," *Torah uMadda Journal*, 1, 1989, pp. 104–112.

13. See Michael Rosenack, "Ha-Adam ha-Yehudi ve-Hamedinah," in *Sefer ha-Yovel Likhvod ha-Rav ha-Gaon R.Y.D. Soloveitchik*, Shaul Yisraeli, Nachum Lamm, Yitzchak Raphael, ed. (Jerusalem: Mosad Harav Kook, 1984), pp. 152–169.

14. See my "Religious Zionism—Compromise or Ideal," *Religious Zionism*, (Jerusalem: Mesilot), 1989, pp. 26–31.

15. See R. Joseph B. Soloveitchik, *Hamesh Derashot*, translated by David Telzner, Jerusalem, Tal Orot, 1974 and "Kol Dodi Dofek," in *Besod Hayahid Vehayahad*, ed. Pinchas H. Peli (Jerusalem: Orot, 1976), pp. 333–400.

16. "Kol Dodi Dofek," pp. 368–377.

17. Naftali Zvi Yehudah Berlin, *Meshiv Davar*, responsum 44.

18. See *Hamesh Derashot*, pp. 89–90

19. "Kol Dodi Dofek," pp. 368–380 and *Hamesh Derashot*, pp. 87–92.

20. See my essay, "Religious Zionism—Compromise or Ideal?" *op. cit.*, pp. 26–31.

21. Aviezer Ravitzki, "Kinyan ha-Da'at Beheguto: Bein ha-Rambam leNeo-Kantianism," in *Sefer ha-Yovel Likhvod ha-Rav ha-Gaon R. Y.D. Soloveitchik, op. cit.*, pp. 141–151.

22. "Imitatio Dei in Maimonides' Sefer Hamitzvot and the Mishneh Torah," *Tradition and Transition,* Jonathan Sacks, ed., 1986, pp. 321–324. See also my "The Centrality of Virtue-ethics in Maimonides," of *Scholars, Savants and their Texts*, Ruth, Link-Salinger, ed. (New York: Peter Lang, 1989), pp. 251–260. See also chapter 5 of my book, *Ethics of Responsibility*, (Philadelphia: Jewish Publication Society, 1994).

23. See Alistair McIntyre, *After Virtue* (Notre Dame University Press, 1981), pp. 49–75.

24. Emanuel Rackman, "Secular Jurisprudence and Halakhah," *Jewish Law Annual*, vol. 8, p. 57.

25. B.T. Kiddushin 55b.

26. "Confrontation," *Tradition* 6:2 (1964), p. 5.

27. See Michael Rosenack, *op. cit.*, p. 169.

28. I am of course aware that in his eulogy on R. Hayyim Ozer Grodzinski ("Nosei Hatzitz ve-hahoshen" in Joseph B. Soloveitchik, *Divrei Hegut ve-Ha'arakha* (Jerusalem: World Zionist Organization, 1991), pp. 187–94), the Rav insists that the authority invested in rabbinic leadership must not be restricted to formal halakhic rulings, but also extends over public policy issues. It must, however, be borne in mind that the Rav referred here to an official Rav of a community whose authority was formally recognized by election or appointment to a position of leadership. This must not be confused with the *Da'at Torah* dispensed by various *roshei yeshivah* who cannot claim a public mandate for guidance of a community.

It should also be noted that the authority of the Priest was based upon the supernatural guidance provided by the "Urim ve-Tumim" and the possession of *ru'ah haKodesh*. See also Lawrence Kaplan's discussion of the issue in his study "Daas Torah," *Rabbinic Authority and Personal Autonomy*, Moshe Z. Sokol, ed. (Northvale, New Jersey: Jason Aronson, 1992), pp. 8–10.

29. See R. Joseph B. Soloveitchik, *Yemei Zikaron*, translated by Moshe Kroneh (Jerusalem: World Zionist Organization, 1986), pp. 9–28.

In this essay (Tradition *24:2*), *Marvin Fox argues that there is "an overarching unity of doctrine, methodology and structure" which informs the Rav's thought. While the Rav's works are written in different styles, this by no means implies a lack of internal unity and coherence in his outlook.*

The unifying principle in all of Rabbi Soloveitchik's work is his conviction that Halakhah is the only legitimate source of Jewish doctrine. Even when dealing with the philosophical issue of evil, the Rav focuses the discussion on how Halakhah governs our behavior and shapes our response.

The Unity and Structure of Rabbi Joseph B. Soloveitchik's Thought

Marvin Fox

A great thinker, especially one who expresses himself in complex and subtle language, always risks being misunderstood. This has been the fate of great philosophers of the past and it continues to be the case among contemporary thinkers as well.[1] The religious and philosophical thought of Rabbi Joseph B. Soloveitchik is no exception to this rule. For the most part, the literature on the Rav's work tends, with some happy exceptions, either to mindless uncritical panegyric, or else to ill-informed and even hostile criticism. One of the criticisms that has gained considerable currency is that the Rav's thought lacks a single unifying center, that it is riddled with a mass of unresolved contradictions. I propose in this paper to show that there are, in fact, a clear and integrating central focus and a fully developed methodology which together serve to unify and structure the work of the Rav, despite the diversity of style and theme which is to be found in his published writings.

I

Before pursuing our study it is important to call attention to certain hazards which confront students of the Rav's thought. First, it is essential to maintain a very sharp distinction between those works which were written by him and published with his authorization and all the rest of the published corpus, whether authorized, quasi-authorized, or not authorized at all. Much has appeared in Rav Soloveitchik's name which purports to be his work, but is in fact only someone else's summary or paraphrase of what they believe him to have said. The very best example of a work prepared for publication by another hand is *Al ha-Teshuvah*, a collection of the Rav's oral discourses which were first given in Yiddish and subsequently rendered into Hebrew by Pinchas Peli. The text rings true and it is as reliable a representation of his thought as one might hope for from someone other than himself. There are, however, a number of far less reliable works which represent themselves as essays by the Rav but have been done by other people. In most cases these have been published without any proper authorization, and in some cases even against the explicit opposition of the Rav and his family. In some instances they are of poor quality and are far from meeting the standards of style, content, and ideas that are characteristic of the Rav's own work. Unhappily, far too many people presume to speak and to write in his name. However well-intended, they do a great disservice to him and to the community of students and scholars who look to him as a teacher of Judaism of unparalleled scope and depth in our generation.

Anyone who seeks to achieve a reliable understanding and appreciation of the Rav's thought should confine himself to those studies which he himself wrote and whose publication he approved.[2] It should always be remembered that he writes with painstaking care and that every word and phrase is carefully chosen. Language and thought are inseparably connected in his work, and one must not rely on someone else's paraphrases or summaries even when they are well done. The Rav's style of meticulously careful writing is rooted in a long tradition. The most striking post-talmudic example is Maimonides who tells us in his Introduction to the *Guide of the Perplexed* that every single word of his book has been carefully and deliberately chosen and that the organization of the entire work is consciously planned at every point. A more recent model is Rabbi Hayyim Soloveitchik, the Rav's grandfather.[3] As the disciple of these paradigmatic figures, the Rav devoted infinite care to his writing. It is clear that no work published under his name should be taken as a reliable source for his teachings unless it actually came from his pen and was submitted for publication with his approval. Even in cases where the actual words may be his own, as recorded on tape or even in a privately held manuscript, a work is not to be taken as authoritative unless it was published with his explicit approval. He alone is the judge of what is in a form that he considers final and ready for publication. To ignore this *caveat* is to risk drawing unfounded conclusions about the Rav's thought based on formulations that he considered not fully finished.

A second danger which confronts the student of Rav Soloveitchik's thought springs out of a certain type of interpretive literature. There are writers who claim to know the Rav's unexpressed inner thoughts, his unspoken aims and purposes, his conscious and unconscious motivations, and who offer accounts of his thought based on this supposed secret knowledge. There is in this style of interpretation a level of presumptuousness which is not only tasteless, but also profoundly and inexcusably misleading. Once such conjectures about private motives are expressed, they tend to assume a life of their own and to become the basis for conclusions about the meaning and import of the Rav's work. It can be demonstrated, and I shall do so later on, that these conclusions are unfounded, that they are not sustained by the texts themselves, and that they derive from the mistaken supposition of the authors that they know the inner and unexpressed dimensions of the Rav's personality and therefore understand in a uniquely accurate way what the Rav "really" was saying.[4] Such claims should always be treated with extreme skepticism and should never be allowed to become the basis for deciding anything at all about the Rav's teachings. Even when practiced by the most skilled and sophisticated professionals, psychohistory is a dubious and ill-founded discipline. It should have no standing as a tool for penetrating into the thought of Rav Soloveitchik. His written and spoken word are all we have. As is the case with all thinkers, even reliable memory of the spoken word will dim as time passes, and it is the written word upon which we must rely.

The Rav's writings need to be studied with the care and thought that they deserve, and no psychologizing can ever be a satisfactory or responsible substitute for such study.

Another danger to be avoided is posed by interpreters who do not understand the Rav's language correctly and draw unfounded conclusions based on mistranslations of his terminology. An instructive example is to be found in the article by Singer and Sokol to which reference was made above (note 4). They address the admittedly important question of the place and function of Western philosophy in the Rav's thought. They conclude that the Rav "uses Western thought to serve his own (Jewish) theological purposes." By itself this is certainly a conclusion which is possible and which may be defensible. They go on, however, to accuse the Rav of deliberately dressing up his Jewish thinking in Western philosophical garb as a way of winning adherents to his position. It is important to see exactly how they express themselves. "Soloveitchik latches on to neo-Kantianism as a way of adding to the prestige of talmudism, he dresses up talmudism in neo-Kantian garb so as to make it more appealing to a modern, secularized audience. . . . he uses neo-Kantian philosophy *as a mere packaging device.*" The authors then add with a triumphant note what they take to be the incontrovertible proof of their claim. They assure us that, "Soloveitchik himself underscores this point when he states (in a footnote in 'Halakhic Man' that has been ignored in all discussions of his work) that he is drawing upon neo-Kantian thought so as to make talmudism more 'palatable' to the reader. Exactly!"[5]

The entire charge rests on a misreading and mistranslation. In the text to which the authors refer, Rav Soloveitchik tells us that he has made use of the example of philosophical idealism from Kant to Hermann Cohen and his disciples, *kedei le-sabber et ha-ozen beniddon ish ha-halakhah, she-ein hakhmei ha-dat regilim bo.*[6] The phrase, *le-sabber et ha-ozen* certainly does not mean "to make more palatable." There is nothing sinister in the phrase, nor does it refer to some hidden propagandistic agenda. It is a standard expression which means "to make intelligible" or "to make more readily understandable." The

Rav is simply saying that the concept of "halakhic man" is totally unfamiliar to people schooled exclusively in the standard literature of Western religious thought. Consequently, in order to make that concept intelligible to readers of that type, he has expressed aspects of the typology in the more familiar language of philosophical idealism. He is not engaged in some kind of vulgar packaging in order to market his ideas successfully. He is certainly not concerned to make his views more "palatable" to properly enlightened Westerners. He is just doing what any good teacher or writer does, namely, making a body of unfamiliar concepts intelligible to his audience by comparing them to that with which he presumes his audience is already acquainted.[7] It should be clear that the works of interpretation need to be read with the greatest care and with appropriate caution. Even seemingly scholarly interpreters can mislead their readers, especially when they are determined to make the Rav fit into their own preconceived mold.

II

One of the recurrent lines of criticism in some of the secondary literature is that the Rav's thought is beset by internal contradictions and conflicting purposes, that it lacks systematic unity and coherence. Here again we can find an excellent paradigm of such criticism in the article by Singer and Sokol. They assert that, "a reading of Soloveitchik's *oeuvre* makes it clear that his theological concerns . . are characterized by tensions, polarities, and outright contradictions."[8] They quote a passage from "The Lonely Man of Faith" and assure us that "the Soloveitchik of the main body of 'Halakhic Man' would find this statement totally alien, while the Soloveitchik of the introduction to the essay would fully endorse it."[9] A superficial reading of the Rav's works might readily lend support to this picture of a figure who is torn between opposed worlds that he cannot bring together, especially if it starts out from an erroneous set of preconceptions. These critics, like some others, see in Rav Soloveitchik a thinker who lives simultaneously in totally inconsistent and contradictory intellectual and spiritual worlds. He is, according to this view, the scion of and superb spokesman for something that they call Litvak-mitnagged talmudism which is described conventionally as coldly unfeeling in its pure intellectualism and without a shred of religious emotion or passion. At the same time he is also portrayed as an existentialist religious spirit (perhaps hasidic or quasi-hasidic), one who has the deepest religious feelings and for whom the life of the intellect alone does not answer true religious concerns. Since it is assumed that these two are intrinsically and mutually contradictory positions, it then follows, in the view of these writers, that brokenness, disunity, and systematic incoherence characterize the Rav's thought.

My primary purpose in this study is to establish and explicate the fact that, contrary to these assertions, an overarching unity of doctrine, methodology, and structure inform the Rav's thought. A sound understanding of the Rav's works will reveal in them an underlying and widely encompassing thematic and systematic unity. We must not rest with superficial first impressions. Let us begin by considering a number of general points. First, it is true that the Rav's works are written in different styles, but this is by itself hardly an indication of internal lack of unity and coherence. The style which is appropriate for *hiddushei Torah*, written in a classical mode, is hardly appropriate for a philosophical or theological essay. What is appropriate when writing systematic philosophy is not the style in which one makes a personal religious statement. From the fact that the Rav writes in different styles (although always in a way that is unmistakenly his own) we can draw no conclusions about the unity or lack of unity in his thought.

Second, we need to keep in mind that not only the style but also the content of any work is determined by its particular purposes. A single thinker may very well write about different aspects of a given topic and do so from diverse perspectives and in diverse frameworks. Tone and content will reflect these variegated aims and objectives. The traditional teaching that the one divine Torah has seventy faces[10] is not just a rhetorical flourish. It expresses the conviction that the Torah is infinitely deep and varied, that it transcends the capacity of any person, no matter how gifted, to contain it all within a single structure. A student of the Torah can only present its teaching from particular aspects and perspectives, exhibiting and explicating some of its facets, never all of them. This is what great figures of the past have always done, and it is characteristic of the work of Rav Soloveitchik in our own time. We know of *tannaim* and *amoraim* who were great masters of both Halakhah and aggadah. Maimonides wrote his *Mishneh Torah* in a manner quite different from his *Guide of the Perplexed*, and these both differ from his style in some of his epistles or in his responsa. The style and focus of the *Shulhan Arukh ha-Rav* of Rabbi Shneur Zalman is strikingly different from his *Tanya*. In these and similar cases there may be those who will argue that we have deep internal conflicts and contradictions, but there is little evidence to support the claim.[11] In the case of Rav Soloveitchik, differences of style, theme, or orientation in his various works do not by themselves support the claim that his work is internally contradictory and is lacking in any systematic unity. The great talmudist, the master of Halakhah, the deeply searching religious thinker, the incomparable preacher, the Jew of simple piety, are all one and they live together in a carefully nuanced and consciously forged systematic unity.

III

The unifying principle in all of the Rav's work is his frequently stated conviction that the only legitimate source of Jewish doctrine is the Halakhah. As he has often expressed it, "The Halakhah is the objectification and crystallization of all true Jewish doctrine." In his various studies, the controlling force and focus is the Halakhah. Religious and philosophical accounts of Jewish spirituality are sound and meaningful in his view only to the extent that they derive from the Halakhah. The deepest religious emotion, the subtlest theological understanding, can only be Jewishly authentic to the extent that they arise from reflection on matters of Halakhah, and are integrated into its disciplined intellectual structure. I propose to focus on a single case which can teach us how this general rule of method is carried out in practice in the Rav's work. The case I have in mind is the Rav's treatment of the problem of evil, the fact that there is human suffering for which we can find no reason and for which we can produce no religiously satisfactory explanation. This is a classic philosophical-theological problem, one which has preoccupied religious thinkers from the Prophets down to the present. I choose this example because of its intrinsic interest and because it illuminates so well the way in which halakhic norms generate theological principles. This case is particularly useful as a paradigm since the Rav's treatment of it is frequently cited, but not always very deeply understood.

His essay, "Kol Dodi Dofek," opens with the statement that suffering is one of the most obscure and enigmatic phenomena that Judaism has struggled to understand from the earliest days.[12] The Rav rejects out of hand a number of proposed solutions to the problem of human suffering which he takes to be fundamentally in error. Prominent among these is the effort to explain away all instances of suffering by treating the very phenomenon as somehow illusory. This is the way in which some philosophers have chosen to resolve the problem. Deny the reality of suffering and the problem has been dissolved. This is a solution which the Rav considers to be so contrary to actual human experience that no one can seriously affirm it. "Evil is a fact which cannot be denied. There is evil; there is suffering, there are hellish agonies in the world. . . . One cannot overcome the reality of monstrous evil through philosophic speculation."[13] He argues furthermore that there is no philosophic solution to the problem of evil. Here he is responding to the long history of philosophic treatments of the subject, not one of which is finally convincing. However, he goes further and takes it to be a fundamental Jewish teaching that philosophical solutions to the problem of evil are in principle not possible. Man's view of the world is only partial. We do not grasp historical or metaphysical reality from the all-encompassing perspective of God, but only from our varying finite and limited perspectives. What may be intelligible just from the divine perspective can never be fully known by any human being, and it follows that a true philosophical answer to the riddle of why the righteous suffer can never be available even to the wisest of men. The tradition teaches us that Moses himself could not arrive at a satisfactory human answer to this agonizing question.

Rav Soloveitchik argues that according to Jewish teaching the proper question to ask is not why is there suffering in the world, but rather what is the appropriate response to the experience of suffering, an experience which no person escapes. He formulates his answer by setting forth two modes of response which he calls *goral* and *yi'ud*, which deal with that experience either as fate to be endured or as a call to destiny to be realized. The *goral* response is simply to endure the suffering and to try vainly to deal with it by way of illusory philosophical or theological solutions. The *yi'ud* response is a call to man to deal with his experience actively and creatively. In this mode one does not deny or minimize the fact of the suffering, but one asks what can I do to transform it into something positive and meaningful. Man should not be a passive object, a plaything of the various forces and events that affect him. Man is rather called upon to "transform fate into destiny, passive existence into active and effective living."[14] The Jew must approach his suffering with a halakhic question, namely, what must the sufferer do to live affirmatively and creatively with his suffering.

The most fundamental question is, what obligation does suffering impose on man? Judaism was particularly concerned with this question and set it at the center of its universe of thought. The Halakhah is concerned with this question as it is with other [more familiar] halakhic questions that focus on the forbidden and the permitted, obligation and absence of obligation. We do not reflect on the mysterious ways of God, but rather on the way in which man should go when he confronts suffering. We do not ask about the cause of the evil or about its ultimate purpose, but only how we can rectify and elevate it. How shall a man behave in a time of trouble? What shall man do so as not to be destroyed by his suffering?[15]

Rav Soloveitchik replies to these questions with what he specifically labels a halakhic answer. The Halakhah requires man to make use of suffering creatively, not just to submit to it passively and hopelessly. It requires us to use the experience of suffering to elevate ourselves, to refine ourselves, to increase our sensitivity, in short, to make ourselves better human beings than we were before.

The great model which exemplifies this response to suffering is Job. The Rav points out the crucial difference between Job before his suffering and after, a point that has gone largely unnoticed. Before his suffering Job is ego-centered. He prays only for himself and his children. When he becomes the victim of great catastrophe, he can make no sense of it. He only continues to affirm his own righteousness and to demand a coherent explanation of his suffering. All of his philosophizing leads him nowhere, until he finally shifts from the attitude of *goral* to that of *yi'ud*. He stops justifying himself and demanding explanations, but instead uses his suffering to elevate himself to a higher plane. It is only at this point that things turn to a new direction. As the biblical text notes at the end of the long Job episode, God rebuked Job's friends for their attempts to give a theological explanation of Job's suffering. He says to Eliphaz, "I am incensed at you and your two friends, for you have not spoken the truth about Me as did My servant Job." They are instructed to offer up sacrifices so that Job might pray for them. The biblical text then notes, "The Lord restored Job's fortunes when he prayed on behalf of his friends." Here we have the transformed Job who prays for his friends with the same concern and the same fervor that he had previously extended only to his own children. The critical point is that Job's suffering becomes meaningful only when it serves to make him a more sensitive, less self-centered person than he was before. The pain he endured was real. His attempts to account for it philosophically were futile. The only positive outcome of his experience is that he learned to use his suffering affirmatively and creatively to transform his character and to make himself a more virtuous human being. His human concerns now extended beyond the narrow circle of his family to encompass other human beings in need of his compassionate help. This is the model which the Rav proposes should guide us whenever we confront our own pain.

The question which arises at this point is whether a response in accordance with the Jobian model has anything to do with the Halakhah. Despite the invocation of the Halakhah, it would appear that we have here a brilliant and moving proposal for dealing with suffering, but we do not see initially its relevance to or dependence on the Halakhah. However, further study will show that what we have here is one of the most clear and explicit cases in which important religious doctrine emerges from a proper understanding of the Halakhah. The Rav bases his views on his understanding of the Mishnah which teaches, "Man is obligated to bless God for the evil which befalls him, just as he is obligated to bless God for the good that befalls him."[16] The point of this halakhic prescription requires explication.

We need first to understand what the significance of *berakhah* is. For this purpose we must grasp a principle which is deeply rooted in the Rav's halakhic analysis. In the act of doing a mitzvah there are, according to him, two elements. The first is the *pe'ulat ha-mitzvah*, that is the purely technical performance of the act which is required. I am obligated to put on *tefillin* each week day, and there are many rules with respect to the correct way to perform this action. The *tefillin* themselves must be constructed in a particular way, otherwise the performance is invalid. They must be put on in the way that is prescribed by law, and at a time which is prescribed by law. This and much more is included in *pe'ulat ha-mitzvah*, the technical performance of the set of actions required by the Halakhah. To perform these actions properly is a necessary condition for the fulfillment of the *mitzvah*. I do not fulfill the halakhic obligation unless I have done these actions in the prescribed way. Exalted thoughts, even the highest level of theological speculation, are no substitute for performing the required action. However, doing the act correctly is only part of what is involved in fulfilling a divine commandment. It is a necessary condition, and it may even be counted as formally satisfactory, but it is not the totality of a proper halakhic performance.

The other element in halakhic action is what the Rav calls *kiyyum ha-mitzvah*, the appropriate internal effects of the prescribed action. The action achieves its total import as the fulfillment of a divine commandment only when it generates the thoughts, feelings, attitudes, state of mind, and inner commitment which are appropriate to it. For example, the rites of *avelut* for close relatives are prescribed in careful detail, but one can hardly consider them to be true mourning if they are only an external performance without any inner feeling. It is obvious that the *kiyyum ha-mitzvah* is only achieved when there is a deep sense of loss, pain, grief, all those attitudes which one expects to accompany mourning for a loved one. Moreover, for the *kiyyum* to be complete the mourner must ask himself what this experience teaches him, what it demands of him with regard to his own life. This point is made very clearly by Maimonides in his *Code*. He sets forth at considerable length the detailed rules for the technical performance of the obligation of mourning. Every aspect of the precise ways in which the *pe'ulat ha-mitzvah* is to be done is explicated carefully. At the very end of his discussion he introduces us to what is required for *kiyyum ha-mitzvah*, the inner state without which one cannot be said to have truly mourned the dead. Excessive mourning is forbidden since it suggests an unwillingness on the part of the bereaved to accept the divine judgment and to recognize that death is an inescapable aspect of the order of the world in which we live. Excessive mourning is, in a sense, a denial of God, and might be construed as nullifying the effectiveness of the technical performance of the mitzvah. On the other hand, "Whoever fails to mourn in the way which our sages commanded is cruel and unfeeling." True mourning, i.e., the *kiyyum ha-mitzvah*, says the Rambam, is expressed not only in the performance of the external rites, not only in the sorrow which is experienced, but in addition the mourner should see his loss as a challenge to his own life. "He should be overcome by fear and anxiety, which should, in turn, lead him to examine carefully his own deeds, and this should be followed by *teshuvah*, repentance."[17] It is fairly easy in the case of such halakhic obligations as mourning or rejoicing to see that the technical performance is incomplete if it does not generate an inner state of mind. It is less obvious in the case of many other *mitzvot* that there is anything more required than the pure technical performance. There may well be some commandments which we fulfill completely and satisfactorily just by doing the prescribed action in the prescribed manner. What the Rav has taught us in his explication of the Halakhah is that this is the exceptional, rather than the normal standard for the true fulfillment of a *mitzvah*.

Let us turn now to the rule of the Mishnah which requires us to bless God for the evil which befalls us as well as for the good. The rules for the technical performance of this obligation are clear enough. We are commanded to recite prescribed liturgical formulas on specified occasions of joy or sorrow. This, however, is incomplete unless it is accompanied or followed by the *kiyyum ha-mitzvah*, a certain inner state. A *berakhah* is more than just the recitation of a liturgical formula. It is the explicit acknowledgment that whatever has occurred to us comes from God and this imposes on us an obligation to respond appropriately to the divine gift, whether it initially brings us joy or sorrow. The *berakhah* is the formal act in which we commit ourselves to treat our fortune, good or bad, as a challenge to transform our experience into a proper service of God.

When the Holy One, blessed be He, gives a person wealth and property, influence and honor, the recipient of these goods needs to know how to make proper use of them. He needs to know how to transform these precious gifts into fruitful creative forces, how to share his great happiness with others, how to perform acts of kindness with the divine gifts which flow to him from the Infinite Source. If the abundance of good which comes to a man does not generate in him complete submission to God, then he has been guilty of a fundamental sin.[18]

It is clear that in the Rav's view the true fulfillment of the obligation
to bless God for the good begins with the recitation of the *berakhah*,
but is only completed properly when we treat our good fortune as a
challenge which refines us and fills us with a sense of responsibility
for others and a spirit of generosity toward them. The evidence of
the sincerity with which one has spoken the liturgical formula lies
in the attitudes and actions which follow. This is the *kiyyum ha-
mitzvah.*[19]

The same is true, *mutatis mutandis*, with respect to our response to
the evil which befalls us. There is a prescribed technical performance,
the recitation of the required *berakhah* at the specified time. This is
the first step in fulfilling our halakhic duty. For it to be complete,
however, it must be followed by the elevation of our suffering to a
level of divine service just as we are expected to do with our rejoicing.
It is the Halakhah, not abstract theological speculation, that teaches
us that we must use our pain as an occasion for self-refinement and
moral growth. If we understand the Halakhah properly, as the Rav
has taught us, then we will know that it requires of us *kiyyum ha-mitzvah*
which is already implicit in the *pe'ulat ha-mitzvah*, in the act of reciting
the *berakhah*. What Rav Soloveitchik has done in this case is typical
of his method throughout his work. The integrating center is always
a proper grasp of the full meaning of the Halakhah. Authentic Jewish
religious ideas are derived from the halakhic sources.[20] At times, as in
the case of the problem of evil, he spells this out explicitly. At other
times the point is implicit. But it is never absent. Careful study of
such a seemingly non-halakhic work as "The Lonely Man of Faith"
will show that its conclusions derive from the Halakhah no less than
the conclusions concerning the meaning and purpose of human suffering.

We can now see the halakhic understanding of suffering in a larger
context. The general halakhic imperative with respect to suffering is
that we are to respond creatively. This emphasis on human creativity
is an overarching theme in the thought of Rav Soloveitchik and serves
to integrate the various facets of his religious teachings into a systematic

unity. At the very broadest level he takes creativity to be the fundamental thrust of the entire Halakhah, the ultimate form of *kiyyum ha-mitzvah* throughout the halakhic system. The Torah itself teaches us that holiness is the aim of all the commandments. "You shall be holy, for I, the Lord your God, am holy."[21] The major halakhic authorities, among them Maimonides and Nahmanides, treat this as an all inclusive commandment which adds a special dimension to the fulfillment of every mitzvah. As Maimonides expresses it, this is a commandment "to fulfill the entire Torah, as if He had said, 'Be holy when you do all that I have commanded you to do, and when you refrain from doing all that I have prohibited.'"[22] Rav Soloveitchik explicates this general commandment as having to do with creativity. He shows that creativity is the *telos* of the Halakhah and concludes that, "The dream of creation finds its resolution in the actualization of the principle of holiness. Creation means the realization of the ideal of holiness."[23] Holiness is identified by the Rav as "the descent of divinity into the midst of our concrete world." To be holy is to make oneself godlike, and imitating God is the ultimate form of human creativity.

The divine creation of the world is an act in which form and structure are imposed on an initially formless mass. Chaos is turned into cosmos. This model of creativity is embedded in the Halakhah as well. To create is always to form and to limit the raw material with which we begin.[24] The aim of the Halakhah is the creation of human beings in whom the divine image is fully realized. The norms of the Halakhah form, structure, and shape the human individual. They are the instruments for actualizing the divine potentiality which is present in every person. "Herein," says the Rav, "is embodied the entire task of creation and the obligation to participate in the renewal of the cosmos. The most fundamental principle of all is that man must create himself. It is this idea that Judaism introduced into the world."[25] This explains in some degree the Rav's great preoccupation with *Hilkhot Teshuvah* over the years, since it is through the process of *teshuvah*, above all, that a person creates and recreates himself.

A study of the proper halakhic sources fully sustains the judgment that human creativity is the teleological and axiological crux of the Halakhah. In the *Mishneh Torah* we find that Maimonides sets forth among the first *halakhot* the obligation to know the existence and nature of God to the extent that man is capable of such knowledge, and then the duty to love and fear Him. These latter *mitzvot* are fulfilled by reflecting on the wonders of God's creation. It then becomes clear that the commandment *le-hiddamot bi-drakhav* means to imitate God in all the ways that are possible for man, but above all to aspire to the fullness of creativity of which we are capable. It is in this way especially that man realizes the divine image with which he is endowed. The Halakhah provides us with the forms and structures which make this self-creating activity possible. The *telos* of each individual Halakhah or complex of related *halakhot* provides us with the occasion and the direction for specific forms of creative striving. Wherever one turns in the works of Rav Soloveitchik, one finds that he reverts to this basic doctrine which emerges from his understanding of the Halakhah and from his mode of halakhic reasoning and analysis. This focus on the centrality of the Halakhah as the only true source of Jewish doctrine is the thread that runs through all his thought, the thread which provides for the systematic unity of that thought in all the diversity of subject matter with which it deals.

IV

The question may well be raised as to whether the Rav's way of understanding the Halakhah is legitimate and whether it genuinely derives from the halakhic sources. Some critics have suggested that Rav Soloveitchik is simply imposing his own theological ideas on the halakhic materials. A similar criticism has been made of the analytic categories which R. Hayyim Brisker developed for the explication of the Halakhah.[26] To resolve this question we must try to understand Rav Soloveitchik's account of Torah learning at its most profound level. As he expounds it, there are two types of learning which stand at the very top of the hierarchy of Torah scholarship. The lower of these is characterized as a state of *erusin*, betrothal to the Torah, and

highest of all is called *nissu'in*, marriage to the Torah. Those who are
described as betrothed to the Torah are *talmidei hakhamim* of unusually
high caliber. They represent standard modes of Torah learning which
have been developed to the best possible level. These scholars are the
typically familiar Torah sages of very high rank. They write important
hiddushei Torah, produce important collections of responsa, and com-
pose analytic and expository books of great value. Through their
teaching and writing they provide us with deep insight into the Halakhah. These *talmidei hakhamim* stand head and shoulders above all
other students of the Torah, but they are still not at the absolute
summit of true creative insight.

That summit is reserved for the small number of sages who achieve
the very greatest depth of understanding and perception.

They are described metaphorically by the Rav as connected to the
Torah in a covenant of marriage. The partners in a true marriage are
united in a relationship of intimacy which breaks down all barriers.
Similarly, the supreme Torah sage lives in a relationship of such
intimacy with the Torah that his perceptions go beyond the normal
limits of intellectual apprehension. We find a secular model of this
mode of understanding set forth in the philosophy of Plato. In the
typical dialogue, a subject is investigated with all the power that rational
discourse can bring to it. This is certainly an achievement of major
significance, but it is not the end of the matter. At the point where
rational discourse has reached its outer limit and can go no further,
Plato normally introduces a myth. The purpose of the myth is to give
literary expression to the philosopher's vision, and this is the deepest
and the most revealing dimension of his work. That vision transcends
the boundaries of purely discursive knowledge, and in all probability
it precedes that knowledge, despite the fact that as a literary-expository
device Plato generally places the myth at the end of the dialogue.
This vision of truth which the true philosopher apprehends is treated
by Plato as the deepest and most illuminating of all philosophic insights.
This vision is only possible for a thinker of the most highly developed
and purified intellect who lives in the closest intimacy with the subjects

of his reflections. On the one hand, it presupposes and grows out of the most complete rational analysis that is possible, but paradoxically it also shapes and directs that analysis. There is a kind of reciprocal movement here, beginning in conventional study, reaching the greatest depths of rational insight, breaking through to the vision which transcends the limits of reason, and then turning back on itself to reshape the materials which were initially understood in the purely discursive mode. To follow out the Platonic metaphor, the philosopher who has left the cave and achieved a unique vision of the ultimate truth must return to the cave to make that vision effective in the world of ordinary men.

Although I am not certain whether Rav Soloveitchik would approve the use of this Platonic mode, I believe that it is a helpful heuristic device for the understanding of his account of the sage whose relationship to the Torah is marriage, not just betrothal. To begin with, he distinguishes between the two by way of a kabbalistic paradigm. The *talmid hakham* who is betrothed to the Torah apprehends it through the *sefirah* of *binah*, while the sage who is married to the Torah apprehends it through *hokhmah*. The former is the highest level of apprehension open to discursive understanding, but the latter opens up supernal vistas of insight available to only a chosen few. The Rav makes the following observation concerning this highest mode of Torah understanding:

> When the last barrier that separates man from the Torah is completely removed, there open before him not only all the modes of halakhic thinking and apprehension, but also all the modes of halakhic perceptivity and vision. The Almighty endows this person not only with an intellectual soul, but also with a soul that is capable of halakhic vision. The purely logical mode of halakhic reasoning draws its sustenance from the pre-rational perception and vision which erupt stormily from the depths of this personality, a personality which is enveloped with the aura of holiness. This mysterious intuition is the source of halakhic creativity and innovative insight. . . . The sage to whom the Torah is married

begins with the teachings of the heart and concludes with the teachings of the mind. Creative halakhic activity begins not with intellectual calculation, but with vision; not with clear formulations, but with unease; not in the clear light of rational discourse, but in the pre-rational darkness.[27]

This is the picture that the Rav presents of the highest level of Torah understanding. The particular context is a description of the achievements of his grandfather, his father, and his uncle, but it can be taken as a model for all of those rare spirits who arise from time to time in our history and are "married" to the Torah. We permit ourselves the judgment, which he himself would never permit, that Rav Joseph B. Soloveitchik is to be included in the company of those rare spirits.

Viewed from this perspective, the deepest level of halakhic study opens up for us an understanding not only of the technical Halakhah, but of the ideal world from which that Halakhah flows and which, in turn, it seeks to realize. The precise conceptual restructuring which R. Hayyim introduced created a revolution in the mode of Talmud study and in the exposition of halakhic thought. The religious-spiritual restructuring of the content of *kiyyum ha-mitzvah* which our contemporary Rav Soloveitchik has introduced has created a comparable revolution in our grasp of halakhic philosophy and theology. Both are the product of the marriage to the Torah which is the special merit of these unique *talmidei hakhamim*. The insights of such sages are not only Jewishly valid and authentic, but they are, in the full sense of the term, halakhically valid and authentic. Their teachings are not the product only of vast learning and incomparable intellectual capacity. They are no less the product of that special quality of halakhic vision with which they have been endowed. Without that vision, no one could achieve their creativity in understanding the deepest levels of the Halakhah. Once they have exercised that vision and worked out its consequences, we are able to grasp their teachings and see for ourselves how they follow from true halakhic intuition.

V

We shall take one final step in establishing our claim that Rav Soloveitchik's thought is a unified structure, and for this we return to
our initial observation that he appears to have presented us with a
body of writing that is riddled with contradictions. In our earlier
discussion we simply noted that one should not rush to conclude that
there are internal contradictions in the *oeuvre* of any serious thinker.
Attention has to be given to the variety of contexts in which he
writes, the particular purposes of each work, etc. Although this is
certainly true with respect to any responsible reading of the Rav's
works, it is important to add another and more telling dimension to
the discussion.

It is characteristic of the Rav's writing, and therefore also of his
thought, that pairs of opposed phenomena appear with great regularity.
Every reader is familiar with the contradictions between *homo religiosus*
and cognitive man, between majestic and covenantal man, Adam I
and Adam II, fate and destiny, loneliness and fulfillment in society,
the drive for moral autonomy and the religious fact of an imposed
heteronomy, sin and repentance, etc.[28] It is clear that we have here
instances of phenomena which are in genuine opposition to each
other. Moreover, Rav Soloveitchik makes no effort to hide or suppress
these contradictory features. On the contrary, he makes a special
point of calling them to our attention and dwelling on their significance.
Does it follow then that his thought is so riddled with contradictions
that there is no hope of finding within it any systematic unity? By no
means!

We must distinguish clearly between the contradictory phenomena
that a thinker discerns in the world which he describes and explicates,
and the actual presence of contradictions in his own thought. The
latter might be a fatal flaw, but the former is the set of inescapable
facts with which the thinker has to deal. We must not condemn a
philosopher or halakhist for being guilty of contradictions if all he is
doing is bringing to our attention the existence of contradictory ele-

ments in reality. The philosopher's intellectual creativity becomes evident in the way in which he deals with this apparently broken reality. In our case the Rav has chosen to confront these contradictory phenomena with full consciousness of their power. He has chosen even to seek them out and bring to our notice instances of which we may not have been aware. He does not seek to dissolve the contradictions or to harmonize them through the use of subtle intellectual gymnastics. Just as he insists that we must face the fact of suffering and not delude ourselves that it is only illusory, so does he insist that we must face the fact of this network of contradictions and not delude ourselves into thinking that intellectual acumen will make them disappear.

Contrary to the expectations of some of his critics, the Rav's program is not to harmonize the contradictories for this would go counter to reality itself. There is in man both the striving of the *homo religiosus* and the cognitive drive. We are called upon to achieve a majestic dignity, and also to experience the redemptive defeat of submission to a higher power. One could go through the entire list of such contradictory phenomena in this same way. What the Rav teaches us is that neither thought nor life itself need be broken by the fact that we are beset by these contradictory drives. He approaches the problem dialectically, that is, he recognizes that we must affirm in each case both of the contradictory elements and strive to live with them in a balanced tension. Neither pole can or should be eliminated. The glory of man lies in some measure in the very fact that he is a complex being whose nature is fully realized only when these contradictory elements are both prized for their individual value and are simultaneously held together as forces forming a unified human life.

The task is a demanding one, but we avoid it only at the expense of denying or trivializing our humanity. We have familiar biblical instances of the tensions within man, for example, between man conceived as the creaturely actualization of the image of God, and man seen as a mere animal. In this particular case, as in all the others, our task is to affirm both dimensions of human reality, to extract the highest value from each, and to balance them within an integrated life and a unified system of thought. It is in just this way that we affirm and give expression to our humanity. Man is both an animal and a creature in the divine image. Man is both a religious being seeking his fulfillment in the transcendent, and a cognitive being whose fulfillment comes from his subjecting all phenomena to the shaping force of his intellect. What the Rav teaches us is that we arrive at the deepest illumination that Judaism can offer us when we recognize that we must affirm the contradictory elements and learn to live with them in that dialectical tension which gives to each its full effective force. This way is far more difficult than a monochromatic harmony, but we cannot escape our own existential reality, and we must not make ourselves less than we are just to be at ease with ourselves and our world.

This may leave us dissatisfied if we are seeking comfort rather than depth of insight, complacency rather than religious and moral challenge, self-involvement rather than the most significant engagement of which we are capable with God and with the world He created. It is human self-conceit to suppose that our finite intellects can encompass the whole of reality in its rich and diverse texture, and that we can create an ontology which will make all the pieces fit together neatly and harmoniously. It is no less a human self-conceit to suppose that we can use our powers to do something similar with the varied modes and dimensions of human existence and with man's experience of himself. The greatest philosophers have always known that our understanding breaks down when we presume to force the infinite and the eternal into the restrictive mold of the finite intellect. This was well known to the greatest of the Jewish philosophers, Maimonides, as it was to the major philosophers who preceded and succeeded him.[29]

This is why the Rav makes such a point of teaching us that the greatest of thinkers also has within himself the soul of a child. His breathtaking intellectual sophistication, the exquisite complexity and subtlety of his insight, are balanced by the openness, and naive simplicity of the unspoiled child. One who is so completely the prisoner of his own maturity that there is no place left in him for the openness of the child "is unable to draw near to God." His oversophistication leaves him with the misplaced confidence that in his philosophic or halakhic categories he is capable of capturing the whole truth about the divine and to penetrate to total knowledge of the Torah. He becomes guilty not only of overweening pride, but also of the fatal error of exaggerating the claims of his intellectual powers. In creating his own neatly ordered world, he tacitly discards whatever does not fit. In the process, he reduces God and Torah to the finite dimensions of the human intellect. Only when that superb intellect is balanced by a childlike simplicity can it recognize its own limits. As the Rav puts it, only the simple faith of the child can break the austere barriers that confine us to our finite world. Only that childlike stance can bring us into a personal relationship with God.[30]

Here again we have seemingly opposed forces brought together in the Rav's thought. There are those who think that he must choose between philosophic and halakhic sophistication, on the one hand, or childlike faith, on the other. Failure to do this presumably leaves him with unacceptable and insoluble contradictions in his work. If this were a sound criticism, it would follow that the Rav's thought rests on methodological practices which are intellectually shoddy, and that there can be no talk of any systematic unity in his work. However, in this case, as in all the others that we have discussed, there is, in fact, both methodological soundness and systematic unity. The Rav is affirming here the subtlest of methodological principles, namely, that no single methodology and no single intellectual stance is adequate to bring us to an understanding of ultimate truth and ultimate reality. Here too there is a dialectical tension between the extremes of intellectual sophistication and childlike simplicity. The former without the latter is, as we have noted, the victim of its own arrogance. The latter without the former denigrates the role of reason which is man's greatest glory. The mark of true maturity is precisely the capacity to develop the intellect to its highest possible level and learn all that it can teach us, while at the same time retaining the openness of the child to the reality which transcends our intellectual categories and can only be known intuitively. We cannot remain permanently and exclusively in either world, but must move between them in our never-ending search for the knowledge of God and of His Torah.

In this brief sketch we have aimed to set forth in outline the grounds for our conviction that the religious thought of Rav Soloveitchik represents a unity in diversity. We have tried to show that the various topics which he deals with, the variety of styles in which he writes, the diversity of methods which he seems to employ, are all facets of a unified system of thought. He has not favored us with a single comprehensive work which brings together all the strands and expounds them in their methodological and metaphysical unity. That work is left to the reader of his collected writings. There is more than enough evidence to establish with confidence the claim that this incomparably great Torah sage has built for us a coherent and integrated system of thought. That systematic structure is based on and is generated out of a deep understanding of the Halakhah. It is an authentic link in the chain of classical Jewish learning, authentic in its faithfulness to the past, and no less authentic in its creative originality.[31]

Notes

1. When Paul Arthur Schilpp established the Library of Living Philosophers some fifty years ago it was with the express hope that we could end disagreements and confusions about the ideas of contemporary philosophers once and for all. For each volume, the ablest scholars would be invited to write critical essays on aspects of the subject's thought and the subject would then reply. In this way, it was thought, we would get final and definitive resolutions about the exact meaning of the philosopher's ideas and arguments. It is one of the ironies of contemporary intellectual history that while the series of volumes is universally recognized as a major contribution to current philosophical literature, its strongest asset has been to continue, rather than end, the debate about what each of the philosophers really meant.

2. From this stricture I exclude, as noted, the work of Pinchas Peli which may not be in the Rav's *ipsissima verba* but which seems to be accurate in setting forth his ideas.

3. See the introduction to *Hiddushei Rabbeinu Hayyim ha-Levi* which was written by the two sons of R. Hayyim, Rav Soloveitchik's father and uncle. They describe there the exquisite care and attention which their father gave to every word he wrote and the gravity with which he viewed the responsibility of giving permanent published form to his teachings.

4. Among the very worst offenders on this score are David Singer and Moshe Sokol in their article, "Joseph Soloveitchik: Lonely Man of Faith," *Modern Judaism* 2 (1982), 227–272. Some aspects of this paper will be discussed later on in this study. One telling example of how these writers do their work can be seen in their reaction to some of the family anecdotes which the Rav relates in his various writings. They render their personal judgment that, "The behavior he describes is so radical, so extreme, as to make his presumed heroes seem grotesque." Having made this judgment, which is peculiarly their own, they assume that the Rav, being an enlightened man, certainly must share their feelings and their perceptions, and they are therefore able to assert with confidence that, "The vein of anger that runs through the anecdotal material in 'Halakhic Man' is not to be missed" (256). It is troubling that these writers are unable to see that they are simply imposing their personal feelings and attitudes on the Rav and then treating them as if they must be his own. An unbiased reader who allows the Rav's text to speak in all of its subtle nuances will certainly see that these anecdotes are always related in order to make or illustrate an important point, and that they are related with love, pride, and appreciation, not with anger. Rav Soloveitchik treats his father and grandfathers as models of the best type of Jewish learning and piety. The assertion that he relates to them and to their halakhic life style with anger and resentment could only come from people who are confident,

for some unknown reason, that they know the Rav better than he knows himself and that they are able to penetrate to truths about his inner life and thought which he has hidden from himself. There is no evident reason why we should take these claims seriously, and many very good reasons why we should not. For other such claims in this article see, e.g., pp. 238, 254, 255, 256, 259, 260, 265, 271 fn. 95.

5. *op. cit.*, pp. 237–238. My underscore. It is puzzling that Singer and Sokol think they have made a great discovery in finding that the Rav does not reinterpret Judaism in some radical new way. It is obvious that he never claimed nor intended to do any such thing. He never says that such radical reinterpretation is his program, nor is there any evidence that this is an unexpressed goal. He sees himself quite properly as standing inside the classical Jewish tradition as it is represented by *gedolei Yisrael* through the ages, not least among them his own immediate ancestors. This is not to say that he does not contribute brilliant new insights or open up new perspectives and new modes of religious understanding. Quite the contrary. In this regard he is also only carrying on the tradition of Torah learning and thought which he inherited and to which he has made his own remarkable contributions.

6. "Ish ha-Halakhah," p. 63, fn. 16, in Pinchas Peli, *Be-Sod ha-Yahid ve-ha-Yahad* (Jerusalem, 1976).

7. It is surprising that Lawrence Kaplan, who certainly knows better, also translated this expression with the phrase "to make the whole subject of halakhic man more palatable to scholars of religion who are not familiar with this type." *Halakhic Man* (Philadelphia, 1983), p. 146, fn. 18. For an example of another mistranslation by Singer and Sokol see their article, p. 261. Here they draw far reaching conclusions as a result of mistranslating a key phrase in a passage where the distinction is drawn between the technical performance of a commandment and the *kiyyum ha-mitzvah*, the inner state which is required in order to fulfill and give meaning to the action. The text reads, *Ha-kiyyum talui be-regesh mesuyyam, be-matzav ru'ah mesuyyam.* They translate, "but fulfillment is dependent on attaining a certain degree of spiritual awareness." It does not require a very profound knowledge of the Hebrew language to know that *matzav ru'ah* does not mean "spiritual awareness."

8. *op. cit.*, p. 229.

9. *Ibid.*, p. 244. Other statements about such seeming contradictions can be found at a number of different places throughout the article. Cf., 239, 241, 242, 243, 247, 256. These statements are often embellished by such expressions as, "startling," "eye-opening," "as if this were not strange enough," "what a claim," etc.

10. Num. R., 13:15; *Zohar* 1, 26a, 47b, and *passim*; *Otiot de-Rabbi Akiva.*

11. Even with respect to Maimonides I do not believe, despite current fashions of exegesis, that the case can be made that there is a deep abyss separating the halakhist from the philosopher. On this point see the discussion in my forthcoming book,

Interpreting Maimonides: Studies in Methodology, Metaphysics, and Moral Philosophy (Jewish Publication Society of America, 1989).

12. See, "Kol Dodi Dofek," in *Be-Sod ha-Yahid ve-ha-Yahad,* p. 333.

13. *Ibid.*, p. 336.

14. *Ibid.*, p. 337.

15. *Ibid.*, p. 339. See also the similar discussion in *U-Vikkashtem mi-Sham,* in *Ish ha-Halakhah—Galui ve-Nistar,* (Jerusalem, 1979), p. 144.

16. *M. Berakhot,* 9:5.

17. *H. Avel,* 13:11, 12. This is not the place for a detailed account of the process by which Maimonides arrives at this description of the *kiyyum ha-mitzvah,* but it can be worked out with little difficulty by any competent student of the Rambam. Similarly, we do not have the space here to work out the *kiyyum ha-mitzvah* of tefillin, although we used it as a familiar example of what is involved in *pe'ulat ha-mitzvah.*

18. "Kol Dodi Dofek," p. 342.

19. For a similar treatment of the nature of *kiyyum ha-mitzvah* with respect to a whole range of *berakhot* see the discussion in, *U-Vikashtem mi-Sham,* pp. 135–137. The Rav refers to the *berakhot* that we are required to recite when we observe various phenomena of nature and when we benefit from the natural world by eating, drinking, smelling or otherwise enjoying its products. He observes that we do not simply speak the words of the *berakhah,* words which thank or praise God for the magnificence and benevolence of the natural order, as a routine formula. Rather, the very moment we speak those words the natural order is transformed into "a supernatural world, a world of marvellous mystery." The *berakhah* bears witness to the fact that the Jew perceives the ordinary things of this world as extraordinary, that in his inner awareness the common has become uncommon, that the fixed order of nature becomes the superb work of the cosmic Creator. "The Halakhah says: Blessed is the Creature who meets his Creator regularly as he makes his way in the world, the creature who recognizes his Creator whenever he drinks a bit of water or eats a piece of bread. Blessed is the man for whom God is a present reality every time he uses his senses and responds to his experience." Clearly, the *kiyyum ha-mitzvah* is only achieved when the technical performance generates in us the appropriate thoughts, feelings, and perceptions. This is as much a requirement of the Halakhah as is the recitation of the prescribed words.

20. Pinchas Peli has argued that this way of deriving theological ideas from the Halakhah is ultimately a mode of highly sophisticated *derush.* Although I admire Professor Peli as one of the best interpreters of Rav Soloveitchik's thought, I cannot agree with him on this point. A sound understanding of the full import of any Halakhah cannot be reduced to *derush,* unless we include under this rubric every mode of thought and analysis which is not part of th. ːchnical practical Halakhah.

The Rav has demonstrated that *kiyyum ha-mitzvah* is as much part of the Halakhah as *pe'ulat ha-mitzvah*, and in this light the halakhic reasoning which brings us to understand the former is no less part of the legal system than is that which brings us to understand the latter. It may be that by *derush* Peli means something akin to the process of *midrash halakhah*, but that is not clear in his discussion. See his article, "Ha-Derush be-Hagut ha-Rav Soloveitchik—Mitodah o Mahut?" *Daat*, 4, winter 1980. An English version recently appeared under the title, "Hermeneutics in the Thought of Rabbi Soloveitchik—Medium or Message?" *Tradition* 23(3), Spring, 1988.

21. Lev. 19:2.

22. *Sefer ha-Mitzvot, ha-Shoresh ha-Revi'i.* See the Comments of Ramban to this section and also his commentary to Lev. 19:2, where he specifically treats this as a general all-inclusive commandment.

23. *Halakhic Man*, p. 108.

24. Of course the fundamental difference between human and divine creativity in our tradition is that God first creates the raw material (*ex nihilo*, according to most views) and then endows it with form and structure. Man always begins with material that is already there and applies to it his creative powers.

25. *Ibid.*, p. 109.

26. Singer and Sokol speak of R. Hayyim as "a talmudist who broke with the past." They suppose that Rav Soloveitchik himself sees his grandfather in this way, but that he tried to suppress the truth "because he had no desire to portray his grandfather" in what might appear to be an unorthodox position. *op. cit.*, p. 237. As I shall try to show this is a superficial and unsound way of understanding the methodologies and the results of one of the profoundest Torah sages of modern times.

27. "Mah Dodekh mi-Dod," in *Be-Sod ha-Yahid ve-ha-Yahad*, pp. 218–219. I have not translated literally the expressions, *mem/tet sha'arei hashivah ve-hakarah* and *mem/tet sha'arei hargashah ve-hazut*. These expressions use the classic number, forty-nine, to convey the idea of the highest level of insight that is possible for man.

28. For a valuable discussion of this subject, see Ehud Luz, "Ha-Yesod ha-Dialekti be-Kitvei ha-Rav Y. D. Soloveitchik," *Daat*, 9, Summer, 1982, pp. 75–89. Luz has an even longer list of such instances of contradictory elements in the Rav's thought. I acknowledge with pleasure my debt to this study. In my brief remarks on this subject I do not claim to have added significantly to what Professor Luz has already taught us.

29. Singer and Sokol in their relentless search for difficulties in the Rav's thought show their misunderstanding of this point. They complain that, "Since he is such an ardent admirer of Maimonides, one would expect him to be greatly influenced by the latter's religious rationalism—the attempt to logically demonstrate the truth of what Judaism teaches. In fact, Soloveitchik completely eschews any such aim, offering . . .

dogmatics in the place of apologetic theology." *op. cit.*, p. 249. This is a misreading of Maimonides who knew very clearly where reason reaches its outer limits, and who explicitly adopted the stance of faith where reason could no longer serve him. He would fully endorse the point that Rav Soloveitchik makes, namely, that rational proofs for the existence of God establish, at best, the necessary existence of a first cause, but cannot provide us with a knowledge of the God who creates the world and continues to relate to it with providential care.

30. See the discussion in "Peleitat Sofreihem," *Be-Sod ha-Yahid ve-ha-Yahad, op. cit.*, pp. 288–291.

31. A final note. When I began to write this paper it was not my intention to devote so much of it to refuting the views of Singer and Sokol, nor did I intend to tie it so closely to some of the topics which they treated. It is clear to me in retrospect that I did so because they represent, in my judgment, some of the best and the worst of what has been done by interpreters of the Rav's thought. They are intelligent and learned. They have read the work of the Rav carefully. They are able to formulate basic issues with clarity. This places them far above many who have written about the Rav's thought. At the same time, they are, in my opinion, singularly wrong-headed in their approach. They begin with their preconceptions of what the Rav says or ought to say, and with their preconceived categorizations of what options are open to him. In the process they misconstrue fundamental aspects of his thought and find the Rav's thought unsatisfactory because it does not do for them what they want it to do. Their extended study became, at first inadvertently, an appropriate foil for this paper. Let me confess that, after the fact, what was initially inadvertent has now become conscious and deliberate.

Much attention has been given to Rabbi Soloveitchik's use of typologies, ideal types of individuals, such as the "man of Halakhah," "man of religion," and "lonely man of faith." Yet relatively little attention has been given to the Rav's use of the Midrashic method. In this essay (Tradition 23:3), Pinchas Hacohen Peli offers a penetrating discussion of the Rav's utilization of derush *in his works.*

For the Rav, derush *is not merely a method, but is part of the substance of his thought. The Rav uses* derush *as a means of integrating modern Western thought and traditional Jewish modes of expression. Derush helps enable the halakhic Jew to confront the challenge of modernity.*

In this essay, Peli illustrates this thesis through an analysis of "Kol Dodi Dofek."

Hermeneutics in the Thought of Rabbi Soloveitchik: Medium or Message?

‏ﻚﻠﺟ‎

Pinchas Hacohen Peli

‏ﻚﻠﺟ‎

Two characteristics stand out in the presentations of Rabbi Joseph Baer Soloveitchik: typology and hermeneutics (*derush*). Both of these are, apparently, matters of form. But are they really? In this case, as in the case of all true creative endeavor, it seems very difficult to distinguish between form and content.

Typology, the first of the characteristics, namely, the creation of *ideal* types in man and in society, and placing them in confrontation with their corresponding *real* types, has been dealt with by almost all students of R. Soloveitchik's thought. R. Soloveitchik himself, in his first published philosophical essay in 1944, defines and delineates this typological approach. When he deals with "The Man of Halakhah" he bases himself upon Eduard Springer[1] and says: "Obviously, the description of the Man of Halakhah refers to a purely ideal type, similar to other types studied by social scientists. Real men of Halakhah, who are not simple but rather compound types, approach the ideal *ish ha-halakhah* in greater or lesser degree, depending upon their social features and spiritual stature." R. Soloveitchik repeats this definition twenty years later in "The Lonely Man of Faith,"[2] where he states that, in actuality, pure typological specimens do not exist and therefore there is sometimes an overlap between two types of personality or community.

Despite these limitations of definition, he does not refrain from structuring his thought around an entire galaxy of typical "Men": Man of Halakhah,[3] Man of Knowledge,[4] Man of Religion,[5] Man of God,[6] Mystical Man,[7] The Lonely Man of Faith,[8] Adam I as the Man of Majesty, Adam II as the Man of the Covenant,[9] all the way to the "Man of Repentance," who is not actually nominated as such by R. Soloveitchik himself, but who does emerge as a specific compound figure from the chapters of *On Repentance*, based on his oral discourses.[10]

Whereas several students and critics of the thought of R. Soloveitchik have referred to this intellectual typology and the problems arising from it,[11] such is not the case with the second conspicuous feature of his thought, the use of the Midrashic method, which has yet to be studied and clarified. The clarification of this question can help us to understand R. Soloveitchik's thought more fully, and to place it properly, despite its external wrappings, within the matrix of contemporary universal religious thought, as well as in its particularly Jewish context.[12] It is to this task that we shall address ourselves.

We shall exclude from our discussion those "sermons" of a popular-publicistic nature which R. Soloveitchik has delivered upon specific occasions. These cannot be integrated into the totality of his thought, as expressed in the remainder of his work, even though certain aspects of his thought processes can be discerned in them.[13] It is clear that in these sermons, the *derush* is primarily directed towards the rhetorical effect upon his immediate audience.

What Nathan Rotenstreich has written with regard to this kind of preaching, in which Biblical heroes are conceptualized as "homiletic archetypes,"[14] applies as well to these sermons of R. Soloveitchik, which should be counted among the best in Zionist homiletic literature. But they contribute little of substance to the body of his thought, the thought of a great, if not the greatest, modern Halakhist. This body of thought, in our opinion, constitutes a complete and systematic theologico-philosophical framework, even if not offered to us as such. Thus, it is neither the Midrashic achievement nor the immediate effect which are paramount, but the construction of a system of thought, independent and original, dealing with God, World, Community and Individual. This system is consistent and comprehensible in terms of objective tools of comprehension, combined with implications for personal subjective existence. And so the question returns to its starting point: how important is hermeneutics (*derush*) to this original and autonomous thought?

II

In order to answer this question we must examine the nature of *derush*, as an overall term inclusive of hermeneutics in all its aspects, such as comes to us from the Jewish sources.[15] These sources constitute the primary resources for R. Soloveitchik, though clearly his output is not of exclusively Jewish interest, but belongs to the general context of modern thought about God, Man, and the World.

Let us begin with the most recent generations, from which R. Soloveitchik proceeds, though as we shall see, he is anchored in all the ages of Jewish thought. "There is no doubt," writes Prof. Yosef Dan in his essay on the Jewish hermeneutics and its literary values,[16] "that in the quantitative sense, the literature of *derush* is central in the life of the Jewish people during the Middle Ages and the beginning of the modern period. Only the halakhic literature exceeds it in historical continuity in the history of Jewish literature, as well as in the quantity of the creativity it embraces. . . . This literature is a universal phenomenon in Judaism: there is not one Jewish community in which the *derush* literature is not a central element of its overall literary product." Yet, "despite its central position," complains Dan, "there is no literature in the history of Jewish literature so neglected by research."

Similarly, Avraham Kariv writes:[17] "There is no branch in the tree of Jewish culture that the 'enlightened' among us belittle as much as homiletics. The very concept *'derush'* has become a synonym for lack of taste and meaninglessness, and yet this attitude is really a deliberate blindness to a powerful source of emotional and spiritual experience in Israel, and a gross ingratitude towards those many and varied preachers who graced our people with this gift called *derush*. *Derush* is a legitimate field of creativity in Judaism, a broad field, fruitful and thriving, as well as a powerful channel of influence upon the life of our people, vital and indispensable."

We have not cited these words in order to defend the honor of the literature of *derush* in recent generations, but to show that it constitutes an accepted and legitimate form of literary expression, which is the very least that emerges from the attempts to define and appreciate it as a specific literary genre in the Middle Ages and the early modern period. In truth it must be said that *derush*, both as method and manner of expression, as well as a *substantive* component in Jewish creativity in Halakhah and Aggadah at once, must not be limited to these periods alone. Its sources are ancient, and it is as old as Jewish creativity itself. *Derush*, in the sense of hermeneutics, is the spinal cord of classical Jewish thought from its beginning—appearing in Scripture itself[18]—up to our own day. In its most recent form, in the Middle Ages and the modern period, *derush* follows in the footsteps of Midrash, and is but its later incarnation. In structure and form it possesses its own recognizable features. Yet it is identical, or almost identical, in its essence, with Midrash, in that it constitutes an autonomous tool of expression, faithful to the internal development of creative thought.

In his voluminous book on Jewish preaching,[19] Rabbi Simon Gliksberg proves with charming naiveté that the first preachers were none other than the Patriarchs Abraham, Isaac and Jacob, followed by Moses and Aaron, on and on down to the Maggid of Kelm and the preachers of our day. However reluctant we may be to accept Rabbi Gliksberg's ingenuous "proofs," the spirit of his simplistic argumentation we can accept, that in *derush* we have uninterrupted continuity of Jewish creativity, spreading over many fields—Halakhah and poetry, history and exegesis and in no smaller measure, thought and philosophy. In the former we refer primarily to *internal* Jewish speculation in confrontation with and in reaction to threatening existential situations; and in the latter, to confrontation with and reaction to *external* trends and philosophical schools.

Already in the earlier and later Midrash of the sages there is a persistent struggle with internal problems as well as with philosophical opinions on the outside, usually without identifying the latter by name. Echoes of Stoic philosophy, Platonism, and the school of Pythagoras reach us via the "implications" of many Talmudic sayings, even if not in what is explicitly said, as proven by contemporary scholars of Talmudic thought, most notably by Prof. E. E. Urbach in his *Beliefs and Doctrines of the Sages*[20] and Prof. Abraham Joshua Heschel in his *Torah min ha-Shamayim*.[21] In a broader and more open fashion than that of the rabbis, Philo of Alexandria struggles with the opposition. His work embodies a meeting point between Judaism and Hellenism. The common element of *derush* in all its manifestations is that it appears as defender in the breach in these confrontations. At times it rejects the opposing viewpoints that attempt to infiltrate from the outside, and at other times it serves as a mediator, recommending the selective adoption of external ideologies by means of the homiletic method. In this manner the method sometimes becomes the very substance of the conscious effort to measure up to external doctrines, and the requisite tool for effecting their legitimate entry into Jewish life.

Such absorption is possible for a Judaism faithful to the tradition of prior generations only by the use of *derush*. When interpretation is strictly literal, collision is unavoidable. Only *derush* smooths out the rough spots; it alone permits opposites to co-exist. Only through *derush* can doctrines and opinions be formulated and constituted, and laws and customs be established.[22] If it is indeed so powerful, it is no longer only a method, but a factor in the growth of Jewish thought through the generations. This growth is nurtured by two sources: inner flow and contact with external worlds of thought.

There are powerful connections between the newer literature of *derush* and the Midrash which preceded it, both in form and in content. Even if it be a new creation of the new era, it is identical to the old in the functions it assumes. The literature of *derush* emerged on the heels of the trauma caused by philosophy in the Jewish culture of the Middle Ages. The view of Harry Austryn Wolfson[23] that Philo was the father of Jewish philosophy in the Middle Ages is strengthened by the similarity of background between him and that of medieval Jewish philosophy, in that in both cases we see a confrontation between the internal culture and the external culture, without either one being ready to retreat from the arena, or to accept second place. The earliest practitioners of *derush* in the 12th and 13th centuries, R. Abraham bar Hiyya (*Meditations of the Sad Soul*), Nahmanides (*Sermon for Rosh ha-Shanah and Other Sermons*), R. Jacob Anatoli (*Teacher of the Students*), and R. Bahya ibn Asher (*Cask of Flour*), employ *derush* to confront Torah with the principles of Aristotelian logic and metaphysics.

In a similar way at a later time, in the era of the expulsion from Spain, we have the sermons of Rabbenu Nissim and R. Yitzhak Arama's impressive homiletics work, *Akedat Yitzhak*. And from there to the 16th and 17th centuries, when we become witness to a direct influence of the culture of the Renaissance, as we find in R. Judah Moscati (*Nefutzot Yehudah*), whose sermons are a mosaic of musical themes, astronomy, philosophy and Italian intermingled with the words of the sages. To these must be added the "militant" preachers—the carriers of the gospel of the "new" to the Jewish world in various generations, up to the wandering Maggidim, the "oppositionist intelligentsia" which was instrumental, in the opinion of Joseph Weiss,[24] in spreading Hasidism in the 18th century. There were also those preachers who expressed opposition to Hasidism,[25] bringing us to the 19th and 20th centuries in which appear the great orators[26] in the cause of Zion, and opposed to them the carriers of the banner of Reform, which placed great importance on the art of preaching, and gave the title of "preacher" to the rabbi. The latter movement promoted the sermon as the unifying factor between past and present, as the ideology which presented the fundamental essence of Midrash, that the new is not new at all, but the old appearing in a new revelation.[27] *Derush*, then, is not a passive partner, but a creative force. It is not a mere method, but a clear and definite substance. This is true of the first philosopher-preacher in Judaism, Philo of Alexandria, and then, crossing over centuries and continents, of Rabbi Loewe of Prague,[28] up to Samson Raphael Hirsch in Frankfurt, Germany[29]—and from him to Rabbi Joseph Baer Soloveitchik.

Side by side with the long and honored tradition of intellectual *derush*, another type of *derush* developed, born as a literary form, motivated by a desire for beauty and artistic playfulness for their own sakes, at times serving as illustration and "intellectual adornment." The distinction must always be drawn between these two types, even though the line of differentiation is not always clear and they sometimes overlap. Thus, Maimonides was able to discern in some Aggadic passages matters of indifferent value, not leading "either to fear or love,"[30] while the sages see in the Aggadah the means to "recognize the One who spoke and thus created the world,"[31] that is, solid theological themes containing fundamentals of the faith.

Thus it is clearly wrong to wrap all preachers and all sermons into one package. Maimonides knows well how to recognize the kind of *derush* which is mere method, thereby constituting a dangerous and revolutionary tool, invalid in supporting or rejecting specific doctrines. "Know that our rejection of the theory of the eternity of the universe is not based on passages in the Torah which speak of the creation of the world, for these verses are not any more conclusive concerning creation than are the verses which imply corporeal aspects in divinity. *The gates of interpretation are not closed to us* in the matter of creation; we could interpret them, as we have done in the matter of the negation of anthropomorphism. In fact, the former would perhaps be simpler for us, since we could easily interpret the verses in question in a manner which would permit the assumption of the eternity of the universe, as we have interpreted verses in order to nullify the concept of a corporeal divinity."[32] Thus in Maimonides' opinion, any doctrine, even that of "the eternity of the universe" which is in fundamental opposition to the principles of the Torah faith, could have been reconciled through *derush* interpretation, for "the gates of interpretation are not closed to us." From the above we should be able to appreciate the absolute refusal to utilize Aggadah and *derush* for the purposes of confirmation or refutation of any particular doctrine. There is no limit to the ability of *derush* to "reconcile" verses for its own purposes. Hence its power is perilous and its usefulness negligible.

All this is true only as long as we speak of *derush* as method, not when it is part of the substance of the matter. In the first case we attempt to "resolve" the contradictions between the verses and their strange content, and *derush* is supposed to serve as some kind of bridge across the abyss that remains after we have tried to span the gaps between the separate worlds. Not so in the second case, in which *derush* is part of the substance. Then, the doctrines which had appeared to be foreign enter into the precincts of the sacred, become naturalized, established within it, and internally blended, so that the process can be considered as *creative hermeneutics*. This process does not bridge or bind two entities but melts them both down, drawing forth from the cauldron a new creation, complete and synthesized.

I. Heinemann in *Darkhei ha-Aggadah* sees two basic guidelines in the creation of Midrash.[33] One, "creative philology," runs as a continuous thread through all of the literature of *derush*. It appears also in the guise of creative etymology,[34] in which each word, every added and subtracted element in the Biblical text, serves as a jumping-off point for fruitful, imaginative creativity. The second is "creative historiography" in which the preacher not only broadens and adds color, names and details to the development of the nucleus of Biblical historical narrative, but also nourishes it from his own resources of meditation and personal experience. However, there is still another line of creative *derush* in which the preacher transports himself, with all his thoughts, beliefs and traits, into the Biblical situation or into the person of the Biblical hero, out of complete empathetic identification. In this situation he seeks to discover himself, without severing his ties to his own time and place.

In most cases, we would find the stimulus for this emanating from an immanent tension, whose source lies in a conscious or unconscious striving for an internal spiritual synthesis of distant, true worlds, struggling within the mind and heart of the preacher-philosopher. To be explicit: we are speaking of a synthesis which leads to unified existence, not a resignation to co-existence in the style of "Torah" with *Derekh Eretz*, or "Religion" and "Science."[35]

The two truths coming into dialectic confrontation here do not *follow* one another in succession, or at the expense of each other—but they are simultaneous, both of them constituting, as it were, one single truth, though at first glance they seem to be not only separate but contradictory. They must be one because they have to dwell within the soul of one man, for whom they assert laws of life, in theory and in practice, and do not remain within the walls of the academy. *Derush*, here, is not an adornment but a primary, essential condition of life.

III

This kind of hermeneutics, flowing from a concrete dialectical existential situation, is the philosophical *derush* of Rabbi Soloveitchik. It arises predominantly from the existential necessity of a new reality, one which, though still striving for self-definition, can only be denied or doubted today with great difficulty. Rabbi Soloveitchik himself is an exemplary representative of this reality.

What we have in mind is the new situation, in which Halakhah, in the sense of a full life of Torah and Commandments, now shares a home with the fullness of Western culture. In this home we meet the Westernized Jew, whose belonging to Western culture is not marginal, derivative or partial, but complete, natural and autonomous. At the same time this very person is also a Jew of the Halakhah, for whom Halakhah is not trivial, a nostalgic vestige, an emblem of ethnic identity, but deeply rooted, profound and all-embracing. Both Western culture and the Torah of Israel are natural truths for him, self-evident; in both does he see a way of life for himself and for the community in which he lives. He does not seek to blur contradictions and cover up the gaps between the two, immanent gaps of which he is quite aware, but which do not deter him or confront him with the necessity to choose between them. He is aware of the tension created by these gaps, this tension itself adding depth and breadth to his existence, fructifying his creative powers, and sharpening his sensations and reactions to the two centers of influence to which he is exposed, not by compulsion but by free choice and recognition of the rightness and worthwhileness of that choice.

Rabbi Soloveitchik represents this Jew, and in his effort to serve as his spokesman, *derush* serves him as a means of passage from one of these poles to the other, enabling him to proceed securely in that one world located within these poles. When he interprets the written sources he is not aiming to "solve" difficulties or give answers in the case of verses that appear to contradict his philosophical thesis; rather, the verses themselves are made to propound that very thesis. The philosophical conception and the Biblical passages, and even more surprisingly the essentials of Halakhah, themselves become spokesmen of the socio-philosophical reality in which he finds himself, while this very same reality on its part, as distant as it seems, actually embraces at many points the halakhic approach and Biblical personalities. The problem is not fundamentally, as it often was in the confrontation between Judaism and forces external to it, one of "verses" standing in contradiction to each other. For Rabbi Soloveitchik it is clear that often verses *do* stand in contradiction, but he accepts axiomatically that a third, reconciling source is available. The tension between the two cultures in which he functions and creates is not destructive, corrupting and shattering, but, on the contrary, constructive, positive, fruitful and creative. Biblical passages and halakhic rulings are not road hazards for him, but traffic signs offering him direction. He brings them together and, as it were, touches them with the magic hand of *derush*. They become "swallowed up" into the meditative-experiential framework he fashions before us, and are set within it as precious jewels. Verses and laws are not foreign transplants which have to be uprooted and replanted, but part of the original intellectual and spiritual landscape. They themselves form the language in which R. Soloveitchik expresses his ideas, even if it does not require any special effort to recognize traces of great contemporary thinkers, most of whom certainly were unaware of and did not recognize at all the interpretation of the passages, to say nothing of the halakhic ambience.

If language be part of the very substance of philosophic thought or personal experience, when the attempt is made to transmit these to others, certainly *derush* in the service of Rabbi Soloveitchik is such a substantive element, and not merely an external, methodological means.

This close integration between modern Western thought and traditional Jewish modes of expression, as found in the thought of R. Soloveitchik—what we have called the *derush* method—is not accidental and is also not a matter of personal style. It is a necessary result of the historical-spiritual situation referred to above. This situation is different from the one formulated by the great neo-Orthodox thinker Rabbi Samson Raphael Hirsch in the slogan "Torah and *Derekh Eretz.*" There Torah and the ways of the world remain separate entities, existing side by side without contact, except that they are embodied in the same person at different times. The situation we speak of is also different from that of the "Renaissance of the Sacred" as propounded by the school of Rav Kook, which seeks to sanctify the new and discern the revelation of the sacred in the development of science, in evolution, and in human progress. In the new situation addressed by Rabbi Soloveitchik, we find ourselves equidistant from, or in equal measure within, two specific worlds, standing in mutual opposition, the holy and the profane. There is no attempt here to secularize the holy or to sanctify the secular. The two worlds exist and persist in their own right, and we live and persist in both of them. In the ladder of priorities both of them together are preferred, with all of the paradoxes and contradictions this involves. This world is aware of its innate contradictions, and the tension produced by them, but they do not lead to hostility and a perpetual state of war. There may not be complete peace between them, but there undoubtedly exists a truce between the armed forces on both sides. The world of Halakhah as it emerges from the situation in which R. Soloveitchik finds himself is mature enough to confront its internal and external enemies. The world beyond the walls no longer tempts and mesmerizes as it did, precisely because I *am already in it and know it.* Winds blowing outside no longer carry everything away and remove everyone from the house of study; the light coming from the outside has lost the power to draw everything to it.

The world of those who observe Halakhah and live according to it on a daily basis has emerged from the *shtetl,* has burst through the walls of the ghetto, and in the process has not thrown the *tallit* and the *tefillin* overboard. The world of Halakhah still sets the Jew apart, but this isolation is a proud one, not a shameful ghetto. The world of Halakhah is now legitimate, socially accepted, even cosmopolitan.[36] It is now possible to observe the strictest standards of *kashrut* on all international flights. It is quite respectable to order kosher meals in many exclusive hotels all over the world, or to inquire of the man at the front desk about the availability of a *minyan.* Torah and *mitzvot* actually exist in theory and practice in exclusive atomic laboratories, in hospitals, in industrial and commercial centers. All this requires a more sophisticated approach to the understanding of Halakhah, and certainly for the purpose of explaining it to others. The old apologetics must now arm itself with more up-to-date weapons, in order to be heard in the higher, contemporaneous levels of society.

Contact between the world of Halakhah and that of secular Western culture is not merely social and external but occurs in basic spiritual terms, in education, entertainment, and in establishing esthetic standards and world views. Jews who are faithful to every iota of halakhic requirement grow up and are directly fashioned by Western culture. For them it is not an external attainment but internally substantive, autonomous, and a spiritual component with which one has to live. Halakhah in its new incarnation, after passing through the tortures and indignities of its inner and outer critics, is not content to be a matter of blind habit, royal decrees, and the like, but demands together with other disciplines the status of intellectual legitimacy and a defensible position. The separation between Torah and *Derekh Eretz*, which worked in its time for the Jews of Germany, no longer suffices for the new-Orthodox Jews of America. The two domains forcibly interest each other and are compelled to co-exist in time and thought.

IV

This reality is confronted in the thought given to us by the mouth or pen of Rabbi Soloveitchik, and includes *derush* as an integral part of it, so much so that it is difficult to describe it otherwise. True, the thought is halakhic thought, but as Rotenstreich[37] has pointed out so well, Halakhah here is not a restricted, specific law, but a matter of anthropology and phenomenology.

From the viewpoint of historical precedent, it seems that what is closest to (although chronologically furthest from) this method of almost complete assimilation of an external culture into established Jewish contents, is Philo of Alexandria in his many-sided literary activity. In this case, it is the Stoic allegory which was "Judaized." This comparison is not accidental. Taking into consideration all the many and profound differences between R. Soloveitchik and Philo, there remains a great measure of similarity between Alexandria of the first century and Boston of the twentieth century. Rav Soloveitchik differs from Philo in his breadth of knowledge of Judaism and in his deep connection to Halakhah, but it seems nevertheless permissible to say that in a certain sense he finds himself in a Philonic situation.

What are the salient features of this situation?

A. The Jewish community and Jewish thought are under the influence of a powerful outside cultural force, which is pagan, anti-Jewish, rejected fundamentally by the Jewish group, and yet is also possessed of an attractive intellectual and spiritual message, clothed in ethical and cogitative values that can easily be identified with ancient Jewish values.

B. There is an urgent need for high-level apologetics for internal and external purposes, which can justify the validity of the Jewish position, especially with regard to the necessity for the observance of the imperatives of Halakhah, within a society and under conditions heretofore unknown. This function is doubly difficult as the Halakhah comes under the fire of criticism from within and deliberate attempts to make it "adjust" and conform to social and cultural pressures of the environment (the old "Hellenizers" and modern Reform and Conservative groups).

C. The apologist holds a thorough and proud conviction of the superiority of Judaism, of Torah, *viz.* Halakhah—which "will not be changed" even in view of the powerful external culture, for "it contains everything," and nothing good, moral or true has been omitted from it if only one knows the way to search for it.

These are among the things that characterized the Philonic situation and gave rise to the allegoric interpretation of Scripture, which only recently has begun to gain the recognition it deserves. These and other similarities characterize the new situation in which Rav Soloveitchik functions. What allegory was for Philo, *derush* is for R. Soloveitchik.

However, unlike Philo's, the goal of R. Soloveitchik is not one of interpretation (were we to assume that this was the goal of Philo[38]), and he makes no pretense of presenting his Midrashim as the authoritative interpretations of Torah. And yet, like Philo, his goal is philosophic and didactic, so that the verses of Scripture (and for R. Soloveitchik also matters of Halakhah) serve as the natural means for him to express his thought, in which there is a synthesis of two distant worlds that have been brought close to each other.

If we were to extend this comparison further, we should substitute for the word "synthesis"—which has been worn out from excessive usage in recent generations—the word "syncretism."[39] That is to say, a total and equal acceptance of both worlds, that of the Western-Humanistic and that of the Jewish-halakhic, with all the imagined and real contradictions between them. This acceptance demands that we perceive the two worlds as one.

With R. Soloveitchik, as with Philo, we find ourselves both at the end of an old long road, and at the beginning of a new one. The meeting between Judaism and philosophy in ancient times was not sudden or of a one-time nature. It took place in several stages, "opening with mere philosophic adornment and wrapping of Jewish ideas, going through a process of introducing isolated ideas of Greek philosophy into Israel, up to the fundamental philosophic purification of Judaism performed by Philo."[40] So Isaac Julius Guttmann attests concerning Philo: "For him philosophy does not serve merely as a means for doctrinal affirmation, and the occupation with philosophic problems is not restricted to details, but he sees Judaism itself as a philosophic teaching, in the sense that it includes within itself a complete philosophic system. . . . With the help of the allegorical method of interpretation created in the Stoic school, he succeeds in dictating into the Five Books of Moses, both into its historical and its legal sections, philosophic content. He thoroughly believed that he was not budging from the ground of Judaism, but was only discovering its deepest meaning."[41]

"The Torah of Moses," continues Guttmann,[42] "is for him the complete truth, and contains all that science can possibly tell, and therefore, the nature of the allegoristic interpretation of Scripture is totally different from that of the allegoristic interpretation of the myths by the Stoic sages, his teachers and predecessors. He wanted to unite the two forms of truth, that of human cognition and that of divine revelation. The position of these two forms of truth together is possible only within the bounds of the religion of historical revelation, and Philo was the first to work diligently to unite them in a systematic fashion. When he was called the first theologian, the title fit him in this sense more than in any other. The manner of questioning later prevalent in theology and in the philosophy of the monotheistic religions, was already familiar to him, and this fact bestows upon him a historical value superior to the value of his thought itself."

This is true also of R. Soloveitchik. He finds in Judaism, especially in Halakhah, a total, unblocked view of the intellectual world of modern Western man, as it is expressed in his philosophic, psychological, or sociological creations. The perspectives of man and world presented by the social sciences and contemporary society do not only not disturb the halakhic view of man and the duties it thrusts upon him, but they are the very same perspectives, from a different point of view. This becomes possible only through the power of *derush* in service to, and under the aegis of, Rabbi Soloveitchik, not only as a methodological tool, and certainly not merely as a literary-esthetic technique, but as a substantive component which raises to realization that syncretic synthesis through which the Jew lives in Halakhah and in time.

V

This phenomenon is clearly evident in many places in the writings of Rav Soloveitchik.[43] Suffice it for us to examine one essay, pregnant with practical implications, though it, too, like most of his writings, is based on an oral discourse. We refer to the essay "Kol Dodi Dofek."[44] This essay is completely marked by the sign of *derush*, starting with its title, and, with its general literary framework, through the many double meanings and the plethora of brilliant Midrashic flashes spread throughout the length of the work, down to the powerful concluding chords—we have before us a profound and powerfully expressed literary-philosophic creation, which cannot be defined in any better way than to call it a *derasha*! Here is a perfect sermon, following all the prescribed rules, though it is not anchored in the classical era of *derush* literature, but is totally rooted in the time and place of its composer, our time. Moreover, the examination of the essay against the background of R. Soloveitchik's other writings and lectures demonstrates that there is no room for any suspicion of deliberate imitation of the style of *derush*, be it in the pseudographic manner or by way of parody. So much for form.

What is important, however, is that every effort to trace the thought content of the essay—containing as it does very significant and weighty themes, as will be clear to anyone familiar with the rich religious thought that sprang up following the Holocaust and the Rebirth of Israel—will find the roots, trunks, and branches of these ideas also existing and maintaining themselves in the world of *derush*. Only in the "Midrashic reality" which tolerates paradoxes and sees things in their prospective and retrospective aspects simultaneously, can the words of Rabbi Soloveitchik on Holocaust and State be acceptable. This reality rescues the thought of Rabbi Soloveitchik from the one-dimensional historiosophic analysis represented so plentifully in the religious thought created in the wake of this complex and many-sided subject.[45]

The essay "The Voice of My Beloved that Knocketh" begins with the ancient religious-philosophic problem of "the suffering of the righteous," in which Rabbi Soloveitchik sees "one of the sealed riddles with which Judaism has wrestled since its earliest days." According to him this is a problem that occupied all the prophets and which "still hovers over our world, demanding its solution: why does God permit evil to rule over creation?" The solution is, and he introduces it in a manner which would indicate much prior consideration, that it is possible to overcome the problem of suffering in the world, when we measure it in two separate dimensions: fate and *destiny*. "Judaism," he says (and it is interesting to test the meaning of this word in the subsequent discussion: Halakhah? Aggadah? Philosophy? Mysticism?), "always distinguished between existence in fate, and existence in destiny."[46]

As for suffering in the dimension of "fateful existence"—it is a riddle and a painful one, agitating and paralyzing, and will ever remain such. Judaism, "with its realistic approach to man and his position in existence" is not ready to accept compromising metaphysical solutions which attempt to obscure the nature of evil. "Evil is an undeniable fact. There *is* evil, there *is* suffering, and there are the pains of hell in the world. He who desires to fool himself by removing his attention from the rent in existence, and by romanticizing the life of man, is but a fool and a dreamer of dreams."[47]

However, in the second dimension of human existence, that of destiny, suffering becomes a challenge to man, calling him to a "face-to-face confrontation with evil. "[48] This confrontation is not a matter of metaphysical speculation but is "halakhic and ethical," in which the emphasis is shifted from the question of the cause of evil to the world of action. "The problem is now defined in the simple language of Halakhah, and becomes relevant to daily practice. . . . What obligations does suffering place upon man?"

Halakhah, Rabbi Soloveitchik establishes, is concerned with the question of evil and suffering "as in other questions of permitted and forbidden, obligation and release. We do not speculate about the inscrutable ways of God, but on the way in which man should walk when suffering befalls him . . . and the halakhic response to this question is very simple."

R. Soloveitchik emphasizes again and again that we are faced here with a halakhic question, that Halakhah provides an answer for it. Yet, is "the halakhic answer to this question very simple" in reality? What really is "a halakhic answer"? Is it to be understood in the limited sense of an answer to be followed in practice? Moreover, is it indeed "very simple" to arrive at this answer? So does Rabbi Soloveitchik rule, and no one will question his position as master of the Halakhah. And what is, according to him, the halakhic answer? "Suffering is intended to elevate man, to purify him and sanctify him, to clean his thoughts and cleanse them from all superficial dross and gross sentiments, to refine his character and broaden the horizons of his life." All these does he include in what he calls "a halakhic answer"! And if that were not enough, he supplements the answer and provides us with "the sum of the matter: the function of suffering is to mend the flaw in the character of man"! And again in the same vein: "Halakhah teaches us that it is a crime on the part of the sufferer to permit his anguish to *go to waste* and to remain without meaning and goal. For suffering appears in the world in order to contribute something to man, to atone for him, to redeem him from corruption, vulgarity and a sunken spirit." These are parts of the "halakhic answer," and what is the first Biblical source quoted in support of this "halakhic ruling"? "'It is a time of travail for Jacob, and from it he shall be saved' that is, from the *travail itself* the salvation will come." The source of the "Halakhah" is then obvious Midrashic novelty, and immediately following is a second Midrash, similar to the first: "'When it is painful for you, when all these things befall you . . . thou shalt return unto the Lord thy God'—suffering obliges man to indulge in perfect repentance before God." Following this Midrash there is a long discussion based on halakhic rulings by Maimonides which stress the tie between trouble and repentance, and are most appropriate for our purposes here. And then, we go on: "Judaism has deepened this concept (of the improvement of man through suffering) by associating the idea of rectifying suffering with rectifying grace."[49] And here he floats far over the waves of the sea of Jewish mysticism to the world of rectification (*tikkun*), both of suffering and of grace, which demand improvement in man. And again, a proof text, apparently halakhic, but in reality thoroughly in the nature of *derush:* "Our great teachers have taught us that 'a man must bless for evil as he blessed for good.' Just as the good obliges man to engage in elevated action, and demands of the individual or the community creative action and renewal (a nice *derush,* but not the simple meaning, of 'to bless'), so does suffering demand improvement of the soul and purification of life . . . in short, it is not man's obligation to solve the problem of rational cause or purpose of suffering in all its speculative complexity, but [his concern is] the question of their amelioration in all its halakhic simplicity, by converting [mere] fate into [meaningful] destiny."[50]

Thus even a cursory reading of a passage in "Kol Dodi Dofek" compels us to recognize this vital methodological and substantive element in the creativity of Rabbi Soloveitchik, as it finds expression in this essay and as it does in his other writings: the concept "Halakhah" is continually broadened under his touch to include a philosophical approach.[51] The justification of this broadening lies in the power of *derush*, which makes it possible to widen and materialize the concept "Halakhah" until it embraces philosophic-existential fundamentals, together with prominent terms from the area of kabbalah and mysticism.

True, the position of Rabbi Soloveitchik in all that relates to the comprehension of "evil" which is expressed in the Holocaust, and the "grace" that is expressed in the historical events ("the calling of the beloved") that are tied up with the rise of the State of Israel, constitutes a "halakhic" approach, that is, an approach that is concerned with real daily existence, and in the obligations that this existence thrusts upon man, and not with metaphysical prophecy beyond this world. And yet, the foundations of this "Halakhah" lean upon the pillars of *derush*, as a result of which, through the enthusiasm engendered by the conception of these matters and their transmission, this "Halakhah" is enabled to pose as the totality of the Jewish scheme of things, as it has been formulated in the modes of practical law, and yet not losing the blazing, living flame which glows in the inner recesses of this practice, from Sinai up to now. R. Soloveitchik represents the "Man of Halakhah" but this "Halakhah" of which he speaks must not be grasped in terms of the four frozen ells; it includes the world and all that is in it, and man together with all his profundities and orbits. These are revealed to us when this "Halakhah" is interpreted in the accepted manner of *derush* over the generations. If we can be permitted a farfetched analogy, we could say that the works of Rabbi Soloveitchik are not a "Mishnah" which contains here and there (as in the *Mishneh Torah* of Maimonides) Aggadic material of an expository and embellishing nature,[52] but a kind of "Midrash Halakhah" in which Halakhah and Aggadah are blended. In this manner, R. Soloveitchik himself passes from his positioning of himself "halakhically" in the matter of evil in the world, expressing the existential obligation towards deeds that carry the force of legal rulings, for the purpose of "rectifying suffering and elevating it"—over to complete formulations, organized statements, or marvelous gems of *derush*, which wander in refrain from subject to subject and from image to image. And the leading image that emerges before us is Job.[53]

The image and events of Job are interpreted to exemplify the thesis that there is no sense in speculation about the nature of suffering. Only after Job is convinced and says: "Therefore do I speak without understanding what is too wonderful for me, and which I know not," only then does God reveal to him "the true, hidden basis of suffering as it is formulated by the Halakhah"! Job never knew the cause or the purpose of suffering, but one thing it is his obligation to know: "the basis of remedial suffering." And here R. Soloveitchik constructs a marvelous Midrashic scheme of Job's situation, which appears at one and the same time in all the various Aggadic-Midrashic eras in which Job lived and functioned. In the manner of Midrash, he pays no attention to the real gap separating the time of Jacob the Patriarch from the time of the return to Zion in the days of Ezra, all the times coalescing for him into one time.[54] The man Job who lived as well in the time of Jacob, the time of the exodus from Egypt, and the time of the return to Zion, he and his pains are woven together in the web of *derush*, which speculates on the nature of Jewish prayer conceived of as public prayer, and on the connection between individual and communal responsibility when the individual is the subject of either a time of grace or a time of suffering. And from here, after R. Soloveitchik has leaped to the wide expanses of hermeneutics that develop around the figure of Job, he returns to the halakhic question: "What is the duty of suffering man that arises out of his suffering? What heavenly commanding voice pierces through the veil of pain?" What are "the laws of the remedying of evil" or "the law of rectifying pain" that we derive from Job? In a broader sense: What is the "Halakhah" we learn from the "echo of the imperative that drives relentlessly upward" out of the event? This Halakhah depends on the manner in which we employ the method of *derush* concerning the special happening occurring in history, in order to derive from it the meta-historical "imperative" of the halakhic principle whose source is godly, and which must be embodied as "Halakhah" within history.

VI

In order to arrive at this compound conception with regard to the historical events of our epoch, centered in the Holocaust and the reestablishment of the State, R. Soloveitchik has need of the classic tools of *derush,* and he creates several new Midrashim for the Scriptural verses, especially for the Song of Songs, from which the name of the essay is taken.[55] From these Midrashim there emerge for us halakhic imperatives of a meta-historical nature, which we are commanded to fulfill within historical halakhic reality.

Before us, in "Kol Dodi Dofek," is one example of this type of halakhic Midrash in our day, formed against the background of the historical events of the last generation. Its starting point is the terrible historical hardship in which the people of Israel were placed after the Holocaust. The Halakhah which emerged from this reality was the meta-historical command not to miss the opportunity. The principle according to which this "Halakhah" was specified flows from the world of Halakhah which stipulates in many cases the prohibition against missing opportunities, and functions out of a keen sense of time in such matters as the desecration of the Sabbath (one moment—permitted, one moment later—prohibited) the time of the reading of *Shema,* etc.[56] The path leading from the meta-historical imperative to its fulfillment in the historical situation is the path of *derush.*

A commandment which is not fulfilled in time can destroy worlds. To illustrate this halakhic principle R. Soloveitchik creates several Midrashim. Here, for example, is a new and moving Midrash dealing with the stories of the sins of Saul and David.[57] While the confession of the latter is accepted and his sin forgiven, that of the former is not accepted because he missed the correct moment, and his kingdom is taken from him. And here is a second Midrash, which serves as the main framework for the essay as a whole and which concentrates upon the image of the Shulamit maiden, and the description of "the tragic and paradoxical hesitation of the beloved, intoxicated with love and nostalgic dreams" who misses the opportunity "of which she dreamed and for which she had fought, and which she sought with all her heart's enthusiasm," so that she does not respond to the knocking of the beloved, who also is very desirous of her. This Midrash upon the Song of Songs created by Rabbi Soloveitchik was not created but to permit us to conceive the meaning of the historical events of the Holocaust and the State, their meta-historical significance and the halakhic imperative that emerges from them.

What is the rise of the State of Israel to Rabbi Soloveitchik? Is it the redemption, or one of its stages? Is it the beginning of redemption? The beginning of the growth of our redemption? Indifferent and unconnected to the course of redemption? False messianism? Satanic?[58]

Rabbi Soloveitchik has prepared us in the preface to his discourse on the conception of the events which led to the rise of the Jewish state, not to ask for the nature of the matter in the metaphysical sense, but for the halakhic imperative which is evoked by it. What then is this command coming to us from meta-history and how does it reach us? R. Soloveitchik refrains from responding with definite answers to this question, as would be expected of him as the *ish ha-halakhah*. For example, he does not rule whether it is obligatory, permitted, or prohibited to recite *Hallel* on *Yom ha-Atzma'ut*. Instead he fortifies himself behind the exalted, mystic Biblical text from the Song of Songs, and by means of *derush* brings forth the "beloved" who knocks on the door of the "friend" entering the specific historical situation which he is dealing with, and this situation itself heralds the Halakhah that emerges from it.

"Eight years ago, in the midst of a frightening night, full of the horrors of Majdanek, Treblinka and Buchenwald, in a night of gas chambers and crematoria, in a night of absolute hiding-of-the-face . . . in a night of unceasing searchings for the beloved—in this very night the beloved arose and appeared. The God who was hiding in his hidden pavilion suddenly appeared and began to knock at the entrance to the tent of the bedraggled and bereaved companion, restlessly tossing on her bed in heaving and tortures of hell. *It is because of the rapping and knocking at the door of the companion, wrapped in grief, that the State of Israel was born!*"[59]

"The knocking of the beloved" is spelled out by R. Soloveitchik in terms of six calls. They result from a hermeneutic development of words and situations taken from the Song of Songs. Are these "knocks" miraculous, outside the bounds of nature, justifying desertion of established halakhic systems? Or are they merely natural developments? Using the *derush* form helps R. Soloveitchik avoid these explicit issues. So, for example, is described the "first knock": ". . . from the viewpoint of international relations no one will deny that the rise of the State of Israel in the political sense was almost supernatural." Notice: "almost" supernatural. Nevertheless, he continues: "I do not know whom the representatives of the press saw, with their eyes of flesh, sitting upon the presiding chair in that fateful meeting (of the General Assembly) in which it was decided to found the State of Israel, but he who looked well with his spiritual eyes felt that the real chairman presiding over the discussion was—the beloved. He was knocking with his gavel upon the table."[60] And this is called "almost supernatural"?

Rabbi Soloveitchik struggles with this matter and here, too, *derush* comes to his aid.

> Do we not interpret the verse in the Book of Esther, 'That night the king could not sleep' as referring to the sleep of the king of the universe?[61] If only Ahashverosh could not sleep, it would not have been important at all and no salvation would have come that night, but if the king of the universe, as it were, could not, or did not sleep—why, then the redemption is born. If so-and-so had opened that meeting of the United Nations the State of Israel would not have been born, but if the beloved raps upon the presiding chair—the wonder takes place. The voice of the beloved knocks.

The way of *derush*, which can move from the Song of Songs to the Book of Esther, affords Soloveitchik the paradoxical opportunity to say and not to say what he wants to say and does not want to say. In all of the Book of Esther the name of God is not mentioned, and yet

Halakhah demands of us to pray for and praise "the miracles" of Purim.

And so with regard to other "knockings." They float on the border between the natural and the supernatural. We cannot, we may not, speculate about the precise metaphysical whatness of those knockings that are expressed in the breathtaking happenings in the political, the military, the educational, and the interreligious spheres after years of the darkness of the hidden face.[62] We should not look for one truth, cut and dried. We should be content with the Midrashic truth of the matter. What it is incumbent upon us to hear from the midst of the wonderful events occurring before our eyes, as a kind of raw material of *derush*, is a meta-historic imperative clothed in real historic Halakhah, and in our case, the Halakhah concerning the prohibition of missing the temporal opportunity in all that relates to the tension of support and assistance to the State of Israel.

The use of the *derush* of "the sound of the knocking of my beloved" is, as we have seen, substantive in the thought of Rabbi Soloveitchik and is not merely methodological. So it is with regard to the "six knockings" of the beloved, and so it is with regard to the distinction at which he arrives by way of a typical form of *derush*, which moves from subject to subject, until the solution to the entire matter is found—the distinction between the covenant at Sinai (the covenant of destiny) and the covenant of Egypt (the covenant of fate), and the difference between them. This distinction leads to other conceptual distinctions, such as between *Mahaneh* and *Edah*, "Nation" and "people,"[63] and "grace" and "holiness" an entire universe of philosophic concepts, all of them rooted in the soil of *derush*, both as method and as substance.

Notes

1. "Ish ha-Halakhah," published first in *Talpiot*, Vol. 1, No. 1, 5704 (1943), and now in: Rabbi Yosef Dov Soloveitchik, *Be-Sod ha-Yahid ve-ha-Yahad* (In Aloneness, In Togetherness), a selection of Hebrew writings edited by Pinchas Peli, Jerusalem, 1978, in the latter, p. 39, note 1. The essay also appears in *Ish ha-Halakhah—Galui ve-Nistar*, Jerusalem, 1979, and has been translated by Lawrence Kaplan in *Halakhic Man*, Philadelphia, 1983.

2. Joseph B. Soloveitchik, "The Lonely Man of Faith," *Tradition*, vol.7, No. 2, Summer 1965, pp. 65–67.

3. See note 1 above and in *Be-Sod ha-Yahid ve-ha-Yahad*, pp. 137–188 (all the citations from "Ish ha-Halakhah" below will refer to this book).

4. *Ibid.*, pp. 45, 55–63; 112.

5. *Ibid.*, pp. 47–48; 84–94; 100.

6. *Ibid.*, p. 48.

7. *Ibid.*, pp. 95–108.

8. See note 2 above.

9. *Ibid.*, pp. 28, 33.

10. Pinchas H. Peli, *On Repentance: In the Thought and Oral Discourses of Rabbi Joseph B. Soloveitchik*, Orot Publishing House, Jerusalem, 1980, pp. 1–343. See especially the Introduction, pp. 117–54.

11. See Eugene B. Borowitz, *A New Jewish Theology in the Making*, Philadelphia, 1964, pp. 164–170, and Lawrence Kaplan, "The Religious Philosophy of Rabbi Soloveitchik," *Tradition*, vol. 14, No. 2, Fall 1973.

12. So writes Arnold Jacob Wolf on the universal significance of the thought of the Rav in a critical essay on *Al ha-Teshuvah* (On Repentance) in the periodical *Sh'ma*, September 1975: "If I am not mistaken, people will still be reading him in a thousand years."

13. Sermons such as were heard at Religious Zionists conventions in the United States appear in Yosef Dov Halevi Soloveitchik, *Hamesh Derashot* (Five Sermons), translated by David Telzner, Jerusalem 5734.

14. See Nathan Rotenstreich, *Iyyunim ha-Mahashavah ha-Yehudit ba-Zeman ha-Zeh* (Studies in the Jewish Thought of Today), Tel Aviv, 1978, pp. 74–83.

15. For an overall review of the traditional Christian hermeneutical method, see *The New Hermeneutic*, ed. by James M. Robinson and John B. Cobb, New York, 1964; also W. Parker, *Hermeneutics*, University of Chicago Press, 1978.

16. *Ha-Sifrut*, Tel Aviv, September 1972, Vol. 3, 3–4. pp. 550–567.

17. In the introduction to his book, *Shabbat u-Mo'ed ba-Derush u-va-Hasidut* (Sabbath and Festival in Derush and Hasidism), Tel Aviv, 5726, p. 5.

18. See Y. L. Zunz, *Ha-Derashot be-Yisrael ve-Hishtalshelutan ha-Historit* (Sermonics in Israel and their Historical Development), edited and completed by Hanokh Albeck, Jerusalem, 5707, chap. 3; and Hanokh Albeck, *Mavo Ha-Mishnah* (Introduction to the Mishnah), Tel Aviv, 5719, pp. 3–10.

19. *Ha-Derashah be-Yisrael* (The Sermon in Israel), a description of the Hebrew sermon and its development from ancient days up to the last period, by Rabbi Simeon Jacob Halevi Gliksberg, Tel Aviv, 5700, pp. 15–519. See also *Torat ha-Derashah* (The Art of the Sermon) by the same author, Tel Aviv, 5708, which is in the nature of a second part to *Ha-Derashah be-Yisrael*.

20. Ephraim E. Urbach, *Hazal: Pirkei Emunot ve-De'ot* (The Sages: Faith and Doctrine), Jerusalem, 5729, chap. 1.

21. Abraham Joshua Heschel, *Torah min ha-Shamayim ba-Aspaklaria shel ha-Dorot* (Torah from Heaven, in the Light of the Generations) Vol. 1, Jerusalem, 5722; Vol. 2, 5725.

22. Comp. Marvin Fox, "Judaism, Secularism and Textual Interpretation," in the collection *Modern Jewish Ethics, Theory and Practice*, Ohio University Press, 1975. See also in that collection the article by Akiva Ernst Simon, "The Neighbor We Are Supposed to Love." On Midrashic interpretation as a living source in Judaism, see the essay "Interpretation" by Simon Ravidovitz in *Studies in Jewish Thought*, pp. 62–84, Philadelphia, 1972.

23. Harry A. Wolfson, *Philo—Foundations of Jewish Philosophy in Judaism, Christianity and Islam*, Harvard University Press, 1947, vol. I, Introd. and p. 63 *et al.* Also in Vol. 2, p. 282.

24. Joseph Weiss, "Reshit Tzemihatah shel ha-Derekh ha-Hasidit, (the Beginning of the Hasidic Way)," *Zion*, vol. 16(5711), pp. 46–105.

25. See Mordechai Wilensky, *Hasidim u-Mitnaggedim—Le-Toledot ha-Pulmus she-beinehem bi-Shenot 5532–5575* (Hasidim and Their Opponents—a History of the Controversy Between Them During the Years of 5532–5575), Jerusalem, 5730.

26. Regarding the preachers for *Hibbat Zion*, see R. Schzipanski, "Hogei ha-Ra'yon bi-Tekufat Hibbat Tziyyon (Thinkers in the Hibbat Zion Period)," in the collection *Hazon Torah ve-Tziyyon* (A Vision of Torah and Zion), ed. by Shimon Federbush, Jerusalem, 5720, p. 83. Comp. further *ha-Derashah be-Yisrael* (The Sermon in Israel), *op. cit.*, p. 10, chaps. 57–60. Also, "Ha-Metifim le-Hibbat Tziyyon (Preachers for Hibbat Tsiyyon)," *Pa'amei ha-Ge'ulah* (Footsteps of Redemption) (Aryeh Zanzifer, Tel Aviv), 5712.

27. According to H. H. Ben-Sasson *Hebrew Encyclopedia*, Vol. 13, p. 219, entry "Derashah" So also does Eduard Maybaum claim in a sermon for Passover in 1879: "For thirty years we have been accustomed to connect homiletically the exodus from

Egypt with our current freedom; then we were aided by miracles, while today science is our salvation."

28. Concerning the Maharal of Prague as a preacher who employed *derush* to react to the challenges of his day, see Andre Neher, *Le Puits de l'Exil, la theologie dialectique de Maral de Prague,* Paris, 1966 and "Ha-Maharal mi-Prague ke-Humanist (The Maharal of Prague as a Humanist)" in the collection of articles *U-ve-kol Zot,* Jerusalem, 5738, pp. 161–177. Also see A. P. Kleinberger, *ha-Mahashavah ha-Pedagogit shel ha-Maharal mi-Prague* (The Pedagogical Thought Of the Maharal of Prague), Jerusalem, 5723; Benjamin Gross, *Netzah Yisrael: Hashkafato ha-Meshihit shel ha-Maharal mi-Prague al ha-Galut ve-ha-Ge'ulah,* (The Messianic Thought of the Maharal of Prague on Exile and Redemption), Tel Aviv, 5734.

29. See the selection of articles on Samson Raphael Hirsch and his special approach to interpretation and preaching in *Ha-Rav Shimshon Raphael Hirsch, Mishnato ve-Shitato* (Rabbi Samson Raphael Hirsch, His Doctrine and Approach), ed. Yonah Emanuel, Jerusalem, 5722.

30. The language of Maimonides in *Mishneh Torah, Hilkhot Melakhim,* 12:2: "A person should not occupy himself with words of Aggadah, and should not pause long over the Midrashim related in these and similar matters, and should not make them central for they do not lead either to reverence or to love [of God]."

31. *Sifre, Ekev, Piska* 49 (Finkelstein edition, p. 115).

32. *Guide to the Perplexed,* Part II, chap. 25.

33. I. Heinemann, *Darkhei ha-Aggadah* (Ways of the Aggadah), Jerusalem, 1970, chap. 1.

34. See Rabbi Issachar Yakobson, in his article *Kavvim Ahadim be-Perusho shel ha-Rav Shimshon Raphael Hirsch la-Torah* (Some Reflections on Rabbi S. R. Hirsch's Interpretation of the Torah), in the anthology *Hirsch* (above note 28), p. 45, on "The Speculative Etymology" in the *derush* interpretation of Hirsch.

35. The first was in the style of Frankfurt neo-Orthodoxy, later incorporated in the version promoted by Yeshiva University in the neo-Orthodoxy of America. See S. Belkin, *Essays in Traditional Jewish Thought,* New York, 1956; also Norman Lamm, *Faith and Doubt,* New York, 1969.

36. For a description of the possible acceptance of the strict Orthodox observer of *mitzvot* in American-Western society, see, for example, Herman Wouk, *This Is My God,* New York, 1961.

37. See *Studies in Jewish Thought* (above note 13), pp. 61ff.

38. See Wolfson (above note 22), vol. 1, pp. 57ff.

39. For the use of "syncretism" with respect to Philo, see David Rokeah, *Chapters of Philo* (Heb.), Jerusalem, 5736, p. 10.

40. Isaac Julius Guttmann, *The Philosophies of Judaism* (Heb.), Jerusalem, 5711, pp. 25–26.

41. *Ibid.*, pp. 28–29.

42. *Ibid.*, pp. 32–33.

43. Examples of the use of *derush* by Rabbi Soloveitchik are numerous and varied. Not only passages of Bible and Halakhah serve as material for *derush*, but even situations and times. Thus, the death of the Brisker Rav on Yom Kippur serves as a starting point for a typological distinction between "The Men of Rosh ha-Shanah" and the "Men of Yom Kippur" (see *Be-Sod ha-Yahid ve-ha-Yahad*, in the chapter "Ma Dodekh mi-Dod"). A similar case is the basic typological distinction between two types of men, based on the interpretation of the passages which relate the story of the creation of man in the Book of Genesis; see "The Lonely Man of Faith" (above note 2) and many similar cases in *On Repentance* (for example, pp. 26–28, 21, 115; 58–60 and many more).

44. First published in the anthology *Torah u-Melukhah* (Torah and State), ed. Simon Federbush, Jerusalem, 5721. A note there (apparently written by R. Soloveitchik himself) states that the words had been delivered orally, at a gathering in celebration of Israel Independence Day, 5716. The essay was later published in abridged form and in full in many places, the latest being *Be-Sod ha-Yahid ve-ha-Yahad*, pp. 333–400.

45. One-sided historiosophic interpretation of the Holocaust and the Renaissance is presented in two diametrically opposed versions. On one side we have the works of Rabbi Joel Teitelbaum, the Satmar Rebbe, *Vayoel Moshe* (And Moses Wished), New York, 5716; and *Al ha-Ge'ulah ve-al ha-Temorah* (On Redemption and Change), Brooklyn, 5727; and of A. Gitlin (Uriel Zeimer), *Yahadut ha-Torah ve-ha-Medinah* (Torah Judaism and the State), Jerusalem, 5719. On the other side we have Rabbi D. Halevi, "Dat u-Medinah (Religion and State)," Tel Aviv, 5729; Rabbi Y. Amital, *Ha-Ma'alot mi-Ma'amakim* (Rising from the Depths), Alon Shevut, 5734; and the works of Rabbi Menahem M. Kasher; *ha-Tekufah ha-Gedolah* (The Great Period),. Jerusalem, 5729, and *Milhemet Yom ha-Kippurim* (The Yom Kippur War), Jerusalem, 5734. So far we do not have a comprehensive study on the subject. Among the tentative overviews are Prof. Uriel Tal's "The Land and the State of Israel in Israel's Religious Life," in *Rabbinical Assembly Proceedings*, 1976; and Pinchas Peli's *Teguvot Datiot la-Sho'ah* (Religious Reactions to the Holocaust), an anthology, Jerusalem, 5733, and *Be-Hippus ahar Lashon Datit la-Sho'ah* (In Search for Religious Language for the Holocaust)," in the annual *Jerusalem*, 5738, and in *Conservative Judaism*, Fall 1978, pp. 86–94.

46. *Be-Sod ha-Yahid ve-ha-Yahad*, p. 333.

47. *Ibid.*, p. 336.

48. *Ibid.*, p. 338.

49. *Ibid.*, p. 339.

50. *Ibid.*, p. 342.

51. On Halakhah as a kind of phenomenology see Rotenstreich (above note 36) and comp. also David S. Shapiro, *Studies in Jewish Thought*, New York, 1972, pp. 112–120.

52. Especially in the concluding sections of the Tractates in Mishnah, and the concluding halakhot in *Mishneh Torah*, but not only there.

53. *Be-Sod ha-Yahid ve-ha-Yahad*, pp. 343–347, on the figure of Job as a classic model for *derush* and interpretation. See the anthology, *The Dimensions of Job*, ed. Nahum Glatzer, New York, 1969.

54. On the stretching of the time element as a Midrashic method, see I. Heinemann, *Darkhei ha-Aggadah*, pp. 27ff.

55. The Song of Songs serves as inspiration for the Midrashic ventures of Rabbi Soloveitchik in other places as well, such as in the late essay *U-Vikkashtem mi-Sham* (Ye Shall Seek Him from There)," *Hadarom* No. 47, Tishrei 5739.

56. On the categories of time as principles in the *a priori* world of the Man of Halakhah, see "Ish ha-Halakhah," pp. 70ff.

57. *Be-Sod ha-Yahid ve-ha-Yahad*, pp. 350–351.

58. All these categories appear with reference to the Holocaust and the Renaissance in the literature of religious thought; see above, note 44.

59. *Be-Sod ha-Yahid ve-ha-Yahad*, p. 354.

60. *Ibid.*, p. 355.

61. A *derashah* found in the Talmud, *Megillah* 15b, on the verse in Esther 6:1.

62. R. Soloveitchik does not enter into the theological explanation of the "Hiding of the Face" that occurred during the Holocaust, which is dealt with by Martin Buber in "Eclipse of the Light of God" in *The Face of Man*, Jerusalem, 5726, pp. 221ff., and by Eliezer Berkovitz at length in his book, *Faith After the Holocaust*, New York, 1973, pp. 94ff. Rather, he accepts it as self-evident.

63. *Be-Sod ha-Yahid ve-ha-Yahad*, pp. 364–366.

In this essay (Tradition 16:2), *Morris Sosevsky summarizes three philosophical writings of the Rav: "Ish ha-Halakhah," "The Lonely Man of Faith," and "Confrontation." He discusses and evaluates some of the critiques of these works.*

The Lonely Man of Faith
Confronts the *Ish ha-Halakhah*

An Analysis of the Critique of Rabbi Joseph B. Soloveitchik's Philosophical Writings

Morris Sosevsky

Rabbi Aaron Lichtenstein, in a biographical sketch of Rabbi Joseph B. Soloveitchik.,[1] notes that Rabbi Soloveitchik's major vehicle for transmitting his vast Talmudic and secular knowledge has always been the spoken word. As a result, there are among Rabbi Soloveitchik's publications but two articles of considerable length and only a handful of shorter articles that provide us with insight into his philosophical thought. Despite the limited publications, Rabbi Soloveitchik's philosophical writings have been critically analyzed in a number of books and periodicals.[2] To date, however, no systematic response to the critique of Rabbi Soloveitchik's writings has appeared. This article will summarize Rabbi Soloveitchik's three most publicized essays[3] and evaluate the critique to which they have been subjected.

Ish ha-Halakhah

In his earliest and perhaps most famous work, "Ish ha-Halakhah,"[4] Rabbi Soloveitchik introduces us to the stylistic approach and the underlying theme that is fundamental to all his writings. Rabbi Soloveitchik does not deal with real existence, nor with abstractions from real existence, but with pure or ideal types. While in reality these types rarely if ever exist,[5] the development of their form and characteristics is used by Rabbi Soloveitchik to clarify the complexities of human existence.

The paradoxes and tensions of human nature and man's awareness of his dual role as both subject and object are the problems of reality with which man must contend. The Man of Science gazes upon the universe with the intention of removing the unknown from nature by means of developing scientific and mathematical laws that categorize and classify nature's perplexities. That which cannot be categorized is not his concern. The Religious Man, uninterested in the mathematical-scientific domain, is completely enveloped in the vast mystery of existence. He too seeks answers. But in his search he finds that as he delves into the unraveling of nature's mysteries they become even more mysterious to him. While his physical existence remains in this world, his spiritual nature becomes dedicated to a supervening numinal realm.

In contrast to Religious Man, the Man of Halakhah is not overwhelmed by the problems of existence. He approaches existence armed with *a priori* concepts contained in the divinely given body of Jewish laws. Because these halakhic concepts deal with all aspects of reality, he uses them to develop a satisfying image of the nature of God, his fellow man, and his universe. Since he applies principles not only to problems of reality but also conceptualizes principles that relate to non-existing cases, the Man of Halakhah attains the lofty level of the pure theoretical Man of Science. Because he is in possession of norms which encompass his entire existence, he, unlike Religious Man, does not find it necessary to escape from temporal to transcendental reality.[7]

Because even God has renounced authority in the domain of halakhic interpretation, the Man of Halakhah takes on full responsibility for the elaboration and progressive refinement of these laws.[8] The Man of Halakhah, with this vote of confidence, is therefore able to rise above the anxiety, helplessness, and awe of human existence by setting standards and norms to otherwise unpredictable religious feelings. Halakhah thus becomes the objectification of religion into clearly defined principles and into a fixed pattern of lawfulness.[9] As a result, the significance of a *mitzvah* is, to the halakhist, not in the feelings it evokes, but in the actual performance in its detailed exactitude. While a surge of religious feeling would undoubtedly be subdued by this cold exacting attitude, it is compensated by a general joyous sense of dedication that accompanies the performance of these tasks.

Because, to Rabbi Soloveitchik, the ultimate level of halakhic achievement is the level of prophecy, he equates the intellectual qualities necessary for the attainment of prophecy with the creative processes used by the halakhist. While the actual reception of the Divine Spirit attained by the prophet is no longer in existence, nevertheless only the ideal Man of Halakhah could have reached the state of preparedness necessary for its attainment.[10]

The halakhist, unlike the Christian saints, is not engaged in a continuous battle against desire since his laws have a moderating effect upon him.[11]

Halakhah may also be considered the most democratic of endeavors since anyone may enter the gates of the halls of study and on his own volition, without the necessity of intermediaries, use the halakhic process to become a creative partner of God.[12]

Neither is the Man of Halakhah fixed in time to a defined and limited period in the historical process. The divinely set laws that are his domain connect him with the history that preceded him and that which will succeed him.

In summary, the Man of Halakhah has a loftier and more totalistic approach to the universe than does the Man of Science or Religious Man. Only he can be successful in developing fully satisfying images of the universe and in removing the major perplexities of existence from his temporal world. He is unified with the entire historical process, is not enslaved by desire, and he alone is capable of reaching the ultimate level of human perfection, that of prophecy.

The Lonely Man of Faith

In "The Lonely Man of Faith,"[13] Rabbi Soloveitchik's second lengthy philosophical writing, he once again embarks on typological categorization in an attempt to explain the paradox and duality of human existence. Rabbi Soloveitchik begins by indicating that there are four major discrepancies that must be reconciled in the Bible's two accounts[14] of the creation of man.

1. While Adam of the first account (Adam the First) was created in the image of God, no information is provided concerning the manner in which he was fashioned. In contrast, we are told that Adam the Second was fashioned out of the ground and received the breath of life from God through his nostrils.

2. Adam the First was commanded to fill the earth and subdue it, while Adam the Second was bidden to cultivate the *Gan Eden* and to preserve it.

3. The female was created together with Adam the First, while Adam the Second initially appeared alone. Only later was he provided with a female companion to be his helpmate and complement.

4. In the first account only the name *Elohim* appears, while in the second it is used in conjunction with *Hashem*.[15]

Rav Soloveitchik explains that the two accounts speak of two distinct "types" of men. Adam the First, formed in the Image of God, is a creator. He expresses his likeness to God through his drive for creative activity and through the immeasurable resources granted him (particularly his intelligence) for confronting his world. Adam the First, as a creative being, is willing to forego metaphysical speculation by asking only: "How does the cosmos function?" and not "Why does it function?" or "What is its essence?" His sole motivation is the discovery of his human identity. He is creative, aggressive, beauty oriented and worldly minded equating human dignity with exercise of control over the environment.[16] He is not interested in what is true but in what is functional, and thereby carries out the mandate addressed to him "to fill the earth and subdue it."[17]

Adam the Second is also intrigued by the universe but approaches the cosmos with the "Why?" question. He is not a creative being but one interested in understanding what exists. He, unlike Adam the First, is receptive rather than dynamic, absorbed primarily in this awe-inspiring qualitative world wherein he seeks to establish a relationship with its Creator. The breath of life breathed by God into his nostrils alludes to Adam the Second's preoccupation with God. To him dignity is not man's sole quest. His method of self-discovery is by means of experiencing a redeemed existence.[18]

Because dignity is linked with attaining recognition, never with anonymity, Adam the First is a communicative social being who could not have been created alone and therefore emerged simultaneously with Eve. The community wherein he exists is a natural one, a reaction of man seeking survival against the challenges of a hostile environment.[19]

While the dignity-seeking Adam the First must control his environment, the redemption-seeking Adam the Second controls himself. Similarly, while dignity can be achieved only through the outside world, redemption may be accomplished in the privacy of one's inner personality. Dignity is acquired when man advances, redemption when man retreats and lets himself be defeated by a Higher Being.[20] Ironically, at the moment Adam the Second discovers his true identity he becomes aware of his aloneness. His covenantal companion, his wife, is granted him through defeat, when an overpowering sleep comes upon him.

Yet we find that only he, and not Adam the First, is introduced to his mate by God who, because of man's sacrificial action, joins in the formation of a covenantal community. *Elohim* signifying God as a source of cosmic dynamics sufficed for Adam the First. For Adam the Second *Hashem* symbolizing the communal relation between man and God had to be substituted.[21]

There are two ways in which the covenantal community between God and man may be formed: either when God addresses himself to man and establishes the covenantal-prophetic community or when man addresses himself to God in the formation of a covenantal-prayer community. Just like the prophet is the representative of others, likewise the inclusion of others is a prerequisite for the prayer community, which requires man to reveal himself to God through prayer and to his fellow man through love and sympathy and communal action.[22]

Halakhah asks man to unite these two Adams within his existence. The same Bible that tells man to "Love thy God with all thy heart" tells him to build a house, cut his harvest, etc. The function of Halakhah is to remind man that he is a member of both a covenantal and majestic community. Halakhah, being monistic in its approach, obviously views the majestic community of Adam the First and the covenantal community of Adam the Second not as contradictory, but as complementary. Man must be creative and conquering and, at the same time, the obedient servant of God.[28]

Contemporary Adam has failed to heed the duality in man. His success in the majestic-creative enterprises has led him to deny that an Adam the Second exists.[24] Although he stands associated with some religious establishment, his religious community is not one governed by a desire for redemption, but is dedicated to dignity and success. Contemporary majestic man, because of his failure to strive for a higher mode of existence, has remained an incomplete being.[25]

If the mystery of revelation could be translated into cultural terms, then Adam the Second could come to peace with, and be understood by contemporary Adam the First. However, because of the uniqueness of the faith experience, it is impossible fully to accomplish this goal. Consequently, contemporary Man of Faith suffers loneliness of a special kind. His loneliness is not only an ontological one, but is also a social one, since he is ridiculed whenever he attempts to deliver the message of faith. Nevertheless it is part of his unique task to continue tenaciously to deliver this message to majestic contemporary Adam the First.[26]

Confrontation

Again basing himself on the Biblical account of creation, Rabbi Soloveitchik sees man on three progressive levels of being.[27] On the first level man feels so totally natural in the universe that he fails to view his existence as a task or opportunity. On the second, man is confronted by nature and attempts to control it. On the third level he confronts others and in doing so realizes that though he finds companionship, he can never again overcome the barrier that separates his inner self from others. While men pursue common goals and thus engage in common enterprise, their ultimate destinies are not the same. Thus man, even when acting as an *ezer*, experiences a state of *k'negdo*.[28] He is a social being yet at the same time a lonely creature. Man's inner personality is never involved in communal existence but always remains in seclusion.

As Jews, we have been burdened with a twofold confrontation. We are human beings sharing with others the general encounter with nature. Yet we are members of a covenantal community which has managed to preserve its identity while being confronted by other faith communities under the most unfavorable conditions.[29] The present proponents of confrontation with other faith communities, despite maintaining a desire for the preservation of the Jewish community, have obviously not fully grasped the real nature and implications of meaningful Jewish identity. They continue to speak of Jewish identity without 'realizing that there can be no identity without uniqueness, a uniqueness that expresses itself in a threefold manner.

1. The Divine imperatives to which one community is unreservedly committed is not to be equated with the ethos and ritual of another.

2. The belief that its own system of dogmas, doctrines, and values is best fitted for the attainment of an ultimate good is essential to the faith community.

3. Each community is unyielding in its eschatological expectations and perceives the "end of time" as an era where their particular faith will be universally embraced.[30]

The second misconception of those advocating full confrontation is their failure to realize the compatibility of a dual confrontation. There is no contradiction between coordinating our activities with others and at the same time confronting them as members of another faith community. It is only because non-Jewish society has confronted us in a mood of defiance that it has been impossible for us to participate in full in the universal confrontation between man and his universe.[31]

Any confrontation with another faith community must therefore be on a mundane level rather than on a theological one. The relationship must be outerdirected to the secular orders in which we function. The great encounter between God and man is a personal affair, incomprehensible not only to the outsider but even to a fellow member of the same faith community. Our commitment to that community cannot be compromised.[32]

Analysis of Critique

In his critique of Rabbi Soloveitchik's thought, Eugene Borowitz[33] dwells upon the difficulty in dealing with typologies. Although their use may be illuminating, it is never quite clear how these types arose, why they and not others were selected, and precisely how they relate to each other. Strikovsky[34] further notes that even within Rabbi Soloveitchik's works there seem to be contradictions regarding the types that he employs. While the *ish ha-halakhah*[35] is portrayed as a scholar who makes use of Halakhah's *a priori* system to construct a meaningful perspective on life, his counterpart, the "Lonely Man of Faith"[84] appears awed and mystified by his surroundings. In a similarly contradictory manner, the *ish ha-halakhah* enjoys both the worlds of knowledge and religion, while the "Lonely Man of Faith" oscillates between two worlds, seeking to be in one just as he begins to accustom himself to the other. To the inner discrepancies cited by Strikovsky, one may add that still another contradiction appears to exist between the types employed in the "Lonely Man of Faith" and "Confrontation" articles. While in the "Lonely Man of Faith" essay, man is portrayed on two levels of existence, that of creative Adam the First and spiritual Adam the Second, in contrast, the "Confrontation" article develops three progressive levels of man's being:

a. natural man, who fails to grasp the nature of his existence;

b. man confronting nature and attempting to control it;

c. man confronting his fellow man and discovering the barrier that separates him from others.[37]

Though Borowitz's general criticism of typologies seems well founded, the inner contradictions cited by Strikovsky between the "Ish ha-Halakhah" and "Lonely Man of Faith" appear to be largely inapplicable. Strikovsky naturally assumed that the chronological order in which the articles appeared is to be used as the guide for their interpretation. It is quite evident, however, that the essay "The Lonely Man of Faith" is to be viewed as a predecessor, in terms of philosophical development, to the "Ish ha-Halakhah" article. If we should view the "Lonely Man of Faith" as a development of the dualism in the quests of men, and the "Ish ha-Halakhah" article as dealing with the unique and superior approach of one who seeks to integrate a redemptive quest into his existence through life-long commitment to the discipline of Halakhah, then Strikovsky's contradictions no longer exist.[38] In this sense Professor Kaplan, in his recent article on Rabbi Soloveitchik's thought[39] proceeds in logical sequence by commencing with an analysis of the "Lonely Man of Faith" essay in his development of Rabbi Soloveitchik's religious philosophy.

Closer scrutiny of the "Confrontation" and "Lonely Man of Faith" articles would indicate that there, too, no true discrepancy exists. Although, at first glance, the "Confrontation" article appears to employ three distinct character types in contradistinction to "Lonely Man's" two, in reality the initial two types identified in the "Confrontation" article (that of man in a natural state, and man confronting nature) represent nothing more than two progressive levels of a creative Adam the First existence. In the initial stage Adam is awed by his environment, but he quickly adapts and proceeds in majestic conquest of it.

Jacob Agus provides further criticism of Rabbi Soloveitchik's thought in his *Guideposts in Modern Judaism*[40] where he argues that even if Halakhah has evolved consecrated religious personalities, as is suggested in "Ish ha-Halakhah," this does not attest to the truth of Halakhah, nor to its enduring significance. Agus fails to recognize, however, that Rabbi Soloveitchik surely had no interest in attempting to establish Halakhah's validity, since the very applicability of Halakhah presupposes a belief in the truth emanating from its Divine origin.[41] Rabbi Soloveitchik simply seeks to indicate in what manner the halakhist, having accepted Halakhah as a tool with which to formulate his mode of existence, emerges as an ideal superior type.

Agus[42] further objects to the use of prophecy as the level of ultimate attainment in the halakhic personality. He claims that by its very nature as a rationally ordained system of law, Halakhah precludes the intervention of non-rational prophecy. Strikovsky responds correctly to this criticism by indicating that precisely for this reason Rabbi Soloveitchik refuses fully to equate the halakhist with the prophet, choosing instead to limit the equation to the requisite intellectual processes that are mutual to both.

As part of his general objection to the use of typologies, Borowitz[43] claims that Rabbi Soloveitchik's types are not essentially Jewish but could easily be applied to personality types within Roman Catholicism.

Strikovsky disagrees. He asserts that while one not adhering to the binding nature of Halakhah may view these typologies as being not exclusively Jewish, a Jew who is accepting Halakhah could make no such error.[44] Based on Rabbi Soloveitchik's position in the article "Confrontation,"[45] each faith community is firmly convinced of both the truth and superiority of its particular doctrine. Thus to Rabbi Soloveitchik it is evident that only one pursuing halakhic doctrine can attain the superior level of the "Ish ha-Halakhah."

Rabbi Soloveitchik's insistence that a basic similarity exists between the halakhist and the mathematical physicist by virtue of their common approach to reality with an *a priori* system, is contested by Agus[46] who cannot see how halakhic principles can possibly be construed to be *a priori*. Kaplan[47] questions this equation further by suggesting an obvious distinction between the two disciplines. While the system of abstract mathematical relations is one that the scientist has himself created, it is difficult to see how the halakhic system, having been revealed by God, can logically be conceived as part of the *a priori* world of the halakhist himself.

Kaplan resolves the difficulty of the science-Halakhah equation by contending that Rabbi Soloveitchik's position can be properly understood only in light of Hermann Cohen's theory of science which suggests that the scientist does not explain the world in its own terms, but constructs abstract-formal mathematical systems in terms of which natural-sense phenomena could be explained.[48] Cohen's philosophy of science may then logically be equated with the halakhic process in view of Rabbi Soloveitchik's contention that his grandfather, Rabbi Hayim Soloveitchik, introduced a similar approach to the study of Halakhah.[49] Instead of explaining the Halakhah in its own terms by merely organizing, classifying, and resolving difficulties and problems, Reb Hayim developed a system of abstract concepts which he in turn used as a vehicle for explaining the Halakhah. Thus, Rabbi Soloveitchik's unique conception of both the scientist and halakhist allows him rightfully to declare that their respective approaches are similar.

Although he contends that Rabbi Soloveitchik's insistence on the objective nature of the Halakhah is basically well-founded, Kaplan[50] nevertheless feels that Rabbi Soloveitchik has pressed the analogy between Halakhah and mathematical physics too far, He argues that we find a number of halakhic categories, i.e., *darkhei shalom, darkhei noam,* (to which may be added, *derekh tovim, ha-yashar v'hatov,* etc.) which are inherently subjective since they can only be applied on the basis of general non-halakhic value judgments. Neither can the Halakhah be viewed as self-sufficient since many conceptual realms such as aggadah, kabbalah, philosophy, and science necessarily impinge upon it. Agus[51] similarly charges that any attempt to develop a self-sufficient philosophy of Halakhah can only meet with futility since a critical examination of the classical formulations of Halakhah would undoubtedly show that there has been much influence from non-halakhic sources.

In response to the rather cogent argument that Halakhah is neither totally objective, nor does it lend itself to the development of a self-sufficient philosophy, we cite an article by Walter Wurzburger, "Meta-Halakhic Propositions,"[52] where he suggests that this form of criticism may well stem from a basic misconception of the precise nature of the halakhist's role in the process of halakhic development. Dr. Wurzburger argues that even if we maintain that differences of opinion on halakhic issues reflect divergent philosophies of life, this does not deny Halakhah its basic objectivity, since the halakhic scholar, though guided by his personal value judgments and his own understanding of the Halakhah, is nevertheless bound by the Biblical and Talmudic texts which serve to provide a framework for his freedom of interpretation. Thus, it may be argued that Rabbi Soloveitchik, in insisting on Halakhah's objectivity, refers only to the objective core within which the halakhist operates, a contention whose plausibility may be supported by the fact that in the very "Ish ha-Halakhah" article in which the Halakhah's objective nature is emphasized, Rabbi Soloveitchik declares that it is precisely the *freedom of interpretation* afforded the halakhist that allows him to become a creative partner of God.[53] Dr.

Wurzburger further contends that just as the halakhist's interpretive role does not violate Halakhah's essentially objective core, neither does the employment of categories of thought that stem from non-halakhic sources necessarily violate the self-sufficiency of Halakhah. Such outside impingement is irrelevant as long as it can be harmonized with an authentic halakhic approach. Drawing an analogy from science, he notes that just as the validity of a scientific hypothesis is dependent solely upon its success in correlating a given set of scientific data, the source of a halakhic proposition should rightfully be evaluated only in light of its use in forming what may be viewed as an authentic halakhic outlook.[54]

Perhaps one may add that rather than undermining the notion of Halakhah's objectivity and usefulness for the formulation of a Jewish philosophy of life, the existence of halakhic categories such as *darkhei noam* and *darkhei shalom* which Kaplan terms inherently subjective due to their applicability solely on the basis of non-halakhic value judgments, may instead be used in support of Halakhah's basic objective core. While there can be little doubt that some halakhic norms like *hayashar v'hatov*, *derekh tovim*, and those cited by Kaplan are situational and denote direction rather than specific action, it nevertheless seems illogical to assume that they would exist as *halakhic* categories (some of which are judicially enforceable[55]) were they to be guided solely by man's independent moral sense. Instead, the very existence of such halakhic norms suggests that the Torah deems it possible to extract from halakhic data metaphysical and ethical propositions which enable man to formulate a philosophy of life to effectively guide him in the spirit of Halakhah even when confronted with situations where one's action is not governed by Halakhah's fixed and rigid objective standards.[56]

Rabbi Soloveitchik's contention that the feeling of loneliness is the universal experience of the "Man of Faith" is criticized by Strikovsky as lacking solid Biblical or Talmudic support. Rabbi Soloveitchik's reference, in an article entitled "Ma-Dodekh Mi-Dod,"[57] to Moses' return from his abode of loneliness after his descent from heaven, is dismissed by Strikovsky as being far removed from the plain and simple meaning of the Torah's narrative which suggests that Moses' seclusion was motivated solely by his disappointment in the nation's fashioning of the golden calf. Although it is true that no concrete source for spiritual man's loneliness is provided in the "Lonely Man of Faith" essay, Rabbi Soloveitchik has elsewhere indicated that the very story of Adam and Eve's creation upon which the "Lonely Man of Faith" essay is founded, provided him his source. In a recently published summary of a public lecture,[58] Rabbi Soloveitchik suggests that the term *levado* of the verse in Gen. II, ("It is not good that he be *levado*"),[59] can have two possible meanings: alone and lonely. Rabbi Soloveitchik argues that the verse cannot logically refer to man's being alone, since Genesis I had amply dealt with procreation and sexual desire, both of which presume the existence of man's physical companion. Clearly the term is meant to refer to spiritual man's loneliness which is founded upon the feeling that he does not share a mutual destiny with those that surround him. Thus it was to partially relieve his spiritual loneliness that Adam was in need of a partner who would at least in some measure share a common destiny with him.

Evaluation

Rabbi Soloveitchik's philosophical thought undoubtedly classifies him as a religious existentialist who seems to have enjoyed many influences, both Judaic and non-Judaic. His understanding of the nature of pure science in the "Ish ha-Halakhah" was clearly influenced by Hermann Cohen's philosophy of science,[60] while his view regarding the universal loneliness of man seems to have had its origin in Kierkegaardian thought. A partial parallel to Buber's "I and Thou"[61] may perhaps be discerned from Rabbi Soloveitchik's development of the I, Thou, He covenantal meeting with God in the "Lonely Man of Faith" essay, and in his insistence that only in such a relationship can man touch upon the inner personality of his fellow man. Despite the vast differences in approach and philosophy, Rabbi Soloveitchik's contention that only through halakhic concepts can one formulate a satisfactory view of the universe is somewhat similar to Hirsch's insistence upon an inner study of *mitzvot* in order to derive God's intents.[62] Although the ideal *ish ha-halakhah* seems to be vastly anti-Hassidic, many of the classical themes of Hassidic thought appear in Rabbi Soloveitchik's writings. Thus two of the major themes of the Hassidic work *Tanya,*[63] the mutual responsibility of one Jew for another and the interrelatedness of all Jews, play a prominent role in the "Lonely Man of Faith" essay. Of course, these notions are so basic to Jewish thought in general that no direct influence need be assumed.

Although we responded to some of the criticism leveled at Rabbi Soloveitchik's philosophy, his use of typologies remains a problem. Borowitz indicates that[64] it is difficult to see how typologies would be of much use to the average reader because of the difficulty in making the deductions necessary for application to reality.

Compounding this difficulty is Rabbi Soloveitchik's relatively limited writings, which greatly frustrate any effort to integrate and thoroughly evaluate his thought. Rabbi Lichtenstein, indicated[65] that Rabbi Soloveitchik had initially planned a doctoral dissertation on Maimonides and Plato which contained as its thesis that general Maimonidean scholarship was mistaken in viewing Maimonides as a confirmed Aristotelian. Perhaps such a work would have allowed us a fuller and richer glimpse into his thought, and would have served to complement the limited material that is presently available to us.

Notes

1. A. Lichtenstein, "Rabbi Joseph B. Soloveitchik," *Great Jewish Thinkers of the Twentieth Century*, Bnai Brith Publications.

2. See Jacob Agus, *Guideposts in Modern Judaism*; Eugene Borowitz, *A New Jewish Theology in the Making*; Eugene Borowitz, "The Typological Theology of Rabbi Joseph B. Soloveitchik," *Judaism*, vol. 15, 1966; Lawrence Kaplan, "The Religious Philosophy of Rabbi Joseph B. Soloveitchik," *Tradition*, Spring 1973; and Aryeh Strikovsky, "The World of Thought of Harav Joseph B. Soloveitchik," *Gesher-1966*. Because of the unnecessary duplication involved in summarizing anew the "Ish ha-Halakhah" article from its original Hebrew, I have used the English language summations found in the works of Agus, Borowitz, and Kaplan.

3. "Ish ha-Halakhah," *Talpiot*, 1944; "Lonely Man of Faith," *Tradition*, vol. 7, no. 2; and "Confrontation," *Tradition*, vol. 6, no. 2.

4. *Talpiot*, 1944, pp. 651–735.

5. While the existence of a pure "Ish ha-Halakhah" and pure Adam the First (of the "Lonely Man of Faith" essay) is within the realm of possibility, the actual existence of a pure Adam the Second would appear impossible.

6. *Talpiot*, pp. 654–662, and 680–684.

7. *Ibid.*, pp. 663–672.

8. *Ibid.*, pp. 701–702.

9. *Ibid.*, pp. 665–689.

10. *Ibid.*, pp. 729–732.

11. *Ibid.*, p. 691.

12. *Ibid.*, p. 679.

13. *Tradition*, Summer 1965, vol. 7, no. 2, pp. 5–67.

14. Gen. 1:26–31, and Gen. 2:4–25.

15. *Tradition, op. cit.*, pp. 17–19.

16. *Ibid.*, pp. 12–16.

17. Gen. 1:28.

18. *Tradition, op. cit.*, pp. 17–19.

19. *Ibid.*, p. 19.

20. *Ibid.*, p. 24.

21. *Ibid.*, p. 33.

22. *Ibid.*, pp. 33–48.

23. *Ibid.*, pp. 51–53.

24. *Ibid.*, p. 63.

25. *Ibid.*, p. 65.

26. *Ibid.*

27. *Tradition,* vol. 6, no. 1, pp. 5–30.

28. Gen. 2:18.

29. *Tradition, op. cit.,* pp. 5–15.

30. *Ibid.,* pp. 20–30.

31. *Ibid.*

32. *Ibid.*

33. Eugene Borowitz, *A New Jewish Theology in the Making,* pp. 161–173.

34. Aryeh Strikovsky, *op. cit., Gesher* pp. 133–150. Dr. Strikovsky is presently preparing a book on Rabbi Soloveitchik's philosophy.

35. *Talpiot,* 1944, *loc. cit.*

36. *Tradition,* Summer, 1965, *loc. cit.*

37. *Tradition,* vol. 6, no. 4, 1964.

38. See sections 1–3 of this article.

39. *Tradition,* Summer 1973. While the sequence adopted by Kaplan aids us with our resolution, Kaplan himself attempts to resolve the inner contradictions between the "Lonely Man of Faith" and "Ish ha-Halakhah" essays by equating the Man of Halakhah, by dint of his *creative* thought processes, to *creative* Adam the First. It seems, however, farfetched to assume that Rabbi Soloveitchik failed to distinguish between the intellectual creativity of the Man of Halakhah and the physical creativity of Adam the First.

40. pp. 37–44.

41. This position has been established by Rabbi Soloveitchik in the "Confrontation" article where he argues that one cannot be "confronted" on basic religious dogma.

42. *op. cit.,* pp. 42–44.

43. *loc. cit.*

44. *loc. cit.*

45. *loc. cit.*

46. *loc. cit.*

47. *loc. cit.*

48. See Samuel H. Bergisian's article on Hermann Cohen's philosophy in *Faith and Reason: An Introduction to Modern Jewish Thought,* pp. 34–35.

49. Rabbi Soloveitchik's view of his grandfather, Reb Hayyim's approach to Talmudic study is formulated in an article entitled "Mah Dodekh Mi-Dod," *Ho-Doar,* vol. 42, no. 39, p. 755.

50. *loc. cit.*

51. *loc. cit.*

52. Dr. Wurzburger's article appears in *Leo Jung Jubilee Volume,* p. 211.

53. *op. cit.,* pp. 701–702.

54. In 1966 Rabbi Soloveitchik was preparing an article entitled, "Is a Philosophy of Halakhah Possible?" for that year's Fall issue of *Tradition*. It is most unfortunate that the article never appeared since it would undoubtedly have shed much light on the subject of Halakhah's objectivity and self-sufficiency.

55. See Bach on *Shulhan Arukh, Hoshen Mishpat* 12. For a further discussion of the enforceability of supra-legal ethical norms, see S. Federbush, *Ha-musar V'hamishpat B'Yisrael*; Z. Y. Meltzer, "Lifnim Mishurat Hadin" in *Memorial Volume to the Late Chief Rabbi Herzog*; M. Silberg, *Kach Darko Shel Talmud*. See also A. Lichtenstein's article "Does Jewish Tradition Recognize an Ethic Independent of Halakhah?" in Marvin Fox's *Modern Jewish Ethics*, for a thorough analysis of the halakhic nature of the Torah's subjective norms.

56. The position that situational halakhic norms exist only because they had been preceded by rigid objective halakhic standards is formulated by Nachmanides in his commentary on the Pentateuch (Lev. 19:2), where he argues that the Torah's broad injunctions always follow rigid objective norms governing that same area of conduct. "And this is the Torah's nature: to detail and then to generalize in a similar manner. Thus, after the admonition concerning the particulars of civil law and all interpersonal dealings . . . it states in a general manner 'And you shall do the right and the good'." See also Nachmanides' commentary to Deut. 6:18 where this idea is expounded in even greater detail. Magid Mishneh, in his commentary on Maimonides' *Mishneh Torah, Hilkhot Shekhenim* 14:5, also appears to adopt the position that the relation of relativistic norms to Halakhah is vital for the definition of general goals, and for molding a halakhic orientation.

57. *Ha-Doar*, vol. 42, no. 39, p. 755.

58. The lecture, originally delivered in December 1971 at Stern College for Women, has been summarized in a recent Yeshiva University student publication, *Shiurei Ha-rav*, under the title "Adam and Eve."

59. Gen. 2:18.

60. See above, footnote no. 48.

61. Martin Buber, *I and Thou*, Scribners & Sons.

62. See Dayan Grunfeld's introduction to Hirsch's commentary on the Pentateuch.

63. *Likutei Emurim*, ch. 32. See Strikovsky, *op cit.*, p. 139.

64. Borowitz, *op. cit.*

65. *op. cit.*

Opponents of halakhic Judaism have lodged a host of stereotypical criticisms of Orthodoxy: that Orthodoxy is characterized by cold legalism; that adherents of Halakhah are mainly concerned with mechanical performance rather than inner spiritual life; that halakhic Judaism suffers from stagnation and a lack of creativity. To these criticisms, Rabbi Soloveitchik offered brilliant and penetrating refutation.

In this essay (Tradition 29:1), Shalom Carmy describes the Rav's confrontation with the challenges of modernity. The Rav's articulation of halakhic Judaism is characterized by intellectual integrity and emotional power.

The Rav has taught that halakhic Judaism demands great intellectual effort and commitment to truth. Halakhah is fulfilled not merely by a technical compliance with the rules, but by an inner awareness of the spiritual meaning of the Halakhah. The Rav challenges us to probe the limits of our own spiritual capacities in our quest to live properly as halakhically-committed religious Jews.

Of Eagle's Flight and Snail's Pace

_{ᐯᴥᐰ}

Shalom Carmy

_{ᑇᴥᐰ}

One of the Rav's best-loved discourses explores the distinction between two aspects of the leadership exemplified by *Bet Din haGadol.* One function of *Bet Din* is to transmit the oral tradition of Torah; the other is to represent the Jewish people, to speak for the *kelal* as an organic entity.[1] One might say that the Rav himself *has* fulfilled both roles. He is, first and foremost, our teacher: for those of us who are his disciples, or the students of his disciples, the study of Torah is forever marked by his accent, the entire fabric of religious life is permeated by his spirit, and our own students, in turn, are haunted by his presence. He has also been called upon to chart a new course for the Orthodox community and has thus spoken for many who are not immediately and intimately affected by his discourses and dissertations. R. Wurzburger's paper identifies, and distills, the inner logic of the Rav's approach to halakhic decision and public policy, emphasizing his response to the unprecedented condition of the Jewish people in our times. I shall turn to a no less important aspect of the Rav's teaching and leadership: his constant and determined effort to draw the individual Jew to a life of intellectual adventure and religious excellence. Can the Rav's vision satisfy the needs, requirements and capacities of the modern Orthodox Jew?

Problems of Modernity

Of the delineations of modernity and post-modernity in academic literature there is no end, and I am free of the desire to increase them. I am satisfied to borrow the characterization of modern man advanced by Charles Taylor, a major philosopher of religious bent, in his influential recent book *Sources of the Self*, Taylor picks out three facets of modern consciousness: inwardness; the affirmation of ordinary life; the expressivist ideal.[2] We shall supplement his list by noting two other factors commanding the particular attention of contemporary Jews.

1) "what might have risen to an eagle's flight has been reduced to a snail's pace by law. Never yet has law formed a great man; 'tis liberty that breeds giants and heroes," proclaimed Friedrich Schiller two centuries ago.[3] Opponents of halakhic Judaism have echoed Schiller's spiritual rejection of law: the objective, externally categorized religious act, in their opinion, is incompatible with the cultivation of inward depth; excellence comes from following the law of the heart. Many Orthodox Jews have implicitly conceded the contradiction between Halakhah and inwardness, ignoring the latter to the detriment of their own, and others' spiritual lives. Even so, emancipation from the law has not bred "giants and heroes" but, at best, mediocrity; not the Nietzschean *übermensch*, but the blinking "last man," the hollow person of the therapist's couch, and the drab eccentric crowned by a halo of exclamation points.

The appearance of *Halakhic Man* made it impossible to deny or misunderstand the singular profundity of the eagles whose lives are sacred to the discipline of "the law." At the same time, the Rav's appreciation of inwardness, and his integration of external performance and inward experience of many *mitzvot* (e.g. prayer, repentance, fasting, mourning, honoring and taking delight in the Sabbath, the joy of holidays), are a hallmark of his approach to the corpus of Halakhah. Most ambitiously, he undertook, in *U-Vikkashtem mi-Sham*, to map the phenomenology of man's encounter with God, with his starting point the fundamental datum of man who is confronted by revealed law, and in the course of which he also achieved a revolutionary reformulation of the venerable faith/reason dichotomy. Moreover, in his writings and lectures he has evoked, time and again, in the manner commonly associated with religious existentialism, the dimension of human depth and the consciousness of loneliness and singularity.[4] More than any other Jewish thinker, his memorable and sometimes brutal honesty has taught us what both conventional piety and fashionable liberalism often seem intent to conceal: that religion is no escape from conflict, but the ultimate encounter with reality.

2) The tendency of conventional religion to edit reality is not limited to the soft-pedalling of existential conflict. It includes the suppression of large portions of human experience. An influential strand in Western culture confines "the religious" to the unworldly and the disembodied, disregarding those weekday activities that take place outside the church, repudiating those, like eating and sex, that are performed by limbs of which one prefers to feign obliviousness. This leads us to the heart of Taylor's second conviction about the modern identity: its affirmation of the everyday life of everyday people.

Though it requires neither great ingenuity nor extraordinary erudition to demonstrate halakhic Judaism's commitment to the redemption of corporeal life and its striving to encompass all domains of human activity, it is not out of place to recall the Rav's consistent, and often sensitive, probing of these areas.[5] The Rav's contribution deserves mention, in part, because there is a vast difference between recognizing everyday life as a principal theater of moral crisis, and the thoughtless, hence meaningless, sanctification of the everyday without qualification. In "Catharsis," for example, the Rav asserted the value of our common everyday desires and aspirations, even while he clear-headedly and uncompromisingly defined the theological perspective from which Judaism evaluates their significance.

3) It is neither easy nor necessary to define the precise parameters of "expressivism," which embraces assorted epistemological, ethical, and aesthetic doctrines. It is sufficient to think of the various "romantic"

or "existentialist" movements for whom the most admirable realization of the individual human being is less a matter of conforming to the laws set down for human nature than of imitating the originating power of nature's Author.[6] For such thinkers creativity is the key concept, allied to a strong regard for individuality expressing itself, whether that expression is the uniqueness of the solitary, perhaps anonymous, hero or the singularity attributable to the genius of the nation.

Despite his unwavering rejection of subjective philosophy, meaning one that would make truth (including, of course, religious and moral truth) dependent on the measure of man, the Rav offers enormous amplitude for the expression of man's creative potential. His celebration of *hiddush*, the creativity exhibited by masters of Torah in developing their novel insights, is the most famous example, but not the one with the most far-reaching implications.[7] For the Rav goes on to explain the fundamental notion of Divine Providence bestowed upon individual human beings on the basis of man's uniqueness, which is, in turn, tied to his/her creative vocation. And when the Rav identifies the penitential act with the work of self-creation, the theme of creativity has become part and parcel of the moral challenge appointed to each existing individual.[8]

4) Modernity is the enemy of Jewish particularity. The democratic affirmation of the everyday goes together with a hostility to morally or spiritually significant distinctions between individuals and groups. The antagonism has a moral face, rooted in principles of ethical universalism. It also has a realistic force: the "Protestant" tradition deriving from Weber, and represented today by the likes of Peter Berger, saw the shift to universal otherhood as the inevitable consequence of the modern world and its socioeconomic institutions.[9] In any event, Jewish thinkers confronting modernity have been forced to explain why "their customs differ from those of other peoples."

Three strategies of response can be extrapolated from the Rav's teaching. One approach draws on the "expressivist" elements in the Rav's thought and specifically on his affinities with Karl Barth and

Kierkegaard. In "Confrontation" he insists that authentic religious experience is ineluctably intimate, hence incommunicable. This insight not only justifies limits on the possibility of interfaith dialogue; by the same token it vigorously counters the assumption that Jewish destiny can be fused indistinguishably with that of humanity. At a different level, the Rav stresses the organic character of the Jewish people, manifest both in our religious destiny and national fate, that transcends all considerations that might incline the modern Jew to assimilate his or her identity.[10]

The third strategy, the most subtle, pervades the Rav's *oeuvre* without ever becoming overt. The dilemma of modern Jewish thought can be summed up as follows: If Judaism is presented as consonant with the current temper, it is superfluous; if it fails to address the contemporary situation of man, it is irrelevant. Thus the would-be Jewish philosopher, to adopt the Rav's anatomy of a parallel problem, must either opt for an apologetic approach that rationalizes religion, or despair agnostically of any solution, or take flight into the mystical; none of these choices is satisfactory.[11] The Rav "calmly but persistently" pursues another path: he proposes to furnish a philosophical anthropology inextricably bound to the fact of revelation in which it is grounded absolutely. Take one instance: in *Lonely Man of Faith*, the "covenantal community" dominates the framework within which the experience of loneliness is to be comprehended. Now when the Rav describes ontological loneliness, it is a predicament familiar to all of us, Jew or Gentile. Yet the central concept of the covenantal community is unmistakably that posited by the Torah as the portion of *Knesset Israel* alone.

5) The Rav's tenacious commitment to freedom of methodology sheds light on the dismissal of Bible criticism and the distaste for many features of academic Jewish studies, to which R. Wurzburger refers. That the Rav was avowedly untroubled by, and manifestly not preoccupied with, the methods and conclusions of these university disciplines, does not signify lack of curiosity. Even in his old age, I can testify, the Rav could allude casually to specific textual issues raised by the Critics. Truly the comments on Biblical subjects that

form a subsidiary current alongside his primary concerns, have contributed more towards refurbishing serious literary modern Orthodox study than the hand-wringing over "correct" methodology typical of the more "open-minded" Orthodox.[12] In *Lonely Man*, for example, he proffered, with the back of his hand, as it were, an interpretation of the two creation stories in Genesis that provided a powerful alternative to the regnant documentary hypothesis. Similarly, in the course of his halakhic discussion of the Yom Kippur ritual,[13] he submits, without mentioning the critical approach, an analysis of the difficulties apparent in the account of the *avoda* recorded in Humash; his treatment overlaps considerably with ideas developed by R. David Zvi Hoffmann and R. Mordekhai Breuer.

If there is an air of paradox to the last paragraph, it is a paradox easily resolved. For the Rav's creative vigor is an outgrowth of his intellectual faith in Torah; it is but another expression of his insistence on the autonomy of the theological enterprise. A letter, dated August 11, 1953, conveys the Rav's judgment that the RCA should refrain from any involvement in the planned JPS Bible translation. The text is instructive, and as it is not readily accessible, I feel justified in quoting two passages from it:

> After all, we live in an age which admires the expert and which expects him to tell how things are and how they ought to be done. The expert, on the other hand, does not tolerate any opposition; all we ought to do is listen to him and swallow his ideas. *I* am not ready to swallow the ideas of the modern expert and scholar on our Tanakh. . .

> I noticed in your letter that you are a bit disturbed about the probability of being left out. Let me tell you that this attitude of fear is responsible for many commissions and omissions, compromises and fallacies on our part which have contributed greatly to the prevailing confusion within the Jewish community and to the loss of our self-esteem, our experience of ourselves as independent entities committed to a unique philosophy and way of life.[14]

These few lines contain a rich legacy: the fierce individual integrity that is not cowed by the authority of experts, the calm and persistent commitment to the truth and uniqueness of Judaism, the unwillingness to attenuate that awareness for the sake of inauthentic displays of recognition, the self-respect that makes superficial approbation no longer needed or desired. It has been maintained that "[a]nyone who has seen Soloveitchik participating in the afternoon prayers with his students (in the classroom!) following one of his Talmud lectures, knows how comical it is to think of him as a modern academic type."[15] If that is the case, then the Rav is indeed deficient in "modernity," and, for that very reason, an inspiration for every believing Jew. Few can benefit more from his example than those of us who interact with the academic world. To be a *talmid* of the Rav is to be emancipated from the burden and the temptation of becoming an intellectual Marrano.

Challenge of a Legacy

My next remarks are not directed to those who disagree with the elements of the Rav's approach to the modern predicament adumbrated above. Instead we must consider the criticism raised within our own camp: the Rav is a giant, but we are pygmies; his standard defies all emulation, however pale; his banner is too exalted, and his trumpet summons none but the elite. We are modern Jews, hence faint of heart and weak of spirit, and we require a system of living and thinking and feeling suitable to our weakness. Such complaints focus on two features of the Rav's outlook: the intellectual and the existential.

Throughout his career, the Rav has championed the predominance of the intellectual gesture, and not only because *talmud Torah* is cherished within the hierarchy of Halakhah in general, and in the Brisker tradition in particular. With keen sensitivity to the malaise of commitment affecting contemporary Jewry, the Rav concluded that religious engagement of the intellect is essential to the cure. First of all, on the Rav's view, a full experiential involvement with *mitzvot* is impossible without understanding their meaning and significance, whence the necessity of learning. But the Rav also deemed our time propitious for the intellectual quest:

> [T]he young American generation . . . is not totally engrossed in the pragmatic, utilitarian outlook. . . . To the degree that average people in our society attain higher levels of knowledge and general intelligence, we cannot imbue them with a Jewish standpoint that relies primarily on sentiment and ceremony.[16]

If R. Kook witnessed the alienation of Jews from traditional religious commitment and decided that his generation needed exposure to a comprehensive Jewish philosophy deriving from the sources of Kabbalah, the Rav offered a simpler, more startling solution: renew the covenant with the exoteric sources that confront directly our concrete experience.

Bereft the vivid fusion of external act and inner appropriation, absent the astonishingly simple yet profound acknowledgment of the human condition, the Rav's thought loses much of its power to galvanize and make existence coherent. Recall, for a moment, his exposition of the *hovot ha-levavot*, those commandments whose very nature requires inwardness; think of the classic essay on the commandment of daily prayer, highlighting the distinction between the "surface crisis" that is felt even by a non-reflective being, and the "depth crisis" that is experienced only by the reflective consciousness. Hundreds of pages in the Rav's published work simply fail to make sense to any reader for whom Judaism and/or life is a matter of surface behavior, lacking the dimension of depth which the Rav never tires of exploring.

There is yet a further face to the Rav's quest for reality in man's relationship to himself. It is not much in evidence in *Halakhic Man* with its exaltation of intellectual assurance; nor does it play a major role in the "existential" Rav, where the *mi-ma'amakim* themes take the foreground.[17] On almost every occasion that I was privileged to consult the Rav on matters that touched upon life, whenever his attention settled on the real-life ramifications of his guidance, he invariably reminded me to act and to speak "with dignity and humility, as befits a *ben Torah.*" Such advice appears obvious to the point of triviality, but what immense reserves of self-knowledge and commitment are required to take it seriously!

Can the Rav's approach, rooted in the majesty of intellect and linked to an intense, hence essentially lonely,[18] probing of human reality, survive our present circumstances? Or must religious education conform itself to a society that is not so much illiterate as post-literate, a society fascinated by psychology, but only so long as the insight is facile, flat and fit for a bumper sticker, a society obsessed with personality, but indifferent to character?

My answer, in brief, is that we have no choice. The Rav is right: no contemporary religious commitment can long stand without an abiding cognitive element. How to sustain that component, and how to combine the intellectual orientation with other formative factors in our religious life, is our task, as individuals and as educators. The Rav has served us well: his production spans a multiplicity of disciplines and genres, and provides a variety of usable paradigms, ranging through Talmud and philosophy, Humash and liturgy, the formal lecture and the classroom laboratory, penetrating homilies and impromptu remarks. If, as we pursue our own growth and the benefit of others, we draw dividends on the riches he has put at our disposal, so much the better.[19] But the responsibility is ours: for this were we created.

The same is true with respect to modern man's capacity for authentic experience, which has been harmed by the inroads of secularism, misplaced in a fog of intellectual confusion, and undermined by the breakdown of the chain of living tradition. The Rav has not always been sanguine about the chances of communicating the lost connection to a more robust experiential past.[20] As to the capacity to live and feel deeply, the Rav frequently relies on Torah and Halakhah to provide the frame of reference within which the healthy emotional responses are to be cultivated. Writing about prayer, for example, he emphasizes that petition, praise and gratitude are not exotic feelings available only to the religious virtuoso, but natural experiences with which we should all be familiar.[21]

Unlike the titans of past eras, who expunged virtually all traces of inner autobiography from their writing, and unlike many contemporary *Gedolim*, whose public posture inspires admirers to romanticize them as a race apart, immune to the vicissitudes of the human condition, the Rav, reticent Brisker though he may be, has painfully, democratically, breached the wall of private solemnity, and acknowledged the vulnerability that he shares with all men: loneliness, grief, fear of death, old age with its attendant indignities, the delights of creativity and the anxiety of remorse, to mention a few of his recurrent themes.[22] He has struggled to evoke, and provoke in his audience, the sense of radical crisis and sheer reality that nourishes the passionate spiritual life.

Once again, one may protest, there are modern men and women who find the task of recovering even the fundamental building blocks of religious existence too much for their frail endowments, and who therefore feel entitled to an easier way than that suggested by the Rav. And once again, it seems to me, we have no choice. What Iris Murdoch said about the task of contemporary literature is true of our duty as individuals and as educators: in the "battle between real people and images," what is "require[d] now is a much stronger and more complex conception of the former."[23] No contemporary religious feeling can long endure that is unearned.

Alexis de Tocqueville, in his well-known diagnosis of modern Western culture, contrasts historians in aristocratic ages and historians in democratic ages.[24] The former concentrate on the "great personages who hold the front of the stage," and the influence that one man can exercise. The latter discount the importance of individual action, seeking after general causes, and ascribing to these an inevitability that makes resistance to the *zeitgeist* pointless. Paradoxically, it is the egalitarian mentality that dangerously undermines the individual's free will and responsibility.

Judaism teaches that each individual bears a unique destiny. It is not altogether surprising, then, that the modern Orthodox community has allied itself to the modern principle that every individual has equal worth. This would entail that each woman and each man be committed to a life of intellectual adventure and religious excellence, cultivating an authentic and passionate inner life, sanctifying his, or her, daily existence, bringing forth that "unique message . . . , [the] special color to add to the communal spectrum."[25] Instead, we submit all too readily to the siren song of mediocrity. There is a type of basketball coach who promotes the illusion of democratic teamwork, while in reality the entire enterprise revolves around the superstar. In the same spirit (or lack of spirit), we expect the exceptional individual to contend one-on-one with the great problems of the day and the relentless challenges of eternity, while the rest of us are reduced to the role of spectators, cheering the *Gedolim* on. The Rav wants more *for* us, and consequently asks more of us. Reluctant and disappointed, we summon the popularizers, the politicians, the polemicists, who, with their unfailing affinity for the superficial and the halftrue, bravely try to make him do, and purvey many anecdotes.

Rather than blame the Rav for demanding too much of us, we would do well to rouse ourselves to take full advantage of what he offers us. R. Levi Yitzhak of Berditchev explains that Israel first confessed the singular greatness of Moses at the parting of the sea, when even the maidservants saw what was denied the prophet Ezekiel. Only because they had reached great spiritual heights themselves, could they grasp that a mortal man like Moses might attain a higher level still.[26]

Until we probe the limits of our own spiritual capacities, we will not appreciate the Rav's, nor will we succeed in coming to terms with the good fortune that made him our mentor. If it is beyond us to soar with the eagle, yet we are not condemned to creep with the snail. Like the eagle, albeit without the eagle's swiftness and sweep, we were made to experience, and act within, a three dimensional world. In other words, it is not beyond us to be men.

Notes

1. *Keviat Moadim al pi haReiyah ve-al pi haHeshbon* (in *Kovetz Hiddushei Torah*).

2. (Harvard University Press, 1989), Preface, x. The scope of these remarks precludes a detailed account of Taylor's complex analysis, or, for that matter, a thorough examination of the Rav's rich thought on these issues.

3. Preface to *The Robbers*, xiv.

4. See, for example, *Lonely Man of Faith*, "The Community," "Majesty and Humility," "Catharsis." For the tension between Halakhic Man and the Rav of "Shir haShirim," see A. Ravitzky, "Acquisition of Knowledge in His Thought," in N. Lamm, et al., eds., *Sefer Yovel liKhevod Moreinu haGaon R. Yosef Dov haLevi Soloveitchik* (Jerusalem, 1984), p. 125ff.

5. See, for example, *U-Vikkashtem mi-Sham*, 17:2 on the elevation of the body; "Redemption, Prayer, Talmud Torah" criticizing indifference to the reality of suffering; *Lonely Man* on the importance of "dignity" for Adam I.

6. On romantic philosophy of language and its pertinence to the Rav's thought, see B. Ish-Shalom, "Language as a Religious Category in the Thought of Rabbi Y.D. Soloveitchik," in *Sefer haYovel la-Rav Mordekhai Breuer* (Jerusalem, 1992) 799–821.

7. See *Halakhic Man* and *Ma Dodekh miDod*.

8. See *Halakhic Man*, Part II and Yitzchak Blau, "Creative Repentance: On R. Soloveitchik's Concept of *Teshuva*," *Tradition* 28:2 (Winter 1994), 11–18.

9. See Berger et al., *The Homeless Mind*. Since the rise of Islamic fundamentalism, Berger has conceded that his prediction of the inevitable triumph of modernity was mistaken.

10. See R. Wurzburger's discussion.

11. Cf. *The Halakhic Mind* 4.

12. I deal more fully with this issue in "A Room with a View, But a Room of Our Own" (in *Modern Scholarship in the Study of Torah: Contributions and Limitations*, ed. S. Carmy [Jason Aronson, 1995]; an earlier version appeared in *Tradition* 28:3, Spring 1994).

13. *Kuntres al Avodat haYom*.

14. Copy in Louis Bernstein "The Emergence of the English Speaking Rabbinate" (YU Diss. 1977), 56ff.

15. David Singer and Moshe Sokol, "Joseph Soloveitchik: Lonely Man of Faith," *Modern Judaism* 2, pp. 227–272, 255.

16. *Divre Hashkafah*, 75–79; quotation on 78.

17. Note the unpublished lecture on *Peshara*, which deals with *Pesak* rather than *Lomdut*. I intend to discuss some implications of the literary aspect of the Rav's *oeuvre*, more fully in my work in progress on the "Category of the Ethical" in his thought.

18. On the tension between the Rav's conviction, which he inherited from his father, that intimate feelings are diminished when paraded before strangers, and the self-exposure that typifies some of his written and oral discourse, see below. On the connection between privacy, creativity and individuality, see, inter alia, the Rav's eulogy for R. Ze'ev Gold and my commentary "Anatomy of a *Hesped*: On Reading an Essay of the Rav," *Bein Kotlei ha-Yeshivah*, 1988, pp. 8–20.

19. See R. Lamm, "Notes of an Unrepentant Darshan" (RCA *Sermon Anthology 1986/5747* ed. B. Poupko), 1–12, for instructive insights on applying the Rav's approach to preaching in different situations.

20. See, for example, *Al Limmud Torah uGeullat Nefesh haDor* (in *Be-Sod haYahid ve-haYahad*).

21. Unpublished notebooks on prayer, circa 1953. See also my "Destiny, Freedom and the Logic of Petition (*Festschrift* for Rabbi Walter Wurzburger)," *Tradition*, 24:2 (Winter 1989) 17–37.

22. The Rav once remarked in my hearing that old-time *Gedolim* refrained from talking about themselves, but that the disconnection of modern man from living exemplars of religious existence has made self-revelation an educational necessity.

23. "Against Dryness: A Polemical Sketch" (in *Revisions: Changing Perspectives in Moral Philosophy*, ed. S. Hauerwas and A. MacIntyre) 50.

24. *Democracy in America*, Volume II, Book II, ch. 20.

25. "The Community," *Tradition* 17:2 (Spring, 1978)10. See also *Sanhedrin* 38a and *Bemidbar Rabba* 21.

26. *Kedushat Levi, B'shallah* 39b.

Rabbi Soloveitchik did not produce a systematic, comprehensive philosophical system. Rather, his works represent a segmented search for a satisfactory stance towards modernity, self and tradition. The Rav was deeply rooted in the traditional yeshiva world of Brisk, and also in the modern intellectual world of Berlin.

In this essay (Tradition 29:1), Moshe Sokol discusses the Rav's modernity and traditionalism. He argues that the Rav fully internalized the worlds of both Brisk and Berlin, emerging as a powerful paradigm of a religious figure dedicated both to traditionalism and to the contemporary situation.

Although the Rav is a thoroughly modern figure, his stance towards modernity is selective—accepting some aspects of modernity while rejecting others. His vibrant intellectual and spiritual life made him a full-fledged hero figure to his numerous students and followers.

"Ger ve-Toshav Anokhi"

Modernity and Traditionalism in the Life and Thought of Rabbi Joseph B. Soloveitchik

ঙ্কৃ৯

Moshe Sokol

ড়ঞ৶

I

Even during the lifetime of Rabbi Soloveitchik, a debate arose amongst his interpreters and closest disciples as to just how modern a figure he was. This debate has only intensified following his death. Was Rabbi Soloveitchik essentially a traditional *rosh yeshivah* who dabbled in philosophy and whose affirmation of certain "modern" positions are exceptions which only prove the rule? Or was R. Soloveitchik essentially a modern figure in outlook and conviction, although anchored in the sea of Talmud and the Brisker tradition?

My thesis in this essay is that Rabbi Soloveitchik was a paradigmatically modern figure for the Jews of his era, and that his enduring contribution to Jewish history derives *precisely* from that modernity. Nevertheless, I hope to show that the traditionalist reading of R. Soloveitchik gets something profoundly important about him right, namely, that in many fundamental ways he *remained* a traditional *rosh yeshivah*. However, I shall argue that the choices he made to retain that past were themselves highly personalized expressions of his own special brand of modernity.

There is of course a sense in which all contemporary Orthodoxy, from the extreme left to the extreme right, is a modern phenomenon, as the historian Jacob Katz and others have noted.[1] The Hungarian *Haredi* heirs of Hatam Sofer represent a distinctive response to modernity no less than the followers of *Torah im Derekh Eretz;* each group is therefore a modern phenomenon. In this respect, R. Soloveitchik is of course no different. Nevertheless, R. Soloveitchik's response to modernity differs from that of the Hungarian heirs of Hatam Sofer and many of their ideological foes in that, first, he chose not to deny all of modernity's values, a point I shall return to later; and, second, his response to modernity's challenges was, as I shall try to show, quite distinctive.

We can begin by contrasting R. Soloveitchik with Rabbi S. R. Hirsch. Whatever one thinks of the *Torah im Derekh Eretz* intellectual program, there is a certain comprehensiveness to it, a univocal worldview which surfaces in just about all of R. Hirsch's writings.

R. Hirsch, after the fashion of the 19th century, believed he had a comprehensive solution to the challenges of modernity, and the ideational initials of that solution are embedded to one degree or another in his entire *oeuvre.*

The same cannot be said of R. Soloveitchik. However one judges the success of the varying attempts to reconcile the underlying contradictions in R. Soloveitchik's writings, and I am a bit skeptical about some of them, there can be very little doubt that there are serious *differences* amongst the writings, even if they do not in the end amount to actual contradictions. The existentialist soul of "Lonely Man of Faith" is altogether different from the neo-Kantian structures of *Ish ha-Halakhah* and both diverge from the phenomenology of *U-Vikkashtem mi-Sham.* This is so even if the audiences for each of the essays are different, the languages are different, or whether R. Soloveitchik is addressing himself to the human condition generally, or to the Jewish condition specifically.[2]

As I shall argue throughout this essay, I believe that in each of R. Soloveitchik's major essays he takes up a problem in Jewish religious life and thought with which he is struggling at a particular period in his life and which he feels himself equipped to illuminate, and seeks to solve it using the approach which he judges to be most appropriate to the problem (in the context, perhaps, of the intended audience), or the approach to which he is then most attached. The sometimes wholly unrestrained (and sometimes restrained but always present) passionate and personal tone of his essays reflects not purely abstract intellectual inquiry, but rather fierce intellectual and spiritual struggle. Indeed, it is precisely for this reason that the essays are so powerful. In effect, then, we have multiple installments of the intellectual and spiritual autobiography of one of the most creative and fertile Jewish religious minds of the century. And this characterization remains true even if the underlying contradictions can be solved one way or another.

The key point I wish to stress now is that this essential approach makes him even more characteristically a 20th century figure, more current than the 19th century "modernists." For amongst the hallmarks of the twentieth century intellectual are the eschewal of comprehensive systems, the dissatisfaction with easy solutions, the readiness to try yet again, with different approaches, and by focusing on different issues. In many ways, then, he is the paradigm of the contemporary thinker in segmented search of a satisfactory stance towards modernity, self and tradition.

It must also be stressed that whatever the position ultimately *taken*, each of the major essays deals with religious Judaism in light of modernity. Whether it is to explain the halakhic life and mind, the religious significance of technology and activism, or the role of creativity, science, nature, and the aesthetic in religious experience, what we find is a consistent struggle to make peculiarly modern theological sense of these themes which recur in his writings, many themselves characteristic of modernity. The varying installments of R. Soloveitchik's intellectual autobiography, then, are themselves varying attempts to come to terms with different aspects of modernity in different ways. It is as if R. Soloveitchik keeps on gnawing away afresh at different dimensions of the problem, and sometimes even the same dimension without even bothering to footnote his own relevant writings, and without ever being fully satisfied that at last he's got it, fully solved the problem of modernity for the halakhic Jew.

This characterization is further reinforced by R. Soloveitchik's use of typology as a philosophical method. For example, Adam I and Adam II in "Lonely Man of Faith" make opposing claims upon the individual, as do *ish dat* and *ish da'at* in *Halakhic Man* and the natural and revelational experiences in *U-Vikkashtem mi-Sham*. The openness to antithetical experiences so essential to R. Soloveitchik's understanding of religious life leads necessarily to a segmented vision and to intellectual and spiritual struggle, which in some instances can in principle never be resolved (Adam I/Adam II in "Lonely Man of Faith") and in others can be resolved if at all only at the end of a long and difficult quest (*Ish Dat/Ish Da'at* in *Halakhic Man* and the natural experience/revelational experience in *U-Vikkashtem mi-Sham*).

Yet another point must be made regarding R. Soloveitchik's modernity: his simultaneous and passionate affirmation of many values of both Brisk and Berlin should not be taken for granted. To use the language of Peter Berger, R. Soloveitchik, "heretically" affirmed Brisk while in Berlin, and "heretically" affirmed many values of Berlin while leading the life of a Brisker *rosh yeshivah* at Yeshiva University. The typical modern religious person, in Berger's analytic framework, is acculturated to modernity yet nevertheless "relativizes the relativizers" and "heretically" chooses religious faith.[3] By virtue of his family heritage, then "heretic" departure to Berlin (for many members of his family, of course, the quotation marks should here be deleted), then return to the life of the *rosh yeshivah*, R. Soloveitchik made not one but *two* "heretic" choices, two self-conscious commitments—he chose not only Berlin while in Brisk, but also Brisk while in Berlin. In R. Soloveitchik, then, we have the distinctive religious faith of modernity squared.

It must be stressed that this is far more difficult and existentially resonant than the choice of so many others who are heir to a path already taken, who may learn *daf yomi* but also dabble with the impact of Dostoevski or Kant for their understanding of the *daf*'s latest *aggadah*. R. Soloveitchik, who embarked alone on the long, long journey to Berlin, took his Kant and Dostoevski with infinite seriousness: he *fully* internalized Berlin, as he had *fully* internalized Brisk. This makes him as well a powerful paradigm of the peculiarly modern religious quest for a theological vision commensurate with the problematics of constructing an identity which simultaneously affirms both past and present. It is hardly surprising, then, that the theological and existential end product for R. Soloveitchik is a highly personalized quest and world-view. The radical embrace of Berlin and radical re-embrace of Brisk would mean, as we shall see, that R. Soloveitchik can never be fully at home in either, that he must be a *ger ve-toshav* in both.

II

I have argued up to this point that R. Soloveitchik must be seen as a thoroughly modern figure. However, this does not imply that the choices he made as a thoroughly modern figure are all that might usually be called modern. A thoroughly modern figure can, in his quest for theological and existential self-definition, make some very traditionalist choices, and that R. Soloveitchik most assuredly did.

Perhaps the best way to see this is by reflecting on Walter Wurzburger's paper in this issue. While Dr. Wurzburger identifies numerous instances in which R. Soloveitchik takes a conservative position in halakhic matters as evidence of his traditionalism, conservative *Halakhah* itself is not *ipso facto* traditionalist. Why shouldn't the modernist too be *mahmir* where his reading of the sources or even his reading of the times leads to *humra?* Instead, I should like to focus on those three areas that R. Wurzburger itemizes as evidence of his *modernity:* (1) R. Soloveitchik's endorsement of secular studies and the study of philosophy; (2) his espousal of Religious Zionism; (3) and his advocacy of intensive Jewish education for women.

There can be very little doubt, as R. Wurzburger maintains, that each of these areas reflects R. Soloveitchik's modernity. Nevertheless, there are strong traditionalist elements in R. Soloveitchik's views on each of these issues.

Consider first his programmatic advocacy of intensive Jewish education for women, including the study of Talmud. What theoretical framework does R. Soloveitchik use to justify this position, either halakhic or theological? We have no *teshuvah* or theological essay from R. Soloveitchik which lays the conceptual groundwork for egalitarianism on this or related issues. Quite to the contrary. Theologically, R. Soloveitchik insists on role *differentiation* rather than egalitarianism. In his "A Tribute to the Rebbitzen of Talne,"[4] R. Soloveitchik maintains that it is the father's task to instill in his child "discipline of thought as well as . . . discipline of action," whereas it is the mother's task to reach the child emotionally and spiritually, to help him "feel the presence of God . . . to appreciate *mitzvot* and spiritual values, to enjoy the warmth of a dedicated life."[5] Talmud study for women hardly emerges naturally from this conception of the female role.

A similar observation must be made concerning the second area R. Wurzburger cites as evidence of R. Soloveitchik's modernity: his Religious Zionism. Without question, R. Soloveitchik here has made a radical break with Traditionalist Orthodoxy and with his own family, a point he makes with great poignancy in *Hamesh Derashot.*[6] Nevertheless, R. Soloveitchik's Zionism is of a clearly traditionalist stripe. As R. Wurzburger himself correctly notes, R. Soloveitchik justifies the State of Israel by conservative religious categories, and these include the amelioration of Jewish suffering after the Holocaust, the biblical command to conquer and settle the Land of Israel, and the promotion of Jewish pride.[7] We have none of the potent eschatology implicit in R. Kook's writings or, at the opposite end of the spectrum, the reconceived religious challenges central to the thinking of Dr. David Hartman.

Finally, and I think most importantly, we come to the first area R. Wurzburger delineates: R. Soloveitchik's openness to secular culture and philosophy. The significance of his position in this area, especially in light of his family heritage and the prevailing values of Traditionalist Orthodoxy, cannot be overstated. As I noted above, R. Soloveitchik does not simply appropriate a nifty bit of philosophical lore to explain the random *midrash:* his entire world-view was shaped by his encounter with secular culture, as his theological essays make readily apparent. Even where he specifically asserts that he is making use of philosophical ideas *le-saber et ha-ozen,* to explain halakhic man to the uninitiated reader,[8] which of course is a thoroughly conservative aim, his systematic use of neo-Kantianism reflects more than a mere casual intellectual parlor trick. The ideas themselves re-orient the conception of halakhic man, and it seems likely that R. Soloveitchik himself intellectually identified to at least some extent with the doctrines he used.[9] This is surely the case with "Lonely Man of Faith" and many of his other major essays. While R. Soloveitchik may have harnessed his secular learning in some instances to traditionalist aims, that learning itself fashioned his own theological world-view to a significant degree.

This said, the picture which emerges is still not altogether straightforward. While R. Soloveitchik assimilated secular culture to a remarkable degree, he did so in a highly selective manner. Perhaps the most striking lacuna in this regard is the almost complete absence of historical sensibility in his picture of Judaism. To confront secular culture but to ignore the findings of Wissenschaft scholarship, especially with respect to the influence of historical factors in both the development of texts and in the development of Halakhah, is nothing short of remarkable.

To assert, as Dr. Wurzburger does, that for R. Soloveitchik Halakhah follows its own logic and *a priori* categories, hardly solves the problem. No doubt R. Soloveitchik did believe that Halakhah follows its own logic and *a priori* categories. But even if this is true, what the halakhic text actually says—understood of course within the parameters of its own logic—surely depends upon getting the text *right.* And critical scholarship has much to say about precisely this question. This is not a matter of applying alien scientific categories to halakhic *reasoning,* but rather, in the case of lower criticism, following common sense in making sure the text one reads is correct, a methodological principle for which there is ample classic Jewish precedent, as is well known.

Moreover, by Dr. Wurzburger's own testimony, R. Soloveitchik's halakhic decisions were profoundly, and often apparently even self-consciously, influenced by his perception of the needs of the times, e.g., his opposition to announcing pages during *hazarat hashatz;* his advocacy of Talmud study for women; his approach to membership in the Synagogue Council of America; and his attitude towards celebrating Thanksgiving, to cite just several examples. As R. Wurzburger himself notes, "A posek is not a computer," and subjective elements necessarily play a role in the halakhic decision-making process.

But to concede this is surely to concede too much, for if this is all true, then historical factors do indeed play a role in halakhic decision-making. The "needs of the times" from the perspective of 1965 amount to historical influences from the perspective of 2010.

Of course, it isn't that R. Soloveitchik was ignorant of the positions of the biblical critics and Wissenschaft scholars. He was surely exposed to them during his student days in Berlin, while at the yeshivah headed by R. Hayyim Heller, and later at Yeshiva University. At least in the case of biblical criticism, he simply asserts that he was never troubled by it.[10] His lengthy discussion of the *a priori* nature of Halakhah is at very best an argument by indirection only. He never in his published writings confronts head-on the challenges posed by history and Wissenschaft. The problem becomes even more striking when one considers that Wissenschaft spawned the major denominational and intellectual competitor to Orthodoxy, Conservative Judaism, and of course did much as well to nourish its other major competitor, Reform Judaism. Here surely we have challenges to Orthodoxy which cry out for a response.

Several factors may have played a role in R. Soloveitchik's avoidance of the problem. First, there is his overwhelmingly philosophical orientation in which abstract ideas and logical categories rather than history and text criticism predominate. Second, he may have understood the grave dangers to the tradition which these disciplines posed, and without any clear-cut solution to the problems, which in any case would have fallen outside his personal and professional expertise, he may have felt it would be best simply not to take the problem on. But according to this second explanation, what might R. Soloveitchik's own rationale have been for denying the problem? This leads me to the third, and I think central, consideration. R. Soloveitchik portrays the simple man of faith, the "man-child" to use his felicitous formulation, as a religious ideal:

> The great man whose intellect has been raised to a superior level through the study of Torah, gifted with well-developed, overflowing powers-depth, scope, sharpness-should not be viewed as totally adult . . . he remains the young and playful child, naive curiosity, natural enthusiasm, eagerness and spiritual restfulness have not abandoned him. Only the child with his simple faith and fiery enthusiasm can make the miraculous leap into the bosom of God.[11]

In this depiction of the religious life, R. Soloveitchik was capturing his own faith with stunning accuracy. R. Soloveitchik secured for himself at least one tranquil island of faith amidst the torrent of existential and theological issues with which he mightily struggled and which occasioned his most creative and brilliant theological works. *Halakhic Mind*[12] is a far more sophisticated statement with much the same thesis: that the life of religious faith is epistemically justifiable.

It must be stressed that R. Soloveitchik's affirmation of the faith of the "man-child" is distinctively modern. It represents a "heretic," autonomous and even creative choice in the face of intellectual pressure from those precincts of Berlin which he was unprepared to confront with the philosophical weapons he had at his disposal. Surely this should not be surprising. It seems altogether likely that most Modern Orthodox Jewish intellectuals have said to themselves at some point in their intellectual odyssey: "In the end, after all is said and done, with a solution or without, I just believe" or, in the pungent Yiddish variant, *Fun a kashe shtarbt min nisht* (One doesn't die from a question). Given all the penetrating intellectual honesty of the Brisker dynasty

to which R. Soloveitchik was heir, we find in his writings no lame
excuses, no half-hearted attempts to white-wash a truly serious problem.
We find instead a fideistic affirmation of faith, out of the secure
corner of the man-child's soul. How self-conscious was R. Soloveitchik
in this regard? Did he choose to make a "heretic" faith affirmation in
self-conscious response to the challenges of Wissenschaft? Unfortunately, this question is difficult to answer with any certainty. Either
way, however, I wish to stress that his stance is in many ways a
prototypic strategy in the Orthodox struggle with modernity. This in
turn helps make R. Soloveitchik into a prototypic Modern Orthodox
Jewish intellectual whose personal struggle with modernity became
paradigmatic for the Modern Orthodox of his generation.

But here we may run into an objection. Isn't R. Soloveitchik the
Maimonidean figure of twentieth century Judaism, courageously rising
to confront the full set of challenges that modernity poses, working
out comprehensive solutions to the *nevukhim*, the perplexed of the
generation?

In my judgment this is the myth of R. Soloveitchik, a myth which
for good sociological reasons found enormous currency amongst many
Modern Orthodox Jews, who required an authority figure to make
sense of and to some degree justify their participation in modernity.
Who better could serve this role than the Rav, brilliant *talmid hakham*,
bearer of the august Soloveitchik name, devoted Brisker interpreter
of the Rambam, and philosopher *par excellence*? I shall have more to
say about R. Soloveitchik's success in fulfilling this role shortly, but
for now I want to stress that this Maimonidean image of R. Soloveitchik
is a mistaken one. To see this, it would be instructive to start by
comparing Maimonides' response to the most serious challenge he
faced in his world-view with R. Soloveitchik's response to the challenge
of history and Wissenschaft. I refer of course to the problem creation
ex nihilo posed for Maimonides.

However one reads Maimonides' true position on this subject, a
question of continuing debate amongst Maimonides scholars, there
can be very little doubt that he met the challenge head-on. Some

thirty chapters of the *Moreh* focus in one way or another on this question, and Maimonides submits the dilemma to the most rigorous philosophical analysis. The absence of a similar discussion in R. Soloveitchik's writings on a central divide between Orthodoxy and its rebellious children is altogether telling. And this is indicative of a much more fundamental difference. Maimonides took up the full range of challenges posed by the philosophy of his day, and wrote a comprehensive, if somewhat veiled treatise to serve as a guide to the perplexed of his day. S. R. Hirsch undertook much the same task for his own generation, although he carried out the project in a very anti-Maimonidean way. The key point I wish to make, however, is that we get no such comprehensive treatment of the challenges posed by modernity in the writings of R. Soloveitchik.

Quite apart from the really critical problem of Wissenschaft, we have no published essay by R. Soloveitchik on the question of whether engaging in secular studies is legitimate, on the very doctrine of synthesis so central to the self-understanding of Modern Orthodoxy, as his son-in-law R. Aharon Lichtenstein produced thirty years ago,[13] and as Dr. Norman Lamm published more recently.[14] We do not have full-fledged studies on the nature of authority and *ta'amei ha-mitzvot*, nor do we even have a fully-worked out philosophy of Halakhah.[15] In addition, as I noted above, we have no full-fledged theological or halakhic study of the role of women and egalitarianism, as we don't have a study in political philosophy on the role and function of the State of Israel, to cite just several more examples of issues which press hard in the self-understanding of Modern Orthodoxy.

The probable reason for these lacunae, I believe, is that R. Soloveitchik simply wasn't interested in producing a comprehensive guide to the perplexed of his era. This is either because some of the issues weren't dilemmas he was struggling with when he chose to pick up his pen and write, or because he may have believed he hadn't anything "Soloveitchikean" to add to the discussion. By and large, I believe he wrote about matters (a) that touched to the core of his own personal struggles with Jewish self-definition in the modern era; and (b) about which he believed that with his unique blend of Brisk and Berlin he had much to contribute. As he explains in the beginning of the "Lonely Man of Faith," he wrote in personal confession; if others benefit, then of course all the better.[16] While there may be an element of coyness here, beneath the coyness lies a profound truth.

III

My argument so far has been that while R. Soloveitchik is a thoroughly modern figure, his modern stance towards modernity, so-to-speak, is selective, reflecting his own highly personal faith commitments. I have also argued that the engine which drove his extraordinarily rich theological output is itself selective, reflecting his own intellectual dilemmas and his own capacity to contribute. Now I want to focus on the question of R. Soloveitchik's role as authority figure for the Modern Orthodox Jews of his era. The point I wish to emphasize is that my analysis should not lead to the mistaken conclusion that R. Soloveitchik was somehow flawed as an authority figure for Modern Orthodoxy, that he didn't or couldn't serve as a *posek* or intellectual role model for a non-traditionalist stance to modernity.

Compelling testimony to R. Soloveitchik's great success in these spheres may be found in Dr. Walter Wurzburger's essay cited above. On issue after issue, R. Soloveitchik's *pesak* served as the basis for the behavior and choices of countless Orthodox rabbis and their congregants. By R. Wurzburger's extensive account, R. Soloveitchik, with acute sensitivity to the needs of the time and to his own values, formulated numerous *piskei halakhah* which help define the stance of Modern Orthodox Jews to the halakhic and policy issues of the day.[17]

It should not be thought that the traditionalist dimension of R. Soloveitchik's response to modernity impeded his ability to serve as an effective *posek* and powerful role model for Modern Orthodoxy. Indeed, I would argue that it was *precisely* his highly personal blend of traditionalist and modern elements which contributed to his success.

This is so for two reasons, one more superficial and the other deeper. At the more superficial (although no less important) level, R.

Soloveitchik's undeniable traditionalism and—although this is a different matter—his capacity for *humra*, contributed to the perceived legitimacy of his *pesak*. His day-in-and-day-out engagement in classic *talmud Torah* as a *rosh yeshivah*, his *rosh yeshivah-like* bearing, and, on occasion, Brisker *humrot*, his faithful denial of some aspects of modernity, his elegiac and potent portrayals of the faith, life and values of the Brisk of his youth and the *gedolim* of another, lost era, quite apart from his truly vast, classical halakhic erudition, all contributed mightily to the legitimacy crucial for Orthodox Jews to accept him as a *posek*. Indeed, were R. Soloveitchik to have bought fully into modern methods and values, he probably would have failed as a *posek* for Modern Orthodoxy at that stage in the history of its development in the United States.

The same is true for his equally important role as a model for countless students and nascent intellectuals struggling with the claims of modernity and tradition. His exacting, even stellar, standards in both Talmud and philosophy made him a kind of hero for the Modern Orthodox Jew in much the same way as, say, Hazon Ish was a hero and role model for yet a different kind of Orthodox Jew. The importance of this point cannot be overstated.

This leads me to the second and deeper way in which R. Soloveitchik's highly personal blend of modernity and traditionalism made him the paradigmatic authority for the Modern Orthodox Jew of his generation. Here again the contrast with Maimonides is instructive. Both, of course, were thinkers of the first rank in their respective generations. Yet each functioned differently in his confrontation with the intellectual challenges of the time. To borrow (and abuse) Plato's concept of the philosopher-king, Maimonides was a kind of Jewish philosopher-as-king. By this I mean that Maimonides regally confronted the full set of intellectual and religious challenges to the Jews of his era, and produced systematic intellectual and legal guidance on every facet of Jewish life for his needy people. Thus we have his comprehensive *Mishneh Torah* on the one hand and his comprehensive *Moreh* on the other. I have argued above (in effect) that to understand R.

Soloveitchik as Jewish-philosopher-as-king is to embrace the myth of R. Soloveitchik.

But that is not the only model for Jewish intellectual and religious leadership. I would argue that R. Soloveitchik embodied what I shall call the Jewish-philosopher-as-hero.[18] By this I mean that R. Soloveitchik's own passionate intellectual and spiritual life made him a full-fledged heroic figure to the legions of students and intellectuals he touched. Surely the ingredients for heroism are there: his struggle to find philosophically illuminating solutions to the dilemmas he confronted in the deepest reaches of his own mind and soul; his desire as a great teacher to share these personal struggles and powerful insights with his students; his uncompromising intellectual rigor and mastery in Talmud and in philosophy; his drive to contribute his special blend of Brisk and Berlin to the ongoing quest of Jewish philosophy, an achievement, it should be added, which would justify his own adventures in Berlin; and finally, of special importance, his "heretic" affirmation in the face of critical challenges of a very traditionalist spirituality, faith, and love and method of learning.

The Jewish philosopher-as-hero need not solve intellectually every problem that comes his way, nor must he project a univocal world-view in solving the problems he does tackle, nor must teach all there is to teach, in order to achieve success. The "heretic" faith affirmation can be as heroic, as important for the student and follower as the comprehensive regal disquisition. Indeed, it is precisely the selectivity of the intellectual enterprise, the sense that the project is not yet complete, that there is yet more work to be done, that sometimes it may be necessary to start over once again, which makes the philosophical task more alive, more engaging. As in Greek tragedy, the *agon* itself is heroic. Moreover, as I have argued above, it is precisely this segmented quest, in which sweeping and perhaps too easy solutions are eschewed, which is so characteristic of the 20th century.[19]

This approach would surely be most appropriate for the Modern Orthodox Jew who must struggle with his own problematic identity, with the need to make sense of the claims of modernity in the context of his attachment to the past. Who could be more suitable as a hero than R. Soloveitchik, himself struggling in lecture after brilliant lecture and, later, essay after brilliant essay, with precisely these problems, with the themes of modernity and the dilemmas they raise for the Orthodox Jew? And to top it all off, who could simultaneously serve as a world class *rosh yeshivah* and *posek* on the one hand, and a legitimizer of such desirable values as Zionism and secular studies on the other. In this very special sense, R. Soloveitchik was the perfect authority figure and role model for the Modern Orthodox of his generation.

IV

No discussion of this subject can be complete without considering some of these questions, if only briefly, *sub specie aeternitatis*, or, a bit more shortsightedly, from the perspective of 2094 rather than 1994. What will be the enduring legacy of R. Joseph B. Soloveitchik?

Unfortunately, we will then no longer have the anecdotal evidence, the rich lore of *Torah shebe-al peh* which has been so critical (and it must be added, problematic, since there are often conflicting accounts, with concomitant revisionism) to conveying his *piskei halakhah* and his positions on various and sundry issues. Some of these already have been, and undoubtedly will continue to be recorded in various books, but they may well lack the halakhically authoritative status necessary to persuade some future rabbi, since they will not be conveyed with the full halakhic apparatus.

Certainly some halakhic traditions and public policy positions will be passed down from student to student, but how many of these will be passed down, how accurately, and with what authority in the face of whole new generations of *poskim* and *gedolim* is very hard to predict. On the other hand, perhaps in the future some *talmid* of a *talmid* of R. Soloveitchik will himself succeed in becoming a world class *posek*, and will do so despite (because of?) his sensitivity to historical influences and textual criticism. Does this strain credulity? But if it does occur, it too in its own odd way will be a legacy of R. Soloveitchik, even if R. Soloveitchik himself would have disapproved.

We will, it is to be hoped, have more and more of the *hiddushei Torah* produced by R. Soloveitchik, either by his own pen or by his students. These, again it is to be hoped, will be studied by generations of *talmidei hakhamim* and considered on their own merits, along with the *hiddushim* of R. Borukh Ber Leibowitz, R. Yitzhak Z. Soloveitchik, R. Shimon Szkop and numerous other future and past world class *roshei yeshivah*.

Jewish life in the mid-late 21st century will have been shaped by R. Soloveitchik's impact as Jewish philosopher-as-hero on several generations of students and students of students, and by his role in the creation and nurturing of the whole Jewish culture we have been calling Modern Orthodoxy, at least in its American guise, with its affirmation of Zionism and secular learning. What this amounts to in the long sweep of Jewish history, however, I leave to others to judge.

And of course, we will have the philosophical writings. Perhaps in the future, in some post-post-post modern era, the problems of modernity will reassert themselves once again, and the essays will be as anguishingly pressing then in exactly the same way that they have been for so many today. But whether or not that is so, I am convinced that future generations will look to R. Soloveitchik's essays for rich insight into a host of issues raised by his encounter with modernity. There is R. Soloveitchik's resonant account of the theological significance of technological advancement and human initiative. There are his powerful, multiple portrayals of the quest for God and the life of faith; his sensitive exploration of the religious significance of loneliness and community and of the nature of prayer; and his discussions of the role of science, reason and the aesthetic in the journey towards religious enlightenment. There are his highly complex treatments of human creativity and this worldliness, themes which run through a number of his essays, and there is his illuminating articulation of the world-view of the Litvak *talmid hakham*, the nature of Halakhah and its functions in Jewish life.

Surely he has left us a rich intellectual legacy. Scholars of the future have much work ahead of them, studying his writings and reconstructing his theological views on a wide variety of subjects, some just mentioned above. Constructive theologians will start where R. Soloveitchik left off, carrying forward their own theological programs by reinterpreting, for better or worse (that is the way of theological programs) his essays. Indeed work has already begun in many of these areas, although much remains undone.

And finally, some 100 years from now a student or class at Hebrew University or Harvard, a *yeshivah bahur* at Gush Etzion or even Mir, and a class at Yeshiva University, will pick up "Lonely Man of Faith" or *Ish ha-Halakhah*, read it, and stand back in awe and illumination, just as so many did, all those years ago.

Notes

1. "Orthodoxy in Historical Perspective," in Peter Medding, ed., *Studies in Contemporary Jewry II* (Bloomington, 1986), pp. 3–17.

2. See, for example, A. Ravitzky, "Rabbi Joseph B. Soloveitchik on Human Knowledge: Between Maimonideanism and Neo-Kantian Philosophy" in *Modern Judaism* 6:2 (May, 1986); Eugene Borowitz, "A Theology of Modern Orthodoxy: Rabbi Joseph B. Soloveitchik" in *Choices in Modern Jewish Thought*, New York, 1983, pp. 218–242; Lawrence Kaplan, "The Religious Philosophy of Rabbi Joseph B. Soloveitchik," *Tradition*, Fall, 1973, pp. 43–64.

3. See, for example, *A Rumor of Angels* (N.Y., 1969), chapt. 2.

4. *Tradition* (Spring, 1978). While this appears in a eulogy for a hasidic *rebbetzin*, and the setting is surely relevant to the traditionalist formulation, it was published later as a formal essay in *Tradition*, and does, I believe, reflect at least one aspect of his thinking about the subject.

5. *Ibid.*, pp. 76, 78. I hasten to add that the point in characterizing R. Soloveitchik's views here as traditionalist is not at all pejorative. The traditionalist perspective, it can be argued, may be entirely right on this question. But even to assert that it is correct is not to deny its traditionalism.

6. Ed. D. Telsner (Jerusalem, 1974) p. 25.

7. See especially *Kol Dodi Dofek* (ed. P. Peli, *Be-Sod ha-Yahid ve-ha-Yahad*, Jerusalem, 1976) and *Hamesh Derashot, op. cit.*, passim.

8. *Ish ha-Halakhah, Be-Sod ha-Yahid ve-ha-Yahad*, ed. P. Peli (Jerusalem, 1976), p. 63, n. 16.

9. Here I have altered somewhat my views on this issue in "Joseph B. Soloveitchik: Lonely Man of Faith," D. Singer and M. Sokol, *Modern Judaism* (October, 1982), pp. 237–238.

10. "Lonely Man of Faith," *Tradition*, Summer, 1965, p. 8–9.

11. "The Remnant of Scholars" in Epstein, ed. *Shiurei ha-Rav* (N.Y., 1974), p. 16.

12. New York, 1986.

13. "A Consideration of Synthesis from a Torah Point of View," *Gesher* (June, 1963), p. 7–15.

14. *Torah U'Mada* (Northvale, 1990) Gerald Blidstein, in his "On the Jewish People in the Writings of Rabbi Joseph B. Soloveitchik," *Tradition* 24:3 (Spring, 1989) makes a similar observation, p. 24.

15. I emphasize "fully-worked out," since R. Soloveitchick does of course touch upon a number of these issues in various essays. With regard to a philosophy of Halakhah, a particularly surprising omission, as Lawrence Kaplan notes, even *Halakhic Mind* and *Ish ha-Halakhah* are not full statements. See Kaplan's essay, "Rabbi Joseph

B. Soloveitchik's Philosophy of Halakhah," in *Jewish Law Annual* B.S. Jackson, ed. (N.Y., 1988) p. 139–197.

16. *op. cit.*, p. 5–6. While "Lonely Man of Faith" is the most personal of his major essays, I believe that this point nevertheless applies to much of his literary output.

17. Here it should be noted that the position R. Wurzburger attributes to me and David Singer, that because of R. Soloveitchik's traditionalism he could not function as a *posek* for Modern Orthodoxy, is simply inaccurate, as a perusal of the article (*op. cit.*, n. 9) will reveal.

18. This distinction, minus the philosopher part, may also be useful in considering the roles of other rabbinic authority figures in modernity. I should add that the distinction is different from that drawn by R. Soloveitchik himself, between the "king-teacher" and the "saint-teacher," in his "A Eulogy for the Talner Rebbe" in *Shiurei ha-Rav, op. cit.*, p. 24–26.

19. Perhaps it should be added that this model for understanding R. Soloveitchik's significance sheds light on another phenomenon as well. Even many of R. Soloveitchik's closest personal disciples perceive him quite differently. The more Brisk-minded take him to be the great Brisker *rosh yeshivah* who of course dabbled in philosophy. The more Berlin-minded take him to be a great Jewish philosopher who of course was also a great *rosh yeshivah*. Absent the comprehensive articulation of a world-view, the critical essay on "synthesis," he can be variously read by various disciples.

Complex, multi-dimensional heroic figures, in the sense I've described, lend themselves to variant readings even by close disciples, to interpretations which reflect the interpreter as much as the individual interpreted. Such widely variant readings certainly occur in the case of the Jewish philosopher-as-king, and Maimonides is a striking example of this, but it is my impression that they take more time to evolve.

Rabbi Soloveitchik has often been described as the philosopher of Halakhah par excellence. In this essay (Tradition 30:2), Shubert Spero argues that Halakhah is not the only source of Jewish philosophy of religion for the Rav. Halakhic Judaism is not derived solely from the Halakhah; rather, it stems from a variety of classic Jewish sources including the Bible, Aggadah, and Kaballah.

The Rav's thought is characterized by deep insight into the complexities of the God-human relationship. He is keenly aware of the dialectical character of this relationship. Religious consciousness is complex, rigorous and imbued with inner struggle. Rabbi Spero suggests that the Rav derived this depth of insight not exclusively from Halakhah, but from a broader range of classic sources. This is true also of the Rav's other philosophical and theological positions.

Rabbi Joseph B. Soloveitchik and the Philosophy of Halakhah

ﷺ

Shubert Spero

ﷻ

Halakhah,[1] while probably the most distinctive component of Judaism and most instrumental in the survival of the Jewish people,[2] has also been philosophically the most problematic. At the beginning of our history, to outsiders looking in, Halakhah appeared as a set of misanthropic superstitions.[3] Later, to groups within Judaism with a sectarian bent—Christians, Karaites and classical Reform—Halakhah embodied all that was objectionable both in content as well as in methodology. However, even within the living environment of Talmudic Judaism which produced Halakhah, there arose philosophical issues which were never resolved and which impinged upon the theoretical grounds of Halakhah: which is greater, study or action,[4] wisdom or deeds?[5] Are there reasons for the *hukim*?[6] Are some commandments more important than others?[7] But even more significant was the fact that from the very beginning of the use of the term "Halakhah," one finds the opposite term, "aggadah," so that it is clear that "Halakhah" was never meant to encompass all of Judaism. Thus, the conceptual stage was already set for comparisons between the two as to their relative role and significance.[8]

While Halakhah itself, from the Talmudic period until the present, has experienced a remarkable development in almost every area—Talmudic commentary and translation, codification, responsa, history of Halakhah—there has been a lacuna in the systematic treatment of the philosophy of Halakhah.[9] As for the medieval period, long considered the Golden Age of Jewish philosophy, conventional wisdom is wont to accept the summary judgment of Gershom Scholem: "Of the two reflective movements in Judaism, the mystical (Kabbalah) and philosophy (rational), the latter failed to establish a satisfactory and intimate relation to the Halakhah."[10]

Our generation, however, has been blessed with the presence and creative productivity of Rabbi Joseph Dov Soloveitchik (henceforth "the Rav"), eminent Talmudist, halakhic authority and charismatic teacher, whose writing has been characterized by a modern philosophic approach. Halakhah and its role in Judaism as a whole has been a central focus of the Rav's writing, as evinced by the titles of two of his major essays: *Halakhic Man* and *The Halakhic Mind*.[11] Indeed, he has been justly called "the philosopher of Halakhah."[12] As the teacher and mentor of the Modern Orthodox Rabbinate, the Rav has been enormously influential in increasing awareness of the centrality of Halakhah in theory as well as in practice, to the point where for many, the term "halakhic Judaism" has come to replace "Orthodox Judaism." Since in Halakhic Man the Rav works with "ideal types," it is extremely difficult to determine whether views of Halakhah attributed to Halakhic Man are to be considered normative for Judaism. I shall therefore begin with his more philosophic work, *The Halakhic Mind*, and consider a single although obviously sweeping claim made by the Rav on behalf of Halakhah which is presented as the conclusion of the theory he outlines in that essay.

H1 . . . there is only a single source from which a Jewish philosophical weltanschauung could emerge: the objective order—the Halakhah[13]. . . . Out of the sources of Halakhah, a new world view awaits formulation.[14]

Others have paraphrased the Rav's views thus:

> Religious and philosophical accounts of Jewish spirituality are sound and meaningful only to the extent that they derive from the Halakhah. The deepest religious emotion, the subtlest theological understanding can only be Jewishly authentic to the extent that they arise from reflection on matters of Halakhah.[15]

> Philosophy is always to be derived from the realm of the Halakhah and not vice versa.[16]

> Halakhah is the visible surface of a philosophy: the only philosophy that could legitimately claim to being Jewish.[17]

I shall consider proposition H1 in three different contexts:

(1) as an independent assertion about Jewish theology;

(2) as the logical conclusion of a theory developed by the Rav in *The Halakhic Mind*;

(3) as a working principle employed by the Rav in the articulation of his own philosophy.

Let us note at the outset that the real problem in the Rav's assertion is his claim that Halakhah is the only source of Jewish philosophy. Certainly it must be acknowledged that Halakhah may serve as a source for philosophy, although even this is not immediately obvious. Halakhah is essentially material which takes the form of norms and practices obligatory upon the Jew. Thus, as imperative and non-propositional, Halakhah as such cannot qualify as philosophy. However, one can conceivably infer a philosophical proposition from a Halakhah. Assuming there to be a Halakhah that one who has sinned is obliged to repent, one might infer that since "ought" implies "can," Halakhah presupposes the psychophilosophical principle of human freedom of the will. As another example, one might argue that since the content of Halakhah is regarded as "commandments," there is the implication of the existence of a "commander." Hence the theological principle of the existence of God as Divine Commander is inferable from Halakhah. There is also the case of a pure theological principle having crystallized into Halakhah. So, for example, Halakhah rules that if a person does not subscribe to belief in the Divine Revelation of the Torah (*Torah min ha–shamayim*), he is classified as a heretic, which has specific halakhic consequences.[18]

Can we, however, insist that Halakhah is the only source of Jewish philosophy? From where have Jewish thinkers in the past drawn their philosophy? If we examine the works of the classical Jewish philosophers—Sa'adya, Yehuda haLevi and Maimonides, we find that the prooftexts they offer are mainly from the Bible, and, if Rabbinic, are generally aggadic in nature.[19] Even if one should disagree with some particular philosophic tenets of these thinkers, one cannot accuse all of them of having looked in the wrong place! Certainly, many of the Talmudic Rabbis perceived aggadah rather than Halakhah as the appropriate place to find philosophic insights: "If you wish to know He-who-spoke-and-the-world-was-created, study aggadah."[20] Particularly if we believe, with Yehuda haLevi, that the God of Israel manifests Himself more tellingly in history than in nature, then we should get ourselves to aggadah. For it is the aggadah and not Halakhah that deals with the significance of history.

Consider, for example, that most crucial of theological questions: Should a Jew seek to justify his religious faith by means of proofs and rational arguments? Bahya ibn Pakuda found the answer in the Biblical verse: "Know this day and lay it to the heart, that the Lord, He is God in heaven above and upon the earth beneath; there is none else."[21] A fundamental question of this kind touches upon the very nature of human knowledge in general and religious knowledge in particular. Bahya reads this Biblical verse as a mandate to engage in whatever rational methods of investigation are available in order to demonstrate the doctrine of the unity of God. Others did not read this verse in the same way. Still, the issue was not one of midrash Halakhah, but hinged upon an *a priori* understanding of religious knowledge and the requirements of Judaism in this area.

We are thus led to conclude that H1 is not acceptable at least as a general description of how Jewish theology has been done in the past. As a proposal for doing Jewish theology in the future, it appears unnecessarily limiting. However, in light of the Rav's own philosophic achievements in certain areas of Halakhah, the following proposition may be posited:

H2 . . . Halakhah is a source of authentic Jewish theology.[22]

Let us return to a consideration of H1 as a conclusion which the Rav derives from an elaborate theory of religion which he develops in that essay. According to the Rav, the God-man relation expresses itself on three levels of human experience:

1. The subjective consciousness with its various contradictory tensions, such as "wrath and love, remoteness and immanence, repulsion and fascination, tremor and serenity, depression and rapture."

2. The objective theoretical level of logico-cognitive judgments and ethical-religious norms, such as: "God exists, He is omniscient, moral, the creator, you shall love God, fear Him, love your fellow man."

3. Concrete deeds, psycho-physical acts, prayer, worship, rituals, cult.[23]

The Rav asserts that religious experiences on both the subjective and objective levels are authentic and veridical and "lie within the ontic zone."[24] That is to say, the Divine manifests itself both "in the (subjective) realm of time and consciousness and in the (objective)

realm of time and space."[25] It is already in this initial presentation
that we grasp the unique nature of the Rav's philosophy of religion
and his overall strategy. Contrary to conventional wisdom,[26] the Rav
insists on the cognitive and veridical nature of the "objectified" elements
in religion, which in Judaism is constituted by the Torah and includes
halakhic as well as non-halakhic elements. What is quite innovative
in the context of Jewish theology is the Rav's acknowledgement of
the ontic and spiritually significant nature of the subjective religious
consciousness. This is the belief that Divinity manifests itself in human
consciousness not only in the rare and dramatic invasion of certain
human beings by the prophetic spirit, but also in the tensions and
conflicts, antinomies and polarities which are part of the general human
condition. In so doing, the Rav is acknowledging the presuppositions
of the phenomenological and existential approaches to philosophy
which he presents, at least in this essay, as a given with no indication
that it is derived from any Halakhah.[27]

However, the Rav goes on to state that because of the obvious
difficulties of reporting and analyzing what goes on in the subjective
realm, it can be reliably grasped only by reconstructing it from the
two objectified levels by a method of "descriptive hermeneutics."[28]
The Rav justifies such a reconstruction by positing a correlation between the subjective and objective levels so that any set of beliefs and
rituals on the objectified levels can be traced to and correlated with
the subjective sphere.[29] What remains unclear is the precise relationship
between these three levels of the "religious act." The Rav claims that
level 1 is "reflected" in levels 2 and 3, levels 2 and 3 are "evolved in
the objectification process," level 1 finds its "concrete expression" in
levels 2 and 3.[30] One has the impression that there is some natural
process whereby the original "spirit" that is experienced on level 1 is
then embodied, in some sense, in the objectified material on levels 2
and 3. If this is what happens, then indeed, one is justified in reconstructing level 1 out of levels 2 and 3, because in a sense its very
ability to appear on levels 2 and 3 constitutes a test of its strength,

durability and therefore authenticity. Thus, if certain sentiments about God appear in man's consciousness and are found reflected in related Halakhah, then the latter can justifiably be used to reconstruct the true nature and import of the former. According to this theory, the ritual and cult is to be regarded as the most fully evolved, concretized and therefore "highest" expression of religion and the Divine spirit. The ritual thus becomes the only reliable key to unlock the vital secrets of our religious consciousness.

In applying this general theory to Judaism, we must ask whether its underlying assumptions can be accepted. Can we say that religious subjectivity has this tendency to "flow" in the direction of objectification and that there is always some sort of "correlation" between the subjective and objective levels?[31] In Judaism, the ethical norms, cognitive-logico propositions and the halakhic rituals are believed to have been revealed to man by God and did not evolve by any natural process. We are under no necessity to assume that they are "expressive" of any antecedent subjective experience. However, in some cases, the rituals may very well be directed at certain recurring human experiences which are accompanied by typical subjective reactions. Thus, the Jewish rituals of mourning are obligatory after the death of close relatives. Here we can agree with the Rav that "the Halakhah is the act of seizing the subjective flow (the grief, the sorrow, and the bewilderment) and converting it into enduring and tangible magnitudes"[32] (the different periods of mourning: *onen*, seven days of mourning, thirty days, twelve months in the case of parents). And sometimes, someone with the insight of the Rav can indeed start with Halakhah and "reconstruct" by a process of "descriptive hermeneutics" the emotional depths of the mourner. However, neither this sequence, nor the correlation, nor the possibility of "reconstruction" seem to hold in every area of Halakhah. For example, in regard to the laws of prayer and the obligation to pray three fixed prayers at three fixed times of the day, the subjective-objective correlation may very well be reversed. That is, in this situation, unlike the laws of mourning, Halakhah may be impressive rather than expressive. Starting out, the worshipper may lack any distinctive religious consciousness, but may under the impact of his prayers begin to feel the Presence of God and other emotions. Here Halakhah is not the means by which to "reconstruct," but the instrument which creates subjectivity and impresses upon it a certain character. Then, there are still other areas of Halakhah, such as the dietary laws, divorce laws, and laws of ritual cleanliness, where there seems to be no obvious antecedent, inner correlation at all that is waiting to be "structured and ordered."[33]

However, the greatest difficulty in viewing H1 as the logical conclusion of the theory of religion developed by the Rav in *The Halakhic Mind* is the following. According to the Rav, the objectification of the religious consciousness takes place on two distinct levels that we have designated level 2 and level 3.[34] The Rav calls level 2 "theoretical," as it contains "logico-cognitive" and "ethical-religious" statements. But it is level 3, called "concrete deeds," which the Rav identifies with Halakhah and which he sees as "the single source from which a Jewish philosophical weltanschauung could emerge." However, the Rav's preference for level 3 over level 2 seems unjustified. The items on level 2 are clearly in the objective realm. Moreover, it is precisely the logico-cognitive and ethical-religious propositions that have, in fact, served as the primary sources for Jewish theology in the past. And, as the Rav himself says: "The canonized Scripture serves as the most reliable standard of reference for objectivity."[35] Indeed, the richest lodes of implicit theology that can be mined for an understanding of Jewish philosophy are still the first eleven chapters of Genesis, the Song of Songs, the Book of Job and Ecclesiastes—and they are part of level 2. Why then does the Rav give preference to concrete deeds, the ritual, as the source for "reconstruction"? Why does the Rav bypass the "ethical norms," although they, in a sense, also belong to Halakhah? If, like the Rav, one accepts the assumption that there is a "trend towards self-transcendence on the part of the spirit . . . that it strives to infiltrate the concrete world and that subjectivity rushes along a path that points towards externality, spatialization and quantification," then it follows that "concrete realization in external and psycho-physical acts is the highest form of objectification,"[36] so that ritual or Halakhah is to be preferred for purposes of reconstruction. However, nowhere is this assumption provided with philosophical justification.

The Rav, however, presents an additional argument for his thesis. He maintains that "religion is typified and described not so much by its ethos as by its ritual and cult" and "the unique character of a particular religion appears only in the ritual," while the existence of an ethical norm is a common denominator in all religious systems.[37] Yet there is good reason to believe that in Judaism it is the reverse. Ritual and cult have instrumental value, while what is unique in Judaism and of intrinsic value is precisely Judaism's understanding of the ethical, the relationship between God and moral values, and the nature of the human being.[38]

Thus, on the basis of the Rav's own designation that religious objective constructs are found in the "norms, dogmas, postulates of canonized Scripture," many of which are non-halakhic, and that from these objective expressions (level 2) the subjective levels can be reconstructed, H1 cannot be allowed the way it stands.[39]

However, in view of the centrality of Halakhah in Judaism, it would seem reasonable to postulate H3:

H3 . . . Any philosophy of Judaism, to be considered adequate, must be consistent with principles logically inferable from Halakhah.

Let us proceed to examine some of the Rav's philosophic writing to determine whether he employs Halakhah as the sole source of his theorizing about Judaism.

In arguing the importance of H1, Professor Marvin Fox focuses upon a particular teaching which he claims is paradigmatic of the Rav's practice of deriving theology from Halakhah.[40] In one of his most important essays, the Rav begins with a discussion of the theological problem of human suffering, which often cannot be explained on the basis of the principle of Provident reward and punishment or in terms of ensuring beneficial consequences.[41] Judaism, says the Rav, with its realistic approach, refuses to cover up or minimize the horror of evil in the world or to overlook the conflict at the heart of existence.[42] There is blatant evil, pain and suffering which cannot be overcome by speculative philosophic thought. This is because the human perspective is never based on more than a fragmentary view of life and history, so that the full picture, accessible only to God Himself, remains unknown.[43] Judaism bids the individual to confront his situation honestly and realistically and must ask: "What must the sufferer do so that he can get on with his life?" We are interested neither in the metaphysical cause of suffering nor in its purpose, but rather in the question: how is the individual to respond to his suffering? How may he elevate his suffering and weave it into the pattern of his chosen destiny in life?

Before the Rav introduces any halakhic source for this teaching, he states that it is the view of Judaism that man is obligated to creatively transform his fate into destiny so that when confronted by suffering, instead of idle speculation, he must perceive his situation as a challenge and seek to use it as a springboard for personal growth.[44] And for this the Rav provides prooftexts from the Bible, Deut. 4:30 and Jeremiah 30:7, to show that crisis can lead to repentance and to personal salvation. The Rav then goes on to show how this "practical" approach to the experience of suffering is reflected in the Mishnah: "Man is obligated to bless God for the evil which befalls him just as he is obligated to bless Him for the good."[45] According to the Rav, "blessing God" means more than saying "Thank You." Man is obligated to reevaluate his entire life in the light of his good fortune. So, too, the experience of suffering obliges the individual to step out beyond the experience and to consider new, creative initiatives in integrating his suffering into a religious blessing for himself and for others.

According to Professor Fox, "We have here one of the most clear and explicit cases in which important religious doctrine emerges from a proper understanding of the Halakhah[46] . . . halakhic norms generate theological principles[47] . . . It is the Halakhah, not abstract theological speculation, that teaches us that we must use our pain as an occasion for self-refinement and moral growth."[48]

Fox seems to be making two different claims:

(1) In "Kol Dodi Dofek," (pp. 65–74) the Rav presents us with a clear and explicit case in which "important religious doctrine" emerges from a proper understanding of Halakhah (Mishnah in Berakhot).

(2) In "Kol Dodi Dofek," (pp. 65–74) the Rav is saying that it is from Halakhah that we learn that we must use suffering as an occasion for self-refinement and moral growth.

I wish to argue that neither of these propositions is correct, i.e., the views attributed to the Rav are not found in this article.

(1) The "important religious doctrine" that Fox is referring to can only be the teaching that "we must use our pain . . . ." But this is a normative statement prescribing a certain attitude and mode of response, hardly an example of the philosophical world-view which analysis of Halakhah is supposed to generate. Even if the Rav does derive the teaching, "that we use our pain . . .", from Halakhah, it hardly is the "clear and explicit case" that exemplifies the general principle. Moreover, even if the "blessing" prescribed by the Mishnah is understood in the full sense of the Rav's interpretation, it implies nothing as to whether, after having made the blessing, one may pursue the philosophical question as to the meaning and significance of human suffering and whether it is reconcilable with God's moral character. From the fact that Halakhah as Halakhah addresses itself to the practical question of how one should existentially respond to suffering, one cannot infer anything as to the attitude of Judaism regarding the philosophical problem of theodicy. In fact, the Rav seems to base his assertion that, according to Judaism, seeking a purely philosophic-speculative solution to the problem of human suffering is futile, upon

(1) the fact that no adequate solution has to date been offered and (2) the argument that the perspective of the human being is too limited to enable him to understand.

Even the lesser claim (#2) does not seem to be borne out by the text. True, the Halakhah in the Mishnah in Berakhot as interpreted by the Rav seems to reflect the teaching that "we must use our pain as an occasion for self-refinement and moral growth," but it is not at all clear that the Rav presents this as his source. Indeed, there seem to be better reasons for considering the Biblical texts cited by the Rav, Deut. 4:30, Jeremiah 30:7, and the Book of Job, as his sources.

Fox makes the following statement: "Rav Soloveitchik replies to these questions (human suffering) with what he specifically labels a halakhic answer."[49] The passage that I believe Fox is referring to is the following:

> The halakhic answer to this question is very simple. Suffering comes to elevate the person, to purify his spirit and to sanctify him, to cleanse his thought and to purify it from all the dross, the superficiality and vulgarity and to broaden his horizons.[50]

A glance at the sentences immediately preceding this paragraph reveals that the "question" referred to is, "How shall a man behave in a time of trouble? What shall a man do so as not to be destroyed by his suffering?" In short, the term "halakhic answer" refers to the practical question: "How should a man react to suffering?" and not to the broader philosophical question of how to reconcile human suffering with God's morality. But surely this is not only the "halakhic answer" to this question, but also the answer of the aggadah: "Should a man see suffering come upon him, let him scrutinize his actions . . . if he does not discover the cause, let him attribute it to neglect of Torah . . . if he still finds no justification, it is certain that his chastenings are chastenings of love."[51] This aggadic answer asserts even more explicitly than the Mishnah that in terms of personal reaction, suffering comes to elevate the person, purify his spirit and sanctify him.

We have argued that no theological principle can be deduced from this Mishnah and that the Rav makes no claim to do so.

In further pursuit of the question of how the Rav treats Halakhah in developing his philosophical insights, let us examine the opening sections of what may be the Rav's most philosophical essay, "U-Vikkashtem mi-Sham."[52] Here the Rav paints on a very broad canvas indeed. He attempts to depict the complex, conflicted and tension-filled relationship between man and God over the vast range of human thought. He notes the areas wherein man has sought to catch a glimpse of a reflection of his Creator: in the drama of the cosmos, in the dark recesses of his own consciousness, in the moral will and in the voice of conscience. Ranging over the entire history of religious philosophy, the Rav shows how man's search for God has been disappointing and frustrating. While doing natural theology, he believes he has discovered God at the end of a rational argument, as a deduction from categorical principles, only to learn in a later period that the entire enterprise was misconceived inasmuch as the finite mind using empirical categories cannot infer anything about the transcendent and the eternal. Then man begins to look elsewhere in the presuppositions of his own consciousness, in his sense of ontological awareness, in his nameless yearning for something that nothing in this entire world can seem to assuage. Sometimes he does catch a glimpse of something sacred, of some transcendent meaning—but in a flash the perception is gone and one is not sure whom or what one has glimpsed. From the other direction, as God turns to man, the results are equally equivocal and disappointing. Often, man does not recognize the Presence of God in his crisis-filled situation. Often, man flees from His demand in fear of the responsibilities involved.

For the Rav, the dialectical character of the history of the relationship between man and God is also reflected in the religious consciousness of the individual. Contrary to those who present religion as "a realm of simplicity, wholeness and tranquility" for "embittered souls and troubled spirits," the Rav insists that the religious consciousness at its profoundest "is exceptionally complex, rigorous and tortuous, anti-nomic and antithetic from beginning to end."

It is in a condition of spiritual crisis, of psychic ascent and descent, of contradiction arising from affirmation and negation, self-abnegation and self-appreciation. The ideas of temporality and eternity, knowledge and choice (necessity and freedom), love and fear (the yearning for God and the flight from His glorious splendor), incredible and overbold daring and an extreme sense of humility, transcendence and God's closeness, the profane and the holy, etc., etc., struggle within his religious consciousness . . . it is a raging, clamorous torrent of man's consciousness with all its crises, pangs and torments.[53]

According to the Rav, these conflicting thoughts and feelings are not the result of confused thinking or psychological pathology, but part of what it is to be man. "This antinomy is an integral part of man's creative consciousness, the source of most of the antinomies and contradictions in man's outlook."[54] "*Homo Religiosus* is suspended between two great magnets, between love and fear, between desire and dread, between longing and anxiety. He is caught between two opposing forces—the right hand of existence embraces him, the left thrusts him aside."[55]

From whence does the Rav derive this depth of insight into the complexities of the God-man relationship? In the opening section of this essay, the Rav poetically portrays the dialectical relationship between the two lovers in the Song of Songs and presents this as the grand metaphor for the relationship between man and God: the going forward and the backing off, the tension between love and fear, searching and not finding, hesitation to respond when the beloved knocks. The following emotional, evocative passages are seen by the Rav as expressions of the conflicted character of the God-man relationship both in history and in the individual consciousness:

Draw me, we will run after thee (1:4)
Rise up my love, my fair one and come away (2:10)
I sought him but I found him not (3:1)

I will seek him whom my soul loveth (3:2)
I sleep but my heart waketh
Hark my beloved knocketh (5:2)
I have put off my coat
How shall I put it on? (5:3)
I opened to my beloved
But my beloved had turned away and was gone
I called him but he gave me no answer (5:6)
Whither is thy beloved gone? (6:1)
I am to my beloved
And his desire is towards me. (7:11)

"When man begins to draw close to God because he hears the voice of God travelling through the world, God distances Himself from him. The Infinite and man the finite seek but do not find each other. This dialectical drama reveals itself in its full strength and loftiness. Man remains alone. Who can save and redeem him from his loneliness if not the God who hides Himself from him."[56]

The analogy fits perfectly. But in what sense can the Song of Songs be said to be the source of the Rav's teaching that the God-man relationship is of this conflicted, tortuous character? After all, it is not literally found in the text. Once again, it is the Rav's "descriptive hermeneutics" that makes the connection.

In what appears to be an attempt to justify his interpretation, the Rav points out that it is the Halakhah which is the basis for the judgment that "if all songs are holy, the Song of Songs is the Holy of Holies," meaning that it is to be interpreted figuratively and never literally as a mere love song.[57] Are we therefore to infer from this that the Rav derived this most innovative teaching from the Halakhah? But all that the Halakhah establishes is that the Song of Songs is to be considered Holy Writ and not to be interpreted as a secular love song; precisely which interpretation should be given remains in the realm of aggadah. Thus, if the Rav decides to give the text a metaphysical-universal interpretation rather than the metaphysical-historical interpretation of Rashi and the tradition, the teaching acquires a midrashic warrant from the text, but hardly from the Hala-khah![58]

A quick survey of the entire essay reveals that in referring to the religion whose doctrines he is analyzing, the Rav uses the term "Juda-ism" at least 16 times, the term "Halakhah" some 12 times, and "Kabbalah," three times. In none of the contexts in which the term "Halakhah" is used is it suggested that a particular item of theology is being derived from the Halakhah. The Halakhah seems always to be presented in a supporting role to Judaism. Once a theological teaching has been declared integral to Judaism, by virtue of some Biblical text or aggadic teaching, it is shown to be reflected in some Halakhah (p. 16) or supported by the Halakhah (pp. 9, 24, 42, 61), or "then comes Judaism headed by the Halakhah . . ." (p. 39). Sometimes, of course, the Rav makes philosophical observations about the Halakhah itself (pp. 49, 55, 62). Of special interest is the Rav's use of the term "halakhic Judaism," which occurs in connection with three different theological teachings. Upon consideration it might be suggested that the Rav uses this term when he wishes to imply that in the absence of the corrective influence of the Halakhah, Judaism might have veered in a different direction: radical detachment from the material world (p. 59), concentration on either love or fear of God (p. 35), or a search for complete mystical union with God (p. 33). For the Rav, therefore, "halakhic Judaism" is not a Judaism that is derived solely from the Halakhah, but a Judaism in which the role of the Halakhah is both practical and philosophical.

Thus, in spite of the many references to the Halakhah in this major philosophical essay, the theological themes that are developed and presented by the Rav do not appear to be derived from the Halakhah.[59]

It was stated earlier that somehow, systematic exploration of the philosophy of Halakhah had been neglected. Yet the basic elements of such a philosophy can be found in Rabbinic sources and in the writing of recent Jewish thinkers, so that the main outlines of such a philosophy can be described. Here in sketchy form is what might be called a prolegomenon to a minimalist view, a theory which will describe the place and role of Halakhah within Judaism and which will do so by making only those assertions which are logically necessary to sustain the enterprise called "Halakhah." The adequacy of this theory is to be judged by whether it accounts for the central importance attached to the study and practice of Halakhah by the tradition.

Methodological Presuppositions

(1) The answer to the question, "What is the purpose of Halakhah?" which is a "second order question," cannot come from Halakhah itself, for the same reason that the answer to the question, "What is the purpose of playing chess?" cannot come from a study of the rules of chess.

(2) The answer, however, must come from within Judaism and not from cultural values outside of Judaism, regardless of how universal or self-evident they may appear. This has been stressed by the Rav: "It is impossible to reconstruct a unique Jewish world perspective out of alien material,"[60] and, before him, by S.R. Hirsch: "We must take up our position within Judaism, to seek to comprehend Judaism from itself, as it represents itself to be."[61] This applies to the efforts to discover the reasons for the individual commandments as well as to the philosophy of Halakhah as a whole.

(3) Halakhah is neither theology nor anthropology, but is based on both.[62] From the Bible and Rabbinic midrash aggadah comes a doctrine of God and a theory of man which are the pre-conditions of Halakhah and within which Halakhah as a whole is to be understood.

On the basis of the above, we may conclude that halakha's being essentially a collection of prescriptions and norms directed to man constitutes the instrumentality by which God, the Giver of Halakhah, brings about the ends He intends for man, His creature. This view locates the purpose of Halakhah in man and not in God or in the world. Thus, the Rabbis noted that the commandments were given "solely to purify" Israel and "make them worthy of life in the World to Come."[63] Deciding to live by Halakhah, behaving in accordance with Halakhah, and studying Halakhah all have crucial effects upon the consciousness, the personality and the moral makeup of man. Unlike some of the medieval Jewish thinkers, who saw only a social benefit in the practice of Halakhah,[64] we are stressing that the study and practice of Halakhah can bring about the spiritual and moral transformation of man which constitutes his salvation as intended by God. Unlike the mystical tradition, our "minimal" theory limits the consequences of halakhic practice to man rather than extending it to the cosmos.[65]

The Rav properly expresses the ultimate goal of Judaism in terms of the category of "Holiness-Kedusha." Judaism believes that the Divine Presence must be brought down into our concrete world so that the Transcendent can be experienced in our everyday lives. "Holiness is created by man, by flesh and blood."[66] Says the Rav:

> An individual does not become holy through mystical adhesion to the absolute nor through mystic union with the infinite nor through a boundless, all-embracing ecstasy, but rather through his whole biological life, through his animal actions and through actualizing the Halakhah in the empirical world. . . . Holiness consists of a life ordered and fixed in accordance with Halakhah and finds its fulfillment in the observance of laws regulating human biological existence such as the laws concerning forbidden sexual relations, forbidden foods and similar precepts.[67]

A similar thought is found in S.R. Hirsch:

> Law purifies and sanctifies even our lower impulses and desires by applying them with wise limitations to the purposes designed by the Creator. . . . Righteousness is the Law's typical end and aim.[68]

And so also A.J. Heschel:

> The deed is the source of Holiness. To the Jew the mitzvot are the instruments by which the Holy is performed. If man were only mind, worship in thought would be the form in which to commune with God. But man is body and soul and his goal is to live so that both "his heart and his flesh shall sing to the living God."[69]

The two divisions of Halakhah, the positive and the negative, the "dos" and the "dont's," are thus accounted for by David Shapiro: The positive in Halakhah reflects on a human level the creative activity of God. The negative bespeaks the finite and unredeemed character of the universe wherein the evil derived from man's freedom is countered by means of man's withdrawal from contact with it.[70]

One should add here the observation of Nahmanides that refraining from the negative commands responds to "fear of God," while observing the positive commands responds to "love of God."[71] This would bring into the very dynamics of Halakhah the dialectical polarities of the religious consciousness which the Rav sees reflected in the commands to love and fear God and in the divine attributes of *din* and *rahamim*.[72] The importance of this approach lies in its focus on the category of the Holy, which is a uniquely religious category and one central to Judaism.

But the ideal of becoming holy by means of Halakhah is given deeper meaning by the Rav by being placed within the broader framework of *imitatio Dei*. The very imperative in the Bible to be holy is couched in terms of *imitatio Dei*: "You shall be Holy, for I, the Lord your God, am Holy."[73]

• By exercising his freedom to choose the good and the true, man is fulfilling part of the Divine Image within him.

• By acting in accordance with Halakhah, man rises above being "a mere random example of his species" and acquires an "I" identity and becomes a possession of individual existence and even individual immortality.[74]

• By being creative in Halakhah, man imitates God, who is the supreme Creator—"Maker of Heaven and Earth."

However, the ultimate instantiation of man as creator in terms of *imitatio Dei* could hardly be one who intellectually creates abstract conceptual worlds in Halakhah. For, as the Rav states: "The peak of religious ethical perfection to which Judaism aspires is man as creator."[75] It is called "religious ethical perfection" because "the most fundamental principle of all is that man must create himself."[76] And self-creation makes sense only in religious ethical terms. Man, utilizing his divine trait of freedom and perceiving God as his model, remakes his personality to become truly merciful, kind, just and righteous. So that from being born in "the image of God" (with potentialities), man becomes in the "likeness" of God in reality. As the Rav acknowledges: "The whole process of self-creation all proceeds in an ethical direction."[77] Therefore, an alternative way of expressing the purpose of Halakhah might be: "Halakhah is the medium for the implementation of *imitatio Dei*,"[78] with the latter understood primarily in ethical terms.

If this sketchy outline of a minimalist philosophy of Halakhah be deemed adequate, how shall we judge the view of the Rav, which stresses the theoretical and cognitive importance of the study of Halakhah?[79]

The Rav states: "The Halakhah is not a random collection of laws, but a method, an approach which creates a noetic unity."[80] "The essence of the Halakhah which was received from God consists in creating an ideal world and cognizing the relationship between that ideal world and our concrete environment in all its visible manifestation and underlying structure,"[81] and again, "halakhic man orients himself to the entire cosmos and tries to understand it by utilizing an ideal world which he bears in his halakhic consciousness."[82] "The foundation of foundations and the pillar of halakhic thought is not the practical ruling but the determination of the theoretical Halakhah."[83]

We would seem to have here first an assertion as to what Halakhah essentially is, namely, a conceptual theoretical system which is directed at our cognition, and second, a value judgment. This latter refers to the classic issue of which in Halakhah is greater, study or deed.[84] And the Rav seems to be saying that intellectual creativity in the study of Halakhah is greater and is of value even in the absence of implementation. Let us first examine this value judgment.

What is the religious significance of discovering systematic connections between abstract concepts of Halakhah? In the words of the Rav: "Halakhic cognition unites the finite with the infinite."[85] In explanation, the Rav cites the views of both R. Shneur Zalman of Lyody and R. Chaim Volozhiner.[86] "When a person understands and grasps any Halakhah in the Mishnah or Gemara fully and clearly, that, for example, it is His will that in case Reuben pleads thus and Simon thus, the decision shall be thus, therefore when a person knows and grasps with his intellect this decision . . . he thereby comprehends, grasps and encompasses with his intellect the will and wisdom of the Holy One. . . ."[87]

"Through studying Talmud and commentaries and all the pilpulim, everything is made to cling to the Holy One, Blessed be He. . . . Since, He, His will and His word are one, by cleaving to the Torah it is as if one is cleaving to Him."[88]

As shown with incisive clarity and scholarship by Aviezer Ravitsky, the Rav bases his theory of human knowledge on the Aristotelian-Maimonidean principle of the unity of the intellect, the intellectually cognizing subject and the intellectually cognized object.[89] Thus, if the thought content of Halakhah is the revealed thought of God, then he who intellectually grasps Halakhah unites in some sense with God.

What is problematic about this theory, however, is as follows:

(1) It does not appear that Judaism is congenial to the proposition that the intellect is to be viewed as the main link between man and God. The views of Yehuda haLevi and Hasdai Crescas have generally been seen to be more "Jewish" on this subject

than those of Maimonides, in spite of the Rav's efforts to temper the strict intellectualism of Maimonides.[90]

(2) While Halakhah as a whole reflects the will of God for man, the content of the different parts of Halakhah might affect its ontological status. Thus, those portions of Halakhah which deal with moral norms, with the demands of the moral values of justice, righteousness and loving kindness can more easily be understood as part of reality and in some sense part of God Himself: "The Lord, the Lord God, merciful and gracious, long suffering and abundant in goodness and truth . . . ."[91] Thus, creative intellectual involvement in moral commandments of Halakhah could be defended as constituting communion with God. However, this would not be the case were we to focus on ritual aspects of Halakhah such as the theoretical concepts behind the dietary laws, which appear to be of instrumental value only.

We saw earlier that the Rav maintains that the study of Halakhah is a cognitive process which somehow is related to "understanding the entire cosmos." This is underscored by his statement in The Halakhic Mind that "the cognition of the world is of the innermost essence of the religious experience."[92] What is the relationship between knowing the theoretical Halakhah and knowledge of the real world?

Certainly, Halakhah itself was given to be "known." These rules obviously cannot be obeyed unless they are understood both in terms of (1) recognizing the situation in which they become applicable and (2) what one is called upon to do. On the theoretical level, Halakhah has constantly undergone a vast development in which the principles behind the practical observances were identified so that further extensions and distinctions could be made in the law. The master of Halakhah in both its theoretical and practical aspects could be said to have amassed a great deal of "knowledge." But knowledge of what? Essentially about Halakhah, which is in some respects an autonomous system.[93] But can it be said that Halakhah provides us with a knowledge of the "cosmos," of the "phenomenological reality?" Only perhaps as an indirect byproduct of our efforts to properly describe those aspects of reality which we must compare to the theoretical model in order to arrive at a halakhic ruling in an actual case.

On the highest level of halakhic scholarship, there is of course a process which might be called "creating an ideal world," which is the development of abstract concepts of great generality that range over diverse halakhic fields, which are useful in resolving contradictions and solving other related problems within Halakhah. However, the more abstract the concept, the more tenuous its link with "phenomenal reality," the less justification there is for calling it "knowledge."[94]

Thus, the sort of "understanding of the cosmos" that one could achieve by "orienting" oneself to it by halakhic concepts would appear to be extremely selective, fragmentary and one-dimensional. One would end up knowing a great number of disconnected particular things about a wide variety of phenomena significant only in terms of Halakhah.

The Rav asserts, "Halakhic man's ideal is to subject reality to the yoke of the Halakhah."[95] This suggests that the religious Jew somehow wishes to transform reality or perceives reality in some radically different way. Actually, the only way the halakhic master could make a proper ruling is to perceive reality just the way it is in all its brute facticity. And the ontological status of the chicken that is consumed after the halakhic ruling that it is kosher is the same and is as "real" as before. The only reality that Judaism would like to submit to "the yoke of the Halakhah" is the will and deeds of man.

It appears therefore to the present writer that the effort to endow creative study of the theoretical Halakhah as such with the ability to provide cognitive insight into the cosmos or mystical communion with the Revealer of Halakhah is open to serious objections. Moreover, it does not appear necessary for a minimal philosophy of Halakhah, which can otherwise meet reasonable conditions of adequacy.

Halakhah was given by God to His people to be developed creatively

so that it might be applied humanely to be observed diligently to
bring about ends which are for the ultimate edification of man and
society: as a medium for the implementation of *imitatio Dei*. Thus,
the real significance of Halakhah is instrumental rather than intrinsic,
"To bring down the Divine Presence into the concrete world," to
inject holiness into all aspects of life. Holiness is created by man
through actualizing Halakhah in the empirical world.[96]

Notes

1. Etymologically, the term "Halakhah" derives from the Hebrew verb, *halokh*, "to walk" or "to go," and, as a noun, refers to that portion of Biblical and Rabbinic lore which takes the form of laws and practices obligatory upon the Jew. In Talmudic literature, Halakhah is used in opposition to the term "aggadah," from the verb *le–hagid*, "to relate," which refers to types of material not encompassed by Halakhah, such as history, poetry, narratives, prayers, and theology. It is important to note that moral teachings are to be found both in Halakhah as well as in aggadah.

2. See Ephraim E. Urbach, *ha-Halakhah* (Yad laTalmud, Israel 1984), pp. 3–4.

3. See H.J. Leon, *The Jews of Ancient Rome* (Jewish Publication Society, Phila. 1960).

4. Kiddushin 40b.

5. Avot 3:2.

6. Yoma 67b on Levit. 18:4.

7. Avot 2:1, Sifra 45.

8. In the Talmudic period both were treated with equal seriousness. Certain rabbis were known as specialists in Halakhah, others in aggadah. There are no sages known as masters of Halakhah who did not also expound the aggadah. However, there are teachers of aggadah in whose name no halakhot have been recorded. There is no halakhic work from the Talmudic period in which aggadic teachings are not found. However, there are works of aggadah in which no Halakhah is found. What must be stressed is the interdependence of Halakhah and aggadah as indispensable constituents of Judaism, and at the same time their distinctive characteristics. Thus Kariv: "The Halakhah is the rigid skeleton of the life of Israel; the Agada is its soul and spirit." For example, the Halakhah of Shabbat treats the 39 categories of work forbidden on the Shabbat, while the aggadah speaks of the Shabbat Queen, the Shabbat as "wedded" to Israel, and the special "over-soul" acquired by the Jew on Shabbat. Heschel put it this way: "Halakhah without Aggadah is dead; Aggadah without Halakhah is wild." Contemporary Yeshiva heads prefer the expression: "Halakhah represents the bread and meat of Judaism; Aggadah contributes the seasoning."

It is difficult to formulate the defining characteristics (necessary and sufficient) of Halakhah in a way that would precisely separate out all that is considered Halakhah from all that is considered aggadah. For example, if we define Halakhah as including all those rules in Judaism which involve "doing," then we exclude what have been called "duties of the heart," which include the important mitzvot of love of God and fear of God and others. Alternatively, the term "Halakhah" can be given to any rule which carries an authoritative, prescriptive character. In this view, anything in Judaism which the individual is obligated to do or say or think or any attitude which he is commanded to adopt is part of Halakhah. This would leave to the aggadah descriptive propositions referring to history, the human being, and the actions of God in the world as well as rules whose observance is optional.

Maimonides, in his halakhic work, Mishne Torah, apparently uses a very broad definition of the term, as he includes material that is clearly of a philosophical, cosmological and psychological nature. Thus, a moral theory based on Aristotelian ethics and psychology is included in a section called Hilkhot De'ot—"The Laws of Moral Character." Another well known section is called Hilkhot Teshuvah—"The Laws of Repentance." But what part of the teshuva process is technically halakhic? Maimonides' own formulation seems to suggest that the mitzvah—obligation—focuses only on the recitation of the confessional (vidui). Are we to conclude that the entire subject of *teshuvah* in Judaism, with its profound philosophical, moral and psychological implications, are all a matter of Halakhah? See Kariv, Avraham, "Tefisat ha-Halakhah ba-Agadah," in *Hagut ve-Halakhah*, Y. Eisner, ed. (Misrad haHinukh ve-haTarbut, 1972).

9. With the important exception, of course, of Rabbi Samson Raphael Hirsch (1808–1888), whose contribution to this subject is of historic importance and whose views we shall cite later in this article.

10. Gershom G. Scholem, *Major Trends in Jewish Mysticism* (Schocken Books, NY, 1941), p. 28.

11. Rabbi Joseph B. Soloveitchick, *The Halakhic Mind* (The Free Press, Macmillan Inc., NY, 1986). Rabbi Joseph B. Soloveitchick, *Halakhic Man* (The Jewish Publication Society, Philadelphia, 1983), p. 137.

12. D. Singer and Moshe Sokol, "Joseph Soloveitchick: 'Lonely Man of Faith,'" *Modern Judaism*, Vol. 2, no. 3, p. 232.

13. *Mind, op. cit.*, p. 101.

14. *Ibid.*, p. 102.

15. Marvin Fox, "The Unity and Structure of Rabbi Joseph B. Soloveitchick's Thought," *Tradition*, Vol. 24, no. 2, p. 49.

16. Aviezer Ravitsky, "Rabbi J.B. Soloveitchick on Human Knowledge," *Modern Judaism*, Vol. 6, no. 2, May 1986, p. 181, note 12.

17. Reported by Rabbi Jonathan Sacks, Chief Rabbi of Great Britain, of a conversation he had with the Rav in the summer of 1967, *Jewish Action*, Vol. 53, no. 3, p. 30.

18. Rambam, *Hilkhot Teshuvah* 3:8.

19. S. Weisblat, "Pesukei Tanakh uMa'amarei Hazal keAsmakhtot leDe'ot Philosophiyyot," *Bet Mikra* (34).

20. Sifrei, Parshat Eikev, see Avraham Kariv, *MiSod Hakhamim* (Mossad haRav Kook, Jerusalem 1976), p. 22.

21. Deut. 4:39.

22. The method by which the theology is generated from Halakhah is called by the Rav "descriptive hermeneutics," p. 98, *The Halakhic Mind.*

23. *The Halakhic Mind, op. cit.,* pp. 68–69.

24. *Ibid.,* p. 75.

25. *Ibid.,* p. 66.

26. Berlin in the 1930's.

27. In his essay, *UVikkashtem miSham,* which we shall deal with later, the Rav associates the dialectic in the religious consciousness with the dialectic in the Song of Songs and the Divine attributes of *din* and *rahamim.*

28. *Mind, op. cit.,* p. 67.

29. *Ibid.,* p. 62.

30. *Ibid.,* p. 67.

31. *Ibid.,* p. 85.

32. *Ibid.*

33. *Ibid.,* p. 59.

34. See p. 6 above.

35. *Mind, op. cit.,* p. 81.

36. *Ibid.,* pp. 67, 68.

37. *Ibid.,* pp. 69, 70.

38. See Shubert Spero, *Morality, Halakhah and the Jewish Tradition* (Ktav-Yeshiva University Press, NY, 1983).

39. What is rather curious is that when Fox cites what he terms "the unifying principle in all of the Rav's work" (p. 49), namely, "the Halakhah is the objectification and crystallization of all true Jewish doctrine," he gives no written source for this quotation other than to say: "As he [the Rav] has often expressed it." However, if there is no other written source for H1 than these two sentences which I have cited from the very end of *The Halakhic Mind* (pp. 101, 102), then perhaps they should be understood strictly within the context of that essay, which, after all, was written in 1944 and published without revision. Perhaps the Rav never meant H1 as a sweeping generalization covering all of Jewish theology. Let us again examine the first crucial sentence of H1 (p. 101): "To this end (the end of discovering what is singular and unique in a philosophy) there is only a single source from which a Jewish philosophical weltanschauung could emerge: the objective order—the Halakhah." The Rav seems to be using the term "Halakhah" here as synonymous with "the objective order." Although we pointed out earlier that the Rav explicitly states that the "objective order" includes norms, beliefs, articles of faith, and religious texts (p. 99) which are not part of Halakhah, perhaps this can be justified in view of the Rav's stated conviction that the Halakhah is the "culmination of the entire process of objectification."

Consider the second sentence of H1: "Out of the sources of Halakhah, a new world view awaits formulation" (p. 102). Here it is possible that the term "world-view" is meant in the narrow sense of developing a unique Jewish vision of such abstract metaphysical concepts as time, space and causality towards which an analysis of certain aspects of Halakhah can be of crucial help (see p. 48 and 101).

Furthermore, this sentence, with which the essay comes to a close, may have a literary function, which is to dramatize what the Rav saw as the important implication of his theory, finding a central if not exclusive role for Halakhah in the development of Jewish theology. The need for this can be better appreciated if we realize that in the essay entitled *The Halakhic Mind*, the Rav does not deal with Judaism and Halakhah until page 91 of an essay which ends on page 102!

40. Fox, *op. cit.*

41. "Kol Dodi Dofek," included in the volume, *Ish ha-Emuna, me'et haRav Yosef Dov Soloveitchik* (Hotsa'at Mossad haRav Kook, Jerusalem, 1968).

42. *Ibid.*, p. 67.

43. The fact is that in Rabbinic literature, this question is repeatedly treated philosophically, as it was by medieval Jewish thinkers, although we do have a point of view among the rabbis that in principle this question does not allow for rational explanation. See Avot 4:19.

44. "Kol Dodi Dofek," *op. cit.*, last two lines on p. 67.

45. Berakhot 48b.

46. Fox, *op. cit.*, p. 52.

47. *Ibid.*, p. 49.

48. *Ibid.*, p. 54.

49. *Ibid.*, p. 51.

50. *Kol Dodi Dofek, op. cit.*, p. 68.

51. Berakhot 5a.

52. Yosef Dov haLevi Soloveitchik, *UVikkashtem miSham*, (HaDarom, Vol 47, NY 1978).

53. *Halakhic Man, op. cit.* pp. 141, 142, note 14.

54. *Ibid.*, p. 68.

55. *Ibid.*, p. 67.

56. "U-Vikkashtem . . ." *op. cit.*, p. 13.

57. *Ibid.* See footnote no. 1 on p. 67.

58. In footnote no. 1, the Rav claims that Bahya and Rambam adopt the metaphysical-universal interpretation. The Rav's claim that in essence both interpretations are one, is not convincing.

59. Fox makes the added claim: "Careful study of the *Lonely Man of Faith* will show that its conclusions derive from the Halakhah . . ." (p. 54). Yet the Rav states

explicitly in that essay: "My interpretive gesture is completely subjective and lays no claim to representing a definitive Halakhic philosophy" (p. 10).

60. *Halakhic Mind, op. cit.*, p. 100.

61. Samson Raphael Hirsch, *The Nineteen Letters of Ben Uziel*, translated by Bernard Drachman (Bloch Publishing Co., NY, 1942), p. 14.

62. See David S. Shapiro, "The Ideological Foundations of the Halakhah," *Tradition*, Vol. 9, nos. 1, 2, Spring–Summer, 1967. See also Shubert Spero, "Is there an Indigenous Jewish Theology?" *Tradition*, Vol. 9, nos. 1, 2, Spring–Summer, 1967.

63. Gen. Rabba 44:1, Makkot 23b. See also Num. Rabba, end of Skeloth.

64. See Maimonides, *Guide for the Perplexed*, Part III, Ch. 27.

65. See Hirsch, *op. cit.*, pp. 100, 138, 143.

66. *Halakhic Man, op. cit.*, p. 47. See also D.S. Shapiro, "The Meaning of Holiness in Judaism," *Tradition*, Vol. 7, no. 1, who claims that kedushah is basically an ethical value.

67. *Halakhic Man, op. cit.*, pp. 46, 108, 109. In a beautiful interpretation of Isa. 6:3 and its Targum, the Rav comments: "The beginnings of Holiness are rooted in 'the highest heavens' and its end is embedded in the eschatological vision of the 'end of days'—holy forever and to all eternity. But the link that joins together these two perspectives is the halakhic conception: 'Holy upon the earth, the work of His might—the holiness of the concrete."

68. Hirsch, *op. cit.*, pp. 100, 138.

69. A.J. Heschel, *Man's Quest for God*, (Charles Scribner's Sons, NY, 1954).

70. Shapiro, *Ideology of the Halakhah, op. cit.*, p. 106.

71. See Nahmanides on Ex. 20:8.

72. *UVikkashtem . . . op. cit.*, pp. 22–26.

73. Levit. 19:2.

74. *Halakhic Man, op. cit.* p. 1259.

75. *Ibid.*, p. 101.

76. *Ibid.*, p. 109.

77. *Ibid.*, p. 137.

78. Shapiro, *op. cit.*, p. 114.

79. There is always the nagging question whether the Rav intended the view of Halakhah he presents in Halakhic Man to reflect the view of normative Judaism or perhaps only as a philosophic rationale for the manner of Talmudic study found in the Lithuanian Rabbinic scholarly tradition.

80. "Ma Dodekh miDod," in *BeSod haYahid ve–haYahad*, p. 81.

81. *Halakhic Man, op. cit.*, p. 19.

82. *Ibid.*, p. 23.

83. *Ibid.*, p. 24.

84. Kiddushin 40b.

85. *UVikkashtem . . . op. cit.*, p. 204.

86. *Halakhic Man, op. cit.*, p. 148.

87. R. Shneur Zalman of Lyody, *Likkutei Amarim,* Part I, Ch. 5.

88. R. Chaim Volozhiner, *Nefesh haHayyim,* IV 8, IV 10.

89. Ravitsky, *op. cit.*, p. 162.

90. *UVikkashtem . . . op. cit.*, p. 68, footnote no. 2. See discussion in Y.J. Guttmann, *On the Philosophy of Religion* (The Magnes Press, Jerusalem, 1976) p. 89. See HaRav S.B. Orbakh, "Ha-Halakhah biTefisatam shel R"H Crescas Ve R"I Albo," page 43, *Hagut ve-Halakhah,* Shana 12, Arukh bi-ydei Dr. Yitzhak Eisner, Misrad haHinukh ve–haTarbut, Jerusalem TSL"G, for the views of Crescas and Albo.

91. Ex. 34:6.

92. *Halakhic Mind, op. cit.* p. 46.

93. It has been shown that the language of Halakhah is not a pure artificial language like mathematics, in which all of its terms bear symbolic meanings given to them by the system. Halakhic propositions are often formulated in terms of the natural language, which means that some halakhic concepts are not a priori. See the excellent article by Tzevi Zohar: "Al haYahas bein Sefat haHalakhah le–bein haSafa haTivit," *Sefer haYovel leHagaon Y.D. Soloveitchik* , vol. 1 (Mossad haRav Kook, Jerusalem 1984), pp. 59–72.

94. The analogy drawn by the Rav between halakhic concepts and the mathematical equations of physicists in regard to their relationship to reality has been subjected to criticism. See Rachel Shihor, "On the Problem of Halakhah's Status in Judaism," *Forum* (Spring–Summer, 1978), pp. 146–153; Kaplan, *op. cit.*, pp. 51–52 and Singer and Sokol, *op. cit.*, p. 236.

95. *Halakhic Man, op. cit.*, p. 29.

96. *Ibid.*, pp. 44–45.

In The Halakhic Mind, *Rabbi Soloveitchik articulates a profound religious philosophy which pervades his later works. William Kolbrener* (Tradition *30:3*) *offers a penetrating discussion of this complex work.*

The Rav argues for a new approach to the philosophy of religion. The quantum physicist, rather than the Newtonian rationalist or the subjective humanist, serves as the new model. The quantum physicist draws on both methodologies, recognizing the objective and subjective aspects which make sense of the world.

Philosophy of religion, for the Rav, is "an act of reconstruction." In order to understand objectified religious norms, one must penetrate into the subjective sphere. Interpretation of Halakhah is not merely a rational activity, but also entails a subjective, emotional involvement.

Towards a Genuine Jewish Philosophy

Halakhic Mind's New Philosophy of Religion

ঞ্চন

William Kolbrener

ড়৹৸

It is not so much the particular form that scientific theories have now taken . . . as the movement of thought behind them that concerns the philosopher. Our eyes once opened, we may pass on to a yet newer outlook on the world, but we can never go back to the old outlook.

—Sir Arthur Eddington[1]

Halakhic Mind,[2] written by the Rav, Rabbi Joseph B. Soloveitchik, in 1944 (but only published in 1986), proposes a new philosophy of Halakhah which emerges through a critique of traditional religious philosophy as well as its scientific and philosophical antecedents. *Halakhic Mind* is a difficult and arcane work, but it provides an intellectually exciting, challenging, and ground-breaking discourse on the integration of quantum physics, philosophy of religion and halakhic methodology. This essay presents an explication of the Rav's basic themes: the interrelationship of physics and epistemological theory, the development of quantum physics and the neo-Kantian theory of knowledge, and the emergence of a new philosophy of religion to replace that which had been shown to be outmoded by these new scientific and philosophical developments. After elaborating a practical application of the Rav's philosophy to Halakhah (the specific mitzvah of shofar), the essay explores how the Rav carried through this philosophy in his later works—particulary his "Kol Dodi Dofek"—in addressing the problem of evil.

It is worth mentioning at the outset that though a critical evaluation of *Halakhic Mind* is surely a desidaratum, the Rav's philosophical *oeuvre* has to a great extent been lost on a potential readership. Even more urgently than critical evaluation, readers need elucidation.[3] This essay is an attempt to provide such elucidation while also demonstrating the connections between one of the Rav's more popular works—"Kol Dodi Dofek"—and the more complex articulations of the philosophical writings examined here. Though the elaboration of the links between these genres of the Rav's writings is preliminary and perhaps skeletal, it will, I hope, demonstrate the value of bringing the various writings of the Rav into fuller conversation.

• • •

The discipline of philosophy of religion had for centuries been dominated by the methodology of first Aristotelian and then Scholastic philosophy, and afterwards by classical Newtonian science. In *Halakhic Mind*, the Rav proposes that the very paradigms which governed the inquiry of the religious philosopher were themselves outmoded. Thus, where the traditional philosophy of religion, like many of the contemporary human sciences, had been dominated by a search for rationalist explanation, the Rav radically undermines this project by arguing that the scientific and philosophical models that governed this quest had become untenable. While for centuries the Jewish philosopher had been forced into the posture of an apologist, defending religious experience in relationship to the apparently stronger truth claims of science or philosophy, the Rav, in *Halakhic Mind*, argues for the priority of Halakhah as the unique and automonous source of religious meaning.

For the Rav, however, the false detour that Jewish religious philosophy had taken through Greek philosophy, Medieval Scholasticism, and Enlightenment science, could be rectified only through those very languages of science and philosophy. That is to say, though the Rav affirms in *Halakhic Mind* that a Jewish philosophy of religion will ultimately emerge only from the Halakhah itself, the re-grounding of religious philosophy in Jewish Law is first and foremost a philosophical and scientific enterprise. In order to establish the priority of halakhic modes of consciousness and interpretation (as opposed to those modes promulgated by Enlightenment philosophy and science), the Rav turned in *Halakhic Mind* to what may seem to us as unlikely sources of inspiration: the neo-Kantian philosophy of Paul Natorp and the emerging scientific languages of the quantum physicist. From out of the new scientific epistemology implied in quantum mechanics, and with help from Natorp's philosophical concept of "reconstruction," a Jewish philosophy based upon the Halakhah could finally emerge.

In demonstrating the poverty of traditional religious philosophy—which was driven by the search for cause and the desire for rationalization—the Rav confronts on the one hand the explanatory arguments of Rambam in the *Guide*, and on the other, the explanatory arguments of liberal theology. Both posit an ideal outside of the halakhic process, a telos towards which the mitzvot themselves tend and under which they may ultimately be subordinated. In this, the arguments of *Halakhic Mind* parallel those of the Nineteen Letters of Rabbi Samson Raphael Hirsch, which explicitly associated the worldview implied in the *Guide* with that implied in the works of Moses Mendelssohn.

Hirsch saw both Rambam in the *Guide* and Mendelssohn in *Jerusalem* as taking their standpoint outside of Judaism, finding external reference points through which to explain and rationalize the Halakhah.[4] The liberal theologian, taking his cue from the rationalist philosopher, claimed to understand the reasons for the mitzvot and was thus able to reject their observance. In presupposing an independent realm of Truth or Reason, liberal theologians like Mendelssohn understood the law to be merely a formal mechanism subordinated to—and in the service of—a higher ethical ideal. As Hirsch explains, Mendelssohn's philosophical and aesthetic view of the Bible ultimately had its roots in the methodology of Rambam in the *Guide*.

In *Halakhic Mind*, the Rav joins a well-established tradition of anti-Maimonist argument: the author of the *Guide* was engaged in an "explanatory quest" by means of which "both mechanistic and teleological concepts of causality" explain religious phenomena "through the existence of an alien factor" (pp. 92, 93). Rambam of the *Guide* understood the mitzvot, especially the *hukim*, as themselves subordinate to an external principle. Such a methodology emptied the particular mitzvah of any positive content, relegating it as a mere means to a higher end. For example, the Rav writes:

> Should we posit the question: why did God forbid perjury? The intellectualist philosopher would promptly reply, 'Because it is contrary to the norm of truth.'

Such a response, the Rav continues, "would explain a religious norm by an ethical precept, making religion the handmaid of ethics"—as Halakhah gets pressed into the service of an abstractly defined Truth. The result of this rationalization is that religion no longer operates "with unique autonomous norms, but with technical rules, the employment of which would culminate in the attainment of some extraneous maximum bonum" (p. 93). Thus Rambam of the *Guide* erases particular halakhot under the sign of a higher ethical end (Truth, for example), to which they themselves are subordinated. To sanction the dietary laws on "hygienic grounds," or to see the Sabbath "against the background of mundane social justice" is to turn to an objective order outside of the Halakhah in order to justify it (p. 93).[5] In the formulae of the *Guide*, Halakhah is subordinated to Reason.

Rambam of the *Guide* had been dominated by a philosophical methodology, one "detrimental to the philosopher of religion" that continually asked what the Rav calls the "why question" (p. 98). Instead of focusing on the meaning of the mitzvah, Rambam of the *Guide* focused on its causes and was thus never able to penetrate into the meaning of the religious act for the Jewish consciousness. If Rambam of the

Guide had sought a justification of Halakhah through philosophical categories, then the modern philosophy of religion, which had emerged as a discipline in the wake of the triumph of the sciences, was even more indebted to rational modes of explanation. To transcend this philosophy of religion which—more obsessed than ever with the "why question"— had stultified in the sociological and anthropological explanations of liberal theology, the Rav turned toward the methodological innovations of contemporary science. The modern philosopher of religion who would explore the content of the religious act (asking "what?" and not "why?"), would have to turn to an unlikely mentor, the quantum physicist.

• • •

In *Halakhic Man*, the homo religiosus, with his mystical, other-worldly tendencies, acted as a foil to the *ish ha-halakhah*.[6] In *Halakhic Mind*, it is the Newtonian man of science who takes on the role of the adversarial anti-type. Aristotelian and Medieval Scholastic philosophy had privileged the objectivity of an independent and abstract Reason; the Newtonian scientist had come once and for all (it seemed) to announce the age of Enlightenment and the objectivity and rationality of a transparently ordered and quantified universe. Newton thus transformed a philosophical principle into a cosmic one, rationalizing the universe. As the Rav explains, the Newtonian interpretation of reality of the eighteenth century, as the Aristotelian and Scholastic interpretations before it, "both adopted a scientifically purified world as the subject matter of their studies" (p. 7). Both of these world views (though especially the latter) assumed the possibility of constructing a "purified" objective world coordinated through "abstract concepts and symbolic relational constructs." The philosopher, inheriting the objective world bequeathed to him by the traditional Newtonian scientist, was thus forced to inhabit the world that classical science had constructed. The philosopher was left to "roam a universe of quantitative relata and mathematical interdependencies"—a realm of quantified relations and causality (p. 7). The Newtonian cosmos worked like clock-work; it was left to the scientist and philosopher to explain its mechanisms.

Starting in the nineteenth-century and continuing through the early decades of the twentieth, physicists like Max Planck, Niels Bohr, and Arthur Eddington began to question the foundations of traditional Newtonian epistemology. The Newtonian philosopher, as we have seen, posited the existence of a universe which was rationally quantifiable and objectively given. The quantum physicist, by contrast, argued against the prevailing Newtonian notion of scientific objectivity. For one, the modern physicist, with new technical methods at his disposal, began to discover quantum—microscopic—phenomena which were unassimilable to the rigid and objective schemes of the Newtonian. That is to say, new technologies enabled the discovery of atomic and subatomic phenomena which did not conform to the Newtonian's rationalist map. The German physicist Werner Heisenberg coined his "uncertainty principle" to account for the uncertainty or indeterminacy in a world that had been presumed to be completely ordered, rational, and quantifiable.[7] And even worse, not only was the specification of the exact nature of objective reality rendered problematic, but quantum physics placed the ostensible objectivity of scientific observation in doubt. Indeed, a new generation of scientists were busy affirming that there was no such thing as the innocent observer standing outside or above an ostensibly pure objective reality. The scientist, practitioners like Niels Bohr demonstrated, was part of the experimental frame. As the experiments of the quantum physicist demonstrated time and again, the scientist helped to create his experimental "reality"; there was no such thing as purely objective data. The quantum revolution had therefore succeeded on two fronts: it assaulted the Newtonian belief in a rationally ordered objective world, while at the same time it questioned the Newtonian scientist's belief in his own methodological objectivity.

But, as the Rav demonstrates, the methodology—not to mention the ideology—of the classical physicist remained extremely durable. This Newtonian methodology is epitomized for the Rav in what he calls (following Max Planck) "atomization and piecemeal summation"—a method which "integrates the whole out of its components" (p. 56). The method applied by the Newtonian scientist "is the so-called explanatory method, which is concerned primarily with interrelations and interdependencies of successive phases in the objective order." Given the scientist's construction of the objective order out of "an aggregate of simple elements" (p. 31), it is left for him to search for a governing principle or cause which will account for their interrelation.

The Newtonian scientist thus "searches for order and regularity, for a causal nexus and a systematic sequence." "Knowledge," for classical science, is not concerned with content, but form. The scientist eschews investigations into the "thickness" of an object, and instead explores the "surface" of relationships, turning to an external source to order a disparate set of phenomena (p. 31).

In the Rav's explication, the methodology of the classical scientist does not "investigate A and B in themselves," but instead "attempts to determine the interdependencies" between A and B. These are nothing more "than ideal points which serve the scientist as a means to the examination of inter-relations, just as the single term in a series serves the mathematician in determining the character of that series" (p. 31). The classical Newtonian man of science who asks for the "relational necessity" between different phenomena "merely dots the path of appearances," constructing an "ideal order" which is coordinated with, but never penetrates into the "anonymity and mystery" of the "cosmic process" (pp. 31–32). Similarly, the traditional religious philosopher, who in an "act of surrender" inherited the method and explanatory telos of the Newtonian scientist, bound himself to a causal analysis which could never penetrate into the inner meaning of religious forms (pp. 7, 34). Burdened by the methods of the traditional scientist and the quantitatively constructed universe which he had bequeathed, "the philosophy of religion could not progress," and was left as a kind of disciplinary apologist for the cold calculus of the Newtonian (p. 39).

In response to the quantification of the world by the scientist and the philosopher, the humanist rebelled, throwing off the yoke of rationality, and cultivating, like the poet William Blake (an earlier rebel against Newtonian science), "impulse" and not "rules." But if the Newtonian scientist had erred in seeing the priority of the objectively quantified world (his world of fact), the humanist would err in his emphasis on subjectivity (his world of the mind and its constructs). Since science had claimed reason as its exclusive province, contemporary humanists were forced to take refuge in various "mystical" (sometimes irrational) movements—whether Henri Bergson's biologism and intuitionism, phenomenological emotionalism, or modern existential philosophy. Bergson, for example, in arguing that "biological and psychical phenomena" resist "a purely mechanistic explanation," sought to elaborate aspects of reality which Newtonian science—with its causal networks—had succeeded in occluding. Against the quantifying tendencies of the Newtonian man of science, Bergson advocated a kind of "intuition" or "intellectual sympathy" through "which one places oneself within an object in order to coincide with what is unique in it and consequently inexpressible" (cited on p. 35). Where the classical scientist had created a rationalist and quantified universe, the modern metaphysician, as a corrective, sought to give voice to those subjective experiences and insights which had eluded "conceptual abstraction" (p. 35).

Although the humanist (or modern metaphysician) sought to go beyond "the path of appearances" posited by the Newtonian scientist, there was nonetheless a "Janus-face" to his enterprise. For while the Newtonian scientist amalgamated the whole from out of its components, the "modern metaphysician" found the "whole" even before he had "apprehended the components." Indeed, the modern metaphysician, so taken with the subjective constructs of his own imagination, altogether denied the existence of the parts (p. 61). Though the humanist might vaunt his ability to explore the "mystery of phenomenal reality," his subjectivism was "pseudo-scientific," leading to both "scientific laxity" and "moral corruption" (pp. 46, 54). Without the "piecemeal contact with reality," presupposed in the world of the classical scientist, the modern metaphysician in his "romantic escape" from reason was left to wander in the "wilderness of intuitionism," falling into the trap of "excessive philosophical hermeneutics" (pp. 52, 60). For where "reason," the Rav writes in a more minatory tone, "surrenders its supremacy to dark, equivocal emotions, no dam is able to stem the rising tide of the affective stream" (p. 53).[8]

Having internalized the paradigms of Newtonian physics, the philosophy of religion had found itself trapped in the causal webs of the scientist—providing the same merely functional explanations of the spiritual world that Newtonian science had provided for the material world. As if to escape these causal webs, humanists and modern metaphysicians had abandoned the objective world of science and sought to found an "impregnable fortress" of "subjectivism"—abandoning any pretense of objectivity, and claiming as their own the subjective and spiritual world which the Newtonian had abandoned (p. 77).

Thus, on the one hand, the Newtonian man of science needed to be rescued from his simplistic view of the universe and the notions of causality which it implied. On the other hand, the humanist, who had come to describe aspects of reality which were impenetrable to the Newtonian scientist (even obscured by his methodology), needed to be rescued from the temptations of anti-intellectualism and irrationalism. The humanist, locked in his subjective constructs, denied the existence of objectivity; the Newtonian scientist, assured of the existence of his objectively posited world, altogether denied the importance of subjectivity.

The quantum physicist, in many ways the "hero" of *Halakhic Mind*, comes to reconcile these two opposed intellectual tendencies and to provide a true model for the religious philosopher by first redefining the assumptions and methods of classical science. The classical physicist had assumed a "purified" objective world and had manifested a faith in what the Rav calls a "copy realism" in order "to photograph reality." The physics of this century, however, began "to regard itself as a postulated discipline of pure constructs and symbols correlated with the given" (p. 31–32). The classical scientist maintained his faith in the objective world; the modern physicist acknowledged that the paradigms and structures of science were themselves merely constructs—artifacts which Eddington himself compared to symbolic or poetic forms.[9] As Planck wrote in the *Philosophy of Physics*, the physicist "merely creates an intellectual structure" which is "to a certain extent arbitrary" (cited on p. 111). If the Newtonian philosopher had assumed a perspective of objectivity, the quantum physicist would acknowledge that the scientist and his experimental paradigms help to create the reality which he surveys.[10]

Niels Bohr's work, in particular, demonstrates the way in which subjective constructs determine the nature of the objective world. Bohr's understanding of the "reciprocal relation of phenomenon and experiment" emphasized that the relation between subject and object must come up for reconsideration, and that the "claim of the natural sciences to absolute objectivity must undergo a thorough revision" (p. 25).[11] Subjectivity and objectivity were not—as both the Newtonian scientist and modern metaphysician had agreed—independent realms. They were instead reciprocally determining. If the humanist (celebrating subjectivity) and the Newtonian scientist (celebrating objectivity) had gone on their own paths, the Rav claims that their methodologies are in fact complimentary. The epistemology of the quantum physicist comes, then, to perform two functions: for one, it corrects the Newtonian view that the world is exhausted by objective description and causal analysis; secondly, it comes to correct the humanist view that the world is completely subordinate to subjective constructs.

The "mosaic" (or piecemeal approach of the Newtonian) and the "structural" (or wholistic approach of the humanist) are not then "two disparate methodological aspects which may be independently pursued." Rather, they form one organic whole. The quantum physicist applies both methodologies, beginning with the Newtonian frame of reference, and then reconstructing from the objectified world "structural patterns that enable him to describe the behavior of the simple elements which the atomistic method postulated" (p. 60). While the mechanist of old was content with a merely quantified and ostensibly objective physical world, his modern successor sought to reconstruct 'subjective' structural aspects which would make sense of the objective order. Thus, where the classical physicist looked outside the system for external causal factors to explain the relationships between components, the quantum physicist acknowledged that the "objective order" could only be understood through reconstructing a subjective "structural aspect" through which, paradoxically, that very objective order is configured.

It is here, the Rav writes, that the humanist and philosopher of religion finally found his "mentor."[12] For just as the quantum physicist acknowledges that subjective structures are part of his epistemological equipment (there is no absolute objectivity), so the modern philosopher of religion would have to acknowledge that the objective phenomena of religious experience must be coordinated with the subjective or qualitative spheres. Indeed, for the philosopher of religion who seeks the meaning of religious phenomena, the subjective stratum is primary: "any kind of relational postulation between the end-products of the series," the Rav observes, "must begin with the subjective phases of the process" (p. 72). The philosopher of religion cannot look outside the system. In order to understand a given objective order, he must understand "the subjective aspect of religiosity" by means of which external religious norms gain their significance. As opposed to "classical science," which "performs an act of construction to determine causality," the philosophy of religion, with its emphasis on "subjective aspects," performs what the Rav calls "an act of reconstruction." The religious philosopher, the Rav suggests, "is powerless to interpret his data unless he traces a positive set of beliefs, dogmas, norms and customs to the subjective sphere" (p. 73). To understand objectified religious norms ("those beliefs, dogmas, norms and customs"), one must penetrate into that subjective sphere through which that objective order has its being and meaning.

• • •

Where much of *Halakhic Mind* has its intellectual pedigree in quantum physics, the Rav's emphasis on the concept of "reconstruction"—the recovery of "subjective aspects" through attention to the objective sphere—has its pedigree in the philosophical work of the philosopher Paul Natorp. Natorp, with Hermann Cohen (about whom the Rav wrote his dissertation at Berlin in 1933) and later Ernst Cassirer, became affiliated with the school of Marburg Neo-Kantianism. In the last decades of the nineteenth century, in reaction to the excesses of Hegelian philosophical idealism and Marxian materialism, Cohen and Natorp turned their critical attention back to Kant—but they qualified Kant's approach in many respects. For one, where Kant's theory of "the thing in itself" seemed to imply a dichotomy between thought and being, Natorp and Cohen argued that thought and being only "have meaning . . . in their constant mutual relation to one another."[13] This emphasis clearly anticipated the relationship between subject and object posited in quantum physics. In *Halakhic Mind*, the Rav turns to Natorp for his articulation of the process of "reconstruction" which is an outgrowth of the general Marburg skepticism towards the distinction between subject and object.[14]

Quantum physics rescued the philosopher of religion from his slavish attachment to the objectivity of Newtonian science. Natorp's method of reconstruction ensured that such an attitude would not result in the subjective irrationalism of the modern metaphysical school. For though the Rav is emphatic that modes of description must follow the "subjective track" (p. 72), he is equally emphatic that the path towards subjectivity begins in the objective order itself. Just as the Rav, in his scientific register, acknowledges the priority of Newtonian "atomization" (though acknowledging its limitations), in a more strictly philosophical language, he also acknowledges the priority of what Natorp calls "objectification." In each field—physics and philosophy—"subjective aspects" can only be reconstructed from out of the objective data.

The Neo-Kantians, who, unlike Kant, "envisaged experience as moving from the objective to the subjective order," provide a groundwork for the Rav's philosophy of religion, where religious experience and consciousness must be understood through their antecedent in the objective world (and not subjectivity, as the avatars of reform theology continue to claim).[15] "Subjectivity," the Rav affirms, "cannot be approached directly." It "is impossible," the Rav continues, "to gain any insight into the subjective stream unless we have previously acquired objective aspects" (pp. 73, 75). As Natorp himself writes more explicitly:

> The constructive objectifying achievement of knowledge always comes first; from it we reconstruct as far as possible the level of original subjectivity which could never be reached by knowledge apart from this reconstruction which proceeds from the already completed objective construction. In this reconstruction we, so to speak, objectify subjectivity as such . . .[16]

For Natorp, as for the Rav who follows his methodology, subjectivity (and by this term the Rav means to include all aspects of religious consciousness), is in and of itself unavailable to the philosopher of religion and can only be reconstructed retroactively through attention to the objectified world. Subjectivity, as Natorp relates, can only be "reached" through objectivity. There are no short-cuts to religious subjectivity and religious consciousness.

Though the Rav, following Natorp, emphasizes the precedence of objectivity, such an emphasis is of "theoretical value only" (p. 66). Pure subjectivity and pure objectivity, in this model, are simply limiting abstract cases (p. 66). Accordingly, the Rav claims, "we do not find two different components, the subjectively given and the objectively constructed, but one unified phenomenon" (p. 66). The religious philosopher, like the scientist, finds that "subjective" constructs and paradigms at once produce and are a product of the already constituted object, and as a consequence, religious knowledge can only be inferred—that is, reconstructed—through reference to that which is already given, the field of objectification. In modern physics, the objectification of reality is the necessary antecedent for exploring qualitative or subjective aspects. Similarly, the religious philosopher—no longer indulging in the excesses of the modern metaphysician—relies upon the objectification of experience before analyzing the subjective or structural constructs which in turn lend them meaning.

The emphasis upon subjectivity finally allows the religious philosopher to penetrate beyond the causal framework which had heretofore been the domain of the traditional humanist. That is to say, where the Newtonian scientist and the philosopher of religion who had followed his causal methodology had been able to construct "abstract general interdependencies" between the data, the new philosopher of religion—freed from the concept of objectivity enshrined in classical science—turned towards what the Rav calls "penetrative description" (p. 98). The new philosopher of religion, understanding that it is "impossible to discover final causation in the spiritual realm" (p. 74), embraces a form of "penetrative description" which leaves causal certainty for the "thickness" of varied descriptions.[17]

Taking up the ostensible causal relation in the history of philosophy between Maimonides and Thomas Aquinas, the Rav elaborates a process of reconstruction by which the "causal nexus" between the two thinkers is rendered "nonsensical." Out of their "philosophical systems," one can reconstruct both their different "philosophical temperaments" and the kinds of "methodological reasoning" which they employed. "Our exploration of the subjective route," the Rav continues, does not stop with this phase but proceeds to penetrate further into the complicated and mysterious sphere of subjectivity. Through the individual subjective philosophizing the clandestine ego emerges from its involuted and ramified recesses. Yet, however far the regressive movement continues, we are never quite able to fathom subjectivity. What we call subjectivity is only a surface reproduction which still needs exploration (p. 73).

The traditional philosopher of religion finds a causal relation of necessity which once and for all unifies a series of disparate objective phenomena. For the modern philosopher of religion, however, the method of reconstruction leads only to an infinite regress. Descriptions become thicker, but they never exhaust the object. There is no decisive endpoint to this analysis, for "any subjective stage to which we may point with satisfaction can never be ultimate." "We may always," the Rav writes, "proceed further and discover yet a deeper stratum of subjectivity" (p. 74). But for the Rav, the fact that "reconstruction" never yields definitive explanations and proceeds infinitely to different levels of description, is not a methodological liability, but rather an advantage. Though it does not yield the certainty of explanation provided in the traditional human sciences, it does however offer "a multidimensional religious outlook to the homo religiosus" (p. 88). No longer "limited to causal designs," the philosopher may survey those subjective aspects in a process of interpretation, which will always require "further exploration."

• • •

It is no surprise that Natorp's emphasis upon objectivity was of such great appeal to the Rav. For with a shift in emphasis, the Rav could transform Natorp's affirmation of the primacy and priority of the objectification of *a priori* mental categories to the primacy and priority of the objectification of Halakhah.[18] Jewish religious subjectivity, then, is accessible only through an examination of the objectified religious norms—an objectification that "culminates in the Halakhah" (p. 99). For the Rav, the "canonized Scriptures," or what he calls the "Deus dixit," serve as "the most reliable standard of reference for objectivity." Through the method of reconstruction, which begins with the objectified world of Halakhah, "God's word, 'the letter of the scriptures, becomes an inner word, a certainty, insight, confession' of the God-thirsty soul." By attending to the objective forms as a point of departure—here the Halakhah—one may gradually "reconstruct underlying subjective aspects," and arrive at that "inner word" of the "God-thirsty soul" (p. 81).

The Jewish religious philosopher who seeks to penetrate into the "thickness" of religious phenomena will turn away from elegant patterns of relation and causality, and towards the subjective aspects through which the objective phenomena derive their meaning. "To analyze the mystery of the God-man relation," for example, "it would be necessary that we first gather all the objectified data at our disposal: passages in the Holy Writ pertaining to divinity . . . , all forms of cult, liturgy, prayer, Jewish mysticism, rational philosophy. . . , etc." Only after examining this "enormous mass of objectified constructs" can the "underlying subjective aspects . . . gradually be reconstructed" (p. 91). The complex explication of quantum physics and Marburg Neo-Kantianism thus leads to an elaboration of religious subjectivity which begins in the realm of objectivity—the Halakhah itself. Where in the past, Halakhah, to adjust Philo's phrase, had been the "handmaiden of philosophy," in The *Halakhic Mind*, philosophy and science become the handmaids of Halakhah.

Which leads us back to Rambam. For though Rambam of the *Guide* anticipated the explanatory methodology of the contemporary human scientist, privileging cause over description, Rambam of the Code pursued an entirely different methodology. In the *Guide*, to use the vocabulary that the Rav developed in the first sections of *Halakhic Mind*, Rambam was obsessed with the "explanatory quest": instead of describing, he explained, and instead of reconstructing, he constructed (p. 92). But Rambam "the halakhic scholar," the Rav argues, "came nearer the core of philosophical truth than Maimonides, the speculative philosopher" (pp. 93–94). To the Rav, for whom the core of philosophical truth lies (paradoxically) within the Halakhah itself, the Code, which attempts to "reconstruct" the "subjective correlative" of the commandments, is far superior to the "causal method of the philosophical *Guide*" (p. 94). In contrast to the methodology of the *Guide*, in which Rambam "objectifies the datum and subordinates it to a superior order," Rambam of the Code, by "exploring the norm retrospectively," preserved the unique structure and autonomy of the religious act (p. 95).

To demonstrate the differences in these methodological approaches, the Rav turns to an analysis of the mitzvah of shofar, quoting Rambam of the Code:

> Although the blowing of the shofar on Rosh Hashana is a decree of the Holy Writ, nevertheless there is a hint to it, as if saying, "Ye that sleep, bestir yourselves from your sleep, and ye that slumber, emerge from your slumber. Examine your conduct, return in repentance and remember your Creator" (p. 94).

By stressing the "reservation that the sounding of the shofar" is a decree of the Holy Writ (a *gezerat ha-katuv*), Rambam, the Rav writes, means to exclude any possibility of "causal interpretation." The very fact that it is a *gezera* makes it unassimilable to causal analysis (in the same way that a *hok* is unassimilable to such analysis). But when he points to "a hint" in the commandment (*remez yesh bo*), Rambam leaves, the Rav explains, "causality and teleology" behind, and "leads us into a new realm of philosophical heremeneutics" (p. 95).

Where Saadia, "entrapped" in the same kind of "causal maze" that Rambam had constructed in his *Guide*, explained that the sounding of the shofar "is reminiscent of an ancient nomadic period when it served as a signal for alarm or as a summons to joyous celebration," Rambam of the Code avoids such causal explanation. Saadia's explanation is "based upon a two-valued logic which entails necessity." Which is to say that the "mechanistic relation" between the mitzvah of shofar and the ancient nomadic custom is, for Saadia, "unique and necessary" (p. 95). Once understood in this fashion, the philosopher's work is done, and he is left only to admire the elegance of his construct. But for Rambam of the Code, who turns from such construction to reconstruction, there is no "relational necessity" that governs and limits interpretation.

Indeed, the new "philosophical hermeneutics" to which Rambam leads us does not end in a singular interpretation derivative from an external cause (a kind of anthropological necessity, as in Saadia's description of kol shofar). But rather, in opposition to Saadia, for

Rambam of the Code, the shofar merely "alludes" to "repentance and self-examination" (p. 95). In this analysis, "it does not follow that the sounding of the shofar is a necessary and sufficient means for the end of inspiring man to penitence and conversion" (p. 95). In contrast to Saadia, who constructs a relationship of necessity, for Rambam, "the call to repent could have been realized in many ways and there is no necessary reason why the Torah selected the means of the shofar" (p. 95).

The fact that there is no "necessary reason" opens the way up for a hermeneutics which is freed from the schematic simplicity of an older philosophical tradition, and is able, through an analysis of the mitzvah itself, to discover those "subjective correlates" which help make sense of what the mitzvah entails. In turning from the "why" question (which, we recall, is "detrimental to religious thought") to the "what" question, Rambam finds a way to grasp "the general tendencies and trends latent in the religious consciousness" (pp. 98, 99). In Rambam's "descriptive hermeneutics" (p. 98), there is no necessary relationship between cause and effect, but a call for continuous description and interpretation.[19]

A cause is determined once and for all; a "hint" or "allusion" demands continued interpretive vigilance. "The reconstruction method," the Rav writes, "neither claims that the subjective counterpart would only be crystallized in one particular way, nor does it explain how it was finally reflected in its objective form" (p. 96). The speculative philosopher whose hermeneutics are governed by such a necessity, may provide philosophical certainty. The "profound religious mind," however, is "averse to the platitudes" which the philosopher constructs to "circumscribe the religious act." For in this process of circumscription, he also deprives it of its "meaningful content" and "essential significance" (p. 97). Though the halakhic mind eschews certainty in interpretation, his triumph is in proving that the quest for meaning in interpretation is unending. Herein lies the (perhaps paradoxical) superiority of the *ish ha-halakhah*: it is a superiority that begins with the knowledge of a demand. Where the philosopher dispenses with his obligation to interpret in a single interpretive stroke, the *ish ha-halakhah* can never free himself from that obligation. For him, the continuing demand for interpretation is the guarantor for a total engagement and immersion in the mitzvot themselves.

Singer and Sokol, in their radical critique of *Halakhic Man*, have perhaps underestimated the extent to which interpretation, for the Rav, entails total individual engagement. For them, the Rav of *Halakhic Man* must have been rebelling against a "Litvak tradition" simply "too cold, too rational," and "too unyielding to the emotions."[20] But, if the Cartesian model for man is the man who thinks, then the Rav's model is clearly the *ish ha-halakhah*—the man who interprets.[21] Though it may be true that the "'book' of Halakhah, replete with triangles, circles and squares," seems separated—by "an enormous distance"—from its "subjective counterpart" (p. 85), the interpretation of this objectified realm is not a merely rational activity obsessively compelled by the details of intellectual geometry (as Singer and Sokol seem to imply).

The halakhic mind, who in his interpretation of the Sabbath, for example, turns from a merely functional interpretation of the Sabbath (as leading towards a goal of "mundane social justice") to a "symbolic strain," is able, the Rav affirms, to penetrate "infinity itself." When Rambam of the Code envisages the Sabbath "as the incarnation of the mystery of creation," he is able to discover in the objective world, in "dead matter and mechanical motion," the "fingerprints of a Creator." In a moment that reveals the extent to which the Litvak ostensibly immersed in the rationalism of Halakhah celebrates the pleasures of interpretation, the Rav confides, "it is superfluous to state that the *homo religiosus* finds delight in such an interpretation" (p. 98). Though it is a moment of understatement, the Rav reveals here that though interpretation is surely a cognitive act, it is the beginning of (perhaps even the prerequisite for) a total relation—cognitive, emotional, and spiritual—to the mitzvot.

• • •

Halakhic Mind is not, despite its difficulty and arcane intellectual debts, a mere eccentricity in the Rav's canon of writings. To the contrary, the Rav's later works are steeped in the religious philosophy articulated in *Halakhic Mind*. In his "Kol Dodi Dofek," for example, which includes an extended meditation on the Shoa and the existence of evil, the Rav extends the arguments of *Halakhic Mind* to their most radical conclusion. Where the Rav had earlier argued for a religious philosophy which would face up to the demands of individual mitzvot, in "Kol Dodi Dofek," he demonstrates how this religious philosophy—which, like *Halakhic Mind*, assiduously avoids causal explanations—requires man to face up to evil. Although this is not an exhaustive analysis of "Kol Dodi Dofek," it should, however, anticipate a fuller study in which the Rav's various works can be understood as forming a more complete whole.

"Kol Dodi Dofek" begins with a type whom we can recognize as a not-too-distant descendant of the philosopher of religion of *Halakhic Mind*. Faced with the existence of evil in the world, the speculative philosopher tracks the intellectual foundations of suffering and evil, and seeks to find the harmony and balance between the affirmation and negation and to blunt the sharper edge of the tension between the thesis—the good—and the antithesis—the bad—in existence.[22]

Such speculations, the Rav continues, permit the philosopher to develop "a metaphysics of evil." But this metaphysics, by means of which the philosopher is "able to reach an accommodation with evil," in actuality only succeeds in covering it up. For the sufferer (following his own speculative tendencies), utilizes his capacity for intellectual abstraction to the point of self-deception—the denial of the existence of evil in the world.[23]

Though the Torah provides the testimony "that the cosmos is very good," this affirmation, the Rav writes, "may only be made from the infinite perspective of the Creator." Therefore, though the Rav of course does not argue against the implicit telos in history, he does claim nonetheless that the consolations that such an end of history may provide are for man—as a temporal creature—irrelevant. "Finite man, with his partial vision, cannot uncover the absolute good in the cosmos." This epistemological limitation is thematized in the story of Job, whose insistent desires for metaphysical explanation and consolation—his desire to transcend the limitations of human knowledge—are repeatedly rebuffed by God: "If you do not even know the ABC of creation, how can you so arrogantly presume to ask so many questions regarding the governance of the cosmos?"[24]

When Job engages upon his quest for philosophical answers to the metaphysical problem of evil, he is fulfilling the role of what the Rav calls Job's character as a "man of fate." Fashioned as he is by a wholly "passive encounter with an objective, external environment," Job, as the man of fate, confronts the evil of his external environment with a sense of astonished and helpless disbelief. Job's passivity before an evil which he cannot comprehend leads him towards philosophy—to the question of "why?" Job, as the first philosopher of religion, "relates to evil from a nonpractical standpoint and philosophizes about it from a purely speculative perspective."[25]

This philosophical attitude may, as we have seen, seem to contain its own consolations: the man of fate can attempt to view his current sufferings retroactively from a hypothetical future which he knows to be wholly good. But the attempt "to deny the existence of evil and create a harmonistic worldview" from a perspective ostensibly external to history, will always end in "complete and total disillusionment." The man of fate who sees his own existence as a function of a providential narrative may look to the end of History to justify a world which seems to depart inexplicably from its promised telos, but this is just a ruse—a recipe for self-deception. The Rav's refusal of metaphysics implies, then, an utterly uncompromising view of history in which the afflictions of the present historical moment do not open up gracefully to a future which guarantees bliss and consolation. Just as the mitzvot in *Halakhic Mind* retain their individual autonomy, so here evil remains "an undeniable fact," wholly unassimilable to any philosophical or theological visions of the future.[26] If the mitzvot of *Halakhic Mind* cannot be circumscribed and explained, so evil in "Kol Dodi Dofek" cannot be contextualized and understood.

We might say that evil, in the Rav's religious philosophy, has the status of a hok; it exists without apparent reason. No amount of philosophical explanation or speculation can erase this existence. Though the philosopher works tirelessly to develop a perspective which will explain evil and nullify its force, the "man of destiny" (who stands, in "Kol Dodi Dofek," at the opposite end of the spectrum from the "man of fate") experiences evil without recourse to the benevolent backward glance of an already fulfilled History. He does not experience such a moment as intrinsically meaningless. That is to say, he does not view history as recapitulating endlessly the "tomorrow, and tomorrow, and tomorrow" of Shakespeare's Macbeth, or the "gray on gray of history" which Hegel associated with a meaningless seculum. There is no despair of a loss of a sense of purpose to history, because for the Rav, purpose or telos is never the proper concern of the subject faced with the complexities of the historical process.

The man of destiny, disburdened of the old philosophical assumptions, faces up to the stark demands which reality makes upon him. Indeed, for the "man of destiny," the evil and suffering in history stand, like the *hukim* of the Torah, as a form of demand. Just as "asking 'why' God issues certain commandments is seeking to comprehend the unfathomable," so the question about the existence of evil, to him, "remains obscure and sealed, outside the domain of logical thought."[27] That is to say, *hukim*, for the man of destiny, neither provide occasions for rationalizations (we do not ask, for example, why God instituted the *para aduma*), nor, however, do they provide a justification for a stupefied silence before God's law.[28] Though we may not ask "why" in relation to these *hukim*, it is incumbent upon us, as the Rav's analysis of Rambam in *Halakhic Mind* reveals, to inquire into what these *hukim* might mean. In the light of the Rav's reclamation of religious philosophy in *Halakhic Mind*, the *hukim* of the Torah, and the hok of evil, become invitations to interpretation, what Pinchas Peli has called "derush"—but not to philosophical explanation.[29] In other words, there is no escape into ostensibly objective causal networks that come from outside to explain away evil (or a seemingly irrational mitzvah like the para aduma), but there is instead a constant demand upon the subject—for cognitive engagement and interpretation. The *hukim*, the Rav writes, must be "interpreted in terms of their subjective meaningfulness to us even if their objective rationale eludes us."[30]

Man's obligation, according to the Rav, in regards to evil and the suffering it imposes, is not then to resolve (and here we can hear distinct echoes of the earlier philosophical work) "the question of the causal, or teleological, explanation of suffering in all of its speculative complexity but rather the rectification of suffering in all of its halakhic simplicity."[31]

Evil, like the *hukim*, contains its own imperatives: "The Halakhah teaches us that the sufferer commits a grave sin if he allows his troubles to go to waste and remain without meaning or purpose." Suffering is pulled out of the 'nightmare of history' not through reference to a perspective external to it, but through "subjective interpretation"—a personal appropriation and "rectification" of suffering. The question, according to the Rav, is not, "how is this suffering resolved in History?" but rather, "What does this suffering mean to me?" The "man of destiny," equipped with a philosophy of religion that has its genealogy in *Halakhic Mind*, leaves the passivity of the "man of fate" through a form of engagement—that is, interpretation—which makes his history his own.

In the stark and demanding arena of the halakhic mind, there is no consolation of metaphysics. Every aspect of reality resounds with a call—a demand. In asking "why?" the speculative philosopher refuses such a demand, remaining satisfied with his impeccable causal schemes and the consolations that metaphysics affords. In contrast, the halakhic mind, in asking "what?" (what is this suffering?; what is this mitzvah?) responds to the continuous demands of life through an unending journey into the "mysterious spheres" of interpretation.[32] This is not, however, merely a cognitive process (pace Singer and Sokol), but a process that ultimately transforms and elevates the individual, from "object to subject, from thing to person."[33] In transcending a philosophical and scientific legacy which turned away from the matters of existence—whether it be the objective religious forms, or evil in all of its unassimilable waywardness—the halakhic mind, with his own religious philosophy, finds an infinite opportunity for individual engagement and self-transformation. Indeed, the halakhic mind responds to this opportunity, foregoing the passive rationalization of the traditional philosopher, and making the choice (albeit the sometimes painful one) for a perspective that leads towards the rectification of the world—not the deceptive consolations of an outmoded philosophy.

Notes

1. A.S. Eddington, *The Nature of the Physical World* (New York: Macmillan, 1929), p. 318.

2. Joseph B. Soloveitchik, *Halakhic Mind* (London: Seth Press, 1986). All page references are to this edition.

3. For early review essays of *Halakhic Mind*, see Michael Gillis, "The Halachic Mind," *L'Eylah* 24 (1987): 37–40, and Jonathan Sacks' more thorough, "Rabbi J.B. Soloveitchik's Early Epistemology: A Review of *The Halakhic Mind*," *Tradition* 23:3 (Spring 1988): 75–87. For a more recent—and less orthodox—approach, see "Joseph B. Soloveitchik's 'The Halachic Mind': A Liberal Critique and Appreciation," *CCAR Journal* 41 (1994): pp. 55–63. Lawrence Kaplan, "Rabbi Joseph Soloveitchik's Philosophy of Halakhah," *Jewish Law Annual* 7 (1988): pp. 139–197, articulates the contours of the Rav's legal philosophy, and demonstrates, among other things, the ways in which the Rav's methodology was indebted to the methodology of the mathematical sciences. Kaplan, in his otherwise comprehensive consideration of the Rav, only briefly comments on *Halakhic Mind*, what he calls "a highly technical and abstract philosophic monograph" (p. 143). Kaplan's approach, it should be emphasized, stresses that the Rav's radically new articulation of halakhic methodology paralleled the revolution achieved in the sciences through the works of Galileo and Newton. This essay, focusing as it does on *Halakhic Mind*, argues that the Galilean-Newtonian revolution only provides part of the groundwork for the Rav's halakhic methodology, while the quantum revolution in physics establishes the other part of that ground.

4. "Moshe ben Maimon, Moshe ben Mendel—are they in fact Moshe ben Amram?" Hirsch caustically asks. Of Rambam of the *Guide*, Hirsch writes: "His trend of thought was Arab-Greek, as was his concept of life. Approaching Judaism from without, he brought to it views that he had gained elsewhere, and these he reconciled with Judaism . . . he delved into speculations about the essence of God and considered the results of these speculative investigations to be fundamental axioms and principles of faith binding upon Judaism." *The Nineteen Letters*, Joseph Elias, trans. (Jerusalem: Feldheim, 1995, p. 265). On Hirsch's complex relation to Rambam, see Elias' notes to "Letter Eighteen," pp. 284–291.

5. Perhaps the locus classicus for this kind of anthropological explanation is the sacrifices. In the *Guide*, the Rav writes, Rambam describes the sacrificial service as "just an educational method of elevating the Jew above such forms of worship." "In order to direct the Jew towards worship of God," the Rav writes, "the Torah made the concession of animal sacrifice." On Rambam of the *Guide*, and the Rav's critique of this of Maimonidean rationalization, see p. 131.

6. R. Joseph Soloveitchik, *Halakhic Man*, trans. Lawrence Kaplan (Philadelphia: Jewish Publication Society of America, 1983), passim.

7. In Heisenberg's own experiments, he demonstrated that it was impossible to identify both the position and momentum of subatomic particles (electrons). As a recent popularizer of quantum physics explains, in the new Heisenbergian world, "we pay a price for our acts of observation. Each act is a compromise. The more we atttempt to measure the position of an electron, the less we can determine its momentum, and vice versa. . . . This uncertainty meant that no matter how accurately one tried to measure the classical quantities of position and momentum, there would always be an uncertainty in the measurement." Indeed, it is this uncertainty that lies at the very foundations of the quantum world. See Fred Alan Wolf, *Taking the Quantum Leap* (San Francisco: Harper and Row, 1981), pp. 114–115.

8. From this subjectivism emerged the "anti-intellectualism" and "cultural decline" which the Rav associated specifically with the emergence of the Third Reich. "It is no mere coincidence," the Rav observes, "that the most celebrated philosophers of the Third Reich were outstanding disciples of Husserl. Husserl's intuitionism (Wesensschau), which Husserl, a trained mathematician, strived to keep on the level of mathematical intuition, was transposed into emotional approaches to reality." Without the mathematical (and rational emphasis) implicit in Husserl's own philosophy, Husserl's "disciples" (in a not very well-veiled reference to Martin Heidegger) transformed Husserlian philosophy into a justification for "racial theories" (p. 53).

9. See Eddington, pp. xiii–xv, 318.

10. While the Rav's work in 1944 was already echoing some of the more theoretical work of physicists like Bohr and Eddington, he clearly anticipated important recent trends in the history of science—particularly Thomas Kuhn's *The Structure of Scientific Revolutions* and Paul Feyerabend's *Against Method*.

11. Since "we have to interfere with the atomic processes in order to observe them at all," Bohr observed, it is "meaningless to ask what the atoms are doing when we are not looking at them." "Nothing is real unless we look at it, and it ceases to be real as soon as we stop looking." Cited by John Gribbin, *In Search of Shroedinger's Cat* (New York: Bantam, 1984), pp. 120, 173. Gribbin provides a useful layman's account of the quantum revolution.

12. The Rav was not alone in seeing religion liberated by the new methodology of the quantum physicists. Eddington, for example, went so far as to say that the year 1927, which saw the "overthrow of strict causality by Heisenberg, Bohr, Born, and others," made religion "possible" for a "reasonable scientific man" (*Nature*, p. 350).

13. Frederick Copleston, S.J., *A History of Philosophy* (London: Burns and Oates, 1965), VII, p. 363.

14. On the Rav's Neo-Kantian cast of mind, see Kaplan, 146–163 (passim), and Aviezer Ravitsky, "Rabbi J.B. Soloveitchik on Human Knowledge: Between Maimonidean and Neo-Kantian Philosophy," *Modern Judaism* 6 (1986), pp. 157–188.

15. Against Kant and the avatars of subjectivism, who argued that qualitative sensation precedes quantitative scientific categorization (i.e., that subjective sense perception precedes organization into the quantitative categories of thought), Natorp asserted the primacy and precedence of intellectual categories. To Natorp, according to the Rav, "even so-called qualitative data are nothing but the product of a spontaneous mental act" (p. 65). From this perspective, there is no such thing as "pure" or unmediated experience, for any "sensational apprehension is conditioned by its antecedent, the act of creative objectification."

16. "On the Objective and Subjective Grounding of Knowledge," *Journal of the British Society for Phenomenology* 12 (1981), p. 263.

17. The Rav's language and methodology anticipate the work of the anthropologist Clifford Geertz, who in his Intepretation of Cultures (New York: Basic Books, 1973), sought to challenge a disciplinary practice governed by "functionalism" and replace it with a "thick description" that "takes us into the heart of that which it is—an interpretation." If the social sciences had been dominated by an explanatory methodology, then Geertz himself emphasizes the importance of description and interpretation of "cultural forms." These forms or "symbol systems," Geertz argues, "draw their meaning from the role they play . . . not from any intrinsic relation they bear to one another." Where the traditional anthropologist arranged "abstracted entities into unified patterns," the Geertzian anthropologist describes and interprets the meaning of cultural practices (pp. 17, 18, 453). Here a methodology very much like the one which the Rav articulated in *Halakhic Mind* serves as the foundation for a revolution in anthropological method.

18. David Sokol and Moshe Singer, "Joseph Soloveitchik: *Lonely Man of Faith*," *Modern Judaism* 1982 (2), have pointed to precisely this shift in regards to *Halakhic Man*. Arguing that in the Kantian scheme, *a priori* refers to a condition of human consciousness, and that for the Rav it refers to a "body of revealed truth such as the Torah," they point to the "far from perfect" mesh between the Rav's philosophy and "talmudism" (p. 236). Without completely rejecting their argument, it is possible to argue that "objectification" for Natorp and the Rav, though differing in kind, both have the status of the "given." As Kaplan suggests, in the Rav's works, "the Halakhah as the objective order of Judaism is pretty much taken as a given" (Kaplan, p. 144).

19. Rambam's method of the Code does not, the Rav argues, permit causal analysis. As the Rav writes, repentance, "which for Maimonides is implied in the sounding of the shofar," cannot "serve as the cause of the commandment that would assure it a

status of necessity, but it must be apprehended rather as an allusion to a correlated subjective aspect" (p. 96).

20. Singer and Sokol, p. 258. For Marvin Fox's trenchant critique of Singer and Sokol, see Marvin Fox, "The Unity and Structure of Rabbi Joseph B. Soloveitchik's Thought," *Tradition* 24:2 (Winter 1989), pp. 44–65.

21. Despite the Rav's emphases on interpretation, it is important to emphasize, as Shalom Carmy has pointed out to me, that as a Brisker, the Rav's primary concern was systematizing the concepts underlying the text. Though I do not fully share Carmy's sense that the Rav did not write about the problems of interpreting texts (and I may be projecting my own concern with hermeneutics onto the texts of the Rav), I nonetheless share the sense that the Rav seemed primarily interested in those conceptual coordinates which produce different interpretations. As Lawrence Kaplan explains, "the concept, the definition, the abstract principle is, then, the light which orders, illuminates, clarifies, integrates and unifes the legal texts and rulings" (Kaplan, p. 165).

22. Joseph B. Soloveitchik, *"Kol Dodi Dofek*: It iś the Voice of My Beloved that Knocketh," in *Theological and Halakhic Reflections on the Holocaust,* Bernhard H. Rosenberg, ed. (Hoboken, NJ: Ktav), 1992, p. 54.

23. *Ibid.,* p. 53.

24. *Ibid.,* pp. 53, 59.

25. *Ibid.,* pp. 51, 55.

26. *Ibid.,* p. 53.

27. *Ibid.,* p. 63.

28. On the Rav's clearly rhetorical suggestion that the *hukim* are "stupefying," see Abraham R. Besdin and Joseph B. Soloveitchik, "May We Interpret *Hukim?" Reflections of the Rav* (Jerusalem: World Zionist Organization, 1989), p. 91.

29. See Pinchas haCohen Peli, "Hermeneutics in the Thought of Rabbi Soloveitchik—Medium or Message," *Tradition* 23 (1988), pp. 21–43.

30. Soloveitchik, *Reflections,* p. 100.

31. Soloveitchik, "Kol Dodi Dofek," p. 58.

32. One does not ask, the Rav writes, "'Why did God legislate *Parah Adumah?*' or 'How does it purify the ritually defiled?' but 'What is its spiritual message to me?' or 'How can I, as a thinking and feeling person, assimilate it into my world outlook?'" (Soloveitchik, *Reflections,* p. 95).

33. Soloveitchik, "Kol Dodi Dofek," p. 58.

In his review essay (Tradition *23:3*), *Jonathan Sacks analyzes* The Halakhic Mind. *In this most technical and philosophic book, originally written in 1944, but first published in 1986, the Rav argues that religion constitutes an autonomous cognitive domain. A proper philosophy of religion must eschew philosophical subjectivism, rationalism and romanticism. In particular, the Rav believes that Judaism can only be properly understood on its own terms and from within its own categories. As the Rav has written: "Out of the sources of the Halakhah, a new world view awaits formulation."* The Halakhic Mind *provides the philosophic foundation for this other works.*

Rabbi Joseph B. Soloveitchik's Early Epistemology

A Review of *The Halakhic Mind*

✿

Jonathan Sacks

✿

In 1941, Rabbi Joseph B. Soloveitchik succeeded his late father as professor of Talmud at the Rabbi Isaac Elchanan Theological Seminary. In 1944, he published the now famous essay *Ish ha-Halakhah (Halakhic Man)*,[1] an epic phenomenological study of the halakhic personality. From then on, for twenty years, almost nothing appeared until "Confrontation"[2]—which argued the impossibility of theological interfaith dialogue—laid the ground for "The Lonely Man of Faith"[3] a year later. This article, at one level an analysis of the perennial conflicts of the *homo religiosus*, at another a prescient critique of what has subsequently come to be known as "civil religion,"[4] firmly established Rabbi Soloveitchik as the outstanding Orthodox philosopher of the age.

To the initiated, however, he had held that position long before. Already by 1963 he was included as one of the three Americans in Simon Noveck's collection of *Great Jewish Thinkers of the Twentieth Century*,[5] and Rabbi Aharon Lichtenstein's essay in that volume did much to project his thought to a wider audience. Those who were familiar with his philosophical positions at that stage knew them as *Torah she-be-al peh*, through the spoken medium of lectures, *derashot* and *shiurim*. Rabbi Lichtenstein explained that this was not to be taken as a distaste for the act of writing, but rather as a perfectionist reluctance to publish. "The fact is, that although R. Soloveitchik has published very little, he has written a great deal."[6] Eugene Borowitz wrote that "I have been present when he has lectured by utilizing a portion of a sizable manuscript, but no book by him has appeared."[7] There was an air of mystery about this submerged iceberg of the unpublished corpus, added to by such tantalizing hints, thrown out by R. Soloveitchik himself, as "The role of the multi-valued logic in Halakhah will be discussed by me, God willing, in a forthcoming paper."[8] This has now been at least somewhat dispelled by the publication of *The Halakhic Mind*.[9]

This, the author notes, "was written in 1944 and is being published for the first time, without any revisions or additions." It is a remarkable work, different in kind from his other writings: a sustained exposition of epistemology and the philosophy of science, quite devoid of the dialectical tension, rhapsodic prose,[10] anecdotal digression and exegetical innovation that so animate the rest of his *oevre*. The most technical of his writings to appear thus far, it displays a yet more awesome command of the philosophical literature than that which astounded readers of *Ish ha-Halakhah*. Most interesting, perhaps, is the reference in a footnote[11] to the essay *U-Vikkashtem mi-Sham*, first published in 1978,[12] which contains some of R. Soloveitchik's most profound theological reflections. It is now clear that a draft of this essay existed in the early forties,[13] and thus a much more complete picture of those years is beginning to emerge.

Epistemological Foundations

The long period between 1944 and 1964 during which no major writings of R. Soloveitchik were published led to a conception of his thought, based solely on *Ish ha-Halakhah*, which had to be radically revised on the appearance of "The Lonely Man of Faith." Here, and even more so in the essays published thirteen years later in *Tradition*,[14] was an existentialism of divided selfhood and ceaseless conflict. The man of faith, wrote R. Soloveitchik, was condemned to move between the "majestic" and "covenantal" communities, "commanded to move on before he manages to strike roots in either," an eternally wandering Aramean.[15] Or as he was subsequently to write, yet more dramatically, "Man is a dialectical being; an inner schism runs through his personality at every level. . . . Judaic dialectic, unlike the Hegelian, is irreconcilable and hence interminable. Judaism accepted a dialectic, consisting only of thesis and antithesis. The third Hegelian stage, that of reconciliation, is missing."[16]

This was not what readers of *Ish ha-Halakhah* had expected. As Eugene Borowitz notes in reference to the earlier essay, "Most readers thought that Rabbi Soloveitchik had restated the *mitnagdic*, anti-Hasidic, tradition of Eastern Europe and wanted intellect, as utilized in *halakhic* reasoning and living, to be the central feature of modern Jewish life. When his later papers appeared . . . it became clear that the early impression was wrong. While an overarching intellectuality is manifest in these later publications, they are concerned with facing the conflicted human situation depicted by modern existentialism, not arguing for a latter-day rationalism."[17]

The discrepancies perplexed a number of commentators.[18] Was the life of faith consummated in a serene equilibrium, or destined to remain torn and divided? Was the man of faith essentially creative (Halakhic Man) or submissive (the Lonely Man of Faith)? Was there, or was there not, a higher synthesis between the messages of creation and revelation? Some suggested that in *Halakhic Man*, R. Soloveitchik was drawing an ideal type, while in *The Lonely Man*, he was projecting his personal spiritual dilemmas.[19] Others argued that Halakhic Man was only the first typological stage in the religious life, and that his full development was closer to the Lonely Man of Faith.[20] A third possibility was that the differences could be traced to the languages in which the various essays were published and the audiences to which they were addressed. In his English essays, R. Soloveitchik warned of the dangers implicit in secular culture and argued that it must be counterbalanced by a different set of values. In his Hebrew essays, speaking to members of the halakhic community, he could afford to be less critical and more harmonizing.[21]

Nor did these exhaust the possibilities. A recent study suggests that the difference lies between the *religious* personality as a general phenomenon—man as such, facing God, the world and his fellow man—and the *halakhic* personality as a specifically Jewish mode of resolving the tensions of the former.[22] Borowitz himself implied the simplest solution. R. Soloveitchik had simply changed his mind: "We cannot now know if there have been major shifts in his thought over these four decades or whether the progress of his thought has come about by slow evolution."[23]

The hermeneutic problem may remain. On this, I will say more below. But the publication of *The Halakhic Mind* allows us to see a full outline of the early philosophical structure. Aviezer Ravitsky has pointed out that *Halakhic Man* and *U-Vikkashtem mi-Sham* are complementary studies.[24] The former is an *analytical* treatment of the halakhic personality, splitting it into its component parts (cognitive man and *homo religiosus*). The latter is a *synthetic* treatment of the same personality, moving in Hegelian dialectic through freedom (active speculation and the search for religious experience) and submission (to the revealed Divine command) to the ultimate union of the Divine and human will. *Halakhic Man* describes human types; *U-Vikkashtem mi-Sham* describes cognitive stages.

The program of *The Halakhic Mind* is essentially prior to both these enterprises. In it, R. Soloveitchik sets out his claim for the cognitive status of religion, for the methodological autonomy of the philosophy of religion, and for the primacy of Halakhah as the basic datum on which a philosophy of Judaism should be based. This looks very much like the epistemological prologue to the two other works. And if *U-Vikkashtem mi-Sham* was indeed extant at least in outline at the time, it would seem that by 1944 R. Soloveitchik had already formulated an impressively complete philosophical system along three disciplinary axes: methodology, analysis and synthesis.

Cognitive Pluralism

The central argument of *The Halakhic Mind* is that religion constitutes an *autonomous cognitive domain*. R. Soloveitchik has no taste for apologetics, for the justification of religion in terms drawn from outside itself. He notes "the passionate desire of every philosopher of religion to legitimate the cognitive validity and truthfulness of religious propositions. Yet the problem of evidence in religion will never be solved. The believer does not miss philosophic legitimation; the skeptic will never be satisfied with any cognitive demonstration"[25]

In the past, rationalization has distorted the presentation of Judaism. R. Soloveitchik singles out for criticism in terms highly reminiscent of Rabbis Samson Raphael Hirsch[26] and Abraham Isaac Kook[27]—Maimonides' treatment, in the *Guide of the Perplexed*, of the reasons for the commandments. "In rationalizing the commandments genetically, Maimonides developed a religious 'instrumentalism.' Causality reverted to teleology . . . and Jewish religion was converted into technical wisdom."[28] Maimonides had subjected the commandments to interpretation in terms foreign to themselves. He had sought the "why" instead of the "what," a failing he avoided in the *Mishneh Torah*.[29]

The avoidance of rationalization does not mean the suspension of the rational. R. Soloveitchik is equally critical of religious irrationalism of the *credo quia absurdum est* kind, and of mysticism and subjectivity, of which he accuses much of late nineteenth- and early twentieth-century philosophy. What, then, is the alternative? Normally there would be none. But the starting point of the book is that the twentieth century has opened up a gap between science and philosophy, and in the void thus created there is room perhaps for the first time for a fully autonomous religious epistemology.

The first and last sentences of *The Halakhic Mind* define the challenge: "It would be difficult to distinguish any epoch in the history of philosophy more amenable to the mediating *homo religiosus* than that of today. . . . Out of the sources of Halakhah, a new world view awaits formulation."[30] The argument between is devoted to two questions: How has this happened? And what would be the shape of a religious philosophy that took advantage of it?

The answer to the first is that traditionally, philosophy and science have been allies. The result has been that "the only realm of reality to which the philosopher had access was . . . the scientifically charted universe."[31] This has placed religion on the defensive, having either to conform to scientific criteria of knowledge (rationalization) or be driven into escapist postures (agnosticism, mysticism). However, the Galilean-Newtonian physics on which philosophy from Descartes to the neo-Kantians is premised, has been supplanted by the counter-intuitive phenomena of modern science: relativity, quantum mechanics and non-Euclidian geometry. This poses a crisis for philosophy which Bergson was the first to diagnose. The result has been the emergence of *epistemological pluralism.*

This pluralism arises from the fact that concepts in the new sciences neither mirror ordinary experience nor remain constant between disciplines. Thus 'space' might mean one thing to the mathematician, another to the physicist, and a third in ordinary experience. Philosophy cannot postulate a unified conceptual world and at the same time embrace modern science. But therein lies the great liberation, for "as long as general philosophy explored a quantitatively constructed universe, the philosophy of religion could not progress."[32] Now there opens up an alternative to the scientific description of reality, namely one which focuses on the *qualitative* aspects of experience. This is where religious experience belongs, in the "concrete world full of color and sound."[33]

R. Soloveitchik insists that the "non-scientific" character of religion does not signify that it is non-cognitive. To the contrary: "The *homo religiosus* must regain his position in the cognitive realm."[34] Against several modern philosophies of religion, R. Soloveitchik argues that the believer is concerned not with a transcendental domain, but with the here-and-now viewed from a religious perspective; not with interpreting God in terms of the world but the world under the aspect of God. The task of a new philosophy of religion would be to uncover its distinctive conceptuality, probing what "time," "space," "causality" and so on mean within its world. Hence the conclusion of the first half of the argument, that for the first time in the history of thought religion can be presented autonomously, as a cognitive system independent of but parallel to science.

From Objective to Subjective

The question now arises: how should such a philosophy proceed? R. Soloveitchik proposes two criteria. The first is practical, or more strictly, ethical. "Epistemology would do well to cast aside such canonized concepts as objectivity and ethical neutrality and survey philosophical doctrines from a subjective, normative standpoint."[35] Such considerations militate against irrationalism, subjectivism and mysticism, for these lead in the end to moral corruption. "It is no mere coincidence that the most celebrated philosophers of the Third Reich were outstanding disciples of Husserl."[36]

The second is theoretical. The philosophy of religion should imitate the method of modern science, namely "reconstruction" or sensing the whole within the parts. "The structural designs of religion cannot be intuited through any sympathetic fusion with an eternal essence, but must be reconstructed out of objective religious data and central realities."[37] Religion may proceed, like art, from subjective experience to objectified forms, but it must be explored in the reverse direction. One may try to gain an insight into the inner world of the artist by examining his works, but the reverse is impossible: from a precise description of his inner state one could not infer the art he will produce. So too in religion. The subjective can only be reconstructed from the objective, the actual forms in which it is concretized in specific traditions. Of these forms, the "cult" is to be preferred to the "ethos" as being more indicative of the unique character of a particular religion.

R. Soloveitchik thus has a series of objections against religious subjectivism which he summarizes as follows. First, it fails to satisfy the *homo religiosus*, who seeks more than inward experience. He wants ethical guidance and a religious community. Second, subjective religion has no defenses against barbarism, to which it frequently descends. Third, it renders religion esoteric and non-democratic. "Aristocracy in the religious realm is identical with the decadence of religion."[38] Religious liberalism errs by proceeding in the wrong direction, from subjectivity to objectivity. But in reality there is no pristine religious subjectivity: "If one seeks primordial subjectivity he would find an evanescent flux, neither religious nor mundane, but, similar to Aristotelian matter, unregulated and chaotic."[39]

The only valid procedure is to travel inwards from the objectified forms of religion, beginning with the received text of revelation. "The canonized Scripture serves as the most reliable standard of reference for objectivity."[40] The halakhic tradition is perfectly suited to this role. "Objectification reaches its highest expression in the Halakhah. Halakhah is the act of seizing the subjective flow and converting it into enduring and tangible magnitudes. . . . In short, Halakhah is the objectifying instrument of our religious consciousness, the form-principle of the transcendental act, the matrix in which the amorphous religious hylo is cast."[41]

The Halakhic Mind ends by dissociating itself from medieval Jewish philosophy. Firstly, the latter never succeeded in shaping the experience of the majority of the Jewish community. Secondly, it is rooted in non-indigenous sources, ancient Greek and medieval Arabic. Thirdly, it cannot meet the requirement of living continuity, since its concepts are by now outmoded. An autonomous Jewish philosophy is possible and necessary, and it can only be constructed on the basis of Halakhah.

Halakhic Mind and Halakhic Man

Such, then, is the argument of the book. What impressions does it leave? First, it is obviously close in spirit to the work undertaken in *Ish ha-Halakhah*. The two books share an admiration for modern mathematics and theoretical physics as cognitive paradigms, and seek to establish their kinship with a philosophy based on Halakhah. There are differences. The *homo religiosus* of *The Halakhic Mind* is not that of *Ish ha-Halakhah*, but this is a matter of terminology rather than substance. The project of the two books is altogether different. *Ish ha-Halakhah* describes Halakhic Man from the inside; *The Halakhic Mind* establishes the philosophical significance of such a description. It belongs, in other words, to the world of the footnotes of the early part of *Ish ha-Halakhah* and constitutes a kind of systematic introduction to it. The two books differ in style and tone too. *The Halakhic Mind* is a sober philosophical work, and the persuasive, evocative style of *Ish ha-Halakhah* would have been irrelevant to its purpose. But the setting is the same in both cases: a sense that romantic religion and philosophical subjectivism have failed, and that the need is for a presentation of religion as a form of cognitive, disciplined perception.

Second, *The Halakhic Mind* is not a prologue to *Ish ha-Halakhah* alone but to an entire program, a new kind of Jewish philosophy. This would undertake to gather the entire corpus of objectified Jewish spirituality Biblical text, halakhic literature, liturgy, mysticism and so on—and seek its subjective correlative. "Out of this enormous mass of objectified constructs, the underlying subjective aspects could gradually be reconstructed."[42] In the light of this, both early works, together with *U-Vikkashtem mi-Sham*, are merely introductory. A good example of the detailed work one would expect, having read *The Halakhic Mind*, would be the lectures gathered in *Al ha-Teshuvah*, where a particular body of Halakhah is treated to "subjective reconstruction." There is thus every reason to suppose that R. Soloveitchik has been faithful to the call he issued in those early years, and that his "philosophy" is to be found as much in his analysis of texts as in his more overtly philosophical statements.

Third, there is a surprising but unmistakable echo of Rabbi Samson Raphael Hirsch in the book's closing pages. There is the same attack on Maimonides and others (Mendelssohn for Hirsch, Hermann Cohen for R. Soloveitchik) for interpreting Judaism through non-Jewish concepts. There is the same call "to know Judaism out of itself."[43] Hirsch writes that "the Bible . . . should be studied as the foundation of a new science. Nature should be contemplated with the spirit of David."[44] For "Bible" read "Halakhah" and we have the program of *The Halakhic Mind.*

R. Soloveitchik's critique of religious liberalism is mounted on the same foundation as Hirsch's critique of the Science of Judaism,[45] namely that any philosophical study of Judaism must live in the details of text and command and be built bit by bit through an extended effort of exegesis.

Indeed, even the weaknesses of *The Halakhic Mind* mirror those of Hirsch. There is the same equivocation between a penetrating methodological critique of Reform and a quite disparate ethical denunciation. Both see humanism as prone to corruption, religious liberalism as arbitrary; both attack the elitism of rarified theologies. Though the temperaments of the two men could not be more different, they share the same movement from emancipation to self-emancipation. The epistemological pluralism with which *The Halakhic Mind* begins is a kind of metaphysical equivalent to the social processes experienced by Hirsch in mid-nineteenth century Germany. Both create space for Judaism to be itself.

Fourth, inevitably, the book has a somewhat dated feel about it. For those raised in the atmosphere of Wittgenstein's *Philosophical Investigations*, philosophical pluralism is not the Copernican revolution it may have seemed forty years ago. Nor is science, after T. S. Kuhn's *The Structure of Scientific Revolutions* (1962), the pristine paradigm of knowledge it once was. Indeed, the "scientific" outlook—cognition, control, creation—came to seem, to R. Soloveitchik of "The Lonely Man of Faith," a more threatening force than the subjective religiosity he attacked in *The Halakhic Mind* and *Ish ha-Halakhah*. Had Hans Georg Gadamer's *Truth and Method* (1960) been available two decades earlier, one of the central arguments of *The Halakhic Mind* (the opposition between physics and modern humanistic sciences[46]) might not have been necessary. None of this is to say that R. Soloveitchik's case has been rendered obsolete. To the contrary, it has been reinforced to the point where it may have been rendered redundant. But the book will remain invaluable as his most explicit methodological statement, his point of departure, the external justification he gave for his long journey inward to a disciplined Jewish subjectivity.

Liberation and Privation

The Halakhic Mind is a deeply impressive work, furnishing new evidence of Rabbi Soloveitchik's unrivalled mastery of secular sources and disclosing a tone of voice we had not heard before, the Dr. Soloveitchik of Berlin rather than the Rav of Yeshiva University. It will raise two questions: Does it succeed in its own terms,[47] in providing a philosophical justification for the cognitive autonomy of religion? And, what light does it shed on R. Soloveitchik's other works and his intellectual development? Both are beyond the scope of this review and the competence of this reviewer. Some tentative speculations, though, seem inescapable.

First, R. Soloveitchik insists at critical stages of the argument that the pluralism he is endorsing is nonetheless a form of *realism*. It corresponds to something real in the world. It is not pragmatism. It does not deny the absolute character of Being. "Teleological heterogeneity . . . does not invalidate the cognitive act, for, in the final analysis, pluralism is founded on reality itself. . . . Pluralism asserts only that the object reveals itself in manifold ways to the subject, and that a certain *telos* corresponds to each of these ontical manifestations."[48]

Yet the very force of the argument suggests that reality can be sliced up and interpreted in infinitely many ways. And if reality corresponds to each of them, is it significant to say that it corresponds to any? This is the conclusion reached by Richard Rorty in his *Philosophy and the Mirror of Nature* (1980), a work which in many ways parallels *The Halakhic Mind*. Rorty's remarks on the implications of twentieth-century philosophy are directly relevant and challenging. "It would make for philosophical clarity if we just *gave* the notion of 'cognition' to predictive science, and stopped worrying about 'alternative cognitive methods.' The word *knowledge* would not seem worth fighting over were it not for the Kantian tradition that to be a philosopher is to have a 'theory of knowledge.'"[49]

Closely related to this is R. Soloveitchik's demonstration that religion is indeed cognitive, namely that its mental acts are *intentional* or "coordinated with an object." He alludes, in footnotes, to the problematic nature of this demonstration. Brentano denied that intentional acts were cognitive; Scheler disagreed; R. Soloveitchik declares his indebtedness to Scheler.[50] But this spreads the net of cognition very wide indeed—to all mental acts—and would not justify the conclusion that he wants to reach, namely, that some forms of religion are more cognitive than others, halakhic Judaism most of all.

This relates to another ambivalence, here as elsewhere in R. Soloveitchik's work, between the universal and the particular. Is *The Halakhic Mind* about religion or about Judaism? Is the *homo religiosus* portrayed in its pages religious man *tout court*, or the Jew? He is "an enthusiastic practitioner of the cognitive act"; he is a "social being"; he seeks ethical guidance and wants to change the world rather than accept it. In short, he has a predisposition to welcome halakhic Judaism. R. Soloveitchik seeks to demonstrate the autonomy of religion as cognition, and then to establish Judaism as the supreme example. But he has provided an argument for the autonomy and incommensurability of religions in the plural, so that the success of the first part of the argument must *ipso facto* weaken the second. He testifies to this at one stage by saying that sometimes one must choose one's philosophy "from a subjective, normative viewpoint."[51] There is a straight road from *The Halakhic Mind* to the argument in "Confrontation" that there is no ultimate dialogue between religions since "the numinous character and the strangeness of the act of faith of a particular community . . . is totally incomprehensible to the man of a different faith community."[52]

These are all symptoms of the dual direction of R. Soloveitchik's thought, projecting the autonomy and cognitive integrity of the halakhic system on the one hand, arguing its supremacy over other systems on the other. The former embraces pluralism, the latter rejects it.

Which brings us back to our starting-point: the relation between R. Soloveitchik's early work and his later, more pessimistic and conflicted essays.

The transition from nineteenth-century liberalism to twentieth-century pluralism-both terms construed in their widest sense seemed to promise much to religious orthodoxy. Instead of having to justify itself at the bar of an enlightenment universal religion or ethic, it could declare independence without forfeiting rationality. Did not the multiplicity of models of knowledge, of which mathematics and science provided ample examples, show that even within the "hard" disciplines there was methodological pluralism? The life of faith too had to be understood on its own terms, in its own concepts, rather than be subjected to the disciplines of science, history, anthropology and psychology. This was liberation indeed, and *The Halakhic Mind* bespeaks the mood.

But the pluralism of knowledge was mirrored in society. It had correlatives in the real world. The single universe of pre-modernity—the universe inhabited by Maimonides, in which the God of Abraham and of Aristotle were indeed one; the universe in which science, philosophy and religion competed in a single arena; the universe whose last Jewish inhabitant was Rabbi Abraham Isaac Kook—was shattered. In its place were not merely pluralities of thought-worlds, but of identities, roles and lifestyles as well. Consider the markers of modernity invoked by one major sociological study: "plurality of life-worlds," "dichotomy of public and private spheres" and "multi-relational synchronization." Personal identity is "peculiarly open, differentiated, reflective, individuated." Modern man is afflicted with a "permanent identity crisis," and suffers "from a deepening condition of 'homelessness'."[53] This world is instantly recognizable. It is the world of "The Lonely Man of Faith."

R. Soloveitchik makes an important point at the beginning and end of *The Halakhic Mind*. Judaism is timeless and autonomous. But how much of it can be expressed in the language of the world depends on where the world is at a given point in time. The pluralism of contemporary culture, which he was the first to recognize, was both a liberation and a privation. It liberated tradition from having to vindicate itself in alien terms. But it prized tradition from its moorings in the collective order and made it seem as just one system among many, either consciously chosen (the *ba'al teshuvah* phenomenon) or validated by an act of faith which is "aboriginal, exploding with elemental force"[54] and eluding cognitive analysis. R. Soloveitchik's genius and the poignancy of his intellectual development are both evidenced in this: that he was the first to explore the positive possibilities of the liberation, and the first to chart the tragic dimension of the privation.

Notes

1. *Talpiot* 1:3–4, New York, 1944

2. *Tradition* 6:2 (Summer 1964), pp. 5–28.

3. *Tradition* 7:2 (Summer 1965), pp. 5–67.

4. See Charles Liebman and Eliezer Don-Yehiya, *Civil Religion in Israel: Traditional Judaism and Political Culture in the Jewish State*, University of California Press. 1983; Jonathan S. Woocher, *Sacred Survival: The Civil Religion of American Jews*, Indiana University Press, 1986. The description given by Woocher of American Civil Judaism exactly mirrors the religion of majestic man described in the last twelve pages of "The Lonely Man of Faith."

5. Simon Noveck (ed.), *Great Jewish Thinkers of the Twentieth Century*, B'nai B'rith. 1963, pp. 281–297.

6. *Ibid.*, p. 287.

7. Eugene Borowitz, *Choices in Modern Jewish Thought*, New York: Behrman House, 1983, p. 222.

8. "The Lonely Man of Faith," p. 51.

9. Published by Seth Press, distributed by The Free Press, 1986.

10. "[Halakhic Man's] affective life is characterized by a fine equilibrium, a stoic tranquillity," (*Halakhic Man*, translated by Lawrence Kaplan. Jewish Publication Society of America, 1983, p. 77). One of the more interesting things about *Halakhic Man*, with its passionate rhetoric, is that it could not have been written by Halakhic Man.

11. Note 98, p. 131.

12. First published in *Ha-Darom* 47 (Tishri 5739). pp. 1–83; subsequently in *Ish ha-Halakhah—Galui ve-Nistar*, Jerusalem: World Zionist Organization, 1979, pp. 115–235. The section on *shinnui* and *hiddush* to which R. Soloveitchik alludes in the *Halakhic Mind* is to be found in the latter, pp. 204–207.

13. Aviezer Ravitsky notes that an early version of *U-Vikkashtem mi-Sham*, under the title *Ish ha-Elohim*, was "already written in the years following the appearance of [*Ish ha-Halakhah*]." See Rabbi J. B. Soloveitchik in Human Knowledge: Between Maimonidean and neo-Kantian Philosophy," *Modern Judaism* 6:2 (May 1986), pp. 157–188, note 17. The present version was clearly written later, and is perhaps a reworking of several papers.

14. "The Community," "Majesty and Humility," "Catharsis," "Redemption, Prayer, Talmud Torah," "A Tribute to the Rebbitzen of Talne," *Tradition* 17:2 (Spring 1978), pp. 1–83.

15. "The Lonely Man of Faith," p. 55.

16. *Majesty and Humility*, p. 25.

17. *Choices in Modern Jewish Thought*, p. 223.

18. In addition to the articles cited below see David Hartman, *A Living Covenant*, The Free Press, 1985, pp. 60–88. In his early writings, Hartman argues, R. Soloveitchik was "struggling to present halakhic man as an attractive model for Orthodox Judaism in the modern era" (p. 71). In his later writings he "senses that if there were a total translation of the halakhic experience into Western rational categories, commitment to Halakhah would be weakened" (pp. 84–85). For much all the rest of the book, Hartman takes issue with the turn in R. Soloveitchik's thought.

19. David Singer and Moshe Sokol, "Joseph Soloveitchik: Lonely Man of Faith," *Modern Judaism* 2:3 (October 1982), pp. 227–272.

20. Lawrence Kaplan, "The Religious Philosophy of Rabbi Joseph Soloveitchik," *Tradition* 14:2 (Fall 1973), pp. 43–64, on the basis of the essay *Al Ahavat ha-Torah u-Ge'ulat Nefesh Ha-Dor*.

21. Lawrence Kaplan, "Deganim shel ha-Adam ha-Dati ha-Ideali be-Hagut ha-Rav Yosef Dov Soloveitchik," in *Mehkerei Yerushalayim be-Mahshevet Yisrael*, 4:3–4 (1985), 327–339.

22. Ravisky, *loc. cit.*

23. *Choices in Modern Jewish Thought*, p. 223.

24. Ravitsky *loc. cit.*, pp. 159–160.

25. *The Halakhic Mind*, p. 118, note 58.

26. Samson Raphael Hirsch, *The Nineteen Letters*, translated by J. Breuer and B. Drachman, New York: Feldheim, 1960, pp. 117–132.

27. R. Abraham Isaac ha-Kohen Kook, *Talelei Orot*, translated in Ben Zion Bokser, *Abraham Isaac Kook* London: SPCK, 1979, pp. 303–305.

28. *Tha Halakhic Mind*, pp. 91–99.

29. R. Soloveitchik offers here a fascinating analysis of Maimonides' use of the term *remez* (*MT Teshuvah* 3:4; *Mikva'ot* 11:12) as signifying "descriptive hermeneutics."

30. *The Halakhic Mind*, pp. 3, 102.

31. *Ibid.*, p. 6.

32. *Ibid.*, p. 32.

33. *Ibid.*, p. 40.

34. *Ibid.*

35. *Ibid.*, p. 52.

36. *Ibid.*, p. 53.

37. *Ibid.*, p. 62.

38. *Ibid.*, p. 80.

39. *Ibid.*, p. 90.

40. *Ibid.*, p. 81.

41. *Ibid.*, p. 85.

42. *Ibid.*, p. 91.

43. Samson Raphael Hirsch, *The Nineteen Letters*, p. 127.

44. *Ibid.*

45. Samson Raphael Hirsch, *Judaism Eternal*, translated by I. Grunfeld. London: Soncino, 1959, vol. 2, pp. 285–286.

46. *The Halakhic Mind*, pp. 30–36.

47. For some other questions, see Steven S. Schwarzschild's review of *The Halakhic Mind* in *Sh'ma*, 1986, pp. 127–8.

48. *The Halakhic Mind*, p. 16.

49. Richard Rorty, *Philosophy and the Mirror of Nature*, Oxford: Blackwell, 1981, p. 356.

50. *The Halakhic Mind*, pp. 41–44, 116 (note 50), 120 (note 62).

51. *Ibid.*, p. 52.

52. "Confrontation," pp. 23–24.

53. P. I. Berger, B. Berger and H. Kellner, *The Homeless Mind*, London: Penguin Books 1973, pp. 62–77.

54. "The Lonely Man of Faith," p. 60.

Repentance is a central theme in the teachings of Rabbi Soloveitchik. His annual Teshuvah lectures were spectacular combinations of profound intellectual insight and heartfelt religious fervor. In this essay (Tradition 18:2), Pinchas Hacohen Peli discusses the Rav's understanding of "repentant man."

"Repentant man" is characterized by four traits: profundity of suffering, a depth of experience, the ability to make decisions with free choice, and the capacity to create. True repentance involves not only an intellectual awareness of one's sins, but a deep inner feeling of pain, shame, and separation from God. Through free choice, one who has sinned may leap from the status of the sinner to that of a penitent. "Repentant man" chooses to create himself anew, to redirect his life so as to come closer to God. Alone, in secret, unaccompanied, "repentant man" undergoes a spiritual transformation. Although the individual Jew works through the process of repentance alone, he always must recognize that he is part of Knesset Israel. The repentant Jew renews the personal covenant with God, and also reaffirms the connection between God and the entire people of Israel.

Repentant Man—A High Level in Rabbi Joseph B. Soloveitchik's Typology of Man

ৎৠ৶

Pinchas Hacohen Peli

ডৡৡ৶

Man stands at the center of Rabbi Joseph Dov Baer Halevi Soloveitch-k's (henceforth, the Rav) religious thought. His study of man is not comprehensive, nor does it attempt to encompass the totality of human experience and behavior. Rather, it is presented episodically with the aim of identifying and establishing a typology of man and of human society.[1] According to this approach, man must be studied and judged in the light of essentially human criteria. Thus, the Rav solidly established the typological characteristics of "Halakhic Man"[2] by contrasting him with "Religious Man" and "Rational Man";[3] thus, too, he anchored his "Lonely Man of Faith"[4] in the prototypes of "Adam the First" and "Adam the Second" as these emerge, according to him, from the two versions of the creation of man in the Torah.

The lines of demarcation between one type and another are not always clear and sharply drawn. Often, characteristics of one type will be shared by another, and though the types portrayed in the Rav's typological system are purely ideal, such as are often used in theoretical philosophy, he was conscious that in reality the types—rarely simple and often complex—at most approximated to their ideal counterparts. That he was aware of this is apparent in his comparison between the ideal Halakhic Man and the real Halakhic Man.[5] Similarly, he occasionally noted the congruence between the different types (by way of shared traits).[6]

The publication of Rabbi Soloveitchik's reflections on repentance seems to compel the addition to his typological categories of another type definable along the lines of the Rav's terminology, as "Repentant Man." Unfortunately, Rabbi Soloveitchik has not yet given a final or systematic presentation of his thought in this matter. We have at our disposal only fragmentary and disjointed evidence upon which to build our analysis. Nonetheless, it appears that "Repentant Man" may be legitimately viewed as inhabiting the highest rung of this typological ladder. To judge from the evidence, "Repentant Man" enjoys an abundance of the positive traits identified by the Rav in the other established types as these endeavor to express their humanity as creatures created in the Divine Image, and are at the same time possessed of independent creative powers coupled with a powerful compulsion to draw near to their Creator. In the person of "Repentant Man" these two ontological tendencies converge and become a unified perfection which propels man toward his ultimate destination: salvation.

Moreover, the depth of the personality of Rabbi Soloveitchik's other types is measured according to criteria of the torments of duality, contradiction, doubts and struggles which issue in the "emergence of a personality shrouded in sanctity whose soul was purified in the smithy of perplexity and contradiction and refined in the fires of spiritual conflict." From the spiritual struggle which is the lot of "Repentant Man," there emerges a perfection of personality "of incomparable splendor and glory unknown among those, whole and simple, who have never undergone the tribulation of internal spiritual conflict."[8] As Rabbi Soloveitchik asserts: "According to the trouble, so the wage: according to the tear, so the patch." In the Rav's conception of human ontology which rests, according to his own testimony,[9] on the dialectical philosophies of Heraclitus and Hegel concerning the general process of being, and on the views of Kierkegaard, Karl Barth and Rudolf Otto concerning the religious experience and religious awareness, immense creative power is vested in the antithesis, "Inconsistency enriches existence, contradiction renews Creation, negation builds worlds and denial deepens and expands consciousness."[10] The portrait of "Repentant Man" rests mainly upon these foundations. Should one seek a parallel in the Rav's typological framework, it would be found in the type defined as the "Man of God," about whom the Rav intimates that "his stature is established in the pangs of redemption and appearance crystallizes in the pains of salvation."[11]

If suffering results in bringing the soul nearer to the object of its yearning, then "Repentant Man" is the type which comes closest to attaining man's goal, for his conception and maturation owe everything to suffering.

Four characteristic traits identify "Repentant Man," according to Rabbi Soloveitchik: profundity of suffering, a depth of experience, the ability to make decisions in the light of free choice, and the capacity to create.

The Rav's conception of ontology is directed to four traits which are to be found, in some measure, in the other types established and described by Rabbi Soloveitchik, but never in so concentrated a form as in his "Al ha-Teshuvah." It comprises man's freedom, his drives, his existence as a repository of the *Shekhinah*, his investiture with free choice (which allows him to adopt a new Law of causation) and his penchant for salvation. God created man free. This liberty, however, does not represent an abandonment on His part. Rather man, born in the image of God, always remains, as it were, in the Divine Presence. He can never completely liberate himself of the religious attraction which draws him to God, which is akin to an unseverable umbilical cord.[12] Man cannot flee from God because God chose the human soul as a dwelling place much like a Temple. "The House of the God of Old"—where is God's house? "Behold, the heaven and heaven of heavens cannot contain thee, how much less this House that I have built?" (I Kings 8:27); Where lives the Almighty and where lives God the Eternal? The Almighty resides in man, in his heart and soul, and He never departs from there even if man sins and defiles the sacred abode. God, as it were, inhabits the deepest recesses of the sinning soul ". . . that dwelleth with them in the midst of their uncleanliness" (Lev. 16:16).[13]

"The Almighty has two dwelling places in man, two temples. One is the temple of the emotions, a holy of holies from which issues human sentiments such as sympathy, astonishment, mercy, goodness, reverence, happiness, sadness, amazement. The other temple is that of the mind. In man's thoughts, as he studies the Torah and refines and sanctifies intellect, there resides the Almighty. One house of the God of Old is in the heart of man, and the other is in the human brain; one is in the emotions, the other in the mind."[14]

The permanent religious affinity, the "living together" of God and man in one house, does not produce a calming or tranquilizing effect. On the contrary, "the religious act is essentially one of suffering. When man and God meet, man is called upon by the Divine to embark on a course of self-sacrifice which is manifested in a struggle against his primitive instincts, in a breaking of the individual will, in the acceptance of a 'transcendental burden,' in an addiction to the bitter and the strange. . . . 'Make sacrifices'—that is the command governing the religious man."[15]

The lot of the religious man is a constant, difficult and tiring struggle, not tranquility. "The beauty of religion with its grandiose vistas, reveals itself to man not in solutions, but in problems; not in harmony, but in the constant conflict of diversified forces and trends."[16] The attainment of sanctity, according to Rabbi Soloveitchik, does not lead man to paradise, but rather to paradox.

The suffering of which man is condemned is not necessarily a punishment; rather, "suffering is there to uplift man, to cleanse his spirit

and sanctify him, to purify his thought and to rid it of all manner of superficial dross and vulgar chaff, to ennoble his soul and to expand his life's vision. In short, the function of suffering is to set right that which is distorted and defective in the human character.
. . . Suffering appears in the world in order to enhance man. . . . It is a time of distress for Jacob and he shall be saved out of it (Jer. 30:7)—i.e., out of misfortune will spring forth eternal salvation. [Man will be] uplifted to a degree incomparably above that possible in a world devoid of suffering."[17] Man's existence in the presence of God involves suffering; man's affinity to God is expressed in constant sacrifice. Only through sacrifice and total subservience to God can man achieve complete freedom and salvation.

Man's subservience to God must be complete and unconditional. This decisive subordination is tantamount to total freedom in relation to the other enslavements to which man is prone. The enslavement to God—which is all-embracing—releases man from a long list of other bondages. Only when a man has one sovereign, to whom he owes unreserved allegiance, is he truly liberated and free. When a man is subservient to more than one being, he is then "taking a hand in some form of idolatry." What then of positive ties of loyalty, such as to children and family? The Torah instructs us to love our children with a great passion—". . . as a father pities his son" is a common simile of compassion and love in our liturgy. Nonetheless, Rabbi Soloveitchik suggests the daring proposition that the narrative of the sacrifice of Isaac was related only in order to teach later generations that parental love must not be allowed to deteriorate into complete enslavement, i.e., into a form of idolatry.[18]

Man attains liberty through self-sacrifice. "Total and unreserved offering of soul and body—that is the foundation of Judaism," asserts Rabbi Soloveitchik.[19] Moreover, he hazards that, in essence, "Judaism does not prohibit the sacrifice of humans"; i.e., he explains, though the Torah forbids human sacrifice and regards the phenomenon as an example of the obscene in idolatry, it does not ban the notion of self-sacrifice. In the words of the Rav, "God demands not tribute

from man, but man himself."[20] Rabbi Soloveitchik sees the central
philosophical idea underlying the act of sacrifice explained in Maimonides' assertion that man is the property of the Creator. Man and
all his belongings, his body and soul, ideas, actions, achievements and
possessions, even his wife and children—all belong not to man, but to
his Creator. And if man is "the property of the Almighty, then he has
no choice when the Voice of God calls out to him to 'take now thy
son, thine only son,' and sacrifice him, but to arise and set out to
obey the command." Abraham has no rights in the disposal of his
son, Isaac; Isaac has no claim over Abraham. Man is free; he attains
that freedom through exercising his right to self-sacrifice in the service
of his Creator.

Were it allowed, the Law would call for human sacrifices, but the
dispensation of grace precludes this, asserting: "Ye shall bring your
offering of the cattle, even of the herd, and of the flock" (Lev. 1:2).
Animal sacrifice is allowed as a substitute for human sacrifice, but the
meaningfulness of the sacrifice remains, as it were, undiminished; so
in the sacrifice of Isaac, and so in all other sacrificial offerings. "As
the sacrifice is burnt upon the altar, so we burn, in the act of confession
over the sacrifice, our entrenched tranquility, our well-nurtured pride,
our artificial lives. Through the sacrifice, or through the suffering
which stands in its stead, we repeatedly feel ourselves 'in the presence
of God.'"[21]

Man's existential condition, in fact, means suffering, doubt, struggles
with the world and within oneself. Only "Repentant Man" can attain
that highest plateau to which suffering can introduce man, for the
very emergence of "Repentant Man" into this world involves conscious
and severe birth pangs.

In order to understand the concept of repentance, it is necessary to
fathom the concept of sin as it emerges from Rabbi Soloveitchik's
reflections on the subject of repentance. The two concepts—sin and
repentance—are interlocked and bound together in a single, dialectical
system, and both constitute stages through which "Repentant Man"
must pass on his way to salvation.

Yom Kippur has two aspects: the experience of that day results first in atonement and, secondly, in purification; as it is written (Lev. 16:30): "For on that day shall atonement be made for you to purify you." Both these elements—atonement and purification—according to Rabbi Soloveitchik, are a direct consequence of sin. For in sin both elements are to be found: (1) sin binds; atonement or pardon provides a counterweight; (2) sin defiles; purification or forgiveness restores the sinner to his original state.

The sin that binds does so, much like obligation and subjection in the juridical sense. There is no sin without punishment, which in a terrestrial or in a heavenly court means pardon (*mehilah*), a word originating in laws of property. As a man foreswears (*mohel*) a sum owed to him by a friend, so God forgoes (*mohel*) and erases (*mekhaper*) the punishment which sin entails. However, the sin that defiles is of another order—the metaphysical one. It exists in the domain of man-God relations. Sin deforms and damages the innermost part of man—his soul, wherein dwells the *Shekhinah*.[22]

Judicial sin, the sin that binds, is revealed to man by his intellect. Repentance of such a sin is generally undergone through calculation, through a desire to erase an obligation, or through fear of the impending punishment. Metaphysical sin, on the other hand, becomes part of man's existential experience and the deeper the sin, the deeper the experience of repentance which follows.

Sin causes man's remoteness from God. The sinner becomes, in the words of Maimonides—whom Rabbi Soloveitchik is wont to quote: "Separate from the God of Israel, for it is written that your sins separate you from God." To be sure, God remains in man also after he sins, but He is so remote that the sinner does not feel his presence at all. Only afterwards he begins, sooner or later, to feel God's absence and, as a result, is beset by existential dread and fear.

Before the stage of "recognition of sin," which is already an integral part of the act of repentance itself, Rabbi Soloveitchik distinguishes a prior stage defined as a "feeling of sin," which is similar to a man's feeling of an encroaching illness. *Het, Holi* (sin, illness) is a parallel concept employed by medieval Jewish philosophers, and already hinted at in the Bible (Ps. 103:3): "Who forgiveth all thine iniquities; Who healeth all thy diseases." It was expanded by Rabbi Soloveitchik[23] to explain the feeling of sin, which is the initial experience and precondition of all repentance or purification. Sin constitutes a kind of spiritual pathology. As there are pathological, physical illnesses in which the tissues cease to function normally and the cells begin to grow wildly, so sin is a sign of a spiritual pathology whose outcome is the disintegration of the whole personality. As in physical disease, so in the spiritual disease of sin. Sometimes a man attempts to erase, to belittle or to deny pain, because of overt or covert fear. Pains begin to engender dread, but man's first reaction is to dismiss them or to belittle their significance.

But belittling them will not diminish their importance; on the contrary, had he taken immediate notice and begun to have them treated, it is possible that a cure for his spreading illness would have been found.

The comparison between sin and pathological illness is complemented by the comparison between sin and mourning. The Torah says of the sin of the golden calf: "And when the people heard these evil tidings, they mourned; and no man did put on him his ornaments" (Ex. 33:4). In the wake of this sin there descended upon the people a strong sense of mourning. Likewise, in the episode of the spies, a sense of mourning overcame the people after the sin (Num. 14:39). Mourning is a reaction to loss; it descends upon man like a vague, almost primitive, sense of loss, of awful incapacity, and develops into a strong feeling of nostalgia, of pining after something, of retrospective memories. The power of mourning, its brutality and loneliness, is centered in the human memory. Were man able to forget, to erase memory, there would be no mourning. The mourner mourns a kindred and loved person who was once and is no more, while the sinner mourns that which has been lost. What has been lost is man's soul, which is like losing everything, for he has lost his closeness to his

Creator, that proximity which allowed him access to purity and sanctity, to perfection and spiritual richness; he has lost the inherence of the holy spirit in man and that which gives meaning and the significance of life to human existence.

"Repentant Man" *in excelsis* reaches repentance not through calculation and fear of punishment, but through the *via dolorosa* of a sense of sin which fills him with powerful longing and sharp feelings of mourning. The experience of sin completely fills man with boundless fear and a wild, vague dread; the more deeply these are felt, the closer man comes to the possibility of overcoming them through the power of repentance.

This dread-filled sense of remoteness from God, isolation, longing and mourning is in the main a powerful aesthetic (or anti-aesthetic) experience. Mourning always contains an element of masochism. The mourner tortures and chastises himself; indeed, he hates himself. This applies equally to the "mourning of sin." The sinner begins to feel contempt and abomination of self, and masochistic self-hatred. In his eyes the sin turns into something abominable, loathsome, nauseating.

"The feeling of sin," says Rabbi Soloveitchik, "is not a moral experience." Man's ethical sense is not a very potent factor. This feeling of sin, which draws man towards repentance, is an aesthetic experience; or rather, a negative aesthetic experience. The sinner senses that which is abominable and corrupting in sin. "The pangs of sin lie in the nausea caused by its obnoxious taint."[24] This sense of abomination 'wonderfully described in the story of Amnon and Tamar [II Sam. 13], as interpreted by the Rav,[25] is also connected to a sense of shame; shame in one's own acts. The sense of abomination intermingles with the sense of shame and opprobrium. The sin appears to the sinner like a terrible monster; he is filled with shame through having come into contact with the "bestial"; and out of the shame, the sense of abomination, of mourning, and of the other emotions which comprise the sense of sin, he begins to ascend the ladder of "Repentant Man," at last attaining repentance itself. This transition from sin to repentance does not occur on the intellectual plane: "The human intellect takes practically no part [in the process]"; it transpires rather mainly on the emotional, experiential and instinctive planes.

Through all the stages of the ascent of "Repentant Man," Rabbi Soloveitchik lays strong emphasis upon the experiential-emotional element which leads the penitent to the feeling of sin in contrast with the intellectual-cognitive element; the latter leads man to repentance by way of "knowledge of sin" of "consciousness of sin," but not to a "repentance through *love*"—*Teshuvah me-Ahavah*—the "higher repentance"—*Teshuvah Me-ulah*—which is the peak attained by "Repentant Man."

This stress on the experiential-emotional element, side by side with the intellectual-cognitive element, runs like a motif through all Rabbi Soloveitchik's descriptions of the essence of the religious phenomenon in general. Thus, for instance,[26] he distinguishes between the *mitzvah* of "belief in the Divine" (in Maimonides' *Sefer ha-Mitzvot*) and "the foundation of foundations and the mainstay of wisdom, to know that there exists a First Being" (with which Maimonides' *Mishneh Torah* opens).

He discerns here two different aspects of the principles of faith and he adds that "this double employment of the *mitzvah* of the existence of God in the sense of 'believing' and in the sense of 'knowing' is not confined to this issue only, but has implications which extend to all the other *mitzvot*, as this *mitzvah* lies at the root and source of all the *mitzvot*."[27] Rabbi Soloveitchik applies this "knowing" to all the *mitzvot* and not merely to the belief in the existence of God, and he interprets it in such a way that the belief in the existence of God will become a continuous and constant awareness of God's reality, a consciousness that never wavers or suffers from absentmindedness.

While the phrase "to believe" contains no prohibition against forgetfulness—for it is possible to believe and yet turn one's mind away from the object of that belief—the phrase "to know" implies "that the belief in God shall be constant in man, a permanent orientation, a living reality from which man cannot divert his attention even for a moment. This awareness of the reality of God must be the basis of our thought, ideas, feelings under all conditions and in all circumstances; all must turn upon this faith."[28]

At this point Rabbi Soloveitchik draws near to the Ba'al Shem Tov's hasidic concept of faith which incorporates this interpretation of faith under the heading of *devekut* (communion).[29] Like the Ba'al Shem Tov, Rabbi Soloveitchik links his interpretation to the biblical corroboration of Prov. 3:6: "In all thy ways acknowledge Him" which, already in the Talmud (*Ber.* 53a) was considered "a small matter upon which the whole body of the Torah hangs," and which explains the passage in a manner almost identical with that presented in the name of the Ba'al Shem Tov (which states: "In all thy ways 'know Him'—that is a great rule, 'know Him' in the sense of a coming together. . . . In all His deeds, even in things terrestrial, it is necessary that his work be done only for a high purpose and let nothing, even the smallest thing, be done for any purpose other than a heavenly one.")[30] (*Zava'at ha-Ribash*, Jerusalem 1969, p. 230). In the words of Rabbi Soloveitchik, "In all thy ways—in everything thou doest, in every path thou takest, in all situations, under all conditions—'know Him,' retain this awareness of the existence of God."

As is his wont, Rabbi Soloveitchik splendidly and at length describes all the places, situations and circumstances in human life in which man can and should "know" God. "To believe is necessary, but it is not enough; one must also feel and sense the existence of God. The presence of the Almighty must be a personal, intimate experience. And if this experience is not common, and if it proves impossible to achieve that *devekut* in Him, blessed be He, and if one feels not the touch of His hand, one cannot be a complete Jew."[31]

This insistence upon experience (which is so close to *hasidic* thought) is rooted in R. Soloveitchik's thought, in *halakhic* categories, and is based on Maimonides' *Mishneh Torah*, *halakhic* code 24. Rabbi Lichtenstein has already noted[32] that Rabbi Soloveitchik has added a new category to the customary division of the *mitzvot* into *hovot ha'evarim* (the duties of the limbs) and *hovot halevavot* (the duties of the heart)—the physical and spiritual duties. Soloveitchik's innovation lies in the identification of a category of *mitzvot* which are of a dual character; they are compounded of both "fulfillable' and "enactable" elements, in which *hovot haevarim* and *hovot halevavot* come together as one. There are *mitzvot* in which the fulfillment and the enactment cannot be separated, the *mitzvah* being fulfilled and enacted at the same time. This, for example, occurs in the *mitzvah* of the *lulav* (palm branch). The Torah states: "And you shall take unto you." When one "takes the *lulav*," one both fulfills and enacts the *mitzvah*. Similarly, with regard to eating *matzah* and "counting the *omer*." In contrast, there are *mitzvot* wherein the enactment and the fulfillment are distinct (occurring, as it were, on different planes and, perhaps, at different points in time). This happens, for instance, in *mitzvot* where the enactment is by hand or through speech, while the fulfillment takes place, perforce, within the heart. Thus a *mitzvah* may be enacted but not, in fact, fulfilled, since the fulfillment depends upon a certain feeling or state of mind. Among such *mitzvot* one may count those of mourning. Acts, such as the removal of sandals, are called for, but without a concomitant fulfillment of the *mitzvah* in the heart of the mourner, the *mitzvah* cannot be said to have been consummated (see *Mishneh Sanh.* 6:6). Other outstanding examples of this distinction between the enactment and the fulfillment of *mitzvot* are the reading of the *shema;* the enactment is in speech, but the fulfillment lies in the acceptance of Divine Sovereignty. Even more so is this the case with regard to prayer and repentance. Prayer is called *avodah she-belev* (worship of the heart) and the *mitzvah* involved is consummated not on the plane of enactment (speech), but on the plane of fulfillment (in the heart), in the experiential happening. The same applies to repentance which is similarly a "silent" or "heart"—centered form of worship.

Rabbi Soloveitchik's teachings about repentance focus on the description of that experiential happening, which he transmits in concepts drawn from the world of Halakhah. From these teachings emerges the character of "Repentant Man"; he embodies the experience which begins with a feeling of sin and ends in the redemption of a wondrous proximity to God. Between these two points stands man as a creator of worlds, as he shapes the greatest of his works—himself. All that is tragic in man, his sense of nothingness and non-being, is manifest in the feeling of sin. Man scrutinizes himself in shame and says: How remote [from God] am I; how abominable and unclean. He sees that his life is a cul-de-sac, that his whole existence is flat and meaningless. He is completely enveloped by Ecclesiastes' cry: "Vanity of vanities, all is vanity." This is a terrible feeling; it leads man to total despair, to a burdensome sense of guilt and to self-destruction.[33]

The sinner feels himself in exile, homeless, marooned on remote shores; his is a schizophrenic personality.[34] His spiritual powers, his feelings and thoughts are bereft of internal cohesion and his character lacks any single focus or center of gravity. When a man begins to feel this way he is at the starting point of the process of repentance. This is the initial stage. The next stage, though the antithesis of the former, is also contained in it and is a part of it. This second stage is fashioned out of the capacity for faith in man's spiritual make-up. This faith posits that, though today a man may be unclean and abominable, he can transcend and escape the constraint of his desperate condition. According to Rabbi Soloveitchik, Maimonides already asserted this when he emphasized again and again in *Hilkhot Teshuvah* that man can shape himself, free himself from deterministic causation and adopt a new system of causality according to his preference. Great is man's power.

It is by virtue of this power that man feels and knows that though all paths are *prima facie* barred to him, yet there remains a narrow and mysterious route somewhere, which meanders and twists between hills and mountains, climbs and descends, turns upwards and downwards and proceeds backwards and forwards. And if a man chooses this route, none can stop him. On more public pathways, man will immediately encounter obstacles: "Who are you and what seek you here?" The "king's way" is barred to the sinner. Neither will the angels of mercy allow him passage, for none can pass through the royal gate wearing the sackcloth of sin and iniquity. But though the king's way be barred, yet one may pass along the secret path in the undergrowth; if the main gate is locked, there yet remains a small wicket through which man may enter. The way to reach the goal is not by the public highway, but along the solitary route—and each man has a route of his own.

And as a man feels and knows that he has at least one further path to traverse, so must he believe that, in the depths of his heart, there still subsists, among the piles of burnt-out cinders, one glowing ember, one flickering spark and from this spark it is possible to rekindle a new flame.

Here is the whole dialectic of the process of repentance. Repentance implies that there are powers in man which allow him to leap from that sense of sin, which profoundly oppresses him and casts him far away, to a different feeling of *hazarti le-fanekha* (I am again in Your presence). "Yester-eve he was unclean and abominable . . . and today, beloved and precious"—a gigantic leap within mere minutes. Here is revealed that complete polarity which pervades the soul of man.

This leap lies at the heart of the act of sacrifice, which is at the core of the worship on the Day of Atonement (*Yom Kippur*). "When a Jew brings a sacrifice for atonement, how are his sins expiated? Is it by virtue of a two-shekel lamb? Certainly not! Atonement comes to him through the recognition and confession of sin embodied in the act of sacrifice. This confession means abnegation and annihilation of self, total submission and subservience, sacrifice of self, of all one's being and possession. . . as though one were oneself laid upon the altar."[35]

As a sacrifice upon the altar—so is the man in the whirlpool of purification. A man goes down and takes a dip and when he emerges, he is a new man, "Repentant Man."

This leap from sin to repentance, from exile and separation back to the Divine is anchored in the principle of free choice. Rabbi Soloveitchik sees this not as a voluntary option wherein a man can choose to do as he pleases, but as a clear exological imperative, as an existential commitment from which one cannot escape. In free choice man discovers his "self." The assumption that man is free and unconstrained, empowered with the courage of free choice and with the ability to do everything to determine the destiny of his religious and moral life—this assumption cannot be satisfied by faith alone; it requires awareness as well ("knowing," in the sense used by Maimonides), a feeling which will fill his whole being with the tension of that God-given "free choice." Choice should implant a feeling of self-esteem and responsibility in man. As Hillel put it (Avot 1:6): "If I am here, everything is here." Hillel the Elder was the most humble of men, yet it was he who stressed the "I," for "without a recognition of the self the feeling of free choice would not arise in man; without awareness of the 'I,' man cannot decide and determine."[36] This possibility of choosing is necessary and man cannot evade it.

Seen in this light, man must look upon himself as a guardian of the fate of the world. As the Talmud puts it (*Kid.* 40:6): "Man must always regard himself as though he were half guilty and half meritorious"; the world, too, should be viewed as if it is half guilty and half innocent. When performing one *mitzvah*, man is blessed for tilting his own and the world's scales to the side of merit; when committing one transgression, man is damned for tilting his own and the world's scales to the side of guilt. Choice is a perpetual feeling of maximum responsibility which permits no absentmindedness even for a moment;[37] choice demands of man commitment, courage, valor and bravery." Thus Rabbi Soloveitchik paraphrases Maimonides' reflection on faith, saying: "It is a positive commandment to know that there is free choice and that man is responsible for his actions."[38]

Man's existence, according to Rabbi Soloveitchik, has two dimensions: fate and destiny. Destiny-directed existence is "an active existence" in which man stands up to the environment into which he has been cast, and defends his individuality and uniqueness, his freedom and his ability not to deprive himself of his essence and independence in his struggle with the external world. The motto of the destiny-directed "self" is: "Against your will you are born and against your will you die, but by the exercise of free will you live." Man is born an object, dies an object, but can live as a subject, as an innovator and as creator, who impresses upon his life an individual stamp.[39]

Salvation, the very possibility of a Messiah, according to Rabbi Soloveitchik, is contingent upon the acceptance of the idea of free choice, which confers upon the man a power of transcendence and a capacity to rise above himself and to reach the infinite and eternal.[40]

"Judaism asserts," wrote Rabbi Soloveitchik in *Halakhic Man*,[41] "that man stands [forever] at a crossroads and wonders which way to proceed. Confronting him is a terrible choice: between the image of God or a beast of prey: the glory of nobility or the monster of the universe; the choicest of creatures or a corrupt creature; the image of a man of God or the portrait of a Nietzschean *übermensch*. Man must always, always determine and decide."

Free choice, which is part of man's being, means that man can create himself at will and, as it were, be born anew. Rabbi Soloveitchik does not completely reject the law of causation which governs mankind, but the distance is great between this and a subscription to total determinism. Following Kant, Rabbi Soloveitchik accepts the dualism of human existence: life unfolding in a mathematical, scientific world governed by physical laws of causation, and the life of the spirit, the internal existence, which is characterized by extreme freedom.[42] But, employing the principle of free choice, Soloveitchik demonstrates that man can fashion for himself a new law of causation which will take effect from a specific moment onwards, i.e., the moment of repentance-salvation, when complete transformation occurs from within.

Indeed years before voicing his reflections on repentance, Rabbi Soloveitchik asserted that "the acme of moral and religious perfection, which Judaism aspires to, is 'man as a creator.'"[43] He wrote: "The Almighty, when He created the world, left room for His creature—man—to participate in His creation. It was as if the Creator spoiled reality so that mortals might set it right and modify it. God transmitted the mystery of Creation—the Book of Creation—to man not only that he might read it, but in order that he might carry on the act of Creation. God left an area of evil and chaos in the world so that man might make it good . . . the abyss breeds misfortune and trouble and chaos lie in ambush in the dark alleys of reality desiring to undermine the Absolute Being and to subvert the radiance of Creation."[44] All this was determined early by the Creator Who, on purpose, "diminished the character and stature of Creation in order to leave room for [improvement] by His own creature and to crown man with the laurels of 'improver' and 'creator.'"[45]

Nothing serves better than the act of repentance "to create a new essence in man; the act of repentance is achieved through the complete application of will and a determined decision of the intellect." These were engraved in man from the commencement of his creation. From here onwards, he was compelled to become a chooser and was obliged to participate in the renewal of Creation; and most important of all is the obligation that man create himself: This is a conception which Judaism gave to the world.[46]

En fin the answer lies in the concept of grace. "The very phenomenon of repentance, the fact that man can transcend his baseness and ascend the mountain of God is one of the great acts of Grace conferred by God on His creations."[47] In justice, sin should have caused man's extinction; man's divorce from the seedbed of his existence should have spelled the end of his life. Thus was sin perceived also by the sages ("the sinning soul shall die") and by the Prophets ("sins will follow evil"). From a metaphysical standpoint, the possibility of repentance is an act of Grace on the part of the Creator, but this Grace becomes explicable through an understanding of the concept of time.

The problem of repentance is tied up with the concept of time, for it involves a future correction of something in the past. According to the definition of time offered by one of the Jewish sages of the Middle Ages, Rabbi Yedaiah Ha-Pnini in his famous epigram, "the past is not; the future—still not; and the present—like batting an eyelid." Man's existence is not rooted in time. For time itself, in the case of the past, appears as "was"—"is not," and as future, as "will be"—"still not." "From this perspective the concept of repentance is meaningless

and hollow. . . . One cannot feel remorse about a past which is
already dead and has sunk into the abyss of oblivion, and one cannot
decide about a future which is as yet unborn. . . . In this sense
Spinoza and Nietzsche did well to deride the idea of repentance."[48]
However, according to Rabbi Soloveitchik, whose thought is based
upon the different classifications one may apply to time in line with
the thinking of Bergson and Heidegger,[49] and especially with Max
Scheler's essay on repentance,[50] there is time which is actually "nothing"; i.e., quantified time, which flows according to the mechanistic
law of causation (in which moment "A" fades and is replaced by
moment "B," which gives way to moment "C"). This time is continuous
and follows the order of past-present-future; each point evolves from
a previous one and is—or is not—self-sufficient. This is physical or
technical-quantitative time; it passes and expires at the moment it
gives birth to the subsequent point in time. In contrast there exists
qualitative time, a dynamic continuity, in which the "past is continuous
and stable, does not pass or slip away through one's fingers, but
remains static. This past obtrudes and enters the domain of the present
which intermingles with the future."[51] In this conception of time, the
future is not of the "still not" variety; is not "hidden beyond the
mists, but is revealed in the here-and-now in all its splendor and
beauty. . . . Such a future infuses from its hidden resources power and
potency, vitality and freshness into the vessels of the past. . . . Both
past and future are alive; act and create in the hub of the present and
determine the appearance of existence." In this perspective the order
of time is not past-present-future; rather all three intermingle and
interpenetrate, and the conception of threefold time erupts and rises
forth beshrouded in the glory of unity—until the principle of "one
after another" often no longer serves as a clear indication of time.
Rather, "man lives in the shadow of the past, future and present
simultaneously," and then "the future determines the direction and
indicates the way. . . . There exists a phenomenon whose beginning is
sin and iniquity and whose end is *mitzvot* and good deeds, and *vice
versa*. The future transforms the trends and tendencies of the past."[52]

This intermingling of tenses occurs within man, who lives and acts not as if from one evolving moment to the next, but lives entirely at once.[53] Thus it is that "man, as he returns to his Creator, shapes himself out of the living and extant past as he looks to the future which offers up a happy visage." This leads us to the conclusion reached by Rabbi Soloveitchik that "the fundamental principle of the essence of repentance is that the future will rule and govern the past unrestrictedly." For repentance, he believes, means nothing other than (1) retrospective contemplation of the past and the distinction between the living and the dead in it; and (2) the vision of the future and its utilization according to the free determination of man.

Man's very existence, according to Rabbi Soloveitchik,[55] is contingent upon these two realms of activity; (1) in the memory of those situations and experiences undergone by man in the past and which, in many senses, have not died or been erased, but rather continue to exist in the inner recesses of his heart; and (2) in his expectations of the future, in his plans and hopes for the morrow and for the day following. In these two realms man responds to the question: Who am I? Memory and expectation come together and focus on the character of man and give significance to the whole of his life, above and beyond the flow of meaningless time, whose flux is devoid of significance and purpose.

Repentance creates and shapes time—in all its tenses—and gives it an image and character in the order of future-past-present. The past returns to life in the light of the future. Occasionally, life is shot—as in the case of the dry bones resurrected by Ezekiel in the Valley of Dura who, according to one opinion among the sages (*Sanh.* 92b), stood on their feet, sang for a short while and immediately returned to the dead. In this case, though the penitent revisits the sinful past, in his confrontation with it he immediately uproots and destroys it, thoroughly erasing it from his personality. While fully conscious, he divorces himself from his past. Among the signs of *teshuvah gemurah* (complete repentance) enumerated by Maimonides, appears the following: "And he changes his name, meaning, 'I am different and no longer the same person who did these deeds.' Nevertheless, true "Re-

Pinchas Hacohen Peli

pentant Man" is characterized by a creative power which enables him to forgo uprooting the past. Rather, on the contrary, it enables him to take up the past and exalt it, and to shape it so that it can be molded with the future to create the present, himself.

Here lies revealed, in all its forcefulness, the whole creative potency of repentance. It issues from the dialectical dynamic of sin, the very thing which severs man from God, which makes him abominable and unclean, the very thing which leads him—after repentance—to that high peak unattainable even by the "completely righteous."

"Repentant Man," if he wishes to attain this high peak, does not forget his sin or tear out or erase the pages of iniquity from the book of his life. Rather he exists in the spirit of "my sin is ever before me" (Ps. 51:3). Instead of uprooting the past and erasing the sin, he carries them up with him to heights he could never have dreamt of had he not sinned.

The force of the sin and the feelings of guilt and shame engendered in man are transmuted in the penitent's heart into an irresistible force propelling him towards the Creator. "The energy of sin pulls, as it were, upwards."[56]

Thus said the sages (*Ber.* 34b): "Where penitents stand the completely righteous cannot." How can it be that the penitent will draw nearer to God than the completely righteous? How can sins turn into a dynamic force propelling towards sanctity? Here, to Rabbi Soloveitchik's mind, is above all a mystery, a manifestation of God's grace, as is repentance in general. The Ruler and Creator of the world was He Who created the possibility that purity might be born out of abomination ("Who can bring a clean thing out of an unclean?" [the only One Who can] Job 14:4). It is also possible that the idea of raising sin to the level of sanctity is contained in this mystery.

Rabbi Soloveitchik does not content himself with indicating the mysterious in this phenomenon. He attempts also to reveal the spiritual, ontological motives underlying the dynamics of sin.

There is a tragic aspect to man's essence: it lies in the fact that people and the things closest to his heart, are not properly appreciated so long as they are alive and present. Man begins to accord them appropriate recognition only after they have moved away and have become distant and inaccessible. "From afar they now entice him like the stars in heaven; he appreciates their value, but cannot touch them."[57] The yearning after one who is gone and no longer lives is extremely difficult to bear and occasionally the soul actually becomes deranged through nostalgia and a craving to return to that original, vanished state. In his lifetime every man confronts this situation of yearning for one who was recently about and is now remote to the point of inaccessibility. Such yearnings are usually accompanied by a strong sense of guilt, which haunts man and may drive him to madness.

In a similar fashion, this phenomenon occurs in the penitent. When a man sins, he expels the Almighty from his presence.[58] God's departure is like that of a dearly beloved soul. After some time, following the initial shock, a man suddenly feels that his life has been impoverished, that his house has collapsed about him, that he has lost that thing most intimate and precious. As it is in the life of the individual, in the disappearance of a beloved soul, so is it in man's spiritual life, in God's departure from man's bosom in the wake of sin. "Mourning the withdrawal, as it were, of the Almighty from the sinner is like the mourning over a beloved father and mother."

Sooner or later the cloud of mourning will inevitably descend, and then will come fear and loneliness, estrangement, alienation, remoteness and separation; sadness will grow and emptiness will spread in the soul, and man will begin to yearn for the Almighty, and when he apparently sights God's Image from afar, he will begin to run towards it rapidly with all his strength. The power of the unleashed nostalgia in man's bosom, after such protracted incarceration, propels him onwards; he will run more quickly now than was his wont before growing apart from God. Through this nostalgic drive the penitent surpasses the completely righteous, who has never sinned, does not know or recognize.

Moreover, the sages of the Kabbalah (and of psychology) assert that in the soul there are two sets of forces: constructive and destructive.

Love is a constructive force; it is opposed by the destructive forces of jealousy and hatred. The positive-constructive forces are by and large static and passive, while the negative forces are dynamic and aggressive. Hatred is more emotional and fiercer than love; the destructive forces are more powerful than the constructive forces. The completely righteous person, who has never tasted sin, is not swayed by hatred and jealousy; he excels in love, charity and mercy, which are by nature tranquil and restrained drives. In contrast with him, the man who has sinned and repented can conjure up the dynamic energy of the destructive forces which once prevailed in his soul, and can channel it into his newly-adopted good ways. The future takes from the energy developed by the sinner and refashions it into a gigantic force for good. The same passion exhibited by the sinner in his thirst for iniquity can now be displayed in the fulfillment of *mitzvot*.[59] The same appetite and commitment previously invested in theft and illegal earning can now be funneled into acts of charity and mercy.

"Through sin man discovered in himself new spiritual forces, a reservoir of energy, of cupidity and obstinacy unknown to him before indulging in sin. Now he can sanctify all these drives and can direct them heavenwards. The aggressiveness within him now will not let him make do with his previous, wonted measure of do-gooding, but will propel him ever closer towards the heavenly throne."[60] In support of this point, Rabbi Soloveitchik elucidates the following passage (Ps. 29:9): "The Voice of the Lord maketh the hinds to calve, and discovereth the forests . . ." and explains:[61] on the Day of Atonement the Almighty demands that man become "a discoverer of forests"; that he endanger himself and enter the "jungle" of his soul, that place where hides the beast that is in man. The Almighty does not ask man to cut down the trees of the forest, nor that he uproot the jungle completely. For as men need fields for grazing and beds in which to raise flowers, so they need giant forests. These contain a great deal of animality and vivacity; a lot of healthy aggressiveness subsists in the depths of the forest. But woe to the forest which is impenetrable to the Voice of God, which maketh hinds calve and discovers forests.

Our aim is not to kill off the hinds, nor do we wish to burn down the dark forests, but rather to turn them into receptacles of the Voice of God. And after this is achieved, as the verse continues: "And in His Temple doth everyone speak of His glory." The rabbis say that the ingredients of incense of the Day of Atonement are alluded to here. In incense there is an admixture of resin and components of perfume. Why must one place resin, whose smell is unpleasant, among the perfumes? In order to show us that one may take the bad and blend it with the perfumes, in order that it may be exalted and enter the Holy of Holies. The exaltation of evil and not its mere purgation, the past itself and not only its eradication—these are the goals of "Repentant Man."

The path of repentance is a lonely road. Alone and solitary, man feels the pain of the sense of sin, and in the inner recesses of his being, he makes his way to repentance. "On the Day of Atonement," writes Rabbi Soloveitchik[62] "we unite with Moses on top of the Mount (to receive the second set of Tablets) as he listened intently to the fine silence which was shattered by the eruption of the wonder of repentance and the Grace of God." The latter presentation of the Law on Mt. Sinai, in which the second set of Tablets were bestowed, does not resemble the first, in which the Tablets were given and broken. On this occasion no public revelation, in the sight of all, occurred. The primal creatures did not tremble; the sound of the shofar was not heard in the camp; nor did thunder and lightning disturb the sleep of the hosts of Israel, who were still in a profound slumber at this early hour of the morning. "Total silence enveloped the mountain and the half-light of a wondrous and secret dawn shrouded it. Moses alone, unaccompanied by friend or disciple, climbed the cold and steep cliffs of the Mount. Even Joshua, who had never left his side, did not join Moses this time." Thus God commanded (Ex. 34:3): "And no man shall come up with thee, neither let any man be seen throughout all the Mount." As God revealed Himself to Moses on the mountain, he underwent spiritual suffering, out of a sense of aloneness, out of a silence of a man whose life is at a standstill and without foundation; in fear, the fear of a creature when he is for a fleeting moment cut off from his Creator.

The Day of Atonement is the day of "Repentant Man," and "the appearance of the Day of Remembrance (*Rosh ha-Shanah*), is not that of the Day of Atonement. On the first of the seventh month, God sets out towards man; on the tenth of the month man sets forth towards God. In the public setting-forth of God towards the community is hidden the secret of sovereignty and judgment; in the secret setting forth of the individual towards God, Who sits hidden in the shadows, is concealed the secret of repentance."[63]

Such is the way of "Repentant Man"—alone, in secret, unaccompanied. Repentance buds and transpires in the heart of the individual. However, "Repentant Man" will not reach his goal and the completion of his mission—salvation—as a lonely man of faith, but only as a part of the community of Israel. His whole endeavor as an individual is worthless to him until he renews his connection with the covenantal community and reintegrates in it. This integration does not abolish his loneliness or isolation;[64] nor does it help to ease his suffering or diminish his pain, but it gives him a certain status that is a prerequisite to salvation.

The individual Jew constitutes an integral part of *Knesset Israel* (the community of Israel). This is not a free and voluntary association; it is an ontological-essential one. As *Knesset Israel* is not a sum total or arithmetic combination of such and such individuals, but a metaphysical personality of singular essence and possessing an individual judicial personality, so the individual Jew does not have an independent existence and is a limb of *Knesset Israel*—unless he commits such sins as cut him off from the congregation and uproot him from the community of Israel.[65] In this manner the way to repentance is sealed off completely. However, remaining tied to *Knesset Israel* through loyalty to that body and its goals,[66] and enjoying the special attitude which such membership elicits—these offer no protection, as it were, except in the one sense of the two compelled by his existential reality as an individual and as part of the community. He still has need of private confession, private spiritual stock taking, individual purification. In this dialectic of individual and community, Rabbi Soloveitchik sees one of the foundations of Judaism.

"A Jew who has lost his faith in *Knesset Israel* even though he may, in his own little corner, sanctify and purify himself through severities and restrictions—this Jew remains incorrigible and totally unequipped to partake of the Day of Atonement which encompasses the whole of *Knesset Israel* in all its parts and in all its generations.

... Only a Jew who believes in *Knesset Israel* will be privileged to partake of the sanctity of the day and of atonement as part of the community of Israel. ... A Jew who lives as part of *Knesset Israel* and is ready to lay down his life for it, who is pained by its hurt and is happy at its joy, wages its battles, groans at its failures, and celebrates its victories. ... A Jew who believes in *Knesset Israel* is a Jew who binds himself with an indissoluble bond not only to the People of Israel of his generation, but to *Knesset Israel* through all the generations."[67] This necessary loyalty to *Knesset Israel* is not, according to Rabbi Soloveitchik's explanation, a matter of mysticism or metaphysics; it is rooted and embodied in the *halakhic* categories which assert, in reference to the sanctity of Israel, that "this sanctity has two roots: firstly, the sanctity of the Fathers, which reaches us as an inheritance transmitted from generation to generation, from the Patriarch Abraham down to the present day; secondly, the sanctity of self. In addition to the sanctity vouchsafed each person of Israel as an inheritance from his forefathers, there is in him a portion of sanctity which the Almighty invests in every man of Israel in every generation." The roots of these two portions of sanctity, explains Rabbi Soloveitchik, lie in the two Covenants between God and His people Israel (in fact there were three but two of these can be counted as one): the Covenant at Horeb with those who received the Torah, and the Covenant of the Wilderness of Moab with those who entered the land. In these covenants, Israel was sanctified and that sanctity passes down to us from generation to generation. That is the sanctity of the Fathers. These two covenants are joined by a third—the covenant in Deuter-

onomy. That covenant was not concluded with that generation only
but with all the generations and with all children of Israel down to
the end of time, as it is written (Deut. 29:14, 15):

"Neither with you only do I make this covenant and this oath, but
with him that standeth here with us this day before the Lord our God
and also with him that is not here with us this day." From here
springs an original sanctity of self, of every generation, and every
individual in every age. Before us, therefore, is a double bond between
Israel and the Lord, both as individuals and as a people, seed of
Abraham.

"The origin of the sanctity is in the making of a covenant, i.e., in a
contract entailing mutual obligations. Sin means that if one party to
the agreement fails to meet the conditions of the contract, the agreement becomes null and void."[68] The sanctity that was conferred by
virtue of the contract lapses. This applies also when the sinner has
sinned through error or under external compulsion. The reference
here is to that personal sanctity of the self. With regard to the sanctity
of the Fathers, the sanctity passes down as an inheritance and it does
not lie in the power of a sinner to breach or break the contract; the
covenant is the inheritance of the whole people of Israel and no
power exists which can revoke it. Nevertheless, though the covenant
with Israel exists, the sinner—as it were—cuts himself off from it
until he repents. Once repentant, "not only does the repentance cleanse
the sinner of the filth of iniquity, but it contains a kind of fresh act of
covenant-making between the individual and the Almighty. . . . Repentance is not merely the purification of the personality, but a special
sanctification of the individual, making him ready once more to conclude a covenant."

The renewal of the personal covenant ("there are no delegates in
covenant-making and if repentance is a renewed acceptance of personal
sanctity, then there is no escape from direct confrontation with God")
leads the individual back to the framework of the complete agreement,
the double one, which rests upon the dual connection between God
and the people of Israel and God and each individual in Israel.

The prophet Elisha was privileged to enter into just such a renewed covenant, as Rabbi Soloveitchik describes him at the end of his essay "The Lonely Man of Faith." In the depths of his soul Elisha remains the lonely man of faith, but in obedience to God's command he returns to participate in the drama of the covenant and to take part in "the great and festive dialogue" between the God and the People of the Covenant.

The ways of repentance are many and varied. Repentance, it is true, is not restricted merely to the ideal "Repentant Man." There are penitents whose repentance is efficacious and perhaps excellent, who yet remain remote from the concept of the typological "Repentant Man." There are also penitents who are not true penitents like the usurer who leaves debt-pledges in his drawer lest he have "need" of them again, and like that sinner who retains the address of the woman with whom he had sinned, lest he "desire" her again. These stand on the borderline of repentance and are light years away from resembling "Repentant Man" who, after deep spiritual torment and personal decisiveness, achieved a total and radical transformation of character "until the One Who knows all mysteries will testify that he [the penitent] will not revert to this sin ever after," without, in any way, damaging the power of free choice that is in man. "Repentant Man" reaches that rung which is above and beyond the momentary, transient choice that determines the nature of the immediate act; he propels himself, as it were, into a state of permanent, standing sanctity, of "sanctity for the moment and sanctity for the future," insofar as he has placed the whole future in his present life which illuminates afresh his past life as well. Moreover, "Repentant Man" does not live with the past, but with the future of which the past has become a part.

Notes

1. On the typological categories and their problematics in the writings of the Rav, see Eugene B. Borowitz, "A New Jewish Theology in the Making" (Philadelphia: Westminster Press, pp. 164–70). Compare the Rav's view on this matter in Notes 5 and 6 below. See also Lawrence Kaplan, "The Religious Philosophy of Rabbi Joseph Soloveitchik," *Tradition* vol. 14, No. 2 (Fall 1973).

2. Rabbi Joseph B. Soloveitchik, "Ish ha-Halakhah (Halakhic Man)," in *Besod Ha Yahid ve ha-Yahad (In Aloneness, In Togetherness). A Selection of Hebrew Writings* (henceforth *IAIT*). ed. Pinchas Peli (Jerusalem: Orot, 1976) pp. 37–188.

3. Soloveitchik, p. 45.

4. Rabbi Joseph B. Soloveitchik, "The Lonely Man of Faith," *Tradition*, vol. 7, No. 2 (Summer 1965), 5–67.

5. Soloveitchik, *Halakhic Man*, p. 39, n. 1, where the Rav deals with the typological system formulated by Edward Sprenger in his book, *Lebensformen.*

6. Soloveitchik, "Lonely Man," p. 48, n. 38: "In reality there are no pure typological structures." See also Note 68 below.

7. Pinchas, Peli, "Al ha-Teshuvah (On Repentance)," from the oral discourses of Rabbi Joseph B. Soloveitchik (Jerusalem 1975), pp. 1–354.

8. Soloveitchik, *Halakhic Man*, p. 40.

9. Soloveitchik, *Halakhic Man*, p. 40.

10. Soloveitchik, *Halakhic Man*, p. 40.

11. Soloveitchik, *Halakhic Man*, p. 41, n. 4. Soloveitchik offers exegesis on the Biblical passages: "Out of my straits I called upon the Lord" (Ps. 118:5) and "From the depths have I cried unto Thee, O Lord" (Ps. 130:1). Out of the straits of contradiction and internal turmoil, spiritual doubts and perplexities; from the depths of the soul riven with anti-nomianism and negation, from the furthest recesses of the spirit, perplexed and suffering. I called unto God, I called You, O Lord.

12. Peli, p. 52. Compare with Rudolf Otto, *The Idea of the Holy*, translated by John W. Harvey (New York: Oxford Univ. Press, 1958).

13. Peli, p. 124.

14. Peli, p. 125.

15. Rabbi J.B. Soloveitchik, "On the Love of the Torah and the Redemption of the Soul of the Generation," an answer to an interlocutor, in *IAIT*, pp. 403–32.

16. Rabbi J.B. Soloveitchik, "Sacred and Profane; Kodesh and Hol in World Perspectives," *Gesher*, published by Yeshiva University, vol. 2, No. 1 (Sivan 1966).

17. Rabbi J.B. Soloveitchik, "Kol Dodi Dofek" (The Voice of My Love Calls)," in *IAIT*, p. 339.

18. Peli, p. 142. The Rav deals with this point at greater length in his essay "On the Love of the Torah and the Redemption of the Soul of the Generation" (*IAIT*, p. 428). "God said to Abraham: 'Take now thy son, thine only son, Isaac, whom thou lovest' . . . (Gen. 22:2). In other words, I demand of you the greatest sacrifice possible. I want your beloved and only son in sacrifice. Do not delude yourself that after obeying my command and offering up your son, I shall give you another in his place. From the moment Isaac is slaughtered upon the altar, you will remain alone and childless. No other will be born unto you. Your existence will be governed by an incomparable isolation. I want your only son, for whom no substitute exists or shall exist. Similarly, do not imagine that you will succeed in forgetting Isaac or putting him out of mind. For the rest of your days you shall brood upon his fate. I demand that son whom you love and will love forever. Your life will turn into one long epic of suffering. Nonetheless, this is the sacrifice that I demand. Of course, at the end of the experience, whose essence is dread and pain, is endless joy. At the moment Abraham removed his son from atop the altar at the behest of the angel, the suffering changed into boundless joy and the dread into eternal happiness. At the beginning of the religious experience lies the sacrifice of essence; at its end, the discovery of essence. Indeed, man cannot discover himself without the sacrifice. For man can find only that which has been lost, and none can retrieve a thing unless it has first left his keeping."

19. Peli, p. 142.

20. Peli, p. 166. Compare with Soloveitchik's *Five Sermons* translated by David Telsner (Jerusalem: Tal Orot, 1974), pp. 14–15. Soloveitchik here explains Deut. 20:29; i.e., the means by which a Jew achieves purchase on the Almighty is through his "whole being," *be-khol nafshekha*, as explained in Rabbi Akiva's sermon (*Ber.* 63a): "Even if it costs one's life." The Almighty can be reached through suffering and obstinate devotion, "in short, one reaches the Almighty through sacrifice."

21. Peli, pp. 65, 167. Compare with Rabbi A. I. Kook, *The Lights of Repentance* (Jerusalem 1970), pp. 46–52. In general, there are many points of convergence between the linking on repentance of the "poet of repentance." Rabbi Kook, and the "philosopher of repentance," the Rav as, for example, on the problem of time, suffering, the individual and the community, etc. A comparative study of the two might prove enlightening.

22. Peli, p. 68.

23. Peli, p. 108 ff.

24. Peli, p. 113.

25. Peli, p. 115.

26. Peli, p. 195.

27. Peli, p. 196, 118. See also Aaron Lichtenstein, "Rabbi Joseph Soloveitchik," in *Great Jewish Thinkers of the 20th Century*, ed. Simon Noveck (Clinton, Mass: 1964) Lichtenstein's assertion (p. 296) that the Rav's emphasis upon religious experience is reflected only in some of "recent writings" dealing with the relation of intellect and emotion, is worth reexamining because, as it seems to us, the value of the religious experience is primary in all of the Rav's published works from *The Halakhic Man* (1944) until today. Compare also: Joseph B. Agus, *Guideposts in Modern Judaism* (New York: 1954), pp. 38–43. Agus argues that one cannot regard Soloveitchik's thought as entirely bound by the confines of the Halakhah and that inevitably it ventures beyond these into the realms of the Kabbalah and philosophy.

28. Peli, p. 197.

29. On the concept of "Dvekut" in *hasidism*, see Gershom Scholem, "Dvekut or Communion with God," in *The Messianic Idea in Judaism* (New York: Schocken 1971), pp. 203–27.

30. Peli, p. 196.

31. Peli, p. 198. Here and elsewhere the Rav reaches unusual intimate and moving confessions, rare in Jewish tradition, of nearness to God.

32. In his splendid biographical essay on the Rav (see reference 27), p. 295.

33. Peli, p. 160.

34. Peli, p. 229.

35. Peli, p. 168: compare *Sefer Ha-Hinnukh*, 91, based on Nahmanides explanation for the sacrifices.

36. Peli, pp. 209–10.

37. Peli, p. 210.

38. Peli, p. 210.

39. Soloveitchik, "Kol Dodi Dofek," p. 337.

40. Soloveitchik, "On the Love of the Torah," p. 405.

41. Soloveitchik, *Halakhic Man*, p. 157.

42. Compare to Borowitz, p. 163.

43. Soloveitchik, *Halakhic Man*, p. 146.

44. Soloveitchik, *Halakhic Man*, p. 148.

45. Soloveitchik, *Halakhic Man*, p. 154.

46. Soloveitchik, *Halakhic Man*, p. 157.

47. Peli, p. 124.

48. Soloveitchik, *Halakhic Man*, p. 162.

49. *Hebrew Encyclopedia*, Vol. IX, p. 448; vol. XIV, p. 52.

50. Max Scheler, "Repentance and Rebirth," in *On the Eternal in Man*, translated by Bernard Noble (London: SCM Press, 1960), pp. 35–65, and in greater detail and

length in a dissertation by Johann Schindler, *Gott and Mensch in ihrer gegenseitgen Zuordnung in der philosophischen Konzeption Max Schellers* (Augsburg, 1968).

51. Soloveitchik, *Halakhic Man*, p. 162.

52. Soloveitchik, *Halakhic Man*, p. 163.

53. Scheler, pp. 40–41. In *Halakhic Man*, p. 72 the Rav refers to his reliance on Scheler's thinking; compare also Kaplan.

54. Soloveitchik, *Halakhic Man*, p. 187.

55. Peli, pp. 170–71. The Rav here develops the idea that the old have more memories and less expectations, and the young less memories and more expectations; the two constitute the elements of the "self" in man. Compare with similar idea developed in Ahad Ha-Am's essay, "Avar ve-Atid (Past and Future)," in *Al Parashat Derakhim*, Vol. 1, p. 150, which begins: "A great philosopher inadvertently was Adam, the first person who expressed the word I. . . the self of each person is the product of the combination of is memory with his will, of the past with the future."

56. Peli, p. 176. Compare with Scheler, p. 42 repentance as revealing in man's soul hidden, untainted corners of youthfulness.

57. Peli, p. 178.

58. Compare Zohar.

59. Here, too, is felt the influence of *hasidic* thought. Compare with "The Book of the Ba'al Shem Tov," Gen. p. 158–61. On the influence of hasidic thought upon the Rav even from his childhood, compare with Lichtenstein, p. 282.

60. Peli, p. 184.

61. Peli, p. 185.

62. Soloveitchik, "Ma Dodekh Mi-dod," in *IAIT*, 189–254.

63. Soloveitchik, "Ma Dodekh Mi-dod," p. 198.

64. Soloveitchik, "The Lonely Man of Faith," p. 22ff.

65. Peli, p. 81.

66. Peli, pp. 93–94.

67. Peli, p. 98.

68. Peli, p. 134.

In this article (Tradition 28:2), *Yitzchak Blau discusses the influence of the Rav on Max Scheler's work on repentance. The Rav moves beyond Scheler's ideas, drawing on classical Jewish sources to create a Torah perspective. Repentance involves the transformation of one's personality. This view of teshuvah also impacts on the creative nature of "halakhic man" and the Rav's understanding of* kedushat hazeman, *the holiness of time.*

Creative Repentance

On Rabbi Joseph B. Soloveitchik's Concept of Teshuvah

ༀ

Yitzchak Blau

ༀ

t is well known that the Rav, Rabbi Joseph B. Soloveitchik, perhaps nore successfully than any other figure in our generation, employs general literature and philosophy to elucidate Jewish texts and conepts.[1] The Rav illustrates aspects of *homo religiosus'* consciousness with the aid of Kierkegaard and others,[2] establishes a model for Halakhic Man which parallels the work of a mathematician,[3] and utilizes a Bergsonian notion of time to explain *kedushat zman*, the sanctity of ime.[4] In all of the aforementioned examples, the Rav openly acknowledges his debt to these thinkers as he reformulates their ideas in Torah categories.

Several writers[5] have noted another explicit source of influence on he Rav: Max Scheler's work on repentance.[6] Scheler (1874–1928), a German phenomenologist who believed in a "logic of the heart," developed ideas that had great appeal for religious thinkers in general and for the German Jewish community associated with the Hildesheimer seminary in particular. Alexander Altmann[7] wrote his doctoral dissertation at the University of Berlin on the cognitive value Scheler assigned to our emotions. Rabbis Joseph Wohlgemuth[8] and Yehiel

Yaakov Weinberg[9] both based their writings on repentance on Scheler's discussion of the subject.

The Rav cites Scheler several times in his discussion of repentance in *Halakhic Man*.[10] The fifth chapter of *Al ha-Teshuva*,[11] (a series of Rabbi Soloveitchik's lectures on *teshuvah* presented by Pinhas Peli) is similar to the discussion in *Halakhic Man* and an analysis of it also reveals Scheler's influence.

We shall attempt here to show how the Rav draws on Scheler's formulations, uses them to decipher a difficult Talmudic passage regarding *teshuvah*, and produces a better philosophical and psychological understanding of repentance. We shall then investigate the echo of Scheler's works in the broader context of the Rav's thought.

The *Yerushalmi* (Makkot 2:6) presents a striking dialogue:

> It was inquired of Wisdom, "What is the punishment of a sinner?"
> Wisdom said, "Evil pursues the wicked." It was asked of prophecy,
> "What is the punishment of a sinner?" Prophecy said to them, "The
> sinful soul shall perish." It was asked of the Holy One, "What is the
> punishment of a sinner?" and He said, "Let him repent and he will be
> forgiven."

This talmudic passage underscores the difficulties in understanding repentance. Both wisdom and prophecy reject any possibility for the sinner to absolve himself of his transgression. It remains for God Himself to affirm the worth of *teshuvah*. We ordinarily assume that what's done is done and that the past is irrevocable. Indeed, the repentant sinner should resolve to improve in the future, but why torment him with the guilt of an unalterable past? Furthermore, our sense of justice demands that acts of wickedness not be dismissed cavalierly without some retribution. Would a civil court allow regret to completely obviate the need for punishment?

Many philosophers concur with the voice of wisdom in the *Yerushalmi*. Spinoza[12] and others regard repentance as worthless or even harmful. Spinoza writes that "repentance is no virtue, and does not spring from reason; but whosoever repents a deed is doubly oppressed and incapable."[13]

Kant[14] expressed the difficulties in understanding repentance from a perspective peculiar to his own thought. His conception of freedom mandated that virtue can be exercised only by the person himself; neither his fellow man nor God can vicariously atone for him. Thus, any achievement of atonement must be deserved by the sinner himself. However, Kant also believes that man must fulfill his duty, the categorical imperative, at all times. Therefore, man can never achieve the extra credit necessary to make up for old debts.

Having asserted the futility of repentance, these writers then attempt to trace the psychological forces that spawned such a pointless concept. One view sees repentance as the "hereditary echo of earlier experiences of punishment."[15] Memory of previous punishment has instilled within us a fear of further pain; we wish that we had not done that. We now call this wish "conscience."[16]

Nietzsche suggests a more extreme hypothesis. Scheler's summation of this theory[17] states that bad conscience arose "when passions of hate, revenge, cruelty and spite of all kinds, which once were allowed free play against fellowmen, came to be dammed in by state, law and civilization, and thereupon turned for their satisfaction against the life-matter of those who felt them." In Nietzsche's own words "Lacking external enemies and resistances, and confined within an oppressive narrowness and regularity, man began rending, persecuting, terrifying himself like a wild beast hurling itself against the bars of its cage."[18]

Some religious thinkers,[19] particularly in the Christian tradition, accept the irrationality of repentance and declare divine forgiveness an act of pure grace. Kant himself was forced to resort to grace though the very concept denies basic assumptions of his thought.[20] This thinking may be responsible for the bizarre penitential rites involving mortification of the flesh. Striving to atone for a misdeed that can't be changed, the pietists imagined greater and more effective ways to damage themselves, the hopelessly guilty sinners.

Although most Jewish writers on repentance (with the notable exception of the *Haside Ashkenaz*)[21] do not recommend ascetic, penitential practices,[22] many of them focus on *teshuvah* as a manifestation of divine benevolence. R. Moshe Hayyim Luzzatto writes[23] that true, untempered justice would immediately punish the sinner and allow no chance for forgiveness. In his view, the possibility of pardon reflects *middat harahamim* more than *middat hadin.*

Rav Menahem haMeiri,[24] among others, offers an explanation for the necessity of *teshuvah*, Man, by his very nature, occasionally fails. If there were no possibility of atonement, man would soon despair and abandon all hope. This approach portrays *teshuvah* as an indispensable concession; it fails to explain how repentance can act positively. Such an approach circumvents the philosophic complaint but does not answer it.

Scheler counters that all the indictments of repentance rest upon a "false notion of the internal structure of our spiritual life."[25] They view our existence as human beings just as we view objective time, like a flowing river in which no later part of the river can exert any influence on a previous part. Time, however, is not onedimensional and one-directional as far as the human personality is concerned.

Every instant of our lives includes the past, present and future. Of course, it is not the material reality of the past or future but rather the memory of the former and the anticipation of the latter. Who we are is, to some extent, determined by how we look at events in our past and what our aspirations are for the future. To be sure, from the perspective of historical reality, the past can not be altered; yet, as far as the human personality is concerned, we can always change that part of ourselves that stands in relation to the past.

Thus, the significance of any previous act remains continuously dependent on how we relate to that act. Scheler writes that "We are not merely the disposers of our future; there is also no part of our past life which . . . might not be genuinely altered in its *meaning* and *worth* . . ."[26] Each human life resembles a book in which the meaning of each chapter only becomes clear with the reading of the final chapter.

II

The Rav builds on this idea in explaining a problematic Talmudic passage (*Yoma* 86b). The Gemara presents two contradictory statements of R. Shimon ben Lakish regarding the greatness of repentance. One statement claims that after *teshuvah*, sins are accounted as if they had been committed unintentionally; the other version states that the sins become converted into merits. The Talmud reconciles the two statements: the former refers to one who repents out of fear while the latter refers to one who repents out of love.

The radical notion that "sins become merits" demands an explanation. As R. Shmuel Edels phrased it, "should the sinner benefit [from his transgressions]?" We might understand that God would absolve the repentant sinner of a punishment he had previously deserved; but why should his earlier errors have positive value?

Rabbi Soloveitchik[27] addresses this issue by posing a psychological question: How does the repentant individual relate to his past filled with iniquity? The Rav depicts two possible reactions. One option involves cutting oneself off from one's past, neither thinking about it nor relating to it, even treating it as if it were somebody else who had lived those events. Indeed, many people prefer never to speak or think about entire areas of their lives.

In the alternative case, *baale teshuvah* do not attempt to erase their past; their reaction is quite the contrary. They remember all their sins but look back at them with a tremendous sense of regret. Knowledge of past sins becomes a motivating factor in their repentance as the remorse they feel drives them on to perform better in the future, to make up for years wasted.

These two alternatives explain the two statements of R. Shimon ben Lakish. People who react in the first way now view their sins as belonging to someone else, as if they were involuntary transgressions. On the other hand, those who chose the latter alternative continue to relate to their sins, but turn those memories into a positive force. In this light the Gemara's assertion that "sins convert into merits" means not that the sins change metaphysically but that sins can serve a meritorious role in the forging of a new personality.

Here, the Rav draws on Scheler's notion but moves a step further Rabbi Soloveitchik begins his explanation[28] by mentioning the philosophic problem of trying to blot out the past and responds, as Scheler does, that memory and anticipation are crucial components of the human personality. Having established that how people relate to their past affects who they are now, the Rav outlines different possible relationships with the past. A sinner's repentance is incomplete to the extent he or she still identifies strongly with his past. Within repentance, two options emerge and the option chosen plays a significant part in the determination of character.

In the lecture presented, the Rav does not explain how those two approaches to repentance correspond to the Talmudic distinction between *teshuvah* motivated by love and by fear. I would suggest that fear is more of a movement of recoiling while love involves a movement of attraction.[29] Whether the Talmud refers to fear of punishment or awe before the Divine, the fearful personality disdains any associations that remind him of his terrifying past. The loving personality, on the other hand, faces that past head on and draws energy from his memories.

Another Talmudic passage can be interpreted along the lines of Scheler's analysis. The Gemara (*Kiddushin* 40b) cites the statement of R. Shimon bar Yohai that a person who has been righteous for a lifetime may yet annihilate his merits by rebelling at the end of his life. The Talmud asks "Let it be [deemed] a mixture of merits and sins?" Resh Lakish explained that we refer to one who regrets his or her good deeds. If one can remake the effect of his sins by looking upon them in a new way, conversely, one can undo the nature of his merits as well.[30] Strikingly, it is once again R. Shimon ben Lakish speaking. In a way, this fourth-century *amora* anticipated Scheler and pointed the way for the Rav some millennium and a half later.[31]

Where Scheler states that regretting the past changes the human personality, the Rav explains how that change occurs. We have already referred to general explanation: memory of misdeeds acts as a motivatng force. Rav Soloveitchik proceeds to develop in greater depth two positive possible orientations for past sins.[32] Firstly, negative traits such as anger and jealousy have a certain aggressive dynamism that the more benevolent characteristics, such as compassion, do not share. The repentant sinner, having experienced the burning force of hatred, can learn to channel that energy towards more positive traits. By the same token, the righteous individual who never sinned will not experience this power and never employ it. The Rav's second approach can best be understood by examining his other writings, to which we shall now turn.

Scheler's concept of repentance is echoed in two of the Rav's significant published works. In "The Sacred and the Profane,"[33] Rabbi Soloveitchik explains *kedushat zman* as a qualitative approach to time. Time is not to be experienced exclusively in quantitative measure like grains of sand dropping into an hourglass or the ticks of a clock, which occupy a finite moment and then vanish. Time is rather to be lived in terms of the values and creativity exhibited in each moment. Hence, the *akedah* and *matan Torah* are not merely historical events belonging to a distant past; they are events that continue to live in our consciousness, and influence us daily.

The qualitative measure of time mandates recollecting the event and analyzing its ramifications. "From the vantage point of the present, we first evaluate the significance of the past."[34] Frequently, we do not appreciate the value of a particular event until its effects wear off and we notice something lacking.

This backward look constitutes the essence of repentance. "God from afar fascinates one more than God in one's immediacy."[35] We first appreciate the wonder of closeness to God when we yearn for that closeness we once knew. Refusing to blot out the memory of his sin, the sinner recalls the pain of being far from God to arouse in himself the desire to be close again.

Here again, the Rav depicts a repentance in which the way one looks at his past defines who he is. In the first approach, the Rav spoke of channeling the dynamism of previous transgressions; in this second approach, the period of sin serves as a point of contrast to illustrate to man how much he has to gain in the realization of his spiritual potential.

Most significantly, Rabbi Soloveitchik employs this theory of repentance as an illustration of the creativity of Halakhic Man.[36] For the Rav, creativity represents an essential characteristic of Halakhic Man:

> The most fervent desire of Halakhic Man is to behold the replenishment of the deficiency of creation, when the real world will conform to the ideal world, and the most exalted and glorious of creations, the ideal Halakhah, will be actualized in its midst. The dream of creation is the central idea in the halakhic consciousness—the idea of the importance of man as a partner of the Almighty in the act of creation, man as a creator of worlds.[37]

From this perspective, the Rav interprets numerous Jewish texts and explains many *mitzvot*, including repentance, in a new light. Here the Schelerian view of repentance is crucial. If one views atonement as the miraculous intervention of God against all logic, then man plays at best a passive role in the process. Repentance would certainly not be so significant a component of man's religious personality.

However, the Schelerian understanding of repentance shifts the focus from God's activity to that of man. Repentance exhibits man at his most creative, as he remolds and refashions his own personality. Rav Soloveitchik points to the Halakhah that repentance is manifested by changing one's name.[38] Through repentance, man recreates himself and truly deserves to be referred to by a different name.

It should be noted that Scheler's approach does not necessitate that man attains forgiveness independently, that is, without any Divine assistance. What his analysis accomplishes is to show how regret and remorse function creatively and positively. Though man may call upon Divine benevolence to achieve atonement, he acts on his own in order to deserve that bestowal of kindness.

A text of the *Yerushalmi* in Makkot found in the Budapest Geniza[39] adds a new dimension to the discussion. In this version, the question addressed to Wisdom and Prophecy regarding the fate of the sinner is asked of Torah as well. Torah responds "Let him bring a sacrifice and he will be forgiven." Even the biblical perspective sees human repentance as insufficient without the aid of sacrifice. At the conclusion of the discussion, God declares that forgiveness depends not on a temple or sacrifices. It depends on *teshuvah*, a refashioning and remodeling of identity.

William Douglass Chamberlain, another thinker cited by the Rav,[40] poignantly expresses the difference between atonement based on penitential rites and a repentance which transforms the personality:

The difference in the two views lies in the fact that the Reformers place the emphasis on the transformation of the whole mind, heart and will of man, while the Catholic view tends to leave the emphasis on the penitential practices of the sinner seeking pardon. In the latter view, the woods cannot be seen for the trees: men lose their sense of sin in their preoccupation with sins. This restricts repentance to particulars when it was intended to touch every phase of life, thought and aspiration.[41]

The anthropological truth that both Rav Soloveitchik and Scheler seek to capture is surely akin to that which Chamberlain identifies with the Reformers. Like the Reformers, both view repentance as a transformation of the personality. Yet Rav Soloveitchik does far more than merely offer a Jewish version of Scheler. The Rav contributes toward greater understanding of repentance from both a general and Jewish perspective.

From a general perspective, the Rav develops Scheler's ideas about the positive effects of remorse with greater psychological depth and precision. Scheler never really explains how recalling sins benefits the personality. From a Jewish perspective, Rabbi Soloveitchik shows how this idea coheres with and even explains in new ways well-known classical texts on the subject. The Rav's work on the theme of *teshuvah* stands out as a magnificent example of how the integration of general and Jewish thought can form a more profound understanding of the latter. Of course, the endeavor to integrate distinct disciplines requires creativity. Thus, the very words with which the Rav calls for the creative gesture are themselves a manifestation of his own creative impulse.

Notes

1. On Rabbi Soloveitchik's use of general thought, see Lawrence Kaplan, "The Religious Philosophy of Rabbi Joseph Soloveitchik" *Tradition*, 14.2, 1973 pp. 43–64, Avi Ravitzky, "Rabbi Joseph Baer Soloveitchik on Human Knowledge Between Mainonidean and Neo-Kantian Philosophy" *Modern Judaism* 6:2, 1986 pp. 157–188.

2. *Halakhic Man* (JPS, 1983) tr. Lawrence Kaplan p. 4, 139 n. 4. The Hebrew original can be found in *Ish ha-Halakhah—Galuy v'Nistar* (Jerusalem 1979). All citations will be to the English translation.

3. *Halakhic Man*, pp. 17–29.

4. "The Sacred and the Profane," *Gesher* 3:1, 1966, pp. 5–29.

5. Kaplan, *op. cit.*, p. 57, 63 n. 68, Pinhas Peli, "Repentant Man—A High Level in Rabbi Soloveitchik's Typology of Man," *Tradition* 18:2, 1979 p. 149, 159 n. 50.

6. Max Scheler, "Repentance and Rebirth," in *On the Eternal in Man*, tr. Bernard Noble (London 1960), pp. 33–65.

7. On Altmann's doctorate see Paul Mendes-Flohr, "Introduction: Theologian Before the Abyss" in *The Meaning of Jewish Existence: Theological Essays* (Brandeis, 1991) pp. xiii–xlvii. The Rav deals with this aspect of Scheler's thought in *Halakhic Mind* (New York, 1986); see index.

8. Wohlgemuth's work on Scheler is cited in Mendes-Flohr *op. cit.*, p. 149 n. 5.

9. Rabbi Weinberg's article is in his *L'Prakim* (Jerusalem 1967) pp. 121–138 esp. 123–126.

10. p. 161 n. 125, 127.

11. *Al ha-Teshuva* (Jerusalem 1975). There is an English version translated by Peli entitled *On Repentance* (Jerusalem, 1980).

12. Barukh Spinoza, *The Ethics*

13. Spinoza *op. cit.*, "Of Human Bondage" Proposition LIV.

14. Immanuel Kant, *Religion Within the Limits of Reason Alone*, tr. T.M. Greene and H.H. Hudson (New York, 1960) pp. 66–72, 106–107, 134.

15. Scheler, p. 38.

16. *Ibid.*, p. 38.

17. *Ibid.*, p. 37.

18. Friedrich Nietzsche, *The Birth of Tragedy and the Genealogy of Morals*, tr. Francis Golffing (Doubleday 1956), p. 218.

19. See Aloys H. Dirksen, *The New Testament Concept of Metanoia* (Catholic University 1932).

20. Kant, p. 70.

21. See Ivan Marcus, *Piety and Society: the Jewish Pietists of Medieval Germany* (Leiden 1981) pp. 75–86.

22. The discussions of *teshuvah* in Maimonides' *Mishneh Torah Hilkhot Teshuva*, Saadiah Gaon's *Emunot v'Deot* and Bahya's *Hovot haLevavot* fail to mention penitential rites. See R. Yehezkel Landau, *Teshuvot Noda b'Yehudah* I, *Orah Hayyim*, no. 35.

23. *Mesillat Yesharim* ch. 4.

24. *Hibbur HaTeshuva* (Jerusalem, 1976) 1:1 p. 23. Also see *Hovot haLevavot*, Introduction to *Shaar haTeshuva* and R. Joseph Albo's *Sefer haIkkarim* 4:28. It should be noted that the previous chapter in *Sefer haIkkarim* includes a different approach.

25. Scheler, p. 39.

26. *Ibid.*, p. 40.

27. *Al ha-Teshuva*, p. 171.

28. *Ibid.*, p. 170.

29. See Maimonides *Mishneh Torah, Hilkhot Yesode haTorah* 2:2.

30. Two recent thinkers who saw repentance as an act of grace were troubled by this passage, with its implications that one can alter the past. See R. Elhanan Wasserman, *Kovetz Maamarim* (Jerusalem, 1991) pp. 23–26. R. Yitzhak Hutner, *Pahad Yitzhak on Rosh Hashanah* (New York, 1986); pp. 72–78.

31. It is fitting that R. Shimon ben Lakish, a *baal teshuvah* himself (*Bava Metzia* 84a), should come to a profound understanding of repentance.

32. *Al ha-Teshuva*, pp. 175–187.

33. "The Sacred and the Profane," pp. 13–22.

34. *Ibid.*, p. 23

35. *Ibid.*, p. 24

36. *Halakhic Man*, pp. 110–117.

37. *Ibid.*, p. 99.

38. *Ibid.*, pp. 112–113.

39. Shlomo Wieder cites the alternate text in *Tarbitz* 17:3 (1946) p. 133. See also *Pesikta d'Rav Kahana*, 24:7.

40. *Halakhic Man*, p. 161, n. 127.

41. William Douglass Chamberlain, *The Meaning of Repentance* (Philadelphia, 1943) p. 22.

A dominant theme in the teachings of Rabbi Soloveitchik is the charge for human beings to be creative. Walter Wurzburger (Tradition 30:2) explores the role of creativity in the Rav's thought.

The Rav, of course, emphasized the need for creativity in the spiritual realm. But he also called for creativity in all aspects of life. Human beings must engage in completing the work of creation by harnessing the forces of nature for the advancement of human welfare, by building a just and ethical society, by working to make this a better world.

In his affiliation with Religious Zionism, the Rav stressed the religious significance of the State of Israel. Jews now have the opportunity to employ their creativity in developing a society in Israel devoted to the ideal of Halakhah. Messianic faith entails human participation in the process of Redemption, rather than passive reliance upon supernatural intervention.

The Rav taught that the Torah must be a Torat Hayyim, a living force in human life. Thus, the ideal Torah personality does not wish to constrict Torah to narrow confines, but values involvement in the development of agriculture, industry, science, technology and commerce.

The Centrality of Creativity in the Thought of Rabbi Joseph B. Soloveitchik, *ztz"l*

ᕼᕋ

Walter Wurzburger

ᕬᕉᕫᕬ

"God wills man to be a creator—his first job is to create himself as a complete being. . . . Man comes into our world as a hylic, amorphous being. He is created in the image of God, but this image is a challenge to be met, not a gratuitous gift. It is up to man to objectify himself, to impress form upon a latent personality, and to move from the hylic, silent personality towards the center of objective reality. The highest norm in our moral code is to be, in a total sense, . . . and to move toward . . . real true being."[1]

This existentialist emphasis upon self-creation is one of the central themes in the philosophy of Rav Soloveitchik *ztz"l*. While it may remind us of Jasper's dictum, "To be a man is to become a man," or of Heidegger's espousal of authenticity, the Rav derives the centrality of creativity from the Torah, not from existentialism or neo-Kantianism or any other secular philosophy.

Significantly, many of the Rav's major writings revolve around the theme of creation and are in a sense commentaries on the first three chapters of Genesis. This preoccupation with creation themes is especially pronounced in his later essays, such as "Confrontation," "The Lonely Man of Faith," and "Majesty and Humility." The Biblical account of creation is not treated just as a metaphysical or cosmological doctrine, but as the matrix of normative teachings, providing guidance and direction for human conduct.

The Scriptural portion of the creation narrative is a legal portion, in which are to be found basic, everlasting halakhic principles. . . If the Torah then chose to relate to man the tale of creation, we may clearly derive one law from this manner of procedure—viz., that man is obliged to engage in creation and the renewal of the cosmos.[2]

According to the Rav, human beings, as bearers of the image of God, are mandated to imitate the Creator. In view of the fact that the commandment, *ve-halakhta bi-drakhav* (*imitatio Dei*) refers exclusively to the divine moral attributes, the Rav treats creation as a moral category.[3] This, as we shall note later, has important implications for his analysis of the Maimonidean conception of the "middle road."

It may appear that his emphasis upon human creativity is inspired by the Enlightenment. In actuality however, it is rooted in Kabbalistic doctrines such as *tikkun ha-olam*, the *itaruta de-letata* (the stirring below), which must precede the *itaruta de-le-eila* (the stirring on high), and the human role in bringing about the reunification of the Holy One, Blessed Be He, with the *Shekhinah*.

R. Chaim of Volozin, a forebear of the Rav, already utilized these Kabbalistic ideas to define the human task as the realization of one's potential for spiritual creativity. In his view, that human beings bear the image of God implies that they are charged with imitating His creativity. It is through novel insights into the meaning of the Torah or through meticulous observance of the mitzvot that man becomes a builder of spiritual worlds, with enormous repercussions in the highest regions of being. In a daring reinterpretation of a classic Rabbinic text, *da ma le-ma'ala mi-mkha*, which literally means that man should be aware of a higher power, he reads into it the thesis that "whatever exists on high must come from you," that the regions of spirituality on high come into being solely as the result of human agency.

He goes so far as to assert that the bliss of the Hereafter can be enjoyed only by those who actually create their own immortality. The World-to-Come is not a pre-existing domain to which God dispenses visas of admission to meritorious individuals. Everyone must, by his own good deeds, create his own spiritual domain in the World-to-Come.

The Rav adopts R. Chaim's interpretation of the Biblical statement, "He created man in the image of God," as referring to the human capacity for creativity. He rejects Maimonides' interpretation that it is the possession of reason which endows man with the divine image. This may be in part due to the Rav's theory of knowledge, which emphasizes the creativity of the human mind. Whereas Maimonides adopts the Aristotelian approach, which defines knowledge as noetic identification with the object known, the Rav, who was strongly influenced by the neo-Kantian theory of knowledge, viewed cognition as a construct of the human mind, not a copy of external reality. Since, according to Hermann Cohen's idealism, even sensation is merely a question posed to the human mind, it is readily understandable why the Rav was far more comfortable with R. Chaim's emphasis upon creativity rather than that of Maimonides, who stressed the capacity for rational contemplation.[4]

The Rav develops R. Chaim's conception of spiritual creativity, expanding it considerably in the process. Basing his ideas upon Maimonidean conceptions, he shows that such fundamental religious notions as *teshuvah*, prophecy, individual providence, personal immortality and freedom of choice represent forms of self-creation.[5]

The task of creation . . . is a triple performance; it finds its expression in the capacity to perform *teshuvah*, to repent, continues to unfold in *hashgahah*, the unique providence which is bestowed upon the unique individual, and achieves its final and ultimate realization in the reality of prophecy and the personality of the prophet.[6]

With respect to *teshuvah*, the Rav focuses upon the emergence of a new personality rather than the attempt to secure atonement or win forgiveness. "Man, through repentance, creates himself, his own I."[7] Insofar as the attainment of individual providence or of immortality is concerned, the Rav resorts to the Maimonidean conception that the sublunar world, with the exception of man, is only subject to general providence. According to the Rav's interpretation of the Maimonidean thesis, individual providence extends only to those human beings who by dint of their intellectual and spiritual development have become genuine individuals and are no longer merely members of the human species.

When a person creates himself, ceases to be a mere species ("man"), and becomes a man of God, then he has fulfilled that commandment which is implicit in the principle of providence.[8]

In the light of the Rav's explanation, we can understand why, in striking contrast with the Torah's description of the creation of various organic creatures, where it is stated that they were created "according to their species," there is no reference to the species in the story of the creation of man.[9] As the Mishnah[10] points out, Adam was created as a single person in order to underscore the importance of the individual.

The highest possible level of individuality is reached when a person turns into a prophet. In the Rav's words:

> The prophet creates his own personality, fashions within himself a new "I" awareness and a different mode of spiritual existence, snaps the chains of self-identity that had linked him to the "I" of old—to man who was just a random example of the species . . . and turns into a man of God.[11]

Although in his Halakhic Man, the Rav, following in the footsteps of R. Chaim, refers to creativity only in the spiritual realm, in many other writings he enthusiastically endorses cultural, scientific and technological creativity as well. For all his affinity to the approach of R. Chaim, the Rav diverges from his radical disparagement of all purely secular creativity.

Insisting that our fate is completely in the hands of God, R. Chaim proclaimed the futility of all human efforts to improve human welfare. From his perspective, human agency directed towards the improvement of socio-political conditions is totally worthless. R. Chaim quotes the Talmudic statement that the destruction of the Temple was not a triumph of Titus' military skill, but was brought about by the sins of the Jewish people. Titus merely "burnt a burnt temple."[12] In other words, the plight of the Jewish people was merely an epiphenomenon of its spiritual failings. Since *galut* was not the disease but merely a symptom, it could be cured only by spiritual therapy, with Torah and mitzvot as the only remedy.

R. Chaim's disparagement of attempts to ameliorate the human condition exemplifies the pietistic quietism which predominated in the Jewish ethos of the pre-Emancipation and pre-Enlightenment Era, when no effort was made to improve the collective socio-political or economic conditions of the Jewish people. To be sure, quietism and pietism play a significant role not only in Judaism but in most religions. William James went so far as to make the exaggerated claim that "the abandonment of human responsibility is the hallmark of religion." But there were many historic reasons why Jews gravitated towards pietistic approaches, especially during the long periods that Jews formed an underclass of European society and were denied the opportunity to participate in the cultural or political life of their respective host countries. Because of their lack of political power and the belief that with the arrival of the Messiah they would be ultimately redeemed by supernatural intervention, Jews were particularly prone to this disparagement of human initiatives. Professor Emil Fackenheim has shown that the reason why Spinoza heaped so much contempt upon Judaism but not upon Christianity was that he felt the religious faith of the Jews was responsible for their willingness to endure powerlessness and rendered them totally uninterested in making any efforts to shape their own destiny.[13]

With all his admiration for the Yeshiva world and its passionate love of Torah, the Rav did not subscribe to the quietistic pietism espoused by R. Chaim. He was convinced that if Torah values were perceived as incompatible with modernity's emphasis upon human responsibility for our socio-political and economic situation, the bulk of Jewry would dismiss Torah as totally irrelevant. It was his fear that a religious ethos which disparaged all human initiatives in ameliorating socio-political conditions and frowned upon any involvement with the trappings of modernity could at best result in halakhically committed Jews being marginalized and relegated to a ghettoized existence on the periphery of Jewish life.

It was his unshakeable faith that Torah is a Torah of life, not an escape from it, that inspired him to search for formulations that would not only grudgingly condone secular studies and scientific, technological, industrial, commercial and political activities, but, as long as they fully conformed to halakhic standards, would fully endorse them as intrinsically desirable and religiously valuable.

What enabled the Rav to formulate a religious philosophy which would enable observant Jews to participate in all facets of modern culture was a reinterpretation of the very text that R. Chaim had relied upon in extolling human creativity in the spiritual realm. From the context of the phrase, "He created man in the image of God," it is quite clear that the Rav's interpretation, which includes all forms of scientific or cultural creativity, is actually far closer to the meaning of the Biblical text, because the very next verse states, "God said to them, be fruitful and multiply, and fill the earth and conquer it and rule over the fish of the sea and the fowl of the heaven. . . ." This shows that it is first and foremost through activities enabling them to harness the forces of nature and help perfect the world that human beings are supposed to imitate the Creator. They are charged with the mission to attain dignity (*kevod ha-beriot*) through imitation of the Creator in Whose image they were created. This is why the Rav links the halakhic concept of *kevod ha-beriot* (human dignity) with the *tzelem Elohim* (the image of God).[14]

One may, argue that this conception betrays the influence of neo-

Kantian categories as formulated by Hermann Cohen. There can be no doubt that, in spite of the Rav's irreconcilable differences with Cohen's views concerning the very essence of Judaism, he adopted many of Cohen's ethical views, especially that Rambam's ethics reflects a Platonic rather than an Aristotelian approach.[15] According to Aristotle, human beings become most God-like through intellectual perfection. Plato, however, maintained that ethical conduct and attainment of virtue constituted *imitatio Dei*. This, in large measure, accounts for the centrality of ethics in the Rav's religious philosophy.[16]

Professor Ravitzky[17] has advanced some cogent arguments against Cohen's interpretation of Maimonides' ethical views.[18] But for our purposes, this controversy is irrelevant, since it is of interest only to the student of the history of ideas. What matters for us is that, basing himself on Rambam, the Rav unequivocally declared that striving for ever higher rungs of moral perfection and participating as a partner with God in overcoming the imperfections of the universe is the pre-eminent approach to *imitatio Dei*.

In opposition to doctrines which delegitimize reliance on science and technology to advance human welfare as a usurpation of divine prerogatives (e.g., the Promethean myth), Rav Soloveitchik developed the notion of Adam I, who is summoned to exercise creativity as a member of the "majestic community." He fulfills his divine mandate of becoming a co-creator with God by not passively submitting to the forces of nature but by transforming them through the employment of rational faculties. In the Rav's view, when human beings engage in efforts to harness the forces of nature to the advancement of human welfare, they are carrying out a God-given task to become partners with Him in completing the work of creation. Scientific and technological activities are not manifestations of hubris but the response to divine directive to conquer the earth.[19]

The Rav remains consistent with this definition of the human task in his approach to the problem of evil. Although, in keeping with the Kantian disdain for theodicies, he shies away from any attempt to provide metaphysical explanations for the existence of evil, he maintains that human beings are challenged to respond to evil. The human assignment is to eliminate want, misery and suffering, as much as possible. If there were no evil in the universe, human beings could not help perfect the world of creation. The Rav goes so far as to declare that God had to leave the world in a state of imperfection in order to provide human beings with a mission.[20]

According to the Rav, seeking dominion over nature and attaining a dignified existence is only one aspect of human creativity. There is another dimension, which is symbolized by Adam II. In his existential loneliness, man becomes aware of the need to enter into a "Covenantal Community," in which he totally surrenders himself and gives up everything to God.

Man, who was told to create himself, objectify himself, and gain independence and freedom for himself, must return everything he owns to God.[21]

In striking contrast with his *Halakhic Man*, which largely revolves around human creativity, his *U-Vikkashtem* is devoted to the analysis of the features associated with Adam II, who remains unfulfilled until he creates a covenantal community with God through total self-surrender and submission.

For the Rav, however, this act of renunciation represents also imitation of the divine Creator. As he points out in his "Ethics of Majesty and Humility," the act of creation, as emphasized in the Lurianic Kabbalistic notion of *tzimtzum* (divine self-contraction), was possible only because God, in a sense, withdrew in order to create space for the existence of the world.

It is precisely because the act of creation involved the utilization of polar values, an ethics of majesty as well as of humility, that the Rav interprets the Maimonidean notion of the "Middle Road" not as an adaptation of Aristotelian ethics, but as the imitation of the moral attributes which the Creator manifested in the creation of the universe. In this respect he sharply differs with Hermann Cohen, whose overall pproach to Maimonidean ethics is, in the main, accepted by the Rav. Whereas Hermann Cohen had contended that the ethics of the middle oad is a "survival" of the Aristotelian elements which do not really fit nto the Maimonidean system, the Rav argues that, far from representing an ethics of compromise, the ethics of the middle road reflects he synthesis of polar qualities which were manifested by the Creator f the universe and which go into an ethics of *yishuv ha-olam*. Hence, ot only the "ethics of the pious," but also the "ethics of the middle oad" reflect not a concession to Greek notions of balance, but an uthentically Jewish ethics, which revolves around the imitation of he divine attributes of action. The Rav calls attention to the fact that he Kabbalistic doctrine of the *Sefirot* similarly operates with polar alues which in turn are synthesized. Thus *Hesed* and *Gevura* yield *iferet*, whereas the blending of *Netzah* and *Hod* engenders *Yesod*.[22]

Like Kabbalah, which utilizes differences in gender to symbolize ctivity and passivity, the Rav suggests that a truly fruitful life is ossible only by the interaction of both the active and the passive oles that are suggested in the Biblical account of creation, according o which Adam was created as both male and female (Genesis 1:27). ust as the Kabbalistic *Sefirot* reflect male and female characteristics, he human personality functions properly only when neither of the wo distinct components is repressed.[23]

Because the dialectical tension between the two components of uman nature (Adam I and Adam II) mandates divergent approaches o concrete situations, the Rav always insisted one cannot simply esolve ethical dilemmas by recourse to formal rules. It therefore ecomes imperative to rely on ethical intuitions, which can be cultivated y the imitation of Torah personalities who can serve as role models.

It was this emphasis upon the need to respond to divergent and ven polar values, which accounted for his espousal of moderation. In ublic lectures he often referred to R. Yohanan ben Zakkai's state of nind before his death. Why was he, of all people, so apprehensive? The Rav contended that since Rabbi Yohanan was not an extremist, e had ample reason to question his place in Jewish history. Perhaps

R. Akiva was right when he ridiculed him for his failure to plead for Jerusalem instead of merely requesting Yavne and its scholars and when he denounced R. Yohanan's moderation as *meshiv hakhamim ahor*. But it might have also been possible that Vespasian, who granted Yavne, would not have been ready to accede to a request for Jerusalem and all would have been lost.[24] According to Rav Soloveitchik, the extremist enjoys the advantage of being self-assured. But whoever has deeper insight and perceives different aspects of issues must forego the satisfaction of dogmatic certainty.

Rav Soloveitchik points to the dialectical tension within human beings as demanding the balancing of *Hesed* and *Emet*. In his interpretation,[25] Hesed mandates involvement in the world to transform it and create conditions conducive to human welfare. Emet, on the other hand, refers to the eternal values of the covenantal community which transcend the world of temporal flux and which alone can provide us with a sense of meaning and purpose and enable us to overcome our existential loneliness. Since, according to halakhic Judaism, it is our task to seek to encounter God's Presence primarily in the lower realms of being (*ikkar Shekhinah ba-tahtonim*), we must not try to escape from this world by a flight into transcendental spheres. The human task is to create an abode for God in this world.

The Rav's emphasis upon creativity explains what prompted him to overcome all kinds of social pressures, defy family traditions, and incur alienation from the so called Torah world by affiliating with Religious Zionism. He thereby affirmed the religious significance of the State of Israel, where Jews enjoy the opportunity to employ their creativity in developing a society in keeping with the ideals of Halakhah.

The Rav categorically rejects the position of the Neturei Karta who claim that any attempt to create a pre-Messianic Jewish state violates the prohibition against "forcing the end." He maintains that the Messianic faith entails human participation in the process of Redemption, rather than total reliance upon supernatural intervention. He also contends that the belief in the ultimate arrival of the Messiah s not merely an eschatological doctrine, but entails that human beings ledicate themselves to the pursuit of the ideals which will be fully realized only with the arrival of the Messiah. But the Rav also disagreed with those who were prepared to grant de facto recognition to the State of Israel while refusing to endow the existence of a sovereign ewish state with intrinsic religious value. In his *Hamesh Derashot*, the Rav described in most moving terms he tremendous price which he paid for identifying with Religious Zionism.[26] To be sure, he was never comfortable in any political role. Ie always referred to himself as a *melamed*. But for all his disdain for political activities, the Rav felt an obligation to formulate an ideology which would enable Jews to live in two worlds,[27] so that they would not feel it necessary to choose between the lure of modernity and the eternal truths of Torah. He felt that those who seek to confine Torah o the "tents" in order to avoid the challenge of "field"—the public arena calling for participation in the development of agriculture, industry, science, technology and commerce—are in no position to implement the ideals of the Torah as a *Torat Hayyim*, which is supposed o guide and mold all facets of human existence.[28]

We thus note that the Rav's affirmation of the value of human creativity manifests itself in the endorsement not only of secular studies and scientific research, but also of Religious Zionism.

Notes

1. Joseph B. Soloveitchik, "Redemption, Prayer, Talmud Torah," *Tradition* (Sprir 1978), p. 64.

2. Rabbi Joseph B. Soloveitchik, *Halakhic Man*, translated by Lawrence Kaplar Jewish Publication Society of America (Philadelphia, 1983), pp. 100–101.

3. Rabbi Soloveitchik emphasizes that the biblical doctrine of Creation makes possible to take freedom and individuality seriously. Whereas for Aristotle, the worl was based upon eternally valid laws, the Torah's conception of creation introduce radical novelty and freedom. See *Halakhic Man*, p. 116 and p. 134 and *U-Vikkashter* p. 223.

4. Because the Rav adopted Hermann Cohen's thesis that Maimonides' ethics w; basically Platonic rather than Aristotelian, he particularly emphasized those aspec of the Maimonidean system that characterize the concluding section of the *Guide*.

5. *Halakhic Man, op. cit.*, p. 110.

6. *Ibid.*, pp. 130–131.

7. *Ibid.*, p. 113. See also HaRav Yosef Dov haLevi Soloveitchik, *Al ha-Teshuva* written and edited by Pinchas Peli, Torah Education Department of the Worl Zionist Organization (Jerusalem, 1974), especially Chapter 1.

8. *Ibid.*, p. 128. See also Zvi Kolitz's discussion in *The Teacher*, Crossroad (Ne' York, 1982), p. 7.

9. See my discussion of this issue in my *Ethics of Responsibility—Pluralistic Approach to Covenantal Ethics*, Jewish Publication Society of America, 1994, pp. 60ff.

10. *Sanhedrin* 4:1.

11. *Halakhic Man, op. cit.*, p. 130.

12. *B.T. Sanhedrin* 96b.

13. Emil L. Fackenheim, *Mending the World*, Schocken Books (New York, 1982 pp. 38ff.

14. HaRav Yosef Dov haLevi Soloveitchik, *Yemei Zikaron*, translated by Moshe Kroneh, Department of Torah Education and Culture in the Diaspora, World Zioni Organization (Jerusalem, 1986), pp. 9–11.

15. See my "The Maimonidean Matrix of Rabbi Joseph B. Soloveitchik's Two-Tiere Ethics," in *Through the Sound of Many Voices*, Leester and Orpen Dennys Limite (Toronto, 1982), pp. 178–179.

16. *Yemei Zikaron, op. cit.*, pp. 85–87. See also the Rav's explanation of the reaso for the recital of *Pesukei deZimra* in his *Shiurim leZekher Abba Mori z"l*, Jerusalen 1985, vol. 1, pp. 17–34.

17. Aviezer Ravitzky, "Kinyan haDa'at beHeguto: Bein haRambam leNec Kantianism," in *Sefer Yovel liKhvod Moreinu haGaon Rabbi Yosef Dov haLevi Soloveitchi*.

Shaul Yisraeli, Nachum Lamm, Yitzhak Raphael, ed., Mosad HaRav Kook and Yeshiva University Press (Jerusalem, 1984), pp. 141–151.

18. *Ibid.*

19. "The Lonely Man of Faith," *Tradition* (Summer 1965), pp. 13–15.

20. Halakhic Man, pp. 105–110; *Yemei Zikaron*, pp. 85–91.

21. "Redemption," *op. cit.*, p. 72.

22. I have dealt with this issue more extensively in my *Ethics of Responsibility—Pluralistic Approaches To Covenantal Ethics*, p. 101.

23. *Hamesh Derashot*, pp. 46–47 and *Yemei Zikaron*, pp. 32–36.

24. *Ibid.*, pp. 33–35.

25. *Ibid.*, pp. 80–81.

26. *Ibid.*, pp. 24–26.

27. *Ibid.*, pp. 112–113.

28. *Ibid.*, pp. 113–115.

For Rabbi Soloveitchik, the individual's religious life is deeply tied to the community. Knesset Israel is not merely an assembly of people who come together for mutual benefit; rather, it is a metaphysical entity, a living whole.

In this essay (Tradition 24:3), Gerald Blidstein analyzes the role of Knesset Israel in the writings of the Rav. The Rav draws two models of Jewish existence: the Jews of fate, and the Jews of destiny and purpose. While the Jew of fate is largely passive in his Jewishness, the Jew of destiny is active and creative in defining his spiritual identity. The covenant of fate is an organic part of the Jewish nation, and its in this framework that Rabbi Soloveitchik understands nationalistic and secular Jews. Yet, the ideal is for Jews to move beyond th covenant of fate to the covenant of destiny and purpose.

The Rav taught that Israel is a community by virtue of the study and teaching of Torah from generation to generation. He frequently uses the imagery of the community of massorah (tradition) which has guaranteed the continuity of the Oral Law. It is through the massoretic community—both in its scholarly aspect as well as in its living experience—that the Jew finds spiritual fulfillment.

On the Jewish People in the Writings of Rabbi Joseph B. Soloveitchik

୨୫୬

Gerald J. Blidstein

ୄୠ

I

It is generally thought, and correctly so, that the individual is at the heart of Rabbi Joseph B. Soloveitchik's thought and writings. The titles of major works tell the story: *Halakhic Man*, "The Lonely Man of Faith." It may be a matter of debate whether the Rav is correctly placed in the existentialist camp, but it cannot be denied that the intellectual, psychological, and spiritual experience of the individual forms the hot core of these and other works. This focus on the person may mark the Rav's halakhic writing as well as his philosophical *oeuvre*. Surely it is no coincidence that major essays, as well as years of classroom teaching, were devoted to *teshuvah*, prayer, and mourning, all topics of individual experience; and that a basic problematic in the Rav's treatment of these topics was the relationship between performance and internalization. Needless to say, the Rav encompassed the entire spectrum of Halakhah in his *shiurim*, from *Kodashim* to *Nezikin*. But at the same time he seems to have taken a special pleasure in demonstrating that *Berakhot*, say, could sustain the rigor of halakhic discussion no less than did *Bava Metzia*.

This stress should not obscure the fact that the community, and specifically the Jewish community of course, has also been a central concern of the Rav, and that much of his written work focuses on the community as a phenomenological and halakhic entity, and grapples with the historical situation of the Jewish people in the modern world. True, the Rav's analysis of the individual provides basic categories through which the community is perceived. More significantly, a basic problematic of R. Soloveitchik's writing is the tension between the individual's personal reality, and his role as a member of a community and people. This tension is rendered all the more stubborn by the fact that the Rav relates to peoplehood on a number of different, and indeed shifting, levels. In a sense, though, all this merely underscores the place of peoplehood and community in the Rav's thought, and his commitment to its inescapable centrality.

II

The tension of individual and community is raised explicitly by the Rav in a number of essays, and in a manner which makes it clear that he is quite aware of the basic modernity of the problematic. Typically, the problem is raised from the point of view of the individual consciousness rather than, say, from the point of view of God or history: so we may say that the ultimate conclusion is given at the outset. Be this as it may, the essay appropriately entitled "Community" opens with the question:

> The very instant we pronounce the word "community" we recall, by sheer association, the ancient controversy between collectivism and individualism. Willy nilly the old problem of who and what comes first (metaphysically, not chronologically) arises. Is the individual an independent free entity, who gives up basic aspects of his sovereignty in order to live within a communal framework; or is the reverse true: the individual is born into the community which, in turn, invests him with certain rights? This perennial controversy is still unresolved.[1]

In this particular treatment, the Rav asserts that no clear-cut choice is possible-though once again the answer itself is formulated from the perspective of the individual consciousness and experience.

And let us give a simple answer; Judaism rejects both alternatives; neither theory, *per se*, is true. Both experiences, that of aloneness, as well as that of togetherness, are inseparable basic elements of the I-awareness.[2]

Characteristically, the community itself is no faceless collective but rather a network of individual relationships-a description which becomes significant as the essay unfolds.

If no clear-cut resolution is possible or desirable in "Community," a decisive set of priorities is articulated in other discussions. The homily entitled "God or People—Which Comes First?" is in fact a discussion of our issue, for "God" = individual spirituality.[3] God, of course, will come first. Here the Rav uses a traditional midrash with striking effect, as he builds on the midrashic priority of *parah adumah* (the Red Heifer) over *korban Pesah* (the Paschal Sacrifice). The Paschal sacrifice symbolizes the national component of Judaism, while the Red Heifer bestows personal purity—and it is the latter which is the more significant.

It is quite apparent that the different resolutions of the tension in these essays reflect, in fact, different aspects of the experience of peoplehood. The priority of God (or individual spiritual experience) over peoplehood expresses the relative insignificance of the people as a political, nationalistic collective. Against this reality, the individual is of far greater significance. This evaluation is revised however when one considers the people not as *collective* but as *community*. As community, the people remain in dialectical equipoise with the individual, and little conflict is felt.

The pattern just outlined provides the basic grid for the Rav's discussion of the Two Adams in "The Lonely Man of Faith."[4] Here too the assertion is made that man is a member of two communities. The prime focus in this essay is, of course, the individual, or more precisely, the type. But discussion of the Two Adams quickly develops into discussion of the different communities produced by these different human types. The Rav cannot discuss Adam without relating him simultaneously to the community he forms: man cannot be understood only as individual. First Adam, we recall, represents majestic, techno-logical Man. Never in search of Eve—as Man and Woman appear simultaneously in the first account of creation in Genesis—First Adam is ontologically complete. The formation of a collective by First Adam (and his coupling with Eve?) is a natural act, rationalized by Social Contract ideology and serving functional need. This collective is, of course, a political entity. Second Adam, on the other hand, appears alone; and his search for Eve is driven by the recognition that loneliness is fundamental to his being. By his commitment in faith to Eve he forms the first covenantal community, a community in which God the Creator is a third partner. This community bears an ontological character and is the pattern for the covenantal faith community of Israel.

"The Lonely Man of Faith" is, of course, devoted to the dialectical relationship of the Two Adams, and asserts the fundamental integrity of each as rooted in the biblical presentation of Man. Technological Man is not merely an instrumental creature in the service of Covenantal Man, but is rather recognized as a unique expression of human striving and fulfillment of a divine command encoded in humanity. Techno-logical man is not to be transcended or conquered; his world-developing activity remains an eternal embodiment of the biblical imperative. In drawing this image of "majestic" First Adam, R. Soloveitchik enthusi-astically endows Western scientific technology with the fullest ac-knowledgment Judaism could offer. And since technological man is also collective man, the acknowledgment extended to First Adam embraces his latter manifestation as well, though it is clear that R. Soloveitchik is much more entranced by humanity's scientific abilities than by its political bent.

(R. Soloveitchik does indeed allow man's technological ability a significant role in the Divine scheme; "majestic" First Adam realized his potential and fulfills a godly mandate by subduing the physical world and perfecting it. But the positive appropriation of this major characteristic of Western civilization is not accompanied by a corresponding imperative to appropriate Western culture, its philosophical or literary achievements. This assertion seems improbable, or at least paradoxical, with regard to the Rav, whose major writings are suffused with modern Western philosophy and literature, and whose very intellectual world is constructed, in part at least, with materials provided by modern culture. Yet the paradox is fact; The Rav is a paradigm of the synthesis of Jewish and Western culture, but he nowhere *prescribes* this move or even urges its legitimacy. Are we to assume, then, that this silence discloses a measure of ambivalence, as though the Rav is hinting that he cannot fully approve of involvement in Western culture, or even that there is no systematic way to make it part of the spiritual curriculum?

My own feeling is that quite the opposite happened. Technology is, after all, concrete and materialistic; it raises the standard of living but does not necessarily enhance our spiritual or even human quality of life—nor is that its intention. Technology, then, needs rabbinic approval and even defense. This is of course not true of philosophy, literature, music. These, despite their potential dangers, are intrinsically related to the noetic and spiritual component of human existence. It is obvious that they should be cultivated and that the Jew who strives for a fuller spiritual existence will be open to their message and impact. The Rav's silence would derive, then, from the very example he provides. How, after reading *Ish ha-Halakhah*, could one imagine that Max Scheler and William James are not required reading? Indeed, that they will not contribute to one's formation?

But despite the enduring dialectic relationship of First and Second Adam, the assertion that neither can or should strive to subdue the other, it is Second Adam who has axiological priority, and the values he embodies which rank the higher. Second Adam, united in covenantal relation with Eve, adumbrates the covenantal community of Israel, which enters a covenantal relationship with God; such community obviously ranks higher than the political collective of First Adam. And—as is implied in "Community"—the human individual, self-conscious and ontologically lonely and searching, will also be seen as more value-laden than the political-technological collective. For spiritual, ethical existence is to be created only within the reality of the community and the being of the person; it is not an aspect of the functional collective.

The fundamental issue for the Rav will be the relationship of this person with this community. R. Soloveitchik often returns to the assertion that the Jewish community is a metaphysical entity:

> The community in Judaism is not a functional-utilitarian, but an ontological one. The community is not just an assembly of people who work together for their mutual benefit, but a metaphysical entity, an individuality; I might say, a living whole. In particular, Judaism has stressed the wholeness and the unity of *Knesset Israel*, the Jewish community. The latter is not a conglomerate. It is an autonomous entity, endowed with a life of its own. We, for instance, lay claim to *Eretz Israel*. God granted the land to us as a gift. To whom did He pledge the land? Neither to an individual, nor to a partnership consisting of millions of people. He gave it to the *Knesset Israel*, to the community as an independent unity, as a distinct juridic metaphysical person. He did not promise the land to me, to you, to them; nor did He promise the land to all of us together. Abraham did not receive the land as an individual, but as the father of a future nation. The owner of the Promised Land is the *Knesset Israel*, which is a community persona.[5]

In halakhic terms—and the halakhic plane provides a highly significant legitimation for any Jewish idea—community is *tzibbur*, rather than *shuttafut* (partnership), which in its functional overtones suggests the collective. Major halakhic phenomena are interpreted in terms of the overarching integrity of the community: the *viddui* (confession) and sounding of the *shofar* on the Days of Awe are structured, in part, as communal acts: the efficacy of the Scapegoat and the very forgiveness on *Yom Kippur* are mediated to the individual through his organic participation (in the dual sense of activity and grounding) in the community;[6] worship too has its communal expression in the prayer of the *sheliah tzibbur*, which is not only a functional repetition of the individual's prayer, but a fundamentally novel and independent ritual act.[7] In all this, the Rav draws upon both ancient and modern thought: midrashic-kabbalistic notions of *Knesset Israel* as well as Hegelian and Romantic concepts of the spiritual uniqueness of peoples. And, as we shall see, the halakhic and conceptual analysis will be supplemented by a deeply emotional stress.

The very examples just cited make the point. However spiritual the Jewish person is as individual, the forms of his spirituality are given him by his rootedness in *Knesset Israel*. More radically, his full relationship with God is mediated through this community-people, for God's promise and commitment is to no individual but only to His people. The people, a metaphysical entity, is possessed of certain existence and continuity and able to enter a relationship with God. The individual is lost without this bestowal; totally alone, he cannot take flight to the Alone, who in a sense, is also not totally alone.

And yet, despite the fact that this community transcends the person and bestows upon him the forms of spiritual life and the possibility of God's forgiveness and acceptance, the matter is surprisingly not so simple or one-sided. For the community is constituted by virtue of the ontological loneliness of the individual, as we have seen; this may not be any more of a historical statement than is Rousseau's Social Contract, but it does describe the essential phenomenon. Immediately after describing *Knesset Israel* as a "metaphysical entity," the Rav asserts that "the personalistic unity and reality of a community, such as *Knesset Israel*, is due to the philosophy of existential complementarity of the individuals belonging to the *Knesset Israel*."[8] It may be, of course, that this latter enlargement upon and modernizing interpretation of Halevi's much more modest analysis of the praying community, ought to be seen in the context of the social workers' conference in which it was made—yet one also ought not to make too much of this fact.

This rather strange situation finds consistent expression in the fact that the community itself is often valorized through experiences that are primarily personal. The political component of communal existence is not highlighted, as we have seen; and when the Rav does focus on the national-historical aspect of Jewish existence (a theme to which we turn shortly), he frequently elaborates on the motif of Jewry's "loneliness" as a people, a motif which owes as much to his understanding of personal life as it does to Numbers 22:9. The individual himself, we hear, is ideally part of his community not by virtue of biology or citizenship, but rather through his appropriation of the community's values—and these values are those concretized in personal spiritual achievement. The following sequence, in which relationship to the organic historical community is in fact mediated through a primarily personal commitment (Torah), is typical:

> The Jew who believes in *Knesset Israel* is the Jew who lives with *Knesset Israel* where she may be and is prepared to die for her, who hurts with her pain and rejoices in her joy, who fights her wars, suffers in her defeats, and celebrates her victories. The Jew who believes in *Knesset Israel* is the Jew who joins himself as an indestructible link not only to the Jewish people of this generation but to *Knesset Israel* of all generations. How? Through Torah, which is and creates the continuity of all the generations of Israel for all time.[9]

The pains and joys, victories and defeats, all the experiences which accompany normal historical-national existence, very much demand the Jew's identification. Ultimately, though, these experiences seem rooted in temporality, in "the Jewish people of this generation." "*Knesset Israel* of all generations" is joined only through Torah.[10] It is a "prayerful, charitable, teaching community, which feels the breath of eternity"—so the concluding sentence of "Community." Certainly, it is not insignificant that two of the three characteristics listed—praying and teaching—are primarily personal acts.

III

"Kol Dodi Dofek" is universally read as the Rav's major statement on Jewish peoplehood. In Israel, I believe, it is often taught as a Zionist statement. Its Zionism, of course, is a very diasporic Zionism: American Jews are asked to provide money and political support, not *aliyah*;[1] and even support for Israel frequently shades into support for *yeshivot*.[12] On the other hand, "Kol Dodi Dofek"—and one cannot overlook the history of Messianic interpretation given this verse in Song of Songs—asserts the providential quality of the State's birth, making its historical emergence an act of divine intervention. It is impossible, then, not to identify with the existence of the State, and R. Soloveitchik does so full-throatedly and whole-heartedly. This act of identification, frequently reasserted, ought not to be underestimated.[13] The Rav has described quite frankly the emotional and social price he paid for his Zionism. The family tradition of Brisk, he reminds us, was quite anti-Zionist—and one need not belabor the Rav's intense attachment to the traditions of his family. Here the Biblical Joseph[14] serves as a powerfully moving paradigm, for he too knew the pain of separation from his brethren, the price knowingly paid for his people's survival in a new and necessary reality:

> I was not born into a Zionist house. . . . If I identify now with Mizrahi, in opposition to my family tradition, it is because I feel that Divine Providence has decided for Joseph and against his brethren . . . I built an altar. . . . The altar still stands today, and the sacrifice still flames. . . .[15]

Actually, though, the Zionism of "Kol Dodi Dofek" is not really its most interesting aspect, though it may dominate most of the essay. Much more interesting, to my mind, is the way the Rav comes to grips with the nature and reality of Jewish peoplehood in the twentieth century, and more specifically, in the generation of *Sho'ah* (and Statehood). Once accepted as reality, it is assimilated into aggadic and philosophic typology, and becomes part of the paradigmatic reality of Torah. The typology which emerges has substantial roots in classical, pre-modern, Jewish thought, but it is nonetheless shaped as a response to a distinctly modern situation and reflects, in part, the modern experience and even value of Jewish peoplehood.

The reality of Jewish peoplehood in the twentieth century is, of course, a largely secular reality. The Jewish people has become a people of non-believers in any traditional halakhic measure. All that is really left is belief in the people itself, whether in its American or Israeli version, belief in national existence in history. This, I think, is the reality the Rav sees. One traditional option is to turn away, inward, acknowledging as "true Jews" only the remaining adherents to traditional behavior and belief. This option is usually complemented by the assertion that, of course, all children of Jewish parents (mothers, that is) remain halakhically Jewish. The Rav does adopt this option—in part. But he goes far beyond it in that he develops a model for identification with this secular Jewish reality, even as he asserts that it must be transcended.

Two models of Jewish existence are posited: Jews of fate, and Jews of destiny and purpose. The first reflects Jewishness as biological fact, as national identity into which the Jew is born. The second reflects Jewishness as chosen commitment to spirituality and *mitzvot*. The first model displays the Jew as passive; the second as active. The Jew of fate is largely defined by the historical role imposed on the people Israel as objects of persecution; the Jew of destiny defines his own spiritual identity as creator of culture transcending physical survival. The Rav realizes, of course, that even physical survival in the context of Jewish fate requires immense energy and organization, so that the "active-passive" distinction does not function as an empirical description. The point, rather, is whether the Jew is responding to the initiatives taken by others as they attempt to impose their vision of the Jews' place upon him, or whether he chooses his own identity. In terms familiar to the student of modern European thought, we may speak of the Jew as object of the will of others or as subject of his own will.[16] And in terms of modern Jewish thought, the distinction reminds one of the Zionist critique of passive diaspora existence as against the self-determining political activity demanded of the Jew. For the Rav, the Jew of destiny and purpose is characterized as the Jew who chooses his halakhic-covenantal identity, though, of course, this identity may also require historical, even political, behavior. These paradigms focus motifs familiar in other works of the Rav: we hear echoes of the distinction between collective and community which has already occupied us (thus the Rav also distinguishes *mahaneh* and *edah*), and the distinction along the active-passive axis reminds us of creative Halakhic Man, though both First and Second Adam are also creative individuals (though in very different ways).

No less significant than the paradigmatic terminology, though, are the biblical models for this typology, models which clearly embody modern concerns.

The Jew of fate is symbolized by Egyptian bondage; the Jew of destiny and purpose, by the Torah received at Sinai. Egyptian slavery, the symbolic embodiment of Jewish historical fate, is a patent symbol of Holocaust, much as the deliverance from that bondage is a patent symbol of the rebirth of national political existence in the State of Israel. Slavery and Exodus precede Sinai, and in the Rav's presentation, are experiences of a people that has not (yet) reached Sinai. Slavery and redemption are, then, in this homily on biblical history, the experience of secular Jews—yet these experiences are inalienable elements of Jewish identity. This move is clearly shaped by the reality of the Holocaust: this happened to secular Jews and this is paradigmatic of classic Jewish existence. The inability to deny these facts leads to an acceptance of the purely national aspect of Jewish existence as rooted in biblical models and as objects of Jewish identification.

Obviously, all this has ancient halakhic and aggadic roots. A Jew remains a Jew, halakhically, whatever his behavior or beliefs. And the aggadah discusses the "sonship" to God of wicked and even defecting Jews. In much later times, one can point to the idea of the *pintele Yid* which remains, inextinguishable, in every born Jew, an idea stressed by both the *Tanya* and *Nefesh ha-Hayyim*. Of special interest in this context is Homily XVI of *Beit ha-Levi*, which develops the distinction between *ani ha-Shem* and *benei ha-Shem* as parallel to pious and impious Jews, with even the latter remaining *benei ha-Shem*.[17] The Rav goes beyond this, however, in one significant sense. These earlier discussions relate, fundamentally, to the Jew *qua* individual and his status. But the discussion in "Kol Dodi Dofek" is devoted to the Jewish *people*: collective and community bear the fate and destiny of Jewry, and the biblical models explored are models of historical, national experience. All this clearly points to the fact that the Rav is interested in contemporary historical reality, which is not a matter of individual behavior but rather a pattern encompassing an entire people; not a question of an individual's status (or providential recompense) but rather of what the nation endures in history. R. Soloveitchik returns repeatedly in his *derashot* to the fact that the Nazis persecuted all Jews equally, irrespective of their religious commitment or lack of same. The *pintele Yid* motif seemingly reflects the eternal focus on the Jew as victim, rather than the ineradicable spiritual imprinting to which he is supposedly heir. It is almost as though the moving force behind "Kol Dodi Dofek," then, is the Holocaust and only secondarily the declaration of the State of Israel. Both these experiences, symbolized by different but related aspects of the Egyptian bondage, focus on the classically Jewish fate of secular Jews and their community. The Rav would not close his eyes to this reality, and so he transmuted it through homiletic typology into Jewish doctrine.

Jewish identity is not defined exclusively by Sinai and Torah—it also includes Egypt and its Jews. Nor is Jewish loyalty directed exclusively to the community of Sinai, as it too is broad enough to include the Jews of Egypt. The Rav frequently stressed (in both oral presentations and in his writings) that a Jew dare not alienate himself from his people. There is a classic halakhic base to all this, of course, inasmuch as a Jew always remains such, but this norm is now filled with historical and especially emotional contents—all this in the crucible of the modern Jewish experience. The Rav would often cite Maimonides' ruling that

:ven the Jew who is not guilty of any sin—the "observant" Jew—may ose his share in eternal life if he alienates himself from the community nd does not willingly share its historical travail.[18] For the Rav, Mai- nonides speaks not only of concrete dissociation from actual Jewish ate, but even of the alienated consciousness.

There is a sense, then, in which the realization that the Jewish)eople exists as a secular reality (with a sacred charge and potential,)f course) is reflected in the content and quality of Jewish loyalty. Fhe Rav will be openly critical of observant Jews ("Jews of destiny .nd purpose") who are unable to embrace secular Jews ("Jews of ate") as organic parts of their commitment to *Knesset Israel*.[19] This .ttitude dovetails with an intense relationship with the entirety of ewish history. On the whole, it is true, the significant moments of ewish history are evoked by Abayye and Rava, Rashi and Rabbenu Fam, the Gaon of Vilna and the *Ba'al ha-Tanya*, that is, by moments)f spiritual-intellectual achievement. But other modes of identification)perate, too. The Rav analyzes incisively the rather tepid response of :eligious Jewry to the State of Israel and more specifically to the idea)f *akvah*, as an indication that this Jewry grasps the Land of Israel in 1ormative halakhic terms alone, rather than by participation in "the /earnings of past generations."[20] Such emotional yearning grows from .n identification with the totality of Jewish life and the totality of [ewish society. Naturally, this society was a traditional society, and its 'yearnings" were pervaded by traditional values and expressed in tra- ditional terms. Yet this focus on historical solidarity remains signif- icant.[21]

Clearly, then, "Kol Dodi Dofek" grapples with the secular reality of Jewish peoplehood, and it may even reflect the growing significance of the idea of peoplehood in modern Jewish thought and life. At the same time, its typology sets limits. Whereas First Adam and Second Adam exist in dialectic tandem, with only a hint of the axiological priority of the latter, Egypt and Sinai, the Jew of fate and the Jew of destiny and purpose, clearly reflect a hierarchical order. Sinai will build on Egypt, and Jewish historical fate is a permanent feature of

Jewish existence, but precious little in the way of Jewish values will emerge from the victimized identity of bondage. Even Redemption, so charged an experience in Jewish thought and experience, occurs to a passive people and does not bear the message of self-transcendence.

"Kol Dodi Dofek" itself does not, of course, develop this tension. On the contrary, its basic thrust lies in the welding of these disparate Jewish experiences into one emotional whole. Indeed. R. Soloveitchik tells us of the values which emerge in a people which must struggle to ensure its physical survival: mutuality, sympathy, self-sacrifice, h*esed.* These are the functional values of the collective to be sure, but they also require the individual to transcend his own selfish concerns and, as *hesed* (the term used in this context by the Rav), resonate deeply in the Jewish consciousness. The Rav also develops the religious symbolism of the "covenant of destiny" and ensures its permanent place in the spiritual totality of Jewish experience. The two ritual acts in conversion-circumcision and immersion-reflect the two covenants which are thus integral factors in Jewish identity. Circumcision symbolizes that which is carved painfully into the historic body of the Jewish people; elsewhere, indeed, no less a figure than father Abraham, first of all Jews to be circumcised and founder of the Jewish people as family, is presented as the forebear of the Covenant of Fate. Immersion, the Rav continues, symbolizes the active spiritual moment in which the potential Jew chooses a life in community, with God.[22] Yet despite this positive appropriation of the Covenant of Fate and of the historic fact of Jewish peoplehood, there is also a deep ambivalence, or better, unease, which is only hinted at by these two disparate symbols of Egypt and Sinai.

Despite R. Soloveitchik's assertion that the national (and in our reading, secular) component of Jewry is an organic part of the Jewish people, for it too suffers the historical fate of Jewry (= Egypt), it is also not uncommon for him to slip into a different literary mode, and both mood and content change. This is best exemplified by his "political sermons," the *derashot* delivered at annual Mizrachi conventions and published as *Hamesh Derashot*. Delivered to religious American Zionists, these talks were really directed at the religious Zionist leadership in Israel, with the American audience serving, apparently, as pretext. The policy issue discussed in these talks is: How ought the religious Zionist party relate to the secular government? What is particularly interesting in our context is not the substantive answer presented by the Rav, who advises a rather aggressive stance, but rather its literary vehicle. In *derashah* after *derashah* secular Israeli leadership is midrash-cally assimilated to the non-Jewish biblical oppressor: Esau, Pharaoh, Avimelekh, Abraham's servant-lads, Amon and Moab. This, of course, is no more than literary and perhaps routine symbolism, yet it ought not to be dismissed out of hand, for it discloses a basic level of consciousness. The secular Jew has ceased being a real Jew, though he too will eventually return. Perhaps, though, it were wise to remember that R. Soloveitchik's hostility is directed at the leadership of an opposing ideology, and that it is evoked in a political context which always stimulates the polemical.[23]

Nonetheless, this literary symptom ought to be pursued more deeply. It would be helpful. I think, to put the matter in terms familiar from the ideology developed by Rabbi A. I. Kook. Rav Kook, needless to say, is also capable of using similar symbols for similar homiletical purposes. But his main thrust moves in quite a different direction. Now, it is likely that the contrast between the Rav and R. Kook reflects different metaphysical orientations no less than differing attitudes towards modern Jewish nationalism and towards Halakhah. I will be concerned nonetheless with the contrast as it appears on the ideological, rather than on the metaphysical, level.

Rabbi Soloveitchik does not seem to think that classical Judaism, as it is presently understood, suffers from any basic flaw. It-as distinct from the Jewish people—displays no moral or religious malaise. Nor is Jewish history, for that matter, a tale of the ups and downs of Judaism which, given at Sinai, has always retained its fundamental divine strength. Halakhah, too, is adequate both in method and substance to its task. Though the Rav will concede that the analytical

method of Brisk cast some much-needed light in a darkening room, i
is significant that the reform in question was intellectual rather than
moral or religious. Perhaps, too, certain forms of Hasidism added
relevant spiritual moments—but nothing more. Certainly, the Rav
does not indicate that a renaissance of Judaism is an urgent need
Hence, whatever growth ought to occur will come out of the healthy
organic stock of Jewish life and thought, from people who are loyal to
Halakhah, its values and patterns. Perhaps the most significant challenge of the Orthodox intellectual (and spiritual?) achievement offered
by Rabbi Soloveitchik (aside from the political critique in *Hamesh
Derashot*) is that which is silently implied by the body of his writing
itself: Why did no one else do anything like this work?

Rabbi Soloveitchik, consequently, finds no legitimacy, spiritual grandeur, or subterranean power in antinomian movements or individuals.
The move to secularism is not seen as an idealistic rebellion against
the inadequacies of the tradition, or an inevitable attempt to reach for
moral and religious realities outside the grasp of Torah as currently
understood or as potentially understandable by its loyal students. He
will not entertain a dialectic according to which religious (and moral?)
antinomianism can be admired as a courageous attempt to scale truths
unattainable within the context of normal halakhic method and life.
The norms of the Torah need not be rejected so that higher spiritual
norms may be disclosed or concretized, or even so that historical
degeneration may be corrected. Halakhah is to be plumbed, not transcended.

Since no substantive renaissance of Judaism is necessary, the function
of a political-national rejuvenation is not to provide such. Zionism is
not, in the broadest sense even, a spiritual movement; and if its history
includes religious and moral excesses, these have no dialectical justification as the necessary price to be paid for the march to higher
spirituality (whether or not that goal is in itself an adequate justification).
If Messianism exists in R. Soloveitchik's vocabulary, it is an austerely
Maimonidean messianism in which a national-political revival provides

a physical base but no intrinsic spiritual content. Zionist leadership will be admired, perhaps even profusely praised, for its achievement in building a physical and social haven. Indeed, the Land of Israel itself is placed on the axis of the Abrahamic covenant of fate.[24] R. Soloveitchik does, I think, go a bit further: I recall his developing the theme that the holiness of the Land was not "mythological" but a function of its providing the context for a holy society-again a fundamentally Maimonidean orientation. The application of Torah norms to an entire society made, then, for a richer and truer concretization of Torah, for a fuller embodiment of the Jew's fundamental task—but even this is no radical renaissance. This image of the State of Israel as a potential embodiment of the broadest ethical and societal vocation of Judaism, a vocation based on a broad covenantal commitment, is perceived by many students of the Rav to be implicit in his teaching.

Curiously (and regrettably?) this positive and challenging image does not recur frequently in the published texts available to us.[25] For the most part, then, the establishment of the State of Israel is a moment in the battle for physical survival and a significant achievement in the ongoing struggle to create a focus of Jewish identity for Jewries which have lost their traditional moorings in the modern world. And, hopefully, this moment of redemption from the victimizations of Jewish fate (though the State fully shares in the "loneliness" intrinsic to that fate) will lead to a fuller flowering of Jewish purpose. But if ever forced to choose between a secular state of Israel and the God of Israel, "we will stand, as one man, for the God of Israel."[26]

IV

I have already noted that the significance of community manifests itself no less on the halakhic plane than on the aggadic. This state of affairs is symptomatic of the Rav's fundamental orientation to Torah as a whole, for he often asserts that the halakhic sphere is the most significant indicator of authenticity; indeed, this is a major burden of *Halakhic Man*. Now, the priority generally attached to the halakhic over the aggadic itself reflects the central role of community. For

Halakhah is normative, obliging all members of the community equally and frequently structured so as to involve them all together:[27] as against the often individualistic, idiosyncratic, and moderately non-normative quality of aggadah. Put another way: the language of Halakhah, its basic forms, are often communal.

The communal aspect of Halakhah is of course expressed in specific ways, some of which were noted earlier: prayer, sacrifice, the *shofar* and confession of the Days of Awe. But R. Soloveitchik devotes considerable attention to another, more general, role of the community within the halakhic scheme—the *community as source of authority*. These discussions are solidly rooted in classical halakhic sources, yet seem at the same time to disclose a modern sensibility. Interestingly, some of the motifs and concerns we have detected in the Rav's evaluation of modern Jewish reality function in his halakhic treatment as well.

It is clear from numerous rabbinic instances that the people Israel function as a legal entity in a variety of spheres, religious as well as civil. As such, Halakhah assumes that the people can express its will, so as to confirm or veto rabbinic legislation, for example. Maimonides, by systematizing the process of rabbinic legislation in *Mishneh Torah*, may have further highlighted this phenomenon; he also claimed that one of the bases of Talmudic authority as a whole is the consent of the people Israel. Rabbi Soloveitchik takes Maimonides one step further: popular consent is given an institutional concretization—the Great Sanhedrin.[28] The Sanhedrin is thus understood as having a dual function, for it expresses the will of the people Israel as well as pronouncing opinions and decisions in its role as the major organ of Oral Law. Thus the Rav points to the interchanging phrases "consent of the majority of Israel" and "consent of the High Court" in Maimonides' definition of national conquest (*kibbush rabbim*). This analysis apparently broadens the scope of rabbinic authority, for the Sanhedrin now speaks for the people as well as for the Torah. Yet a study of the broader context in which this analysis figures indicates a more complex situation. If the Sanhedrin speaks for the people, it is no less clear that its authority, in certain spheres at least, is derived from the people.

This discussion of *kibbush rabbim* is actually a springboard for a much more extended treatment of the principles of authority constituting the Jewish calendrical year. Ideally, according to Maimonides, calendrical decisions are to be taken by an ordained court, a subcommittee as it were of the Great Court. This ideal construct encounters difficulties, obviously, in current (and Maimonidean) historical reality; the Great Court and ordination no longer exist, and yet the calendar does continue to function authoritatively. This is not the place to rehearse in detail the various Maimonidean texts relevant to the problem, of course. The Rav finds a solution in the idea, supported by these texts, that what is really crucial are the calculations done by *benei Eretz Yisrael* ("the Jews of the land of Israel"), or in a later version, the practice of Jewry as a whole.[29] In normal circumstances, of course, the Great Court would itself have the calculations done and issue the proper directives. Yet the fact that this can also be accomplished by "the Jews of the Land of Israel" indicates that the Great Court is in fact the representative of this Jewry, speaks for it, and actually derives its authority (in this and similar administrative matters) from it. As I have pointed out, R. Soloveitchik (in one treatment of this problem, at least) vests the authority of the calendar, ultimately, in the practice of the entire Jewish people, in the holiday celebrations of the entire Jewish people which legitimate the normative calendar: "Now, *Knesset Israel* in its entirety sanctifies . . , the holidays and New Moons by its ritual practice. . . . The entire people fixes the calendar through the calculations, and the celebration of the holidays and New Moons according to these calculations functions to set the calendar." And in a charming aside, the Rav explains the familiar phrase in the synagogal announcement of the New Moon, *haverim kol Yisrael* (in the comradeship of all Israel) as no rhetorical flourish, but rather as the liturgical statement of our doctrine.[30]

Halakhic theory, it thus seems, accommodates the changed reality of the Jewish people very well. Yet from another perspective, the theory spun out above reflects an ideal situation; or in terms mor familiar from *Halakhic Man*, it expresses the *a priori*. For if this theor absorbs with little shock the reality of a destroyed Temple, and ar abolished Sanhedrin, it is predicated on the assumption of an idea people, a people which observes the Sabbaths and, holy days of th year as of yore. But we all know—and so does R. Soloveitchik—tha "the entire people" no longer celebrates the holidays. The theory indeed, seems appropriate for a pre-modern age, for a people whicl exists as a memory. What now?

At this point, of course, we enter the realm of the speculative. *F* number of options ought to be raised, then. The Rav may think, for one thing, that even if the majority of the people no longer sanctifie the holidays in a halakhic mode, it does recognize them as its own don't most Jews continue to identify with Pesah, for example? *F* possible implication of this argument is that if even this bare identifi cation were to be restricted to a minority, the people would no longe have a calendar, for which the legitimation of the entire *Knesset Israe* is necessary. This would be radical doctrine indeed, as the piou minority would then be unable to function, abandoned as it were by the mass of the Jewish people! The opposing alternative, of course, is to assume that the Rav recognizes the observant minority itself a *Knesset Israel*, the remnant which becomes the "entire people." Actually none of these options seems terribly convincing. Rather we retreat to the admission that no "solution" exists, and we discuss matters on a different level.

Put plainly, we must admit that R. Soloveitchik here seems to be writing pure halakhic theory, as he explicates Talmud and Maimonides which are read as ideal texts. And he rests his case on an ideal under standing of the Jewish people as a nation of purpose and destiny. Jewry as a nation of historical fate and nothing more simply does not enter the picture. *Hurban ha-bayit* has, in a sense, been absorbed into this theoretical model; *hurban ha-Am* has not. A terrible chasm does, in fact, exist between halakhic theory and modern reality: theory simply refuses to grasp reality. But something more ought to be added.

Halakhic theory, in this case at least, is perhaps more than analytic description. It is also a statement of faith. Here (and elsewhere), the Rav asserts that the Jewish people, which is incomprehensible to him outside its covenantal commitment, will return to its vocation of holiness. Messianic faith, he declares, is "faith in the Jewish people."[31] Thus, despite the two-tiered historical model of "Kol Dodi Dofek," no halakhic model exists for a bifurcated Jewish people. The Jewish people is ever Sinai, Torah. (Interestingly, the halakhic theory behind the workings of the calendar also led Maimonides to one of his more daring statements of faith when he asserted that the Lord would never allow the Land of Israel to be totally emptied of its Jews. That, he wrote, is a concomitant of God's commitment to the ongoing existence of His people.[32]) Ironically, it is precisely the ironic description of the authority immanent in Jewish life which suggests how far contemporary Jewish life actually is from its sacred vocation; and the argument for the indispensability of this authority, which suggests how fragile the sacred existence of this people is today. The calendar—at least on the theory developed by the Rav—is living on borrowed time, and not the calendar alone.

V

The very being of the Jewish people is inextricably tied up for the Rav with Torah. Usually the people is identified with Oral Law, rather than Written Law.

> In its power and authority to decide halakhic issues—an authority greater than that of the scholars, whose decisions are based on intellectual grounds alone—is expressed the mystic, holy, idea, that Torah and Israel are one.
> Israel is holy because it is identical with Torah, because Israel is itself Torah and Torah is itself Israel.[34]

The force of the identification with Oral Law specifically seems to be that Torah is then immanent within the people itself, rather than being an external standard alone, which is what the Written Law apparently symbolizes. The latter statement cited explains, in context why the Jewish people, however sinful, remains eternal.[35] But rather than exploit this idea to the fullest degree, R. Soloveitchik continues to say that the Torah as Oral Law is always within the people because "the mind and memory, the very soul of the Jew, contains hidden myriads of letters and crowns of the tradition: bits of prayer, memories of a festival . . . echoes of a Torah-idea. . . . there always remains a divine spark which cannot be profaned." And while it is true that R. Soloveitchik speaks here of "authority to decide halakhic issues," the Rav is actually quite far from the modernist exploitation of this identity as a basis for innovation. Many modernists, of course, value the idea of the immanent authority of the community precisely as it counters and dislodges the normative tradition. This is simply not the drift of R. Soloveitchik's discussion. For the Israel of which he speaks is still the ideal people of purpose discovered in our discussion of the calendar, and the Torah of which he speaks was given at Sinai. The two basic foci of the identity of Israel and Torah, then, are that (1) Israel is a community whose positive historic continuity has been forged through the study and teaching of Torah; and (2) alongside the tradition of study there has always flowed the experience of the life of Torah itself. Indeed, the Rav finds the tension and complementarity of the intellectual and the experiential a fascinating and charged topic. The sensitivity to this problematic does not grow from a sense of the gap between theory and the demands of the real world. Rather it grows from a sense of the richness and variety of the spiritual experience, and of the frustration encountered within the intellectual act. The limitations of the intellectual experience will be felt, obviously, only by one who is so fundamentally committed to it. Be this as it may, the story of Jewish history is not, for the Rav, a tale of dislocations, discontinuities, gaps. Rather, it is a conversation across the age by generations linked not only in common purpose but in common understanding. The passage of time does not produce distance or aliention; rather, it adds partners to the ever-enriched conversation. It is not necessary to add that, even casting metaphysical assumptions aside, the question of what is history—How is it to be perceived, written? What is significant in the record of the past?—can only be answered in the most subjective way.

R. Soloveitchik frequently returns to the imagery of the community of the *massorah* (= tradition), the community whose continuity is the essence of Oral Law. This continuity is represented, of course, in the experience of "learning," which is an intensely personal, indeed emotional, experience:[36]

> When I sit to "learn" I find myself immediately in the fellowship of the sages of tradition. The relationship is personal. Maimonides is at my right. Rabbenu Tam at the left, Rashi sits at the head and explicates the text, Rabbenu Tam objects, the Rambam decides, the Ra'abad attacks. They are all in my small room, sitting around my table. . . . The study of Torah is a staggering experience of generational comradeship, of the mating of spirits, the fusion of souls. Those who transmit Torah and those who receive it meet at the caravanserai of history.

Or again:[37]

> . . . the *massorah* society was founded by Moses at the dawn of our history and at the point of eschatological fulfillment of our history will be joined by the King Messiah.

What characterizes that society? An unqualified dedication to learning and teaching, its motto is—teach and let yourself be taught. It demands that every Jew be simultaneously teacher and pupil, that every member of the society hold on with one hand to an old teacher while the other hand rests upon the frail shoulders of a young pupil. This society which represents the very essence of Judaism cuts across the ages and millennia and holds the key to our miraculous survival.

On the long Sabbath afternoons in the summer, we preface the recital of *Pirke Avot* with a declaration concerning our total involvement in the massorah community; "Moses received the Torah from Sinai,

and handed it on to Joshua, and Joshua to the Elders, and the Elders
to the Prophets, and the Prophets handed it on to the men of the
Great Assembly." In other words, Judaism expresses itself through
the *shalshelot ha-kabbalah*, the chain of tradition. Hands are linked
generations are united. One society encompasses past, present and
future. As I mentioned before, admission to that society is a difficult
and complex affair.

Though open to all, and even demanding that all enter, this society
is admittedly elitist. At the same time, it is not peripheral to Jewish
peoplehood. Indeed, one senses that for R. Soloveitchik, this society
is the very essence of Jewish community; in it and through it does
one discover the meaning of Jewish commitment.

There is another aspect to the *massorah* community and the Rav is
careful to insist on this second reality. It forms part of the community
of the tradition, but does not contribute to its intellectual substance
Occasionally R. Soloveitchik will identify it again on a personal level
with dominant maternal figures on other occasions it is embodied in
the people as a whole, which bears the responsibility for the concretization of Jewish commitment through history. There is, on the one
hand, his description of his mother and of the *rebbitzen* of Talne:[38]

> People are mistaken in thinking that there is only one Massorah and one
> Massorah community; the community of the fathers. It is not true. We
> have two massorot, two traditions, two communities, two *shalshalot ha-
> kabbalah*—the massorah community of the fathers, and that of the mothers.
> "Thus shalt thou say to the house of Jacob (= the women) and tell the
> children of Israel (= the men)" (Exodus 19:3), "Hear my son the instruction
> of thy father (*mussar avikha*) and forsake not the teaching of thy mother
> (*torat imekha*)" (Proverbs 1:18), counseled the old king. . . .
>
> I admit that I am not able to define precisely the massoretic role of
> the Jewish mother. Only by circumscription I hope to be able to explain
> it. Permit me to draw upon my own experiences. I used to have long
> conversations with my mother. In fact, it was a monologue rather than a
> dialogue. She talked and I "happened" to overhear. What did she talk
> about? I must use an halakhic term in order to answer this question; she
> talked *me-inyana de-yoma*. I used to watch her arranging the house in

honor of a holiday. I used to see her recite prayers; I used to watch her recite the sidra every Friday night and I still remember the nostalgic tune. I learned from her very much.

Most of all I learned that Judaism expresses itself not only in formal compliance with the law but also in a living experience. She taught me that there is a flavor, a scent and warmth to *mitzvot*. I learned from her the most important thing in life—to feel the presence of the Almighty and the gentle pressure of His hand resting on my frail shoulders. Without her teachings, which quite often were transmitted to me in silence, I would have grown up a soulless being, dry and insensitive.

The laws of Shabbat, for instance, were passed on to me by my father; they were part of *mussar avikha*. The Shabbat as a living entity, as a queen, was revealed to me by my mother; it is a part of *torat imekha*. The fathers *knew* much about the Shabbat; the mothers *lived* the Shabbat, experienced her presence and perceived her beauty and splendor.

The fathers taught generations how to observe the Shabbat; mothers taught generations how to feel the Shabbat and how to enjoy her twenty-four hour presence.

The Rebbitzen, as I mentioned before, was one of the few women to whom the maternal massorah, *torat imekha*, was entrusted. She represented the Massorah community with great loyalty and dedication. She was a devoted, good keeper of the treasure which was put in escrow with her and she knew how to guard it and how to transmit it to another generation. She was an outstanding teacher.

Now, this description dovetails perfectly with the Rav's analysis of 1e two forms of traditional authority; that of scholarly analysis and ecision, and that of life lived by the explicated on that broad level, eople itself. Proverbs 1:8 was to the verse and the too: and needless ɔ say, the midrash kabbalistic imagery of *Knesset Israel* should be ecalled.[39] And though the essay devoted to this idea is in fact titled Two Forms of Massorah," there is, again, no indication that the uthority immanent in Israel's experience is perceived as in conflict ʾith its normative heritage; nor is there much interest in discussion f this problematic.[40] Though not identical, experience and norm ow in the same direction and supplement, rather than conflict with, ach other. (Needless to say, any analysis of Rabbi Soloveitchik's halakhic posture will also have to take into account his responsiveness to modern reality—a phenomenon which does not come to the for in his published writings.) This, then, is the second component o community as Oral Law: the community whose very life is an ongoing embodiment of Torah.

It is through this massoretic community—in both its aspects—that the Jew finds God:

> Individual and community must take the historical identification with the past and future of the people, with its fate and its destiny. . . . Thus does the individual adhere to God fully and absolutely and irrevocably.[41]

Once again, the individual and his quest are the center of concern And once again, the Jewish individual can attain his ultimate goal only with the community of Jew's, past, present and future.

Interestingly, the Rav opens two avenues of *devekut* in *U-Vikkashten mi-Sham*, an essay devoted largely to the possibility and modes of communion with God. There is *devekut* through the study of Torah in which, as Ravitzky has shown,[42] the Torah shared by man and God creates an epistemological basis for communion. But there is also *devekut* through ethical behavior within the community, though it theoretical basis is less developed and though this community, the Rav insists, is the committed covenantal community alone.[43] In the passage cited above, which is virtually at the close of the essay, Rabbi Soloveitchik apparently collapses this distinction.[44]

Notes

All works cited are by Rabbi J. B. Soloveitchik, unless otherwise noted.

1. "Community," *Tradition* XVII, 2 (Spring 1978), p. 7.

2. *Ibid.*

3. A. Besdin, ed., *Perakim be-Mahshevet ha-Rav* (Jerusalem. 1984), pp. 80–88. A imilar evaluation of the relative weight of individual and community emerges from he following, mildly ambiguous passage the Halakhah is concerned with man as entered mainly on the individual Man is neither an idea like humanity nor a superinividual (*sic*) unity like society, philosophical systems, including that of Marx have lealized and idolized. They have tune the praise of society which is supraindividual nity. The Halakhah insists that nothing nor the idea nor the collective should upplant the single transient, fleeting, frail individual. I mean it I may use a Hebrew hrase *shehayom kan umakhar bakever*, who is right here on the platform, and the next ay, who knows where he will end up. Of course the Halakhah is not saying that the ommunity particularly the community of the committed, of the elected, is the arrier to the divine eternal message. Yet the individual constitutes a reality, whose ntic legitimacy must not be questioned and whose interest the Halakhah, like a evoted mother, has at heart." (From the typescript of an unpublished lecture, "Mental Iealth and Halakhah," delivered in December 1961, pp. 20–21. The typescript, vhich is apparently an unedited transcription of a tape recording, is found in the brary of the Jerusalem Mikhlala for Women and was brought to my attention by)r. Joel B. Wolowelsky.)

4. "The Lonely Man of Faith," *Tradition* 7:2 (Summer, 1965), pp. 5–67.

5. "Community," p. 9.

6. P. Peli, ed., *Al ha-Teshuvah* (Jerusalem. 1974), pp. 69–100.

7. *Shiurim le-Zekher Abba Mari, z"l*, II (Jerusalem, 1985), pp. 17–34.

8. "Community," pp. 9–10. For elaboration of this idea in kabbalistic terms, see *emei Zikkaron* (Jerusalem, 1986), pp. 59–62.

9. *Al ha-Teshuvah*, p. 98.

10. See *Perakim*, pp. 84–5. Cf. *Beit ha-Levi* (by the Rav's great-grandfather), Homily .VIII, printed as an appendix to *Responsa Beit ha-Levi*, II (Warsaw, 1874). Comparison f this and other aspects of the Rav's essays with these homilies is beyond the scope f this essay. In general, the homilies of *Beit ha-Levi* also ought to be read in the light f the 19th-century haskalah and other social developments in the Jewish community.

11. But see A. Eisen. *Galut* (Indiana U. Press, 1986), p. 166.

12. Indeed, the Rav occasionally seems discomfited by the halakhic value of certain hysical aspects of Israel's involvement with its land. Thus, in interpreting the rabbinic ssertion that the land's holiness was established more permanently by *hazakah* (pos-

session) then by *kibbush* (conquest), the Rav understands *hazakoh* in two distinc
ways—neither, though, elaborates the meaning of physical occupation. See *Al hc
Teshuvah*, pp. 300–308 (= *U-Vikkashtem mi-Sham*, in *Ish ha-Halakhah—Galui ve-Nista*
[Jerusalem, 1979], p. 191, n. 17). and *Hamesh Derashot* (Jerusalem, 1974). pp. 42–4
(Naturally, I am aware that this is, in a sense, an argument from silence, and that
makes ideological capital from halakhic *hiddush*. Nonetheless—*devarim be-go?*) No
the parallel spiritualizing moment in the Rav's assertion that "holiness" of Ramba
and Yehuda HaLevi was no greater in the Land of Israel than in *galut*: "Personall
emotionally, I simply cannot accept the fact of the diminished holiness of thes
matters while in *galut*. . . . For in a spiritual sense, they never were in *galut* (*Hames
Derashot*, p. 93).

13. See also M. Rosenak, "Ha-Adam ha-Yehudi ve-ha-Medina," in S. Israeli, ed
Sefer ha-Yovel li-Khevod ha-Rav Yosef Soloveitchik (Jerusalem, 1984), I, 152–3, on th
significant impact of the Rav's religious-zionist affiliation and involvement.

14. Rabbi Soloveitchik frequently returns to the figure of Joseph in his *derashot*.
discussion of this theme is beyond the scope of this essay; I would simply point o
that the Joseph material, which often focuses on either cultural pluralism or famili
separation and reconciliation (often interweaving both these themes) is especiall
poignant.

15. *Hamesh Derashot*, pp. 24–5. Actually, the move towards religious Zionism ha
already been made, and the sacrifice brought, by R. Moshe Soloveitchik, the Rav
father. Nonetheless, the integrity of the anti-Zionist position possessed its attraction
as "Ma Dodekh mi-Dod," the Rav's eulogy of his uncle, indicates. See Eisen, *op. ci
p. 169.

16. These categories figure prominentlv in the analysis of a self-creation in *Halakh
Man*.

17. The distinction, along with appropriate terminology, is of course much olde
see, e.g., Ramban to Exodus 14:10. But similar ideas also figured in modern Jewis
thought: see N. Rotenstreich *Ha-Mahshavah ha-Yehudit b-Et ha-Hadashah*, 1, p
166ff, on Buber's distinction between *am* and *umah* and on its roots in moder
European thought.

18. *Hilkhot Teshuvah* 3:6.

19. *Hamesh Derashot*, p. 94.

20. P. Peli, ed., *Be-Sod ha-Yahid ve-ha-Yahad* (Jerusalem, 1976), pp. 417–418.

21. See David Hartman's account of Rabbi Soloveitchik's charge to students as h
ordained them to he rabbis:

> I have entrusted to you the spiritual message and treasure of the Jewish people throughout
> history. Halakhah says that if one harms a person, one must ask for forgiveness. And if the
> person in question has died, Halakhah demands that one goes to the cemetery, that one

finds his grave and that one publicly declares one's guilt and begs for forgiveness. Now—I want you to remember one thing always: we do not know where all the graves of more than three thousand years of Jewish history are. I entrust to you the heritage of the people of Israel. (D. Hartman, *Joy and Responsibility* [Jerusalem], p. 223).

2. "Kol Dodi Dofek," in P. Peli, ed., *Be-Sod ha-Yahid ve-ha-Yahad* (n. 19, *supra*), pp. 83–390. See also *Al ha-Teshuvah*, pp. 134–7; here too Abraham and the *avot* in general signify the inescapable element in Jewish fate, as does circumcision, while *abbalat mitzvot* (the convert's acceptance of *mitzvot*), ratner than *tevilah*, symbolizes the freely chosen moment of integration with Jewish destiny. See also n. 24.

23. *Hamesh Derashot*, pp. 30, 68–9,72, 118–9; see Rosenak, *op. cit.*, p. 153, and Eisen, *op. cit.*, pp. 167–8. A second major theme of these talks, generally is that Mizrahi—rather than the anti-Zionist entities—represents authentic Judaism and this claim will be further buttressed by attacks on the secular Zionist leadership. Interestingly, these talks betray no illusions as to the likelihood that their audience could be proselytized into *aliyah*; it is clear throughout that American Jews and Israeli Jews were and will continue to be two distinct populations.

24. *Hamesh Derashot*, pp. 91–2. It is to be recalled. of course, that this Abrahamic community is no mere nationalistic collective. but a metaphysical *tzibbur* to which the land has been granted; see at n. 5.

25. See Rosenak, *op. cit.*; the survey in A. Ravitzky. "Ha-Kol Tzafui . . .," in A. Hareven, ed., *Yisrael Likrat ha-Me'ah ha-Esrim v'e-ha-Ehad* (Jerusalem, 1985), pp. 85–191, with the careful summary at p. 191; A. Lichtenstein, "Introduction," in J. Epstein. ed., *Shiurei ha-Rav* (New York, 1975), p. 4.

26. *Hamesh Derashot*, p. 76; Rosenak, p. 166 and n. 36.

27. *Halakhic Man*, trans. L. Kaplan (Philadelphia, 1983), pp. 42–43.

28. The following discussion is based on two essays dealing with the calendar and other problems: *Kovetz Hiddushei Torah* (Jerusalem, n.d.) pp. 47–65 and *Shiurim le Zekher Abba Mari*, I (Jerusalem, 1983), pp. 129–134. The latter treatment is apparently reworking of the former. It is not unlikely that the stress on the representative function of authoritative institutions and on the role of consensual elements reflects modern thinking. But see, too, *Hiddushei R. Yitzhak Ze'ev ha-Levi* (Jerusalem, 19761) to *Hilkhot Sanhedrin* 5:1 (as Prof. Abie Feintuch pointed out to me—or is even R. Velvel a child of modernity. For the role of these notions in classic halakhic materials see my "Individual and Community in the Middle Ages," in D. Elazar, ed., *Kinship nd Consent* (Ramat Gan, 1983), pp. 217–259: *Ekronot Mediniyyim be-Mishnat ha Rambam* (Ramat Gan, 1983), pp. 154ff. See also Y. Ben-Sasson on R. Meir Simha of Dvinsk in *Sefer ha-Zikkaron le-Mordekhai Vizer* (Kevutzat Yavneh, 1981), pp. 346–366 Heb.).

29. See *Shiurim*, p. 130 and n. 14; this comment, incidentally, is of special relevance to our discussion.

30. *op. cit.*, pp. 130–1: see also p. 228.

31. *Al ha-Teshuvah*, pp. 93–98.

32. *Sefer ha-Mitzvot, Aseh* 153.

33. *Yemei Zikkaron*, p. 59.

34. *Ibid.*, p. 249.

35. As Rabbi Soloveitchik indicates (*op. cit.*, p. 247), the terms of this distinction and its application to the Jewish people are found in *Beit ha-Levi* (Homily XVIII) interestingly. the issue of the sinfulness of the people is not raised in that context.

36. *U'Vikkashtem*, p. 232. See now M. Oppenheim, "Kierkegaard and Soloveitchik," *Judaism* 37, 1 (Winter, 1988), pp. 38–39. who points out that participation in the chain of the massorah community is, for the Rav, an answer to the ravages of time.

37. "Tribute to the Rebbitzen of Talne," *Tradition* 17:2 (Spring, 1978), pp. 75–6.

38. *Ibid.*

39. *Berakhot* 35b; *Pesahim* 50b; *Hullin* 93b.

40. *Shiurim*, pp. 220–240.

41. *U-Vikkashtem*, p. 234. One wonders whether the terms *goral* and *ye'ud* ("fate" and "destiny"), used here in a work roughly contemporary with *Halakhic Man*, have the same meaning as would be assigned them in "Kol Dodi Dofek." If so, we see the fusion of concern for the two communities, See also below at the conclusion of this essay.

42. A. Ravitzky. "Kinyan ha-Da'at be-Haguto," in S. Israeli, ed., *Sefer Yovel* (n. 1 *supra*), pp. 138–140.

43. *U-Vikkashtem*, pp. 192–193. Remarkably, the Rav's discussion takes as its point of departure the rabbinic dictum to "adhere to the sages"; Rabbi Soloveitehik chooses to take his saying as directing the Jew to his community, rather than to the masters of Torah. See also Ravitzky, *op. cit.*, pp. 146–151.

44. Though our citation seemingly focuses on the community and its history alone these sentences conclude a discussion of the role of prophets and sages.

The relationship between Halakhah and ethics is a topic of broad concern. Are they in fact identical categories? Or are they separate but overlapping, with Halakhah in the more authoritative position?

In this essay, (Tradition 30:4), Professor Carmy analyzes the category of the ethical in the published writings of Rabbi Soloveitchik. The Rav, keenly aware of the dialectical nature of human beings, did not shy away from the complexity inherent in moral and religious life.

Pluralism and the Category
of the Ethical

ఆఈ

Shalom Carmy

ఆఈ

The ethical implications of any philosophical theory, as to its beneficence or detriment to the moral advancement of man, should many a time decide the worth of the doctrine.[1]

It is obvious that dialectical man cannot be committed to a uniform, homogeneous morality. If man is dialectical, so is his moral gesture. Judaism has indeed formulated such a dialectical morality.[2]

Once the very formulation of the question eluded us, and now that we know how to pose it, the teacher to whom we had always looked for illumination is no longer with us, and though we seek him in the mountains and the valleys, he will never return to us. Our Rebbi, *maran ha-Rav* Yosef Dov Soloveitchik *zt"l*, the master eulogist of our times, never tired of reminding his audience that the act of eulogy is inherently an absurd performance: "it is the absurd will to turn the third person into the second person, having failed to recognize the real live presence when it faced us. Mourners and eulogists occupy themselves with the building of bridges across that gap that will never be bridged."[3]

A large portion of any philosophical endeavor is clarifying the nature of the problem to be addressed. To think purposefully about the reality of the ethical, which is the subject of this paper, we shall first try to understand exactly what it is that troubles us about our initial, unreflective conceptions. At that point, we will be ready to consult the relevant remarks in the Rav's literary corpus. Insofar as the Rav does not explicitly address the problem in the manner that I formulate it, merely to enumerate his sayings on the ethical will not be sufficient. To the contrary, because the Rav discusses the ethical in a variety of contexts, an anthology of sources will confuse rather than enlighten. Thus it will be our task to create a coherent account from the Rav's statements as they pertain to our subject.

A prefatory comment on my use of the Rav's texts: I have limited myself to text written and prepared for publication by the Rav himself. Any unauthorized version runs the risk of inaccuracy, but the danger of misrepresentation is even greater when discussing issues that did not occupy a conspicuously central place in the Rav's oral discourse, and the nuances of which would therefore be more likely to escape the ingenuous reporter. I have likewise abstained from referring to unpublished manuscripts that the Rav made available to me. Examination of this material, in my opinion, does not alter, but rather confirms and enriches, my analysis and conclusions; proper evaluation should await publication of these documents in their entirety.[4] In any event, the published record is ample for our purpose.

Halakhah and the Ethical: The Nature of the Problems

Nowadays, whenever it is claimed that some action is right or wrong on both halakhic and moral (ethical) grounds, someone is sure to point out an apparent redundancy: halakhic *means* ethical, and vice versa. Upon further reflection, however, the equivalence becomes less straightforward. Actions may accord with the letter of Halakhah, which are nevertheless reprehensible because our moral judgment condemns them: the recent resurrection of *kiddushei ketanna* is a spectacular and, one hopes, indisputable example. There are circumstances where to act in accordance with Halakhah entails violating firmly held, and justified, moral intuitions: e.g. the tragedy of an intractable case of *mamzerut.*

Less dramatic than these conflicts, but perhaps more revealing at a philosophical level, are the incontrovertible facts of linguistic usage. When we contrast *mishpatim* (usually interpreted as those laws which human beings would have adopted even in the absence of divine instruction) and *hukkim* (the laws that do not readily appeal to our reason), however the difference is defined, we all have a good idea what is meant.[5] Whatever our theories, we commonly recognize that people who are devoid of religious commitment may nonetheless execute their moral obligations conscientiously, and meet a standard that many of the religiously observant neither aspire to nor fulfill.

So clear is the evidence of our practice that one is tempted to blame the facile equation of the halakhic-religious and the ethical on some manifestation of ideological blindness. The rationalist, convinced that all divine imperatives must be reducible to the ethical, strains mightily to demonstrate that all *mitzvot*, without exception, when properly understood, fulfill his or her ethical values. The fideist, by contrast, denigrates human moral insight, except as guided directly by revealed illumination. Because human moral judgment is fallible, lends itself to self-deception, and offers little guidance when faced with difficult dilemmas, he or she concludes that human morality is an illusion. The rationalist is like a person familiar with fish, who insists that a whale is a fish, and must be classified as fish, despite its mammalian features. The fideist is like a physicist who observes his less sophisticated fellows succumbing on occasion to optical illusions, and decides that they must be blind, and see nothing.

Despite our habit of distinguishing between the ethical and the religious, there is one serious philosophical consideration that encourages their identification. When we compare the ethical to other ascriptions of value (as when we nominate an action aesthetic or rational), two features indicate its unique status:

a) The claim of the ethical is absolute. Ethical imperatives take precedence over other types of value pursuit; to use a phrase popular among analytic philosophers, ethics "trumps" other values. A policy may be prudent or efficient, an endeavor may promise pleasant, interesting, or enchanting fruits, but we must not undertake a course of action if it is morally wrong. If, as Yeats declared, "the intellect of man is forced to choose Perfection of the life or of the work," then ethics has no trouble determining in favor of the former.

b) The characteristic inner feeling we experience in the face of the ethical imperative is unmistakably different from our feelings with regard to the realization of other values. Ethical obligation has something sacred, inviolable, unutterably exalted about it. Kant called it *achtung*: that unique feeling of awe and reverence that accompanies the apprehension of moral principle.

Now Halakhah exhibits the features we have just adumbrated, both with respect to the absoluteness of the norm and to the sense of awe appropriate to its fulfillment. Both Halakhah and the ethical thus lay claim to absoluteness over all other spheres of value. But if Halakhah reigns supreme then the ethical must, in principle, submit and be dethroned: "two monarchs cannot wear the same crown" of absoluteness. In order to retain the unique authority of the ethical we must either identify it with the religious, so that the two kings are really one and the same, or we must redefine our conception of absoluteness so that the authority of the ethical is no longer a challenge to the sovereignty of the religious.

If Halakhah and ethics are identical, it follows that they have the same essential characteristics. A religious duty is one commanded by God; likewise, to judge an act or attitude to be ethically good or obligatory, means to assert that it is required by God. The content of Halakhah encompasses many norms not usually assigned to ethics, but this does not establish a distinction between them; it merely testifies to the limited intellectual horizons of ethical outlooks not rooted in revelation. Many duties enter Halakhah through the side door of ethical intuition, rather than deduction from revealed halakhic premises (via *ve-asita ha-tov ve-ha-yashar* and similar principles). By the same token morally repulsive actions are contrary to the will of God even when the formal Halakhah doesn't rule them out. These obligations and prohibitions, like the formally codified *mishpatim*, belong to the ethical insofar as they are generally laws that human reason would have adopted on its own; to that extent ethics differs from those revealed religious norms usually called "ritual." Once introduced into Halakhah, however, these norms are part and parcel of the halakhic system, assuring them a standing no different, in principle, than that of Shabbat and Kashrut.

In reality, of course, the identity theorist would have to concede that norms associated with "ethics," deriving from human ethical judgment, are often treated differently than revealed, determinate *mitzvot*. When ethical intuitions conflict with formal religious obligation, for example, the latter nullifies the former. This phenomenon, however, can be regarded as a legal principle within the halakhic system, which carries no more philosophical weight than, let us say, the rule that a positive *mitzvah* overrides a negative one (*aseh dohe lo taaseh*).[6]

What about the more violent conflicts between seemingly clearcut ethical judgments and uncompromising religious imperatives? The identity theory would be forced to maintain that in every such case, the Halakhah, being the will of God, is by definition the ethical. What appears to be the ethical is not truly the ethical. Thus Rabbi Walter Wurzburger's admirable exposition of the identity thesis includes the following assertion:

This explains why Judaism has no need for the Kierkegardian doctrine of "the suspension of the ethical," which demands that whenever moral imperatives clash with religious commandments, we must subordinate our ethical concerns to the higher authority of the religious. Once God is defined as the supreme moral authority, obedience to divine imperatives emerges as the highest *ethical* duty. Thus, Abraham's readiness to sacrifice Isaac cannot be invoked as a paradigm of the "suspension of the ethical."

On the contrary, it was a perfectly *moral* act. Abraham does not cringe before the absolute power of a demon, but rather obeys the command of the supreme moral authority.[7]

According to this view, the prohibition of murder, in the case of the Akedah, does not define Abraham's ethical duty, but merely his *prima facie* duty, what his duty would have been were it not for the fact that obedience to God supersedes the normal obligation after all, and thus constitutes the true moral requirement. In other words: with two candidates for the position of Abraham's duty, the prohibition of murder, on the one hand, and the obligation to obey God, on the other hand, the identification of God's will with ethical duty ratifies the latter and disqualifies the former. It is a problem about the adjudication of an ethical dilemma, and not a very difficult one at that, rather than being the confrontation of two conflicting awe-inspiring categories of value, each of them employing a voice of authority, each reaching for the quality of absoluteness.

If the ethical is not the same as the religious, but represents a different category of value, and we wish to preserve our intuition about the absoluteness of the ethical, in the face of the supremacy of the religious, then the ethical, in effect, must be treated as both real (absolute and awe-inspiring) and distinct from Halakhah. At the same time Halakhah, the revealed expression of God's will for man, occupies a higher rung on the normative ladder than the ethical. The question returns in full force: how can Halakhah and ethics share the crown of absolute dominion over other spheres of value? To which the plain answer is that we must recognize a hierarchy of axiological transcendence: the ethical is absolute in relation to non-ethical values; the divine imperative, while it endorses, indeed annexes, the ethical in principle (as is evident from *ve-asita ha-tov ve-ha-yashar* and the like) is absolute in its relation to the ethical as well. The sense of awe reverence and solemn responsibility is appropriate both to our consciousness of ethical duty (as distinct from halakhic commands) and to our apprehension of God's commands (although aspects of these eelings will differ, insofar as the respective objects of the feeling are not the same).

We have sketched two alternative approaches, the identity thesis equating ethics with Halakhah, and the hierarchical, pluralistic theory, according to which the ethical and the religious, in spite of their broad overlap in content and scope, denote distinct realms of value. Both the identity and the hierarchical approaches explain the basic facts of human axiological experience: the feeling of awe and reverence when contemplating our duty, the significance of human moral intuitions and that the will of God must be obeyed even when it conflicts with human moral intuitions. The subtle difference between the two interpretations is that the identity thesis only allows ethical intuitions to generate *prima facie* duties, which are obliterated in the face of higher ethical imperatives communicating the will of God, whereas the hierarchical view grants reality to the ethical as a category unto itself, albeit a category axiologically inferior to the religious sphere that is identical with the revealed divine command.

Before turning to the Rav's writings, let us raise, without attempting to answer, two more questions about the status of the ethical: First, can ethics (as distinct from Halakhah) be made into a science? If by science we mean an inquiry that aims at the delineation of fundamental concepts, the discovery of systematic principles underlying these concepts and accounting for phenomena in the field, then it seems that a science of ethics is as worthy an object of pursuit as a science of sociology or aesthetics. The hierarchical approach would appear to encourage such an endeavor, insofar as it regards ethics as a distinct sphere of value, albeit not the supreme one, which is the religious. If, however, we operate with the identity thesis, then ethics, as distinguished from Halakhah, cannot constitute a complete discipline in itself, but only a subfield of the religious.

If the previous puzzle is too esoteric to perturb the average man's speculations, the same cannot be said of another persistent question: why be moral? I refer here, not to the purely psychological problem as to what motivates people to do what they acknowledge to be the right thing. There is a deeper metaphysical issue: what gives the category of ethics its special air of command, its absolute power, its reverential aura of authority? For most people, the unique status of the absolute norm is not simply a fact about the universe, unrelated to the rest. The meaning of normative ethics is embedded in the broader context of our existence as a whole. Whether the power of the norm is two-headed, as the hierarchical approach would have it, or has a single undifferentiated basis, as the identity thesis maintains, its absoluteness is bound up with the question of man's relation to God. In looking at the Rav's outlook on questions of ethical theory, it is worth assessing his potential contribution to this area as well. And in taking as our subject the relation of the ethical to the religious, we are particularly interested in how the Rav's understanding of the ethical-religious dimension of philosophical anthropology may shed light on the interaction of the two putative categories.[8]

Rav Soloveitchik and Ethics: The Textual Record

Unlike most primary sources in Jewish thought, each one of the Rav's major compositions creates a distinct literary-philosophical context. Certain themes appear with regularity—Torah study, creativity, individuality, the significance of this world, for example—yet each recurrence of a favorite concept is intended to contribute towards the better understanding of the problems in that essay. This is one reason for the inconsistencies that obstruct the progress of the superficial reader. Moreover, awareness of the Rav's mode of exposition should deter us from lifting juicy nuggets of sage wisdom from their appropriate connection. What is true of the Rav's *oeuvre* in general will guide us in examining his statements about the ethical in particular. We shall first attend to the variety of the Rav's reflections before attempting their systematization.

1. *Omitting the ethical.* Several central passages in the Rav's corpus give implicit support to the identity thesis. In these texts either the ethical is not mentioned, in connections where the hierarchic approach

would expect to find it, or else ethical norms are treated in a manner that downplays their absolute and awe-inspiring nature.

In a famous section of *Ish ha-Halakhah*, the Rav dramatizes the cognitive agenda of halakhic man, who measures each phenomenon, be it sunrise, sunset, or the flowing of a spring, from the perspective of the Halakhah. He builds on an analogy to neo-Kantian epistemology, according to which fundamental *a priori* principles create the framework for the formulation of scientific laws. For Kant himself, the three critiques dealt, respectively, with scientific (mathematical-physical) knowledge, with the moral law, and with the principles underlying aesthetic and teleological (meaning, in effect, biological) judgment. The Rav, however, following the late nineteenth century revival and transformation of Kant associated with the Marburg school, is prepared to recognize a more generous menu of fundamental objects of knowledge. When he states that halakhic categories determine truth about a broad spectrum of phenomena, he produces a long list, ranging through the physical and biological sciences, and including human intellectual constructions referring to the state, the family and human psychology.[9] The Rav refrains from treating the realm of moral judgment as an independent object of knowledge which Halakhah either supplements or interprets. Whatever normative significance can be annexed to the ideal type of "cognitive man," must come from Halakhah and from no other source.[10]

An obliviousness to the ethical as an autonomous source of ethical commitment can be more clearly discerned in *Lonely Man of Faith*. The Rav has delineated the project of Adam the First, dedicated to conquering reality, his goal the enhancement of dignity. Lest one regard this ideal type as a depiction of the scientist-technologist alone, the Rav elaborates:

> Adam the First is not only a creative theoretician. He is also a creative esthete. He fashions ideas with his mind, and beauty with his heart. He enjoys both his intellectual and esthetic creativity and takes pride in it. He also displays creativity in the world of the norm: he legislates for

himself norms and laws because a dignified existence is an orderly one. Anarchy and dignity are mutually exclusive.[11]

What the Rav here labels "the world of the norm" appears identical, in its content, to what is customarily called ethics. It defines duties and values and goals that obligate and guide individuals who recognize their claim. What is lacking from this account is the peculiar reverence which is, we have seen, an essential property of the ethical. The Rav's avoidance of the conventional term "ethics" signals that the norm of Adam the First is literally unworthy of the name. For Adam the first the norm, that is to say the rules governing ethical behavior and attitudes, is one more means towards a dignified existence, one more value of human culture. It is, to be sure, an indispensable value, insofar as its absence is positively opposed to dignity. Nonetheless the norm is appropriately relegated to the same paragraph as the aesthetic values to which it is assimilated.

2. *Ethos and cult:* In *The Halakhic Mind*, an essay devoted primarily to the philosophy of science, the category of the ethical, omitted or downplayed in *Halakhic Man* and *Lonely Man*, achieves a measure of recognition. The Rav adopts the terms "ethos" and "cult" from the literature of comparative religion, and asserts that prohibitions of acts like murder and perjury, and injunctions to help the neighbor, "though included in any system of secular ethics, are nevertheless specific religious commandments."[12] He then explains why cult is more important when it comes to objectifying the unique religious experience:

> Religion is always typified and described not so much by its ethos as by its ritual and cult. The existence of an ethical norm is a common denominator in all religious systems. The unique character of a particular religion, however, appears only in its ritual. Positive religion must always be measured by the yardstick of ritualism, not by that of the ethos. This does not mean that religion can, in any way, dispense with the ethos. Far from it. Both ritual and ethos inhere in the religious act. The cancellation of morality in religion would render it synonymous with barbarity and paganism. The dissociation of the religious act from its non-rational worship and ritual is identical with the resolution of the religious experi-

ence into a secular morality and a mundane ethical culture. The superiority of ritual is to be understood only from the viewpoint of religious typology which treats of the unique in religion.[13]

A bit later in his discussion, the Rav accuses theological "liberals" of trespassing upon the territory of ethics and/or aesthetics in the mistaken belief that they are studying religious subjectivity.[14]

What can we learn, from the passages cited above, about the nature of the ethical? First, that it refers to a realm of experience distinct from that of religion although, to be sure, religion must embrace the content of ethical norms, if it is to avoid degenerating into "barbarity and paganism." But (partly because the Rav is not consistent in his use of the term[15]) it is not clear whether the ethical, taken by itself, partakes of the awe and authority that we associate with the absolute imperative. The reader of *Halakhic Man* and *Lonely Man*, coming to *Halakhic Mind*, is apt to subsume the "secular system of ethics" under the mundane rubric of culture. The unique power of ethical duty, on this understanding, appears only when the content of ethics is apprehended as the specific content of religious imperatives.

3. *Morality as theological anthropology.* Many of the Rav's discourses and longer essays revolve around the nature of the human being. Invariably the Rav isolates two aspects of human nature and explores what is, at times, an irresolvable tension between them. Frequently the dichotomy deals with relatively localized regions of the human condition: man as individual and man as social being; man of majesty and man of humility; man as cosmic explorer and man yearning for his roots, and so forth.[16] In *Lonely Man* and *U-Vikkashtem mi-Sham* the dualities discovered permeate virtually all domains of human existence. For our purposes the following observations are in order:

(i) The Rav's statements about human nature convey normative information: if it is human nature to be such-and-such, then it is, in principle, legitimate for human beings to pursue the triumph of that nature. Of course, when the Rav speaks of human nature, he does not mean that which comes naturally to man: the ubiquity of human cruelty, for example, does not make it a legitimate human impulse. The Rav's insight into empirical human psychology is often dazzling, but the normative judgments that flow from his vision of the human condition are anchored in an explicitly religious standpoint. Majesty and humility, individuality and social commitment, are legitimate human goals because they partake of the nature that God bestowed upon man. In the blunt language of *Lonely Man*:

> Before beginning the analysis, we must determine within which frame of reference, psychologico-empirical or theologico-Biblical, should our dilemma be described. I believe you will agree with me that we do not have much choice in the matter; for, to the man of faith, self-knowledge has one connotation only—to understand one's place and role within the scheme of events and things willed and approved by God, when He ordered finitude to emerge out of infinity and the Universe, including man, to unfold itself.[17]

(ii) "Man is, quite often, a captive of two enchanting visions, summoning him to move in opposite directions. . . . The Halakhah is concerned with this dilemma and tries to help man in such critical moments. The Halakhah, of course, did not discover the synthesis, since the latter does not exist. It did, however, find a way to enable man to respond to both calls."[18] If man is summoned by conflicting values, and if it is the Maker who willed the schism and contradiction in man's moral gesture, then it is obvious that morality cannot be the articulation of any one principle, however important.

This central thesis of the Rav's thought forces us to rethink much of our previous discussion. Thus far we have posited the category of the ethical as standing for something uniform and homogeneous. Our problem was whether, and in what ways, the ethical could be distinguished from the religious. Now, however, we are told that the ethical picks out a variety of values and goals, frequently in conflict with each other. The territory of ethics, upon exploration, calls for further division and for the multiplication of subsidiary categories.

To this point we have tried to maintain a distinction between the ethical as a distinct category and the ethical as a descriptive sub-field of Halakhah. The texts we are now discussing, for which human existence becomes the meeting ground of incommensurable values requiring a dialectical moral gesture, further complicate the picture. Morality, which in the context of these essays can be defined as the fulfillment of the human nature ordained by God, entails the agony of integrating heterogeneous values. This depiction of moral experience certainly grants it a grandeur and absoluteness that sets it apart from the merely cultural creativity characteristic of the unconfronted Adam of *Lonely Man*. "The clash is staggering" only because the decision is indeed momentous and all-important. At the same time, the moral gesture is not quite identified with Halakhah. Halakhah provides guidance for the human being who is struggling within the thicket of moral choice. It does not render the moral experience superfluous.

   (iii) It would seem that the Rav's anthropological inquiries tend to affirm the independent value of ethical experience and moral judgment. It is in this part of his work, however, that he also insists upon the ultimate incommensurability of religious commitment and ethical intuition. "Catharsis" vigorously champions man's march to victory, the striving to satisfy one's legitimate desires and goals. Yet man must also learn to accept defeat. Even the most valuable human telos must be sacrificed, when God calls upon man to do so. No area of human existence is spared: the pleasures of the conjugal bed, the bittersweet consolation of grief at the death of a beloved, the intense quest for knowledge, even the search for God. The student of these texts can have little doubt that the Rav sanctions man's quest to actualize the nature bestowed upon him by the Creator. At the same time, he insists that man's legitimate desires must be sacrificed to God through the gesture of withdrawal. Furthermore, the fulfillment of human nature is contingent upon the individual's willingness to purify his desires by submitting to God. Without that commitment, that performance which could have been sanctified becomes an ugly affair.

Let us recapitulate the three themes we have distilled from the "anthropological" strand in the Rav's thought. The proper realization of human nature is not mere culture; it is rather man's aspiration to march forward victoriously, apprehended as the fulfillment of the destiny willed by God for man. Therefore the manner of that realization is a matter of immense significance; the great choices confronting man are indeed awe-inspiring. The choices facing man are predicated upon the existence of plural values not given to synthesis. One such arena of conflict, and clearly the most radical, takes place when the entire range of legitimate human values is pitted against the transcendent imperative of obedience to God.

Natural Consciousness and Revelational Consciousness

The ultimate tension between the dual aspects of man, that fashioned for fulfillment and that destined for obedience, which is presented most explicitly in "Catharsis," and is probably most familiar from the *Lonely Man of Faith*, receives its most profound justification in *U-Vikkashtem mi-Sham*. Here the Rav undertakes to produce a map of man's relations with God and the inner logic correlating the various stages of religious existence. The most fundamental elements are man's search for God and God's willingness to reveal Himself to man. The human search engages, potentially, every aspect of existence. It extends to the awareness of the cosmos without and the spiritual dimensions within, the world of logical concepts and the uncanny feelings of the mystic. Yet man's capacities are necessarily limited. God is infinite. Hence the search for God, conducted from the human side of the infinite gap separating creature from Creator, must fall short. Unless God makes Himself available to man, the encounter cannot occur.

It is beyond the scope of this paper to review the Rav's textured account of the different types of revelational consciousness (*toda'a gilluyit*) engendered by the reality of God confronting man, and their interaction with the natural consciousness (*toda'a tiv'it*) that is the fruit of man's own initiative. Both are mandated by God: "Man is

commanded not only to have faith in God but also to know God."
What matters most, however, is "belief in His revelation to man and
man's readiness to fulfill His will unconditionally."[19]

In the course of demonstrating the significance of man's dual experience, even while emphasizing the essential commitment to revelation,
the Rav warns of the danger in reliance upon man's natural faculties
as a self-sufficient source of ethical norms:

> In such a situation, it seems to man as if he were the father of the
> commandment, as if he determined the aim and purpose of religion. It
> seems to him that both the formulation of the law and its fulfillment are
> given to man. Hence he is permitted to choose one law and reject
> another law . . . as if all derives from man's free creation and all returns
> to it. The end of this liberty is moral anarchy. . . . A religious imperative
> (a secular ethical norm is insufficient) irrupting with titanic power, is the
> foundation of objective religious existence. . . . Religiosity lacking an
> objective-revelational basis that obligates man to deeds and actions, cannot
> conquer the beast in man. The subjective faith, wanting command and
> law, of which Saul of Tarsus spoke, even if it masquerades as love of
> God and man, cannot sustain itself if it is without specific commands to
> do good deeds, and to fulfill specific commandments, which do not
> always find favor in the eyes of reason and culture.[20] The terrible devas-
> tation (*sho'ah*) of the Second World War is proof. All those who spoke
> about love remained silent and did not protest. Many of them even took
> part in the destruction of millions of human beings.[21]

Much of the Rav's moral argument in this passage, and elsewhere,
is psychological, rather than ontological, in its import. Insensibility to
the revelational aspect of human existence, he maintains, brings about
disastrous moral consequences. To understand fully the significance
of revelation, however, it is not enough to concentrate on the track
record of the human race. If revelation were only a prophylactic
against human wickedness, then a human psychology substantially
altered for the better, a human beast a bit more tame, and a mind less
prone to self-deception, could safely dispense with the yoke of "specific
commandments which do not always find favor in the eyes of reason
and culture."

But this is not the case. The Rav's critique of modern man's illusions about himself is not the whole story. We need determinate revealed commandments not merely as a means to help avert moral catastrophe. We require *Torah u-mitzvot* in order to encounter God. For, as we have seen, human initiative, however ambitious, disciplined and sustained, cannot bridge the measureless gulf that divides finite creature from infinite Creator. If God is really and truly God, then we encounter His presence not only when and where we are prepared to recognize it, but precisely when He overtakes us and commands our attention and commitment, in moments unguarded and circumstances uncontrived by human hands.[22]

The Primacy of God and the Pluralism of Ethics

We have reached a vantage point from which we may survey the Rav's treatment of the ethical, understood as a normative realm characterized by awe and absoluteness. In some texts (*Halakhic Man* and the presentation of Adam the First's creativity) the ethical is ignored as an independent category. Elsewhere (*Halakhic Mind*) the Rav seems to recognize the ethical as an autonomous mode of apprehending reality. In much of his work he affirms morality as a powerful and complex component of human existence, and it is in these texts that he invariably makes the authority of ethics dialectically dependent upon the supremacy of revealed commandments.

In the opening section of this paper, we raised three questions: First and foremost, what can the Rav teach us about adjudicating the conflict between identity and hierarchical theories with respect to the relationship between the ethical and the religious? Is the Rav disposed to consider the ethical as given to scientific development? And why does the ethical occupy such a central place in human life?

It would be best to begin with the last question. The absolute subject of human existence, the only matter of ultimate concern, is man's relationship with God. The ethical, like the religious, does not materialize in an anthropological vacuum. Both the creative human esture, the polychromatic search for meaning, which the Rav, in *J-Vikkashtem mi-Sham*, calls "natural consciousness," and the gesture f submission, obedience and sacrifice, the "revelational conscious ess," arise from that relationship, as is their dialectical interrelation hip.

Grasp the primacy of the God-relationship for the man of faith, nd the various remarks about the ethical in the Rav's writings are eadily understood. From a phenomenological standpoint, the ethical s frequently experienced as a realm of absolute value distinct from he religious imperative. This is a fact about human consciousness nd thus a part of any real account of human experience: hence the ⟨av indeed takes it seriously (in *Halakhic Mind*, for example). It is also fact, according to the Rav, that ethical consciousness is pluralistic; n other words, that legitimate desires and goals are incommensurate nd that there is no formula whereby they can be synthesized. No ess real is the dialectic engendered by the confrontation between the ethical and the religious: inexorably and inscrutably, God commands specific commandments which do not always find favor in the eyes f reason and culture." Furthermore, because of the primacy of God's vill as the absolute source of value, the ethical, for all its significance, s incomplete by itself; for this reason, the Rav may be disinclined to reat the ethical as a subject for systematic scientific construction.[23]

Finally, in the light of the above, we return to our initial question ibout the ontological status of the ethical in relation to the religious: he identity theory vs. the hierarchic thesis. As we have noted, some f the Rav's texts point one way; some, the other. To me it seems hat everything depends on the point of departure. From a God's-eye ⟩erspective, as it were, the ultimate justification of human existence is heological, how man is to go about fulfilling the will of God. What ve define as the ethical is no more, and no less, than a subset of the ·eligious: this outlook fits the identity theory. Perceived through human ⁊yes, the ethical, to the degree that its content is not exhausted by ⟩pecific halakhic injunctions and prohibitions, expresses man's "natural

consciousness" of value, the human attempt to encounter God. Thi:
attempt, when divorced from commitment to "revelational conscious
ness" is doomed to failure or worse. It is nonetheless real, and it
reality is best described by the hierarchic model.[24]

The Rav and Our Present Crisis

It is impossible to survey that segment of Jewry denominated "moderr
Orthodoxy" without being impressed by the frequency with whicl
the Rav *zt"l*'s name is invoked and the infrequency with which hi
work is studied. To take a conspicuous example, he is often extollec
as a paragon of the integration of liberal arts education and Torah
But how often do the spokesmen who generate the publicity grappl
with the reality of that integration as practiced in his life and in hi
writing? How frequently do they effectively gloss over anything tha
would furrow the brow, or prick the conscience, of amiable insignif
icance?

The blank obliviousness with which the Rav's legacy has been receivec
extends to his remarks on the ethical as well. The hard pluralism tha
required real men and women to take seriously their dialectical experi
ence of the ethical and the religious, never had much of a chance in ;
community that all too easily slipped into a confounding of its owr
ethos with that of the Creator. Pluralism of this sort is difficult because
it forces us to treat as crucial decisions to which Halakhah provides ;
frame of reference, but not a clearcut resolution. Thus, for example
one who appreciates the spiritual opportunities and challenges tha
flow from the choice of a spouse or a professional career cannot
despite the absence of specific halakhic dictates, regard such decision
as a matter of religious indifference. There is even greater pain wher
the choice of one value entails the sacrifice of another. Pluralisn
means that the dethroned value is still there; it has not been discarded
and still exercises its influence over the individual who cannot full
realize it in practice. A community that prefers either the self
congratulation of success or the resentful self-pity of frustration i
impatient with the dialectic of triumph and retreat. Its ethos car

oscillate between unbalanced hope and reckless despair. It is incompatible with sober, and sometimes tragically complex reality.

In the good old days the regnant ethos was one of Western bourgeois achievement and comfort—the American dream of the post-war years. Back then it was the Rav's emphasis on sacrifice and retreat, on the religious imperative that estranges the individual from the crowd and offends against conventional reason and culture, that left the public relations wing of Orthodoxy with a bad case of intellectual amnesia. Times change, and a new generation, disenchanted with the promise of Western culture, diverted itself with a more sullen and ethnocentric vision, contracting spiritual deformities whose cost we only began to measure when some of us chose to act them out.

Through the tergiversations of our history, the Rav continued to preach the dialectical truth. He knew that modern men and women were not always insensible to their deficiencies, that they experienced a genuine yearning for the sense of meaning which religious faith was expected to provide on the occasion of services and lectures, and the donation of money to religious institutions. And yet he did not compromise his vision or tailor it to their preferences.[25] When people borrowed pleasing insights from religion it was not religion: it was merely "religious culture."[26] And when the tide turned, and it became fashionable to deprecate the ethical in the name of an exclusively national ideal, he was prepared to warn against that confusion too.

"Judaism has indeed formulated a dialectical morality." Not the least of the Rav's many gifts to our century is his keen awareness of the complexity inherent in moral and religious existence, and his tireless commitment to make that complexity real. The present essay is an attempt to keep that legacy alive. We need his guidance more than ever.[27]

Notes

1. *Halakhic Mind* (Seth Press, 1986), p. 52.
2. "Majesty and Humility," p. 26.
3. Rabbi Joseph B. Soloveitchik, "A Eulogy for R. Hayyim Heller" in *Be-So. haYahid ve-haYahad*, ed. Pinchas Peli (Jerusalem, 1976). I here improve upon my translation in *Shiurei HaRav*, ed. Joseph Epstein (Hoboken, 1994). p. 49.
4. I refer most particularly to the analysis of the ethical and the aesthetic in the notebooks on prayer, composed in the 1950's. I hope, God willing, to prepare thi material for publication in the near future.
5. For a good recent analysis of the distinction in its early stages, see S.Z. Havlin "Hukkim and Mishpatim in Torah, Rabbinic Literature, and Maimonidean Thought," *Bar-Ilan Yearbook* 26–27, pp. 135–166.
6. Let me observe that the Rav's pluralism, as expounded later in this paper, i eminently compatible with a halakhic phenomenology recognizing positive and neg ative commandments as expressing dual aspects of religious experience. See Ramba to *Shemot* 20:7 and later authors cited in Chavel's edition of *Perush haRamban* (Jerusalem 1962) I 399. In the same manner, one may distinguish the phenomenological feel o different categories of mandatory and prohibited actions e.g. those for which court imposed punishments are ordained, those where the debt is imposed by Heaver (*dinei adam* and *dinei Shamayim*), and those where vigilante action (*kannaim pog'im bo* is an option.
7. Walter S. Wurzburger, *Ethics of Responsibility: Pluralistic Approaches to Covenanta Ethics* (JPS, 1994), p. 19. Overall Rabbi Wurzburger's book, and several of his othe writings, are consonant with much of my essay, particularly in subscribing to pluralism by which I mean the idea that Jewish ethics cannot be derived from one principle.
8. My revered teacher Rabbi Aharon Lichtenstein, in his essay "Is There a Morality Independent of Halakhah?" (in *Modern Jewish Ethics*, ed. Marvin Fox [Ohio State U 1972]), pp. 62–87, deals with subject matter similar to that of this paper. My focus however, is not on the delineation of spheres between morality and Halakhah, bu rather on the *experience* of apprehending the values and imperatives emanating from each sphere. For this reason I have also paid attention to conflicts between, anc within, the two domains. I have also refrained from discussing the practical implication of taking the category of the ethical seriously, for example how ethical insight can and should, influence halakhic analysis. On this subject, see Rav Lichtenstein's brie but suggestive remarks in "Kevod haBeriyot (Respect for Human Beings)," *Mahanayin* 5, Iyyar 5753, pp. 8–15).
9. "Ish ha-Halakhah," in *Talpiot* Vol. 1, pp. 665–667.
10. Compare to the section on the normative character of halakhic man, for whom

ethos has teleological priority over logos (690ff).

11. "The Lonely Man of Faith" (*Tradition* 7:2, Summer 1965), p. 15.

12. *Halakhic Mind*, p. 69.

13. *Ibid.*, pp. 69–70.

14. *Ibid.*, p. 90.

15. Take, for example, p. 67, where ethical subjectivity is objectified by being converted into "propositions, norms, values, etc." (here the ethical is presumably distinct from the religious). The paragraph ends by identifying the aggregate of religious objective constructs with "ethico-religious norms, ritual, dogmas, theoretical postulates, etc." (and here the adjective "ethical" describes the realm of the religious).

16. See the first four essays in *Tradition* 17:2. Though they were composed at different times, the edited text and arrangement of these articles deliberately constitute a unified presentation.

17. *Lonely Man*, p. 9.

18. "Majesty and Humility," p. 26.

19. *U-Vikkashtem mi-Sham* (in *HaDarom* 47, Tishre 5739), p. 19.

20. Note that the Rav does not speak of irrational commandments, or commandments that contradict reason. He is not making a metaphysical statement about what is categorically rational and what is not; rather he is describing ordinary human moral judgments. He takes such judgments seriously, but without turning their essentially anthropological character into an unqualified absolute. Such locutions, in my opinion, are not accidental. I vividly recall, for example, a lecture on *Hukkim* (circa 1975) during which, in response to the Rav's rhetorical question, members of the audience called out that *hukkim* are irrational and/or illogical. Seemingly accepting their answer, the Rav subtly reformulated it: the *hukkim*, he said, do not lend themselves to the understanding of the logos.

21. *Ibid.*, pp. 25–26.

22. Abraham Sagi and Daniel Statman, in their pioneering and, in many respects exemplary, integration of Jewish thought and analytic ethics *Dat uMusar* (Bar-Ilan, 1993) count the Rav among thinkers who make ethics dependent on religion for psychological reasons (see their discussion of the *U-Vikkashtem* passage p. 235). They cite several suitable passages in lectures whose printed versions were not prepared by the Rav himself. The ontological conception that I develop here on the basis of *U-Vikkashtem mi-Sham* coheres with a pluralistic model that does not appear among their classifications. In a recent discussion of R. Shimon Shkop, "The Religious Commandment and the Legal System: a Study in the Halakhic Thought of R. Shimon Shkop," *Daat* 35, pp. 99–114, Sagi discovers a two-tiered framework of natural ethics and revealed Halakhah with affinities to the pluralistic model proposed here.

23. In principle, of course, a scientific domain may be dependent upon another and

yet capable of autonomous systematic development. One can formulate a coheren account of thermodynamics, for example, while recognizing its reducibility to me chanics. By the same token, a disciple of the Rav might recognize that ethics ultimately derives from the religious without despairing of the possibility that the field of ethic can be systematized on its own. Whence the uncertainty in my phrasing above.

24. The hierarchic theory arrived at here posits, not only that the ethical is axiolog ically inferior to the religious, but that it is incomplete, in the absence of submissio to the religious. This conclusion flows from the dialectic described by the Rav ir *U-Vikkashtem mi-Sham.* Question: is this picture consistent with the phenomenologica reality, in which the ethical makes awesome and absolute demands on individual who do not recognize the "revelational consciousness?" A dismissive and purely psychological explanation, that the ethical commitment of such individuals break down under pressure, is inadequate; from a phenomenological perspective, it is enough to establish the ontological reality of the ethical that some individual case is authenti cated. In *Lonely Man* (p. 48, n.1), the Rav observes that "[i]n reality there are no pure typological structures," and that when the characteristic covenantal conception o time appears in the majestic community as well, it has been taken over by the latter from the former. Presumably he would offer the same answer for the present case Such an approach would seem to be supported by the historical evidence: our sense of the ethical as absolute and awesome may be predicated upon Christianity and the type of vestigial Christianity represented by thinkers like Kant. Greek ethical view diverge significantly from this model (see, among recent writers, Bernard Williams *Shame and Necessity* [University of California Press, 1993]) and the therapeutic ethic of the psychologists, proud in its repudiation of both guilt and shame, threatens to achieve an even more radical emancipation from the ethical in the post-moderr world. See also P.S. Greenspan, *Practical Guilt: Moral Dilemmas, Emotions and Socia Norms* (Oxford, 1995).

25. Note that "Catharsis," which is the Rav's sharpest formulation of the need to sacrifice, was delivered to a collegiate audience. In general, the theme of withdrawal in the Rav's published writings, is more sharply delineated in his English works. The major exception, *Al Limmud Torah u-Geullat Nefesh ha-Dor*, corrects the statement of a French-American correspondent for an Israeli newspaper whose concept o religion tended to treat the religious as a means of serving the national culture.

26. I am building on the concluding pages of *Lonely Man of Faith.*

27. Coming to grips with the spirit and substance of the Rav's work willy nilly renews one's joy in the community of kindred religious-intellectual spirits. Among those who commented on my first draft, let me mention Rabbi Yitzchak Blau, Rabb Adam Ferziger, David Hazony, Dr. William Lee, Rabbi Moshe Wohlgelernter, Dr Joel Wolowelsky, Rabbi Walter Wurzburger.